Philosophy and Education in Western Civilization

SUMMARIES AND INTERPRETATIONS
FOR SCHOOLMEN AND CHURCHMEN

Philosophy and Education in Western Civilization

SUMMARIES AND INTERPRETATIONS
FOR SCHOOLMEN AND CHURCHMEN

BY

John A. Stoops

DEAN, SCHOOL OF EDUCATION
LEHIGH UNIVERSITY

The Interstate
Printers & Publishers, Inc.
DANVILLE, ILLINOIS

To the Memory of Charles C. Stoops—
Archytas of the American Tarentum

Preface

It has been often said that there is an eternal novelty in basic ideas. With each fundamental change in western civilization a new light is thrown upon fundamental notions in western thought. Certain aspects are seen to have added importance, and elements of previous significance are seen to fade. This alone justifies continuous reworking of the philosophical legacy left by the ancient, medieval, and renaissance thinkers. Once a tradition of thought becomes established in a civilization it remains as new as the newest part of that civilization.

No one doubts that the character of change underway in modern schools and churches is fundamental. Modes of faith and valuation are altering in decisive ways. Although the pedagogical effort of our times is massive, and the level of social consciousness unprecedented, the young of our times display a lostness reminiscent of that discussed by St. Augustine in his *Confessions*. Writing of the alienation of his younger days he said, "I lost myself in a multiplicity of things." How is such lostness overcome? There is little help for the young when elders are similarly lost.

In response, the churches and schools are turning away from *man* as a collective idea and turning toward *person* as a particular identity. Much that goes on in general pedagogy is being adapted accordingly. Modern education focuses less upon what is true of the world in general and more upon what is true of the self in particular.

It has been always recognized that philosophy is not produced independently of life, but frequently philosophy is abstracted and taught as if it were something apart. Now, in a time when each person may become his own personal philosopher and educator, philosophic thought should be revealed as it really is, namely, the efforts men have made to give meaning to the problems and passions of their lives. The summaries and interpretations in the first twelve chapters are written to this end.

However, it is folly to think of persons philosophizing as if independent of social arrangements. Each person must come to terms with himself, but he must also come to terms with civility and civilization. To help the young resolve this paradox, schools and churches require a theory of civilization which grows out of a theory of person. The final two chapters of this book suggest possible grounds for this resolution through conceiving civilization as a body of enspirited forms. These last two chapters are part of a continuing work.

Acknowledgements

A project of this length and variety requires many contributors. This author is fortunate in being associated with a number of capable men and women who derive satisfaction from the sharing of their talents. Their expertise and personal support of the author have made this work possible. A special tribute must be reserved to Mrs. Mary Barch who helped with the organization and typing of the manuscript. Mrs. Faye Fenstermacher and Mrs. Roberta Lareau also shared in the typing. Miss Phyllis Furst, Professor Robert Leight, Miss JoAnna Wentling, Mrs. Betty Soler, and Rabbi Stephen Schafer read portions of the manuscript, indicated needed corrections, and offered useful suggestions. The materials which compose this work have also been used and commented upon by a number of students over the past few years. These reactions have been helpful.

Finally, a great appreciation is expressed for this assistance and encouragement of my wife, Muriel, who carried some part of every burden this task imposed and cheerfully instituted the priorities needed to insure its completion.

Table of Contents

CHAPTER I

The Handles and Harnesses

All students of education must harness and handle ideas. This is true of those whose work is technical or scientific, as it is of those who devote themselves to concerns which are called humane. There are a number of great traditions in Indo-European thought. Anyone who aspires to a significant responsibility for the educational development of others should have the ability to grip and handle these traditions with understanding. They flow as streams through western civilization. In some places they appear apart and alone. At other places two or more of them will be discovered to merge and flow as one. Wherever men gather to talk of education, of teachers, or of institutions, words and sentences take meaning from these traditions. Those who study education and work in schools, while associating closely with one or more of these traditions, must understand and appreciate the others.

Education and Philosophy

To achieve this understanding one must acquire the handles and harnesses which philosophers have fashioned for this purpose. In western scholarship those designated as philosophers have performed many tasks. When thought first rose to the level called philosophy, that word literally meant the love of knowledge. We have attributed the term to Pythagoras, a remarkable schoolmaster of the Sixth Century. Inspired by philosophy, men have been able to establish knowledge systems such as physics, mathematics, and history and establish these systems with an identity which appears to be separate from philosophy. Even so, philosophy and philosophical problems remain in each knowledge system, philosophy remains apart itself as a field of scholarship.

How can this be? The answer is that specialists in philosophy serve all knowledge systems by working to improve the tools for the analysis of the philosophical problems which plague them. For example, many modern philosophers work on languages, classification, quantification, conceptual models, and theoretical systems. In a sense, one could call such philosophers the "tool and die makers" of the modern knowledge industry. They also provide instruments of detection, measurement, and evaluation. In modern man's unprecedented quest for knowledge such philosophic services are as vital as ever.

Another view of this can be obtained by imagining that all of knowledge is divided into two categories: art and science. It can be further imagined that the knowledge men call *science* is that which has been gained by looking *out* at the world, and the knowledge that men call *art* is that which has been gained by men looking *within* themselves. The distinction between art and science cannot really be resolved so simply; but, if we can imagine that it is, then we can set these two categories apart and understand that all we call knowledge is of one kind or of the other. That is, all but philosophy; this cannot be assigned to the arts or to the sciences. Then what role does it play? In this imagined scheme of the extremes of knowledge (arts and sciences), philosophy can be said to operate between the arts and sciences, and it is on this middle ground that the general meanings are developed which are of interest to students of education. Philosophy and education, therefore, can be said to be transdisciplinary. In this way philosophy and education not only serve the individual knowledge systems but work among and between them to illuminate the whole.

In turning to philosophy for the equipage needed for the management of ideas, the student of education is not himself becoming a professional philosopher. He is going to the field of the professional philosopher to acquire the conceptual or analytical tools and terms necessary to grip and handle with understanding the issues in his own practice and to acquire the probes needed to examine relationships with and among other fields. This encounter with philosophy becomes successful when his mind is furnished with the various *implements of analysis* which students of education need to perform such tasks.

The "implements" appropriate to the field of education now include virtually every tool that philosophy produces. This is because education is joined with philosophy as a transdisciplinal study. Its transdisciplinal nature becomes clearer with the realization that there is no knowledge system (or discipline) that does not constantly present its own special problems to education. The moment new knowledge of any kind is produced, the problem of transmitting it to others is born, and the *field* of education is thereby changed. Thus it is proper to reason that students of education should study philosophy with greater intensity than students of restricted academic disciplines such as physics or mathematics. Unlike the physical chemist, the ecologist, or the historian, the student of education has no domain of knowledge to which his inquiry is restricted. He is not, of course, omniscient, but there is no knowledge problem that is not (in part at least) his problem.

The History of Thought

Moreover, the study of education has historical dimension. The traditions of thought which educators must grip with understanding are traceable to the various personalities of the Indo-European civilizations. It is important for students of education to understand as much as can be understood of how these traditions originated and what influences have modified them as they made their way to the Twentieth Century. Philosophy has been produced by men in time. Very often it was not produced by a man who was making a direct effort to originate a philosophy. Such philosophies were produced "on the job." A philosopher such as Plato may have had before him the object of designing a perfect government or a basis for civil order. That which we call his *philosophy* emerged in the logic of justification which supports his scheme for government. This is very like a carpenter producing a miter box in order that he can construct a frame for a doorway. His theory for the doorway was worked out in the angles he cut in the miter box. Now other carpenters could take the same miter box and produce similar doorways. But if the theory of the doorway is to be significantly altered, that particular miter box will have less use. Perhaps it will have no use at all. So as we look at what is called a man's philosophy it is usually relevant to look also at what he was doing at the time.

As another example, it is vital for the student of education to know something of the circumstances under which St. Augustine prepared his powerful and influential book called *The City of God*. Not only does such knowledge add greatly to comprehending the work, but it also helps the student to see whether or not the uses of Augustine's arguments in later times were appropriate uses. Likewise, one does not sense the urgency which led to the speculations of Thomas Aquinas, the courage which produced the views of Occam, or the intrigue which surrounded Bacon, without a study of the men, issues, and events of the times in which they lived.

Historical relevance also contributes to the study of Locke, Hegel, Marx, and Berkeley. Men who are familiar with contemporary events and issues will certainly apply them in giving meaning to works such as those of Dewey, Buber, and Sartre. Only a few philosophers seem to speak across the centuries, seemingly detached from the civilization which nurtured them. Certainly this claim could be made in behalf of Heraclitus and Spinoza and also for Kant and Peirce. However, any list of such men would fail to do justice to many others. Of importance here is not the contents of such a list but the fact that only a few philosophers have a kind of existence which is not related to their times.

Does this then deny the earlier assertion that a student must consider the historical relevance of philosophers and philosophy? The answer is no. Although a philosopher may have been so possessed of originality and independence that he was unaffected by his time, his work—once recognized—became an influence upon history; and it is through the study of influences such as this that we come to a fuller appreciation of their source. Those who are in the profession called education must study the historical relevance of ideas and the men who seem to originate them. In many cases the most important handle one connects to the idea is the name of the man who presented it to the western mind.

The Preeminence of Metaphysics

In addition to a belief in historical relevance, the approach to educational philosophy used in this treatise is distinguished by the preeminence of metaphysics. Is this true of all philosophy? It is not. Many, perhaps most, who work in this field strive to diminish the role of metaphysics or eliminate it entirely. This tendency to avoid metaphysical considerations is not shared by this author.

To explain the issue it is necessary to offer a meaning for metaphysics as it relates to education. In classical times it was commonly said that if one wanted to possess ultimate wisdom he should consult an oracle. Students of education would want to know a great many things; certainly, one of these things would be the nature of goodness in men. If there existed an oracle, or anything else in the world that men could go to see, which would tell what is the Truth about goodness in men a great many issues in education would cease to be issues. But there is no place where this answer can be found and given out convincingly enough to be accepted as true.

Nothing in the form of word or object has yet appeared which can convince all men that one tradition of thought is true and all others are not. To say it another way, no physical reality has appeared which can compose the differences, establish the ultimately true, or assign the one to a station above others. It is necessary to accept the origin of the differences as being somewhere beyond physical reality. The word for that which lies beyond physical reality is *metaphysics*.

To further discriminate between questions which are physical and those which are metaphysical, let us imagine that we are asked how many shad were in the Delaware River at 3:00 p.m., on July 4, 1776. This question would be very difficult to answer. We do not possess the means to obtain a precise answer. However, it can be agreed that a certain number of organisms of this kind were located within a geographic entity called the Delaware at the time indicated here. Even though we cannot answer the question with the means now at our disposal, we do not doubt that a physical answer exists. Therefore, the question is not understood as a metaphysical question. However, on that same day, in a building now called Independence Hall, in a city on the banks of that same river, certain events were culminated in a document called the *Declaration of Independence*. The authors of the document called it righteous. It contains references to a *Creator*, to rights *inalienable*, to truths which are *self-evident*. These were and are matters of some importance on the scale of public concern, far more important in fact than the exact number of shad in the river. Was the action righteous? Does or did the Creator create? How do rights come to be inalienable? The answers to these questions are not contained in any known physical form. The answers are somewhere beyond physics. To answer directly one consults his beliefs, and the men who authored the document in question were firm in their beliefs. Another way of saying this is to say they were firm in their metaphysics. These men bet their lives on metaphysical assumptions.

All knowledge systems are based on metaphysical assumptions. Once they are accepted, scholars build knowledge upon them. If the knowledge turns out to be reliable, coherent, or prophetic, it offers support of the base assumption. However, no matter how tenable a metaphysical assumption is made to seem, it remains metaphysical. But because it seems tenable most scholars in most disciplines can set the metaphysical issues aside as did the authors of the Declaration of Independence. They simply believed them.

For example, a physicist may assume that the weight of an

object is the set of operations a man goes through in establishing the weight of an object. By so assuming and so believing he can build knowledge without getting further engrossed in cosmic meanings. Similarly, a geometer can assume and believe that a perfect circle can exist even if it never has existed anywhere except in the minds of geometers. It is interesting and fruitful to examine each knowledge system to see what the base metaphysical assumptions are. Education students who specialize in curriculum are increasingly active in this kind of inquiry.

Because many metaphysical assumptions reward their believers with reliable, coherent, or prophetic knowledge, many authorities are not disposed to offer metaphysics so large a place in philosophy. They say, for example, that we have ideas, objects, language, and various methods for dealing with them. Some propose that problems in knowing and valuing need not be metaphysical and the metaphysical issues must be disposed of before any really useful work in philosophy can begin. They assert that models for "thinking" and decision making can be developed, and that "language" for computers can be devised. Certainly men have long been engaged in an effort to produce better descriptions of the world which appears in their senses. These things hold promise of highly practical benefits, and metaphysics plays little part in them.

But the educational philosopher cannot dispose of metaphysics so easily. The student of education is warned that his profession is one which is constantly redefining its goals. The practicing educator whose work is done in the schools and colleges is constantly forming and articulating a *vision of man* which stands as the foundation of his art. The practicing educator is producing a man, and in some way all that the educator does relates to his vision. What kind of man is he producing? If educators could agree on one, if there was a kind of oracle they could consult and believe, they could dispose of metaphysics and build knowledge as do scholars in specific knowledge systems.

This is the reason metaphysics keeps sticking to the fingers of an education student. His working faith is a metaphysical vision of man which takes on whatever level of reality he chooses to give it. When he presents his vision to others a series of metaphysical beliefs furnishes the syntax of description. Moreover, certain modern trends in educational and theological thought which have advanced the tradition of existentialism in the formation of educational policy give metaphysics even greater prominence. The reader will soon discover that the plan of this treatise strongly orients other traditions of thought in a metaphysical context. In this study of educational philosophy, metaphysics is pervasive.

Origins of the Handles

Having explained that this work is characterized by an attempt to show historical relevance and that it is a philosophic version freighted with metaphysical issues, the way is clear to expose a few of the most important handles. If the student is to grip with understanding the dominant traditions in western thought he must acquire the use of special terms and develop precision in meanings which are usually overlooked or undetected in conventional discourse. He will find that commonplace words such as universe, society, cause, and self are not always used analogically as in ordinary language. At times they may be used univocally (i.e., with exactly the same meaning) and at times they are used equivocally (i.e., with wholly different and unrelated meanings). Part of the student's training in the philosophy of education must be directed to being keenly aware of these issues in the nominal aspects of language. The student will also discover the general terms used by students of philosophy to identify various philosophical positions. He will be told, for example, that Plato (428-348 B.C.) was a formal idealist and the originator of a philosophy which is known as formal idealism. Now how did this come to be? Did Plato invent his philosophical position and then call it formal idealism? No. Plato wrote a number of books in the form of dialogue. He wrote also in the more conventional expository forms. He was certainly interested in presenting or revealing the reality of certain abstract nouns such as knowledge, love, piety, and justice. He explored concerns such as the soul and man's quest for immortality. Much of his work was didactic in that he was devoted to teaching his ideas to others.

If Plato were incarnated today and introduced to an audience as the first of all western philosophers to develop a complete philosophical system, as the inventor of a system known as formal idealism, as a profound influence on the early Christian church, and as the teacher of Aristotle, one whose philosophy has stood through the centuries as formidably as his own, Plato would probably be astonished. If Plato did not invent formal idealism, who did? Formal idealism was invented by students of philosophy who found that term a convenient and appropriate name for Plato's work.

The written commentaries on the work of Plato are beyond counting. Plato has been created and re-created many times. Somehow the works he did set in motion were influences which tended to shape much of the western thought. How fascinating it would be to hear what he might have to say about it all! One suspects that both he and Aristotle would be amazed at how much has been made over the differences between them. There are indications that Aristotle himself never thought he had departed from the circle of Platonists. One also suspects that Plato would be surprised that his philosophy would be so prominently reflected in a religion which was founded over three centuries after his death. Plato's work was associated with the pagan religions of his time. The point of this is that when we study Plato we study much more than Plato ever knew about, but we have no way of knowing how much we now have of him with which he would himself agree. We can be certain he would not agree with all.

How does this happen? When students of Plato or other philosophers begin to analyze his work they develop categories. For example, they may begin by asking what was Plato's theory about reality, or what did he consider to be ultimately real? Some philosophers call the answers to this Plato's *ontology*. Then they ask how or by what manner did Plato accept as true that which he claimed to be true? The answer to this is called Plato's *epistemology*. Finally, they ask what did Plato think to be good or how did he establish standards for goodness, and what are those standards? And the answer to this is called his *axiology*.

What is real? How is it known? And what is good? These questions are called ontological, epistemological, and axiological in that order. A complete philosophical system (or a complete philosophy) is expected to answer these questions. Because, in the work of Plato, rather complete answers to each of these three questions are found, we can call his philosophy a complete system. This does not mean that the system answers all of the questions which could be brought. It simply means that a basis is established for dealing with all of the questions which could be brought.

It is possible to think of *ontology* (the problem of reality), *epistemology* (the problem of knowledge) and *axiology* (the problem of good) as being the basic handles a student reaches for in his quest to grip with the understanding of a philosophical system. When a teacher who himself has studied the system sets about to explain it to students he will do so by presenting these handles to his students and inviting them to grasp them as he has. How would Plato himself teach Platonism? We are pretty certain that he would not have done it just this way. Most of his work has been preserved, and it seems clear that this mode of analysis did not occur to him; or, if it did, he found no use for it.

But our problem is different. Plato obviously wished to present only his views to his students. We have a number of other systems to teach. Therefore, we need a mode of analysis which enables us to make comparisons and to delineate differences. After we take note of Plato's ontology we can look into the work of Aristotle to find his ontology. After this we can discover the ontology of Aquinas, Descartes, Locke, Hegel, James, Dewey, Sartre, etc. By comparing and contrasting ontologies we can note the similarities and differences in how these philosophers described reality. Similarly we can note similarities and differences in their epistemologies and axiologies. As our skill grows, we have a means of analysis and criticism.

Even though comparison and contrast are among the oldest, most respected, and best established modes of analysis, there is always present the problem of distortion. Distortion occurs when the work of any philosopher is taken from its natural form and reshaped in the form of answers to these three fundamental questions. We must accept this as a limitation, and any student is put on notice that the only way really to study a philosopher is to study him as he presents himself and not as he has been managed and massaged through this or any other analytical mode.

However, students of education usually take only one, two, or, at best, three courses in philosophy. It is not possible within the scope of so limited an effort to go through all of the major works of western philosophy and do all of the things which professional students of philosophy do in developing analytical methods. Students of education must be shown the handles which have been selected for their use. We justify such usage by calling it *philosophy applied to education, philosophy of education,* or *philosophical foundations of education.* Such terms not only describe the field of study, they also imply the limitations inherent in the method.

By using these handles it is possible to inspect certain traditions in western thought which are called by words such as idealism, realism, Thomism, experimentalism, and existentialism. Early in his training the alert student will ask what kind of reality these traditions have? Do they exist? Are they illusions which have been fortified as delusions? A teacher of philosophy cannot fail to be pleased by such questions because they indicate that the questioner has begun the intellectual behavior which is called philosophizing. How does a teacher justify thrusting these traditions at his students as if they were real?

Again, it is the problem of handles. There are certain differences which can be perceived in how men act and value. There are differences in how they govern themselves, how they establish institutions and delineate the purposes of their institutions, and how they seek knowledge and use what they know. Some men call one thing good and others will say of the same thing that it is not good. Men can be found who will sacrifice anything they have, even life itself, for an idea. Other men feel all ideas are open to compromise and are willing to work things out. We have called these differences metaphysical. It is reasonable to suppose these differences are the consequence of some kind of belief. When a man recognizes that these differences in belief exist then he is bound to think they are caused.

If a student of philosophy was led to a consideration of these differences, and his time was unlimited, he could examine them in detail, notice consistencies, and develop his own theory of cause. However, the time of an education student is limited, so it is believed best to inform the student of education that this extensive historical and philosophical work has been done and much of this work has led scholars to sense the existence of these traditions. We, therefore, initiate our study by accepting their reality. In other words, we start off by believing in them and then we work very hard to understand that which we believe. Do the traditions really exist? We have not said that they do, but as theories they offer us the best explanations we have of why men differ as they do in what they accept (ontology), know (epistemology), and value (axiology).

Therefore, we might note five traditions which are well known to students of education by the following names:

1. Idealism
2. Realism
3. Thomism
4. Experimentalism
5. Existentialism

Each of these is to be subjected to analysis based on the three questions: (1) the ontological question, (2) the epistemological question, and (3) the axiological question. The five traditions are given historical reality; the three questions to be asked of each tradition give the student handles by which he can grip the issues.

Are there more terms? As indicated above, nearly all the tools which philosophers produce have some relevance in education and to the work which students of education do. Yes, there are many more terms. Indeed, there are enough to fill a good-sized dictionary. Philosophy has been going on for a long time. So there are many more handles than just the names of five fundamental traditions of thought and the three categories of questions. However, by basing our studies upon these traditions and questions, we determine which of the hundreds of technical words or phrases are of greatest importance.

Ontological distinctions between the five traditions just named are easily drawn. One simply asks of each what it is that followers of that particular tradition assume to be real. In each case a reality statement is given out which differs from all of the others. For example, idealism presupposes that idea is real and that it is cosmologically anterior to act, relationship, or thing. This is to say that thinghood comes before the thing; or, more specifically, the idea of workmanship precedes the rendering of a task, the idea of friendship precedes friends, and the idea of treehood comes before trees. To the idealist ideas not only come first, but also preside. By contrast, realism presupposes the reality of matter; it also presupposes that matter is anterior to form. Realistic philosophizing generally begins with material. The realist asks: What is the basic "stuff" of the world? Matter, in this case, is anterior to idea. Ideas are something men have about matter. The Thomist presupposes that ultimate reality is some kind of intellect. Aquinas himself followed each proof of the reality of this being with a remark such as "and all call this being God." Experimentalism, the first of the two exclusively modern traditions, tends to look to the reality of process. The world operates. There appear to be procedures in force. Existentialism, the second modern tradition, emphasizes the reality of personal awareness. General metaphysics is subdued and personal metaphysics is emphasized.

Epistemological distinctions are similarly sharp and, therefore, easily seen. Here one asks of each tradition what kind of test it offers of the truth of any proposition. The idealist is fond of dialectic. He uses it to test the coherence of discourse on ideas. If discourse remains coherent through the rigor of dialectic the discourse is generally thought to be a true expression of the idea. This brings to mind that charming passage between Socrates and Agathon in the Symposium. Agathon said, "I cannot refute you Socrates," whereupon the teacher replied, "say rather, beloved Agathon, that you cannot refute the truth; for Socrates is easily refuted." Realists, on the other hand, begin knowing with careful observation. Ideas are true when they are found to correspond with that which is observed in the world of matter or things. Thus, the realist uses the test of correspondence. Thomists use both coherence and correspondence; but they add, in addition, a quality called intuition. This latter is an aspect of man's natural tendency to know and is explained by the presence of microcosmic elements in his intellectual make-up.

Of the modern positions, the experimentalist epistemology is especially strong. It holds that man learns through his active efforts to reduce an identified problem. Man is constantly testing hypotheses. Out of the pragmatic test comes information about what works or does not work in reducing dissatisfactions. This, of course, is knowledge, and is as true as any knowledge. Existentialists endow truth to a belief, object, or idea simply by personal acceptance of it. Existential truth is a matter of personal choice.

Axiological distinctions are more difficult because there is greater diversity and a degree of overlapping among the various traditions. Questions about the good involve man in ways that questions about the real and questions about the known do not. Man is constantly and actively valuing. Can there be a good which is independent of man's valuation? The idealists think there can. The active good is paradigmatic (or approximating the perfect idea). A paradigm is conceived as a form or as an ideal. However, other forms of idealism look upon the good in other ways. Absolute idealism recognizes it in the resolution of antithetical forces; and, in the spiritual idealism of Kant, the good is recognized as good will. There are other versions of the good which emanate from the idealist tradition. Realism also offers variations. Aristotle argued that happiness is the highest good for man. Other realists propose to discover good in function. Bentham suggested pleasure as the basis for moral standards in his principle of utility. Experimentalists offer the good as instrumental. This is to say that the good is "good-for" some end-in-view. Other variations parallel those of certain realists who represent the good as a public judgment. Existentialists measure good in terms of personal freedom and personal authenticity.

A summary of this kind raises more questions than it answers. But this is true of all philosophy. Philosophers make no apology for raising questions. On the contrary, philosophy begins with questions, and in the end it produces nothing more or less than better questions.

Along the way, however, there are a number of gains. One of them is perspective; another is an increased propensity to inquire. A. N. Whitehead described these gains as a sense of the immensity of things and a purification of emotion by understanding.

There are even more specific benefits to students of education. Not only do they become familiar with the intellectual traditions of their own civilization and become familiar with the names commonly attached to these traditions, but also they learn to read the literature of philosophy. Literacy in any field requires a familiarity with the "handles" the vocationers of that field attached to the key concepts. Literacy also requires that the reader be able to make distinctions between the key concepts as they appear in the context of the professional literature. It is of relevance here to note John Dewey's remark that education is "philosophy in working clothes." If this is true then a large part of the vocabulary of philosophy is also in the vocabulary of education. Indeed, this composes a very convincing argument for students of education to consider extensive studies in philosophy.

Let us consider what value, if any, the work of educational philosophy has. There are, in modern times, those who take this on as a profession. They are trained in the field and make it a full-time concern. As a consequence, certain standards (or rigors) are anticipated when a professional vocationer of the field speaks. But one does not have to be a professional philosopher of education to philosophize about schools. It is a mistake to think that a professional philosopher of education has any more wisdom about what a school should be than have parents, teachers, or school administrators. However, a professional can help by keeping minds free from nonsense. This can be a formidable undertaking; and, if successful, it can be a remarkable contribution. But many times professional philosophers fail to eliminate nonsense simply because the layman becomes embarrassed or angry if his ideas are shown to be incoherent or irrelevant. The philosopher who can gently pluck such maladies from public thought without attracting the ire of public thinkers is a valuable man to have around.

The Profession of Educational Philosophy

Another way of saying this is to repeat an old slogan, "philosophy bakes no bread." At first, it is difficult to see where professional philosophers of education perform a salable service. They can hardly hope to support themselves by writing books. A few could, but this accounts for only a small portion of the whole. In truth, most of them support themselves by teaching philosophy of education to prospective teachers and school leaders. So the educational philosopher serves by ministering rigor to the present and future thought about education.

How are philosophers of education distinctive, and what distinctive tasks do they perform? Most professional groups tend to take themselves rather seriously. Nearly every month of the year large motels or hotels about the country (usually in off-season) are packed full of conventioners. In these gatherings such great themes are considered as: Who are we? What must one do to become one of us? How can we prevent there being too many of us? How can we be assured that there will always be some of us? What steps are needed to better our lot and, incidentally and hopefully, the lot of mankind as well? To their everlasting credit, educational philosophers do not tend to discuss these questions. In fact, of all groups in education they are among the few who have not taken themselves too seriously. This, of course, is as it should be. If philosophers of education should ever weld themselves into a closely knit professional body they would cease to be philosophers of education or philosophers of any kind. Such society as they have meets mainly to hear papers read and views exchanged. It is directly related to at least one journal. In 1953, a statement was developed on *The Distinctive Nature of the Discipline of the Philosophy of Education.*

This statement reported the distinctive nature to be characterized by (1) the acquisition of theoretical tools and techniques common to all philosophy; (2) the application of these to make and evaluate assessments, judgments, and choices, with particular reference to the field of education; and (3) a scholarly acquaintance with the events in education as viewed or analyzed in the various theoretical modes. Stating these three points more briefly, the philosopher of education must have a working knowledge of general philosophy, an ability to apply this knowledge in developing and evaluating educational decisions, and an ability to develop theoretical interpretations of educational events.

On these grounds the educational philosophers build their claim to a distinctive discipline. As it turns out this is acceptable until one asks: What are the boundaries of the field of education? What decisions are not educational decisions? What events fail of educational relevance? Some answer this by saying, "Only those things which have to do with the running of schools." The Society in the second part of its statement defines institutionalized schooling and goes further by saying what this means. But upon reflection, it becomes clear that the philosophers of art, philosophers of history, philosophers of music, and, indeed, even philosophers of philosophy have a great deal to say about the running of schools. Their work clearly bears upon procedures, resources, and goals (methods, means, and ends) and the employment of criteria, guides, and reasons why these procedures, resources, and goals are established. Thus, the philosopher of education is deprived of an exclusive domain because he, like a man without a country, is destined to wander across the earth visiting all domains, and when he settles upon a specific task he usually finds himself in the company of persons from other parts of the academic profession.

But the philosopher of education is needed virtually everywhere. He is needed because of the distinctive nature of the *task he performs*. Even though this author finds reason to question the first part of the Society's statement on the distinctive nature of the discipline, he is warmly attracted to the second part of the same statement which deals with the task which the educational philosopher performs. It is a distinctive task, and one which deserves more recognition.

As reported by the Society it is observed at three levels:

1. The *descriptive analytical* task of the philosopher of education may be in the articulation of (making explicit) the criteria which, in fact, guide the choices made in educational circles. This task may include relating these criteria to philosophic positions, and examining them in terms of consistency, meaning, expectation, and method.
2. The *critical evaluation* task of the philosopher of education may be in the forming of alternative criteria provided by the philosophy of education. This task may include locating criteria for assessing these alternatives for purposes of determining more adequate or "reasonable" criteria.
3. The *speculative* task of the philosopher of education may be in the forging or framing of new alternatives for use in philosophy, education, and/or the discipline of the philosophy of education.

Although there may not be a distinctive domain of educational philosophy with sharp boundaries around it, the task which educational philosophy performs is distinctive. Therefore, more is to be said about this task than of the supposed profession which performs it. But, again, this would be a wholesome outlook for all of the supposed professions of the modern world. Many of these are tormenting themselves in the righteous rigor of self-definition and have lost sight of the work which they might do.

To Higher Ground in Education

One way to think happily about the work of the philosopher of education is to think that he is moving education to higher ground. How is this done? Let us consider the three tasks outlined above: (1) description, (2) application of metacriteria, (3) speculation; and apply them to a very common enterprise in education—namely, the teaching of reading.

Phase one is description and analysis. Education suffers greatly because the work of description is so poorly done. Because it is so poorly done there is much looseness in language and lack of rigor in discussing outcomes. The result is confusion and, at times, distortion of meaning. This is particularly true of reading, where established practices have been introduced again and again, each time in the name of innovation or reform.

For example the descriptive work of a philosopher of education might begin by his saying that the elementary schools in America developed their curriculum in response to the growing technologies of the farm, market, and church. Chief among the needed technologies was reading. We can call it a technology because of specific application which governed both its presence and manner of presentation in the school program. The philosopher would then go further by analyzing what was meant by universal educational opportunity, and he might conclude from his analysis that the meaning must be taken from a metaphysical belief that the opportunities for economic success and religious participation should be universalized for American children.

Now, he might reason, this belief determined the original nature of the reading program; namely, it was instrumental to other purposes and not an end in itself. Therefore, teachers and schools were disposed to draw satisfaction from the extent to which children could make printed words and sentences intelligible.

Then the philosopher might evaluate and describe other influences such as the development of achievement testing and the establishment of achievement norms. He could go further and point out that the tests, as developed, were not inconsistent with the purposes of the reading programs, and the norms which were invented for such phenomena as vocabulary, word attack skill, and comprehension reinforced all that had gone before. Now, however, he might point out that the testmakers were setting the goals for the reading program.

In the perspective of time the philosopher could review all of this as a monumental achievement. A vast and diverse population had been taught the complicated task of reading the English language. That is, they could derive meaning of a kind from English words which appeared before them in print. Moreover, they could write and communicate their descriptions of events and such thoughts as they had to others. The philosopher who can observe, analyze, and record this development with clarity and precision performs a distinctive service for his civilization; and in regard to the reading enterprise in public education, this has been done.

Then the philosopher moves to the next phase, the application of metacriteria. Actually, this is usually done in the later stages of description or as a part of it. However, it is discussed separately here. The application of metacriteria is not a popular thing because it involves making people unhappy with themselves and each other. In newspaper stories it may appear that so and so denounced the reading programs in Farmville schools as being inhumane. What is happening here?

The philosopher of education has begun asking hard questions. For example, he asks: Is this all that can be done with reading? What accounts for the remarkable yen for pornography? Is the reading program furnishing only one more way of satisfying primordial appetites? Has the reading program of our schools been a civilizing force? Are we merely developing literate barbarians? What are the human consequences of reading? *What does reading do to the child?* When has a person really learned to read? Suddenly teachers, schools, communities, and agencies of government are no longer fully pleased with themselves. Criticism mounts. Articles in weekly magazines and Sunday supplements begin to ask, what is wrong with our schools?

Nothing is really wrong. The educational philosopher has been probing and simply has struck a nerve. It hurts and it goes on hurting. Reading teachers begin to register for workshops. Reading specialists begin to revise their books and monographs. The Federal Government begins to revise its guidelines for funded programs and the Congress provides funds for scholarship in the humanities. Innovations spring forth like a thousand flickering lights. Most flicker for a while and then seem to go out; others begin to burn more brightly. Even computer specialists who have committed their lives to "hardware" and "software" speak in their own unique vernacular about personalizing, individualizing, and humanizing, as if this needed to be done to each child (who when he comes to school is more personal, individual, and human than any school could ever make him).

Perhaps it would be good if the philosopher of education could stop here, but he can't. He has the further responsibility to offer ideas about how the schools might meet the objectives inherent in his meta-criteria. He must *speculate*. Now, others have opportunity to be critical of him. Despite this, he cannot fulfill all aspects of his mission unless he leads the way to higher ground. This, of course, requires that he show the others where he thinks it is. He cannot very well do this unless he has some knowledge of instructional materials, teaching methods, and the great body of information about how schools are financed and administered.

It is in this third task that educational philosophers are frequently least equipped to render. The rigors of training for the first two of the three often leave little time for the educational philosopher to become professionally competent in the details of institutional processes. This, as much as any other single thing, prevents him from withdrawing into a tight little world of his own. He must (to resume our example in reading) establish communications with authorities in children's literature, with developers of classroom technologies, with students of school finances, and with the profession of teacher educators. He must be sufficiently perceptive and creative to pull from these resources the elements needed for a speculative response to the issue which he, himself, has created.

It is reasonable to claim that as a consequence of this kind of activity, education moves to higher ground. This simply means that we have looked at a practice, criticized it, and eliminated the basis of criticism. This is a rational model for the improvement of education and a meaningful description of the task of the educational philosopher. It is hard work. The philosopher is often unpopular, and frequently (in a figurative sense) he gets his hands dirty. John Dewey of our own century offers perhaps the world's most meaningful example of a competent philosopher (and was so rated). He brought new criteria to bear; he operated a laboratory school; and he proposed new foundations for pedagogy in America. Thus, he fulfilled all three aspects of the philosopher's task; but unlike many others, he was distinguished in all three.

Few have done so well. Dewey ranks with Plato, Aristotle, Cicero, Quintilian, Rousseau, Pestalozzi, Froebel, Comenius, Mann, and a few others, who succeeded in doing it all even to the point of implementing their speculations, thereby giving their theories a reality which the world could not fail to notice.

Other Reading

Belth, Mark. *Education as a Discipline.* Boston: Allyn and Bacon, Inc., 1965. Chapters I-III.

Brameld, Theodore. *Education as Power.* New York: Holt, Rinehart & Winston, Inc., 1965. Chapters I-III.

Broudy, Harry S. "How Philosophical Can Philosophy of Education Be?," *Journal of Philosophy* LII, (October 1955), pp. 612-622.

Burns, Hobert W. and Charles J. Brauner. *Philosophy of Education.* New York: The Ronald Press Co., 1962, pp. 3-73.

Butler, J. Donald. *Four Philosophies and Their Practice in Religion and Education,* New York: Harper & Brothers, 1951, pp. 1-41.

Dupuis, Adrian. *Philosophy of Education in Historical Perspective.* Chicago: Rand McNally & Co., 1966. Chapter I.

Gruber, Fredrick C. *Foundations for a Philosophy of Education.* New York: Thomas Y. Crowell Company, 1961. Chapters I, & II.

Morris, Van Cleve. *Philosophy and the American School.* Boston: Houghton Mifflin Company, 1961, pp. 3-23.

Nakosteen, Mehdi. *The History and Philosophy of Education.* New York: The Ronald Press. Chapter I.

Peters, R. S. *Ethics and Education.* Atlanta: Scott, Foresman & Company, 1967, pp. 1-20.

Price, Kingsly. "Is a Philosophy of Education Necessary?," *Journal of Philosophy* LII, (October 1955), pp. 622-633.

Shermis, Samuel S. *Philosophic Foundations of Education.* New York: American Book Co. Chapters 1-4.

Shields, Thomas E. *Philosophy of Education.* Washington, D.C.: Catholic Education Press, 1921, pp. 21-32.

Smith, Phillip G. *Philosophy of Education, Introductory Studies.* New York: Harper & Row, 1965, pp. 7-71.

_____. "Philosophy, Educational Theory and Pedagogy," *Educational Theory* VI, (July 1956), pp. 129-134.

Villemain, Francis T. *Philosophic Research in Education.* New York: New York University, 1953, pp. 1-12.

Wingo, Max. *The Philosophy of American Education.* New York: D. C. Heath & Co., 1965. Chapters I-II.

CHAPTER II

The Origins of Philosophy

Who Needs It?

For several centuries men have been sifting through the rubbish and rubble of antiquity to discover more about their own origins. It has been a serious effort and not without its ironies. Often accounts of archeological adventures are enlivened by photographs of hundreds of perspiring but indifferent denizens carving out neat trenches under the gaze of academic aliens in white linens who have somehow conscripted the diggers into unearthing debris about which they know very little and care even less. Such pictures convey an obvious implication that the portion of mankind obsessed with its earthly navel is small and confined to sections of the planet where little serious digging is needed. There is some irony in this.

There is even more irony in recent efforts of men in one part of the world in giving their considerable wealth in order that tons of ancient statuary can be rescued from the flood plain of a new dam erected by an impoverished people whose main concern is water. And there is irony in the impoverished of other lands selling relics, and irony in the duties or taxes which are charged for the removal of artifacts to distant museums. It seems those most closely tied to this past by legacy of land and blood are reduced to selling it to strangers in order that the strangers can know more of themselves. One of the most curious things about man is the kind of things about which man is curious.

Those who have wealth or leisure seem more curious about origins than those whose daily concern is their own survival. The authentic descendant of early Incan, Sumerian, or Egyptian groups, scratching out a bare existence in uncongenial environment left to him, usually has no serious doubts about who he is or what his purpose is. Paradoxically, it is the inquiring foreigner jetting across the skies in air-cooled comfort who seems troubled with an ever-deepening and ever-darkening enigma. Is philosophy, therefore, the curse of leisure?

Or, is philosophy that which is lost by leisure? Thus, philosophy is its own first question.

The Long Conception

Modern man is not the first to form great questions or to develop abstract expressions of doubts, fears, and aspirations. There is reason to think meditation and teaching have gone on in all kinds of organized groups. The relatively recent probes into the past have produced enough evidence to require that modern man rethink his creation story. One could argue that the creation of man began when the first hairless biped of the general nature and style we call *Homo sapiens* awoke one morning and formed with his tongue and lips a sound equivalent to: "Why?" If this was not the beginning of man it was the beginning of philosophy. No one knows for how many thousands of years men and civilizations struggled with the question: "Why?" These struggles gave birth to countless animistic suppositions, personalized mythologies, and mystical dogmas. Clearly, in these struggles men also found purpose, produced beauty, developed meanings, acquired technologies, and schooled men of priestly and contemplative natures. Many of these achievements have been called remarkable; but, generally, they have not been called philosophy.

The accolades for beginning philosophy among Indo-European people are usually awarded to the Hellenes, so named for the male figure whom mythology records as their ancestor. Here and elsewhere in this discourse reference to this gifted and enterprising race will make use of the modern appellatives, Greece, Greek, or Grecian. Thus, it is said that the Greeks began western philosophy, and this is one of many honors due them. But as do all human achievements, theirs was accomplished by standing on that which had gone before.

The great civilizations in the Nile Valley had produced a vast laboring population "divisible into husbandmen, shepherds, artisans, boatmen—indeed, a multitude of special functional classifications."[1] This industry was supportive of an advanced institutional order featuring agencies of government, education, medicine, philanthropy, and religion. The Egyptians recorded the events and feelings of their lives in systems of hieroglyphics which tell of games and festivals, tools and trades, art and dance, war and peace, dynasty and age. The chronometrics of this great people are recorded by millennia, commencing before 5000 B.C. These rhythmic developments of their civilizations included the rise and fall of several scholarly traditions. So

complex an institutional order required a class of men who knew
letters, and it has been said that everyone was a scribe who knew how
to read, write, and cipher, and who knew the administrative routines
of the government and market, and who could apply the principles of
bookkeeping.[2] There were also those whose work required arithmetic,
geometry, chemistry, and other technologies of the higher secular professions such as astrology, architecture, and medicine.[3]

However, it was the priestly class whose avocation, and in some
cases vocation, was the pursuit of learning for its own sake. The temples were sources of learning and the Greeks, who later succeeded in
bringing human inquiry to the level of philosophy, had traveled to
Egypt, studied at the great priestly colleges, and knew the mathematics
and physics of Ptolemy. Both Thales and Pythagoras, originators of different and divergent traditions in Greek thought, studied in Egypt.
Legend holds that while there, both made original contributions of
their own. Thales is reputed to have demonstrated a means for measuring the height of a pyramid by measuring its shadow at the same time
of day that a man's shadow is equal to his height.[4]

Gifts to the Greeks

Egypt was not the only source of stimulation to Greek thought.
Any review of the origins of philosophy must take account of the
legacy and the life of the Hebrews, the Semitic nomads who traveled
the fertile crescent outlined upon the plains of Mesopotamia, anchored
on one side by the Tigris and Euphrates rivers and on the other side
by the Valley of the Nile. This region is spotted by mounds of random
shapes which commemorate the life and repose of communities now
vanished. Here once were Babylon and Nineveh. Six thousand years
ago barley and wheat reputedly grew on these arid wastes, and those
who lived here produced the heritage of literature and elements of
wisdom we call Biblical Antiquity.

The Greeks knew Babylon and they knew the Semites who
traveled the crescent. It is difficult to think that they were unaware of
the intricate political and social schemes which found expression there.
Parts of Babylonian mythology seem to have counterparts in Greek
mythology. The code of Hammurabi and the Babylonian sense of
justice are said to have influenced nearly all contemporary antiquity.[5]
The Semites who produced our Biblical heritage were bonded in Egypt
during the time when the Achaean invasions from the north were
establishing the basis for the Mycenaean civilization in Southern

Greece. At about the same time Moses led the "forty years" sojourn into the wilderness of the Sinai Peninsula, Mycenaean culture matured in Greece. The great city of Mycenae formed upon the hills that rise above the plains of Argos on the Peloponnesus; Gnossus fell; and Cretan (or Minoan) influences spread to the north. While the Israelites became unified under great leaders, formed a nation, and became the sovereign of their neighbors, the Homeric age was in its glory, the Dorian invasion began, and the aggressive colonization effort of the Greeks was started.

The rise of the Greek city states corresponded with the decline of the Kingdom of Judah. The Jews made continuing efforts to revive their political heritage. But from the Fifth Century B.C. onward, many dispersed and took with them the sense of prophesy, proverbial wisdom, commitment to law, and devotion to idea which placed them in or near the center of every intellectual movement in the history of western civilization. There were sons of Judah among the Greeks.

To the east, in Persia and India, highly developed civilizations had flourished for thousands of years prior to any state of organization among the Greeks. Indeed, it has been thought that many of the pre-Achaean, Neolithic Greeks, were Indo-Ayrian migrants from the east. Certainly the religious ties of Ionians give reason to link the origin of these Asian Greek with the lands and peoples to the east. There may have been ties to the Mohenjo-Daro on the Indus River. Those who have investigated the site of this ancient city compare it favorably with Egyptian and Sumerian cultures and from the ubiquitous presence of baths infer it to be hygienically superior.

India, of course, is universally regarded as the source of Brahmanism, a system of religious ideas which was well known to the Greeks and which seems to have made a special impression on Pythagoras. Persia also made its contribution. From the Indo-Iranian peoples, particularly those who lived in the high plateau of Iran, came Zoroastrianism, a religion far different from Brahmanism. In terms of influence it may have registered more strongly on the thought of Plato than did the beliefs of the Brahmans, although he, too, was clearly aware of the latter. Zoroastrianism—so called from Zarathustra, its founder—is credited with clarifying the teachings of the Magi who were recognized in Biblical literature for their wisdom. After the Seventh Century B.C., Zoroastrianism apparently became the official religion of the Persian rulers.

Zoroastrianism, sometimes called Magianism, is understood as a vision of contest between good and evil. The two central figures are

Ormazd (Mazda) the creator of all things, who stands for light, truth, goodness, purity, virtue, and beauty; and Ahriman, whose characteristics are such things as decay, darkness, sloth, and death. "Man according to his deeds belongs to Ormazd or Ahriman."[6] The noteworthy aspect of this religion is the high reality it proposes for abstract nouns (light, truth, purity, etc.) and the active place it assigns them in the lives of men. The religious nature of man—i.e., whether he is good or bad—is identified by his association with these abstract qualities. The religion of the Zoroastrians tended to be an ethical force in the lives of men and its adherents were answerable to ideals of conduct rather than rules of obeisance. Zoroastrianism has not been called philosophy but it is very close to philosophy. Many of the traits of Ormazd turn up in the Grecian Apollo and some of the characteristics of Ahriman are found in Apollo's counterpart Dionysus. Some of Mazda's power in the moral life of men has been preserved in the theology of the Christians.

So those who seek the origins of philosophy are indebted to those who sift through the rubbish and rubble of man's past. As the digging goes on another tomb is opened, new hieroglyphics are found, a battered weapon is unearthed, a fragment of a pot is collected, and archeological detectives assign them significance. They add more details to what can be known about the lives and lusts of early men, their migrations, their civilizations, and their problems with themselves and others. In producing philosophy the Greeks did not begin at the beginning any more than the inventor of the mathematics of relativity began by inventing number systems. The poets, priests, and scholars of Egypt, Crete, Sumeria, Persia, India, Phoenecia, all contributed something. When all was gathered and added to by Greek scholars of Ionia and southern Italy, it became philosophy. When the first hairless biped formed on his lips a sound which meant "why," philosophy was not born, but it became inevitable.

The flame came alive in the Sixth Century B.C., it flickered with some uncertainty in the Fifth Century and it radiated with strength and brilliance in the Fourth and Third Centuries, and then it began to fade. At the beginning of the Christian era there were only smoldering remains, but the coals were sufficiently alive to be rekindled. They did not vanish entirely. The Greeks persevered and are acknowledged as the progenitors of our modern knowledge systems. Thus do we recognize their eminence. Those who become teachers in western civilization should know well the Greeks of Antiquity.

The Cradle of Philosophy

The part of the world into which philosophy was born is not imposing when compared with the various land masses of the earth. At the most Greece encompasses no more than 50,000 square miles.[7] Its geographical territory is roughly equivalent to the state of New York. However, there is an entrancing quality about this setting which has always touched the poet in man. But few poets have done justice to its almost melancholy mixture of stone, water, and clay. There are scores of surrounding islands, each one with its own enchanting history. There is a background of light brown mountains which stands out against what Homer once called "the wine-dark sea." The ranges are creased by tiny river valleys—dry in the summer, often flooded in the seasons of rain. Few of them are more than ten or twelve miles long and six or eight miles across, and seldom does one lose sight of the sea. As Plato once said, "like frogs around a pond we have settled upon the shores of this sea."

Continental Greece is divided into three parts. The first of the three is Northern Greece which consists of Macedonia, Thessaly, and Epirus. Central Greece includes the territory between these northern lands and the Gulf of Corinth. This region contained such important places as Thebes, Delphi, and the region called Attica with its principal city Athens. South of this is the Peloponnesus which is saved from being another large island in the Mediterranean by the Isthmus of Corinth, an isle of land a few miles in width which joins the Peloponnesus to the mainland. The land is not fertile. Earthquakes are commonplace. During long periods of the year there is little or no rainfall. The climate of the north is temperate, and the climate of the south is tropic. From the sea the view of the hills is screened by mist. Storms strike with an overwhelming suddenness. There is much in this setting to urge reflectiveness in men. Perhaps the setting itself contained the progenitory forces of western civilization, but this is the base whence they came.

Although the topography of Greece is not exceptionally congenial to the basic needs of man, men came to it. In the third millenium B.C. there was a neolithic culture which by the year 2500 B.C. seems to have acquired the use of copper.[8] As indicated before, these early residents of the peninsula were probably migrants of civilizations to the east. The first external influence to be exerted came in the form of visiting sailors from the island of Crete where a highly advanced form of civilization had developed. The Cretan culture which is frequently referred to as Minoan and the influence exerted upon the early Greeks was profound. Indeed, Minoan civilization has been called a prologue to the classical age. The classic Greek language is found to contain many words of Minoan origin including place names that end in "inthos" and "ssos" or "enai." And although the most fruitful exchanges between the Cretans and the indigenous Greeks occurred in a time after the Minoan culture had passed its peak, there can be no question that the interactions of the two sparked the first surge of civilization on the mainland.[9]

While the cultural influence of Crete was being assimilated new invaders came to the peninsula from the north. They were Alpine and Nordic in origin. Their ancestors had lived in the Danube and Rhine valleys. Their language was Indo-European and they entered Greece at the time the Hittites entered Asia Minor about 1900 B.C. These conquerors we know as the Achaeans. They came on by infiltration and by invasion. The inundation lasted three or four centuries. They intermarried with those who preceded them and settled into local groups. Thus amalgamated, they formed a new and richer civilization and a culture which is called by the name Mycenaean. At the same time some of the long-established residents of the area moved across the Aegean Sea to the shores of Asia Minor and laid foundations for the great Ionian civilization on the coast of Asia.[10]

But it was the virile and aggressive Mycenaeans who occupied the center stage of early Greek history. They were characterized by the bold and resolute Agamemnon, who led the confederation of Greeks against the Asian Troy. Their adventures in civilization furnished the legend and lore of the heroic age. It is difficult to separate fact from fancy, but there can be no question that the great legends contain much history. This history is so bound up in sculpture, poetry, drama, and art, that we are driven to believe that these were people rich in imagination, vigorous in life, and expressive beyond any which preceded them in time. Homer belonged to a later time but it was of the Achaeans and the Mycenaean life that he wrote. It was an unmeditative age which seems to have produced almost no literature, but it produced an art which had near purity of form. Those times were colorful, exciting, and dominated by men of action. The Achaeans were not men to stand idly by. We hear much of their deeds, but little of their thoughts.

Then in the Twelfth Century there began a second massive invasion from the north. These invaders were the Dorians; and like the Achaeans they, too, appeared to emigrate from the Balkans, and their presence brought a renewed and heightened sense of enterprise and adventure to a people who were already enterprising and adventuresome. By the Ninth Century B.C. the Greeks began to colonize the northern shores of the Mediterranean, establishing living groups in southern Italy, southern Spain, Sicily, and Sardinia. Greek settlers moved northward to the shores of the Black Sea, southward to the island of Cyprus, and finally to the African southern shores of the Mediterranean at Cyrenea.[11] The Greeks had no coordinated national identity as such might be understood today. They were scattered in colonies and organized in small towns. However, because of common origin and elements of culture they became in fact a great maritime empire, and they developed commercial institutions around which men seemed to gather and accumulate wealth. All was not peaceful. The Greeks were vigorous and quarrelsome. They appear to have been at war with each other as much as they were at peace with each other. Even so, these internecine conflicts seemed not to arrest the ascendancy of their influence in the world.

Many modern scholars look upon commerce as the activity which explains the Greek city state (polis).[12] The tenability of this belief can be observed by noting that the great city states appeared on the natural trade routes of the then civilized world. Although trade or commerce may have determined the origin and location of the city states, it is very clear that the requirements of defense and military tactics determined the organization of the city itself. A state of war was the normal condition of life in Greece. Whether engaged by foreign enemy or fighting with each other, the fortunes of the city-state were generally in the hands of its military leaders.[13]

We have no standards by which to judge which town or settlement was a *city* and which was only a *village*. Nevertheless, this geographical entity now called Greece was, in antiquity, peppered with small but thriving communities, each one independent of the other, cooperating, conducting trade agreements, forming military alliances, exchanging artists and teachers; but, nevertheless, they were governmental or political entities. As such, they were set apart from each other. If one were to set about the business of creating western civilization and decided the first step would be to construct a laboratory for the purpose of experimenting in government, in education, in religion, in military organization, in monetary systems, in postal systems, and in economic systems, one could not fashion a better laboratory than the seventy or more great city-states of Greece. These political entities, over the period of seven centuries, conducted nearly every experiment possible in institutional life. There is virtually nothing in modern life which was not tried at one time or another by the Greeks. Indeed, many experiments in living were tried in Greece which have yet to be replicated. Those who study social process or wish to know the effects of various political or economic systems can look upon this great period of experimentation and make the sensible inferences. Athens and Sparta, Thebes and Corinth offer only two of the many vivid contrasts. Although scholars have been studying these diverse cultures for two thousand years, it is very clear that all of the ore has not yet been removed and much that is out in the open has not yet been fully refined. Of course, Greece was not conceived as a laboratory for experiments in civilization, but it would be difficult to conceive a better one. As the discerning scholar faces the complexities of modern civilization, the Greeks still teach him. At the level of principle there are few problems today which were unknown to antiquity.

One cannot summarize all the contributions of Greek antiquity without mentioning one which eludes the critical historian but which may, in terms of force, be the greatest. Indications are reasonably clear that prior to the Greeks the state of civilized man tended to be wretched. His religions were fearsome. His princes were oppressive. His neighbors were menacing. His arts revealed obsession with power. He was starved, butchered, and enslaved. The Greeks did not bring these things to an end. But they did show man how to rejoice in life, to find the world beautiful and delightful to live in. They did show man institutions which turned primitive passions into forms of art and inspired competition. The pagans laughed and mourned with their Gods. Life was shown to be harmony, fellowship, and joy.

The joy of life is written on much that was left behind. Joy and sorrow, comedy and tragedy, move stride for stride through Greek art and literature. Vase paintings reveal the merriment which the Greeks took from the predicaments of gods and men. There is a perspective on the brevity and futility of human endeavor. The Greeks, the most enterprising of the ancients, tended to see the enterprise itself as the thing and would not stake their happiness on whether the enterprise succeeded or failed, for all ended the same. The fire of life burned briefly and it may just as well have burned brightly. There were no little pleasures.

All of this was further highlighted by an evolving notion of personal freedom. Tyranny was so brief that its brief existence in Athens has been regarded as a benchmark in the struggle for democracy. In the *Persians,* a play written by Aeschylus to celebrate the great sea victory at Salamis, there is a vigorous comparison between Greek and oriental styles. The Greeks, so the Persian queen was told, "fight as free men." She asked, "have they no master?" She is told, "No. No man calls the Greeks slaves or vassals." At Olympia the Greeks competed for a wreath of laurel, at Athens for a cup of olive oil harvested from the sacred trees. A prisoner taken at Thermopylae was asked by a Persian general what the winners of the games were given. On being told, the general reputedly turned to Xerxes with the comment, "and we must fight men like these."

Despite the discomfort this seemed to give aristocrats like Plato, the Greeks set limits on the power of the state over the individual. More than this they set limits on the priests. Prior to the Greeks, tribal priests had reserved to themselves the thinking that men were permitted to do. Except for certain notable moments of backsliding, particularly at Athens, the Greeks maintained that all things are to be called into question, and no limits were set upon thinking. There is in fact no trace of sustained domination of the Greek mind by priests of any kind. Homer's account of the Trojan War states it was fought by gods and men together. No priests were in camp to interpret one to the other.

These qualities of joy, enterprise, and freedom tended to disappear in western Europe during the middle periods of the Christian era. But they survived. All considered, their emergence in Greek antiquity was as much responsible for the emergence of philosophy as anything. Socrates spoke to Theaetetus of "the ease which free men always command. They can have their talk out in peace, wandering at will from one subject to another, their only aim to attain truth." Even today, it is characteristic of the Greek that he will express himself. The joy in life comes to expression at various times and places. It is not uncommon to hear a Greek in one of his native restaurants break out in song or enter into an impromptu dance. Why not? He is free, and his greatest beneficence to western man may be his liberal spirit.

When western man seeks the origin of that which we call Greek philosophy the eyes of his memory are inclined to first fall upon Athens—the city of Pericles, home of the Academy, abode of the great Socrates, and reportedly the intellectual center of classical antiquity. Indeed, it was Athens which became a stage for the dramatic events which brought enduring renown to Plato, Aristotle, Diogenes, and numerous others who did so much to shape the western mind. But we do not find the origins of philosophy in Athens. Although Greek philosophy had exciting days in Athens, the Athenians were never especially hospitable to free and open discourse. Now that the record is clear, it is apparent that Greek philosophers who wished to accomplish longevity, serenity, or both, were well advised to stay out of Athens.

Some authorities assert that philosophy began east of Athens, across the Aegean Sea, among the Ionians on the coast of Asia Minor. They speak of Thales of Miletus. Others say that philosophy came to life west of Athens on the coast of southern Italy, and they claim the honor belongs to Pythagoras and his society of followers in the city of Crotona. It is clear that in the Sixth Century philosophy burst forth in both Ionis and Italy, but the Ionians and the Pythagoreans differed in what they did and thought. This difference is important.

The Ionians and Metastasis

The first Ionian scholars lived in a city called Miletus. Therefore, in the literature of thought they are referred to as the Milesian School. Doubtless many were involved in the activities of the Milesian School, but the approbations of time and tradition do major honor to only three. The first of the three was Thales. He was born about 640 B.C., probably at Miletus, and reputedly of Phoenician parentage. Thales obtained much of his early education during his travels through Egypt and the near East. Our vision of him reveals a tall, graceful, sensitive, and alert man who was much honored in his days, which lasted into a ninety-fourth year of life. As a young man he engaged in a business venture which succeeded so well that he was able to devote the remainder of his life to the study and teaching he so obviously loved. He has been accredited with the introduction of mathematical and astronomical science into Ionia. One of the great legends of antiquity records how, at the time he was in Egypt, he measured the distance from the ground to the top of a pyramid by determining the length of its shadow at the same time of the day when a man's shadow equaled his height. Returning to Miletus, Thales pursued the study of geometry as a deductive science. Later he was to astonish all of Ionia by successfully predicting an eclipse of the sun for May 28, in the year 585 B.C.

Thales would be accepted into that tradition of philosophy called realism. He is best known for his mode of materialistic speculation about the *basic stuff* out of which the world is made. He was not disposed to accept accounts furnished by mythology. Thales thought there was a single substance out of which all other things were derived. He asked of *himself*: "What is this base out of which all matter is derived? If all was once again resolved to its primordial substance, what would this substance be? Where would it be? What would be its name?"

Applying his very considerable powers of observation and reason to the material realities which appeared in his senses, Thales took notice that water surrounds the land; that it comes forth from the earth and down from the heavens; that water is a constituent part of every living thing. He noticed that when the stem of a plant is cut there is moisture found within. When a seed is taken apart, moisture is found within, and that when a thing dies and it begins to decay, the moisture begins to depart. Thales assumed, and reasoned as true, that the basic stuff of the world is water, and for this he came to be known in later ages as the "water philosopher."[14]

In retrospect, it is easy to recognize his error. Yet he was a man of his time, and as such, his remarkable faith in observation and reason set him apart from the others of his time and all who preceded him. He made demands on his powers of observation and reason which few, if any, had made before him. The obstinate and persistent faith which he vested in his own capacity to know marked the arrival of a new kind of man. In later times when Greece came to name its seven wise men it placed the name of Thales before all of the others.

The second of the three great Milesian scholars studied under Thales. His name was Anaximander. He lived from 611 to 549 B.C., and in his later years he passionately advanced the methods of his teacher. His central question was the same as that propounded by Thales: what is the basic stuff out of which the world is made? Unlike Thales, he concluded that the basic material of the world or of the cosmos is a boundless *mass* possessing no specific qualities but developing out of its inherent forces the multiformed realities of the world. The *mass* of which he spoke is indeterminate (without purpose) and infinite (without boundaries), and all substances of the world which have specific identity are in the process of being derived from this indeterminate, infinite mass, or in the process of being resolved once again into it. Out of this characterless infinite emerge new worlds; in an unending procession they return. Within this original, primordial infinite, all opposites are included: hot and cold, moist and dry, motion and rest, solid and gas.[15]

Anaximander believed that the earth in its earliest form was fluid and that a great heat, which was external to the earth, dried some of it into land masses and evaporated much of it into clouds. He declared the living organism emerged by gradual stages from the original moisture and that land animals were at first animals of the sea, and he reasoned that only with the drying out of the earth did they acquire their present shapes. He indicated that man, too, was once a fish and deduced that it is impossible that man in his original form could have been as he is in his present condition, for in his present state man is too weak to secure his food, protect himself, and compete among other living things for the substances of life.

The third great figure of the Milesian school was a younger contemporary of Anaximander whose name was Anaximines. Asking the same question which was raised by his two predecessors, Anaximines concluded that the first principle of matter was air. He believed that all other elements are derived from air by rarefaction, which is usually taken to mean out of fire. He declared the soul, which is air, holds men together, so the air of the world is a pervasive spirit, its breath, and even its god.[16]

These three speculations into the physical nature of the cosmos created much excitement in Miletus; and, without question, in the Sixth Century B.C., Miletus was the intellectual stronghold of Ionia. But, as a great city, Miletus soon faded. Prosperity and the pursuit of wisdom seem at times to make a people soft. In any case, softness and decay soon pave the way for the conqueror, and so it was for Miletus. Class strife broke out; control of the government shifted from faction to faction; and the great age of Miletus and Milesian philosophy was soon over.[17] The center of intellectual power in Ionia shifted northward to the most enduring of Ionia's famous cities, Ephesus. This great metropolis of pagan antiquity was known for its art and its religious shrines. For centuries it was the center of Artemis worship and those to the east who worshipped this oriental goddess of fertility and motherhood made pilgrimages to Ephesus to visit its famous altars and holy places.[18]

Christians will recognize Ephesus as one of the locations where, in later days, the great apostle, Paul, established a primitive Christian church. On one of his visits to Ephesus it is said that Paul found himself sorely beset by, among others, the metalsmiths of the city. They were angered at the presence of a stranger who taught the citizens of a God for whom no gold or silver images could be built, so they rioted and would have brought him to a violent end had he not been arrested. His escape is a well known part of Biblical record.

In the Sixth Century B.C., Ephesus became known for its poets and philosophers. Probably the best known and remembered of the poets was a man called Hipponax (the original hippy), who midway through the Sixth Century was composing poems so coarse in subject, obscure in language, pointed in wit, and refined in metrical style, that all Greece spoke of him and all Ephesus hated him. "He was short, thin, lame, deformed, and completely disagreeable."[19] In one of his sur- viving fragments he claims that women can bring only two days of happiness to a man, "one when he marries her, and the other when he buries her."[20] He was a sharp-witted satirist. He attacked every notable of the city with apparent impunity. Accounts vary as to how he met his end. Some say it was suicide and others attribute the violence to others. There can be little doubt that the event, however it occurred, seems to have been well received by just about everyone.

But the most illustrious son of Ephesus was the philosopher Heraclitus. Born about 530 B.C., he belonged to an aristocratic family. This may have accounted for some of his hatred for democracy. He argued against it endlessly, claiming it a diversion for fools and a destroyer of distinction among men. Frequently, he denounced the democratic aversion to quality and distinction, and one of these indict- ments survives:

> The Ephesians deserve to be hanged, every one that is a man grown, and the youth to abandon the city, for they cast out Hermodorus the best man among them saying;—Let no one among us be best, and if he be best, let him be so else- where and among others.[21]

Heraclitus saw no basis for postulates of equality. Said he: "to me one man is ten thousand if he be the best."[22] Accounts of his life reveal that he was disinclined to make congenial accommodations to the dif- ferences between himself and his fellow citizens; and, in turn, they referred to him as "Heraclitus the obscure."

Heraclitus depicted a world of endless change and universal motion. His answer to the question raised by the Milesians was that the *basic stuff* of the world was and is an everlasting fire. He said: "all things are exchanged for fire, and fire for all things. . . ."[23] Thus, he seemed to believe that all matter is in a state of warming or cooling. This related to his notion that change in all things is both ubiquitous and unending. Nothing is static; all is moving. Involution, evolution, and revolution are constant and forever. Everything is ceasing to be what it was and is in a state of becoming something else.

All that remains of his writings is contained in one hundred and thirty-four fragments. The most famous of these relates to this theory of change. He said: "you cannot step twice in the same river for other water is ever flowing on to you."[24]

Heraclitus is regarded as one of the most brilliant men of all time. He gave added inertia to the materialistic Ionian philosophy which was so well started by the Milesian scholars. The validity of some of his observations on physical reality, though often contested, has not been overthrown. The nebular hypothesis lives on as one of the most plausible explanations about the origin of the earth. In the Nineteenth Century Hegel, the great German idealist, described the world as a vast becoming dominated by the massive fact of change through the interaction of opposites. Also, in the Nineteenth Century, Nietzsche led an assault on democracy with a polemic reminiscent of the Sage of Ephesus. In fact, the student of philosophy is struck by the many ways in which Heraclitus and Nietzsche are similar in their lives, thoughts, and manner of expressing themselves.

But the poet in man is most deeply moved by the Heraclitean quest for meaning through the unity and interdependence of opposites. It occurred to Heraclitus that all things take place by strife and all things are given meaning by their opposite. Youth takes its meaning from age; good takes its meaning from bad; and if one will understand or appreciate peace, he must know and appreciate war. Opposites are different forms of the same thing and, like the two ends of a string being pulled taut, create vibrations and harmony[25]; opposites pull and thus create in their strife the interplay, the fluxation, the harmony, and the discord of life. He said "from that which draws apart results the most beautiful harmony."[26]

So in day against night, satiety against hunger, man against woman, youth against age, color against color, generation against generation, the strife goes on. Each of the contraries is essential to the meaning and reality of the other. Thus the tensions, alterations, and interactions of class and class, nation and nation, idea and idea, organism and organism become the dynamics of the sensible world. By knowing that upward and downward are simply directions on a single path, a man comes to understand that opposites express meaning to the unity of which they are contrary parts.

All is generated by fire. Heraclitus pointed out that "the sun is new every day."[27] This regenerating vision lived on. Plato put a fire in his analogy of the cave. A divine fire was postulated by the Stoics and seems to have passed ultimately into the theology of the Christians as the Divine Word.[28] Perhaps Heraclitus may have obtained his notions about fire from the Persians. Whatever the source of his ideas, it is generally recognized that Heraclitus is one of the few among the men who are called philosophers who stepped apart from his age and, through a creative intelligence surpassing all others of his time, put forward notions about physical reality which cling to us, even today, with the tenacity of truth.

The Ionians presented a world dominated by the massive fact of change. To them nothing survives except change. All material is in the process of becoming something other than what it is. Permanence and immutability have no existence except in the musings of the romantically minded who refuse to look, see, and accept the world which surrounds them. So devastating was the Heraclitean's notion of change that it was to unsettle the minds of philosophers for two centuries. Cratylus, a devotee of Heraclitus and an early teacher of Plato, was so fixed in his thinking about the ubiquity of change that he criticized Heraclitus by saying that a man cannot step even once in the same river because as he is stepping in the river, the man himself is undergoing change.[29] In subsequent years, Greek philosophers were to speculate further as to how this change occurred. The notion of the eternal and endless transformation was firmly planted in western thought and no philosophy which has since been constructed can fail to give it consideration.

The Pythagoreans and Metempsychosis

But the Greeks, who settled on the shores of southern Italy, originated a philosophy which was generated out of a wholly different view of reality. The hero of this movement was Pythagoras. According to legend he was born in the city of Samos about 580 B.C. As a young man he studied extensively and traveled widely. Like Thales, he visited Egypt where he attended the priestly colleges. There he probably learned astronomy, geometry, history, and perhaps a great deal of mysticism. He also was a man of imposing presence. At the age of fifty he organized a school at Crotona on the coast of southern Italy. It was not an ordinary school. For one thing, Pythagoras implemented a policy of equal opportunity for both sexes and was probably the very first schoolmaster to do so; but the rules he established and imposed upon both himself and his students gave the school many of the aspects of a medieval monastery. Strict dietary laws were enforced which included the prohibition of the drinking of wine.[30] It is supposed that even then such a regulation would be difficult to enforce in Italy. Pythagoras seems to have been obsessed with a belief which in modern times has been doctrinized as *metempsychosis*. This is a transcendental view of life which reputedly originated among the Brahmans. In general, it holds that the soul of a dying or dead organism passes into another organism; thus souls may live successively in the different bodies of men, animals, or plants. This is not to be confused with the conception of reincarnation which envisions more than the transmigration of souls. Metempsychosis gives no thought to the destiny of the body in which a soul is housed.

However, the important point is that Pythagoras and his followers were convinced that there was much more to reality than could be seen in the materialistic and temporal life of the senses. Whereas Thales and the Ionians philosophized on the basis of what their senses presented to them, Pythagoras and his followers seemed to think that meditation or reflection in which the senses took only a minor part constituted a more fruitful path to ultimate truth. Thales and the Ionians found only change. Pythagoras and his followers searched for permanence. The Pythagoreans were excellent astronomers and mathematicians. Virtually every school boy is familiar with the Pythagorean theorem which enables him to discover the length of the hypotenuse of a right triangle by squaring the lengths of the right angle sides, adding them together, and extracting the square root of the sum. Pythagoras also reduced musical notes to numbers and thereby established a mathematical basis for sound and harmony. But Pythagoras was not interested in the applications of mathematics to the sensible or material world of time and motion. Mathematics was an intellectual probe into regions beyond the senses, and its purpose, if anything, was religious.[31]

It is little wonder Pythagoras and his followers were interested in things that do not change. As geometers they doubtless considered the circle. The circle, of course, is an idea. It can be represented in the sensible world of objects, but it has never been constructed there because error is a constituent part of a man's every physical performance in the world of objects. Therefore, a perfect circle has never been made on paper or incarnated by material reality. However, it can and does exist in the mind. The Greeks selected the letter "π" to represent the relationship between the radius of the circle and its circumference. The idea of the circle is the same to the American schoolboy as it was to Pythagoras and the society. *Thus one can argue that the idea of a circle has not and will not change.* The same can be said of the Pythagorean theorem and the other like discoveries which he or members of his school (society) left to posterity.

Initiation into the Pythagorean society was based upon the purification of the body by abstinence, asceticism, and self-control. The mind was to be purified by scientific study. Arithmetic was not considered as a practical means of solving problems; it was approached as an abstract theory of numbers. It is important that once again we compare the world which Pythagoras depicted with the metastasis of Heraclitus. Whereas Heraclitus observed endless change, Pythagoras postulated permanence. Although there was great respect in each of these philosophical camps for what was happening in the other, there was a fundamental disagreement. Out of this difference emerged the first great metaphysical issue: is reality ever changing or ever permanent? Other issues inherent in the difference are: is thought of the body, or is it of the soul? And if the sensible world is real, then what is the quality called thought? And if thought is real, then what is the sensible world?

The Pythagorean society scattered but lived on after the death of its founder. He wrote three books—one on education, another on statemanship, and a third on nature. Another book which passes as the work of Pythagoras is by Lysis of Tarentum. At least one famous philosopher followed in the Pythagorean tradition. Accounts differ as to whether he himself was a member of the society. His name was Parmenides. According to legend, he was first taught by Xenophanes who was of the Ionian persuasion and a stern critic of the Pythagoreans. Both of these men were from the city of Elea, and together they are said to have formed the Eleatic school. Parmenides, in particular, presented a theory of permanence by developing his concept of being. He said the one way of assuming that *being is* is that it is impossible for it not to be. Not being is impossible. Then he went on to point out that *thought* and *being* are the same thing.[32]

Parmenides' argument presents a rational basis for permanence in the universe. It establishes that the seat of all being is in *thought*, and in *thought alone*. Thus, the metaphysical line in behalf of permanence was more clearly drawn. Parmenides argued the reality of mind and believed that the quality called thought was not subject to destruction. He implied that thought is *real;* it is the whole of being, without beginning or end, and questions about generation and destruction simply do not apply to it. Thus, the Pythagoreans and their kindred gave us a vision of a life of mind that is apart from the life of objects. Life of mind is an abode wherein permanence, and invariance, and immutability, can dwell. Moreover, when one enters into the world of thought and engages in the life of mind, he has connected himself to the eternal train.

The Pythagorean society appears to have been what we might call communistic in its organization. There was a common sharing of goods and property by members of the cult. Some authorities state flatly that beyond this, nothing is or can be known about how this experiment in living ended. Others, however, who harken with greater faith to details taken from the legends of antiquity and write with unbridled imagination have given full accounts of how the Pythagoreans were finally dispersed. Being Greeks, it is pointed out, they could not stay out of politics. And in the perennial political struggles between the democrats and the aristocrats the Pythagorean society was decidedly on the side of the aristocrats. According to one account, Pythagoras attempted to make his society the governing body of Crotona, whereupon the enraged popular party burned down his house, overtook the fleeing leader (who must have been at least eighty at the time) and put him to death. In another story, he escaped to Metapontum where he indulged in remorse to the point of not eating for forty days and died of starvation on the forty-first.[33]

But the Pythagoreans lived on. A few of them started schools of their own. Their ideas were given further momentum and freshness by Parmenides and during the period of enlightenment which followed, these ideas took hold in many of the traveling teachers (or sophists) who found the young men of Greece eager to enlist intellectually on one or another side of the metaphysical combat between the Ionians and the Italians of Sixth-Century Greece.

Notes

1. Thomas Woody, *Life and Education in Early Societies* (New York: The Macmillan Company, 1949), p. 50.
2. *Ibid.*, p. 51.
3. *Ibid.*
4. Will Durant, *The Life of Greece* (New York: Simon and Schuster, 1939), p. 136.
5. William Morley, *Morley's Ancient Peoples* (New York: American Book Company, 1943, Countryman's Edition), p. 66.
6. Woody, *op. cit.*, p. 179. Quoted from F. M. Muller, *The Sacred Books of the East* (The Clarendon Press).
7. J. W. Swain, W. H. Armstrong, *The People of the Ancient World* (New York: Harper and Bros., 1959), p. 151.
8. *Ibid.*, p. 160.
9. Woody, *op. cit.*, p. 197 ff.
10. Swain, Armstrong, *op. cit.*, p. 166.
11. *Ibid.*, p. 177.
12. *Ibid.*, p. 180.
13. *Ibid.*, p. 182.
14. Aristotle, *Metaphysics, I.*
15. Durant, *op. cit.*, p. 139.

16. Aristotle, *Metaphysics, I.*
17. Durant, *op. cit.*, p. 140. Quoted from *Athenaeus.*
18. Morley, *op. cit.*, p. 100.
19. Durant, *op. cit.*, p. 143.
20. *Ibid.*
21. Heraclitus, *Fragment* 114.
22. Heraclitus, *Fragment* 113.
23. Heraclitus, *Fragment* 22.
24. Heraclitus, *Fragment* 41-42.
25. Heraclitus, *Fragment* 46.
26. *Ibid.*
27. Heraclitus, *Fragment* 32.
28. Durant, *op. cit.*, p. 147.
29. Aristotle, *Metaphysics.*
30. T. V. Smith, ed., *Philosophers Speak for Themselves* (Chicago: University of Chicago Press, Vol. I, *Thales to Plato*, 1934), p. 48.
31. *Ibid.*, p. 54.
32. *Ibid.*, p. 15.
33. A widely accepted account of the Pythagoreans is Hicks' translation (Loeb Classical Library series) of *Diogenes Laertius* (II, 323-331 and 335-337).

Other Reading

Butts, Freeman. *A Cultural History of Western Education.* New York: Mc-Graw-Hill Book Company, 1955. Chapters I-III.

Chamoux, Francois. *The Civilization of Greece.* New York: Simon and Schuster, 1965, pp. 1-161.

Copleston, Fredrick. *A History of Philosophy.* London: Burns, Oates, and Washbourne Ltd., 1946. Volume I.

Durant, Will. *The Life of Greece.* New York: Simon and Schuster, 1939, pp. 4-41, 66-374.

Gomperez, Theodor. *Greek Thinkers, A History of Ancient Philosophy.* Tr. G. G. Berry. New York: Charles Scribner's Sons, 1908. Volumes I, II.

Good, H. G. *A History of Western Education.* New York: The Macmillan Company, 1960.

Gulick, C. B. *Life of the Ancient Greeks.* New York: Appleton-Century-Crofts, Inc., 1905, pp. 1-87.

Gutherie, W. K. C. *A History of Greek Philosophy.* Cambridge: The University Press, 1965. Volume II.

Jager, Werner. *The Theology of Early Greek Philosophers.* Oxford: The Clarendon Press, 1947, pp. 1-155.

Lawton, W. C. *Introduction to Classical Greek Literature.* New York: Scribner's, 1904.

Mulhern, James. *A History of Education.* New York: The Ronald Press Company, 1959, pp. 130-177.

Raven, J. E. *Pythagoreans and Eleatics.* Cambridge: The Cambridge University Press, 1948, pp. 1-65.

Russell, Bertrand. *Wisdom of the West*. London: Rathbone Books, Ltd., 1959, pp. 1-58.
Sidgwick, Henry. "The Sophists," *Journal of Philosophy* IV, (1872-1873), pp. 288-307.
Woody, Thomas. *Life and Education in Early Societies*. New York: The Macmillan Company, 1949, pp. 197-465.

CHAPTER III

The Rise of Formal Idealism

Thales and the Ionians sought ultimate reality in matter, and are henceforth called materialists. They belong to the tradition of philosophy called realism. Pythagoras and the Italians sought ultimate reality in spirit and, henceforth, are frequently called spiritualists or mystics. They belong to the tradition of philosophy called idealism. It is not possible to know whether Greek philosophy began first in Ionia or in Italy. Thales preceded the Pythagoreans in time but Pythagoras himself gave the word philosophy to our language. It is said that he found the term *sophia* or *wisdom* immodest and insisted that philosophia, which we take to mean the *love of wisdom,* was more fitting. Thus humility, or lack of pretense, was the mark of the philosopher. In the Sixth Century the words philosopher and Pythagorean had identical meanings.

The philosophers traveled widely. As we have seen, Xenophanes, one of the Ionian materialists, turned up in Italy and aroused Parmenides to philosophy. Anaxagoras, another Ionian, journeyed to Athens for a misadventure giving him the honor of heading what soon became an impressive line of philosophers who were denounced or menaced within that sullen bastion of religious conservatism. Parmenides came to Athens about 450 B.C., and although he seems not to have antagonized the Athenians he certainly aroused their interest. Clearly, the issue of change versus permanence was now before all of Greece. The Heraclitean doctrine was reduced to the words *Panta Rei* (all things change). The Parmenidean doctrine was resolved to the phrase, *Henta Panta* (all things are one and never change).[1] Permanence became the target of constant criticism by the materialists; and those Greeks who revered the ancestral gods were shocked by the seemingly irreverent doctrines of the Ionians.

There were, as might be expected, philosophers who attempted to create mediating theories. Empedocles produced a thesis on evolution and sought to reconcile materialism and spiritualism by explaining them as aspects of the inherent forces which brought about evolution. It has been said that his system anticipated the late Nineteenth-Century philosophy of Herbert Spencer.[2] Zeno of Ela made a gesture in the direction of mediation by showing that extremes of permanence and change were both theoretically impossible. This pre-Socratic reactionist was said to have had the sharpest tongue in antiquity. One of his contemporaries declared, "say what one would, Zeno would argue it untrue."[3]

This atmosphere of intellectual contention contributed to the advancement of learning which took place midway through the Fifth Century and produced other great figures such as Democritus who responded to the issue of materialism by saying that matter is composed of atoms moving in a void.[4] Democritus theorized that the differences we observe in the material things of the world are explained by differences in the shape and size of atoms, out of which materials are composed. In this way science acquired one of its most famous and enduring hypotheses. Democritus shared the same stage of time with the great physician, Hippocrates. Prior to Hippocrates the most famous Greek physicians had been associated with the Pythagorean school. Hippocrates gave medicine to science.[5] Although he wrote widely and in many other fields, his treatises on the human body, its needs and cures, stimulated the advances in Greek medicine which reached a level not surpassed until the Nineteenth Century A.D. Perhaps he has been better known as author of the physician's creed. The Hippocratic Oath still stands as a plenary definition of the relationship between physician, patient, and the civilization of which both are part.

The Sophists

We have established that Athens was not the source of philosophy. It is equally clear that neither Athens nor Attica, the region it governed, was a major source of Greek philosophers. None of the great scholars before Socrates were citizens of that city; and of all those who followed him, Athens can claim only Plato. Antisthenes was but half Athenian, and Epicurus was not born there. But as the Greek intellectual spirit began to animate the region, Athens increasingly became the center to which men of thought were drawn. The whole of Greece became a kind of university during the Fifth Century B.C. As interest in philosophy grew and the great metaphysical issues agitated the populace; traveling teachers became more and more commonplace. They scheduled appearances at one or another of the city states, advertised, and collected fees. These teachers were accredited by their mastership of one or more of the issues of interest which Sixth-Century philosophy had produced. We are assured that these men were not given to self-abasement, nor were they afflicted by the sense of modesty which compelled Pythagoras to call himself only a lover of wisdom. The traveling teachers called themselves *sophistia* which meant *teachers of wisdom.* They learned to speak wth clarity, precision, and grace. They knew the languages of city, town, and country. Often they were in great demand. One, in particular, whose name was Protagoras, was able to command very high fees for his lectures and we have been reliably informed that he received ten thousand drachmas for the education of a single pupil.[6] The fees, of course, varied in accordance with the market. On occasion, very high fees such as those charged by Protagoras, were challenged on moral grounds and Protagoras, in particular, was frequently called upon to account for his high tuitions. But, according to Plato, even Socrates, who objected very strenuously to teachers charging for their work, held high respect for Protagoras.

Protagoras seems to have been a forerunner of the modern existentialist. Of humble origin, in youth he earned his livelihood as a porter, but he became an itinerant teacher and ultimately was attracted to Athens where he became a friend of the great Pericles.[7] He reputedly professed that contradictory assertions can be true for different persons at different times. In the *Theaetetus,* Plato quotes him as saying, "Man is the measure of all things; of those that are, that they are, and of those that are not, that they are not." Protagoras seems to have been possessed of the strength of his convictions. He aroused the Athenians by declaring that he did not know whether the gods existed and then went on to say he did not think men could know such things. As a consequence of this he became (at least) the second philosopher Athens honored by expulsion. Moreover, Protagoras may have been the first to be celebrated by having his books burned in the market place. According to some accounts, after his banishment from Athens he attempted to reach Sicily, but was drowned on the way. Presumably, this melancholy result was reassuring to the Athenian governors. However, there were many more problems on the way.

Another well known sophist, whose name was Gorgias, originated from the city of Leontini. His fame as a teacher was almost equivalent to that of Protagoras.[8] He exceeded Protagoras in having the good judgment not to visit Athens in a professional capacity. He spent time there as an ambassador from Sicily and seems to have made a hit with the Athenians by a lengthy oration which aroused their patriotism against a threat from Persia. It is said that his teaching fees were as great as those of Protagoras, and he wrote numerous books; but, unfortunately, very little of his writing remains.

In these times there were other great sophists such as Hippias of Elis and Prodicus of Ceos. These and many others spread enlightenment to the far colonies of Greece. They made language a vehicle capable of transmitting knowledge. They gave further inertia and credence to rationality in human affairs, and they made it fashionable to doubt, question, and discuss. But it is also true that much dishonor has been attached to the name *sophist*, and authority has been divided as to whether this infamy was deserved.

Criticism of the sophists came mainly from the "big three" in Greek philosophy; Socrates, Plato, and Aristotle. The criticism stemmed from two practices. The first was that as competition among them grew in intensity sophists tended to become "crowd pleasers," and their sensitivity about fees mounted. It was charged that the sophists, especially the lesser or weaker ones of the group, tended to tell their hearers what they wanted to hear, ask believers to believe what they already believed, and make unworthy appeals to emotions. Such things, it was said, were accomplished through clever but empty rhetoric which, in itself, grew to a fine art. So clearly was the charge made and so firmly did it stick that sophistry is still a word used in describing this kind of elegant deception. The second charge rested primarily on the matter of fees. Socrates, who wanted nothing in the material world and cared very little about possessions of any kind, found it easy to criticize teachers who accepted money. He called them "prostitutes of wisdom" and thus castigated them along with prostitutes of any kind. Plato, who was born into a family of Athenian aristocracy, and was not obliged to seek his own support, was unsympathetic to the idea that anyone would charge for teaching. Aristotle, who, to use a modern term, was "funded," apparently by Alexander and other patrons, likewise found it easy to criticize the sophists for charging tuitions. He declared that a sophist is one "who is only eager to get rich on his apparent wisdom."[9]

The reputation of these traveling teachers was further damaged by the fact that the time of their greatest prominence corresponds with what some observers have called a decline in morality and other aspects of the Greek institutional life. It is obvious that Athenian vitality was diffused by the latter part of the Fifth Century. The early years of this century were marked by the magnificent Athenian victories over

Persian aggression and the emergence of democracy; but its later years were marked by civil unrest, war with Sparta, and a decline in capacity for consistent political action. Some, of course, attributed this to the questioning, doubting, and quibbling which seemed to follow in the wake of the traveling teachers.

However, in fairness it must be noted that this kind of argument can never be settled. What some men take for vitality others will call dissension. What some observers insist is morality, others claim to be dogma. Some observers of civilization will claim that enlightenment weakens the people, makes them soft, and opens gates to their enslavement by others. At the same time others argue that enlightenment liberates a people and frees them from the evils of prejudice, blind adherence to authority, and regimented thought.

In the ten years 450-440 B.C. Athens was the Imperial City. Pericles governed, and the majestic Parthenon with its Sanctuary of Athena was erected atop the Acropolis and consecrated by religious ceremonies so great as to be commemorated in stone. But at that same time the greed of Athenian merchants and the arrogance of Athenian statesmen were casting seeds of bitterness and resentment which one decade later grew into forces which ultimately brought the City to its knees. It was in this period of decline that the Socratic denunciation of sophistry was leveled.

Modern commentaries are more sympathetic to the sophists. Educators of today, confronted as they are with the problems of finance are disinclined to take seriously the charge of "prostitution" made by Socrates and echoed by Plato and Aristotle. Despite the eminence of its authors, the accusation that teaching for money is a criminal rapacity is seldom heard and never accepted in modern times. It is also clear that the sophists, though not in every case creative philosophers, nevertheless spread philosophy. Therefore, it can be argued that they spread the doctrines which were, in time, to inspire greater philosophy. The Platonic dialogues alone present convincing evidence that Socrates himself may have been elevated to the level of philosophy by men such as Protagoras. In the Platonic dialogue which bears his name, Protagoras defends realism, democracy, and established educational practices from challenges by an aggressive Socrates who is testing Protagoras for meaning and clarity. Socrates in this role is a young adversary to the established political and educational traditions. But if it is credible to think that sophists such as Protagoras inspired Socrates to philosophy, then the enduring honor of the *sophistia* is assured. For we have Plato's own view that he was inspired by Socrates. We also have Aristotle's admission of his debt to Plato. It is therefore an ironic probability that the sophists gave intellectual birth to their most uncompromising critics.

The Gadfly and His Forum

It is said that his father was a stonecutter and that he himself carved a Hermes and the three graces which stood near the entrance to the Acropolis.[10] This is the kind of legend through which we know Socrates, the most famous man of antiquity. Constantly, the modern intellectual world is amazed and amused by the fact that he never published; we have nothing which came from his pen. His mother was a midwife, and later he drew upon this circumstance to form a self-characterization as a "midwife" whose mission it was to bring forth ideas from men.[11] It is reliably recorded that he served Attica as a soldier, and he seems to have gained something of a reputation for valor.[12] He won the enduring sympathy of the male portion of mankind by his cheerful forbearance of his wife, Xanthippe, apparently a waspish nagger, whom he married late in life and whose wifely malevolence is also institutionalized in western literature. Like the Greeks of his time, Socrates was disposed to honor and respect a deep affection among and between men. His passion for Alcibiades, a comely young man (destined for notoriety as a military officer with dubious loyalties), bewilders and concerns modern western scholars who are nurtured to conceive such relationships in the relatively narrow context of homosexuality.

One purpose inherent in the study of philosophers and philosophy is to relate the specific characteristics of a thinker to his more general characteristics as a man. In some cases the relation between the thoughts and the lives of great men is remote. However, in no other case does thinking and living seem so closely bound as in the instance of Socrates. That which he taught was not carefully written down either by him or by his students. Therefore, we do not have from Socrates himself a form of discourse which can be directly imparted to future generations. Instead of writing, Socrates went about stirring up others to a state of mind similar to his own. Even though he claimed it was not his style to make pronouncements, he is the most quoted man in antiquity. A casual examination of several texts which describe the life, the times, and the philosophies of Greek civilization reveals his name as the most frequently indexed. One book quotes him directly on twenty-five different occasions and another quotes him directly, frequently, and in length, at least fourteen times; and yet, directly, from Socrates himself we have nothing of what he said. Most of the knowledge which we have of the historical Socrates comes from two sources. One, of course, is Plato. The other is Xenophon.[13] Other writers refer to him, and the general picture of his nature and of his activities seems to be clear and consistent. Specialists can be found who disagree on this or that aspect of his nature, but even these disagreements fail of the magnitude of those which exist about many men who are alive today.

Socrates was born during the last years of the Persian war and, therefore, was a near contemporary of all the outstanding figures who adorned the Age of Pericles. He considered it to be his special mission to work upon the moral and intellectual improvement of himself and of others and seemed to feel this so strongly that it apparently became the religion of his life. He tried, through self-denial and abstemiousness, to rise above the primordial needs of his body. As a great consequence of this effort, he was able to boast with great sincerity that his life was freer from trouble and less vexed than the lives of his friends. As a consequence of this he could devote more nearly the whole of his power to the business of examining the ideas of men. He conducted these examinations for their own sake and without extraneous end, aim, or motive. Apparently, he had no ambitions to hold office or to become prominent in any other way. Again, he seemed convinced that he would best serve mankind by acquiring a greater knowledge of himself.

It seems that Socrates was never weary of discussion. He was constantly alert for opportunities to give an instructive turn to conversation. Every day he was in the Agora, the parks, the forums, or the fields, ready to talk with friend or stranger, citizen or soldier, teacher or student, freeman or slave. One cannot stand today in the ruins of the Athenian Agora without musing that here he came day after day calling hearty greetings to his students. It was here, in the dust and heat of the city that he taught them. Nearby must have been the court where he was tried, and on yonder hill is reputed to be the prison where he was held and executed. The western world knows something of what he did. But what was he trying to do? In every case, he was devoted to bringing issues to higher levels of abstraction, and he apologetically insisted that this was his only way of public service. There is no question that even in his time his fame was great, and that he had a circle of enthusiastic admirers which, for the most part, consisted of young men often from wealthy families. He made it his business to teach his young friends and to advise them on anything they chose to discuss. There was no common doctrine. Out of this welter of discourse and colloquy there seemed to emerge a critical spirit and a disposition toward rationality. The story of his last days is one of the epics in western listerature.

The death of Socrates is described by Plato, one of his most devoted and certainly the most famous of his students. The account is carried in a work which Plato called *Apology*. We are assured that it was written within a few years after the hemlock, and although it is really Plato's version of the defense Socrates made at the trial, the fact that the trial and execution were well within the memories of those who first read the *Apology*, offers some assurance that the account is not overly fanciful. It is known, of course, that Plato was present at the trial. It is also known that Plato, even then a man of thirty, was deeply shocked and disillusioned by the conduct of his fellow townsmen who condemned and killed his teacher. Socrates had been accused by three men, Meletus, Anytus, and Lycon, of the crime of corrupting the youth of the city and professing disbelief in the ancestral gods.[14] As we know from other examples, Athens was a bastion of religious conservatism; but, in addition, there was great political unrest and more than the usual number of abrasions in the relations between the older and younger generations. We can assume, therefore, that public opinion in Athens was not then disposed to sympathy for an aging sage who seemed constantly to stir the rebellious propensities of the younger men.[15]

Even more specifically, during a recent Spartan occupation of the city the democrats were out of power. The oligarchy of artistocrats who governed in this brief interval behaved very badly. Many democrats were ruthlessly killed. When the Spartans withdrew and the democrats returned to authority, there was an ugly mood upon the city. Socrates tended to be *a political*, but his style of questioning seemed to place him in the camp of the aristocrats. He tended to dispute whether democracy produced virtue. Obviously, the democrats were discomfited. Some of his followers, like Plato, were aristocrats. Such were the times and circumstances when the charges were brought.

As we have it the *Apology* is in three parts. In the first, we find Socrates, apparently without fear, not only refuting but disparaging the indictment. He explains his way of life, religious attitudes, and exposes a lack of sincerity on the part of his accusers. Now the jury of such a trial in Athens was composed of any number of citizens who might care to sit and hear the case. At the close of the trial the jury voted and the majority ruled. In those days it was the custom to use fragments of broken pottery as ballots. Each citizen scratched yes or no on a shard given him for that purpose. Socrates was convicted by the comparatively small margin of sixty votes. The jury then had the problem of determining the punishment. His accusers demanded a verdict of death, but it was the custom that a convicted man might propose an alternative and the jurors then chose between death and the alternative punishment proposed by the convict.

Socrates' response forms the second part of the *Apology*. In it Socrates appears even more defiant. Instead of proposing a reasonable punishment, he suggested that he be given an award and be allowed to continue living, but at public expense. At last he said that if he must pay something he hoped his friends would scrape together enough for a moderate fine. The jury, undoubtedly angered by what a modern court would most surely call contempt, voted a punishment of death.

In the third part of the *Apology* Socrates accepts the decision. He pronounced upon his jury his own verdict which must surely have been understood by many who were there. As he entered mid-passage of this he said,

> . . . there will be more accusers of you than there are now accusers whom hitherto I have restrained, and as they are younger they will be more inconsiderate with you and you will be more offended at them. If you think that by killing men you can prevent someone from censuring your evil lives you are mistaken. That is not a way of escape which is either possible or honorable. The easiest and noblest way is not to be disabling others but to be improving yourselves.

He concluded this memorable oration with the words: "The hour of departure has arrived and we go our ways, I to die and you to live. Which is better God only knows."

The leaders in Athens must have sensed their folly for it is reliably recorded that the way was made open for Socrates to escape.[16] He chose not to do so. He was seventy years of age. By comparison with other Greek philosophers, he was not an old man, but he chose to accept the immortality that his fellow citizens thrust upon him and in the presence of his students he accepted the cup of poisoned hemlock. Before expiring, he reminded one of his students to repay a small debt he had incurred by borrowing a rooster from one of his neighbors.

We look for a reason, one which in his own words accounts for his almost cheerful agreement to end his own life. The reason is quite important and anyone who is truly a part of the profession of teaching cannot but thrill to hear it recounted. In the second part of the *Apology*, after Socrates proposed a silly punishment, one which he must have been perfectly certain would not only fail of acceptance, but also would anger the jury into its ultimate reproach, Plato quotes him as saying:

> "Some will say: Yes, Socrates, but cannot you hold your tongue, and then you may go into a foreign city, and no one will interfere with you! Now I have a great difficulty in making you understand my answer to this. For if I tell you that to do as you say would be a disobedience to God, and therefore, I cannot hold my tongue, you will not believe that I am serious; and, if I say again, that daily to discourse about virtue and of those other things about which you hear me examining myself and others, is the greatest good of man, and that *the unexamined life is not worth living* you are still less likely to believe me. Yet what I say is true although a thing of which it is hard for me to persuade you."

The key words in this, of course, are contained in the phrase *"the unexamined life is not worth living."* Socrates, in effect, informed his judges that if they would take from him the privilege of examining men on the subjects of love, justice, piety, knowledge, truth, and wisdom, they would take from him the only activity that he found to be of value in his life. The rest of it was of no consequence. In this way this kindly, perceptive, patient, cheerful, and (at times) tactful man gave teachers both a slogan and a hero. Those who propose to lead modern teachers may find profit in reminding their colleagues of both this heroism and this ideal. Socrates does not come through as a martyr in the sense that he died for a cause. He would probably have thought that to be pretentious. There were too many doubts in him for the martyr's role. Instead we find him somewhat embarrassed by the whole episode like a man who blundered into the wrong century and into the wrong civilization. He seems a little apologetic and his departure appears marked by his own sense of relief. In the final hours one of his disciples remarked, "you do not deserve to die." The old man teased him, "Would you have me deserve to die?"[17] in accepting the hemlock he offered words of comfort to his executioner.

Socrates left no doctrine. There is a Socratic method but there was no Socratic system. As a teacher he seemed more determined that his students make up their own minds. This they seemed to do. A number of them went on to establish schools. Some became philosophers, scientists, or statesmen. Certainly, of all of the teachers in the history of western civilization, only Jesus Christ rivals him in the fame of his students. Most, but not all, turned out well. There was, of course, Plato, and much more will be said of him. There were also Xenophon, the historian and general, and the excitable Appollodorus. Eucleides of Megara left Athens and stirred his native city into a rage of disputes.[18] There was also the elegant Aristippus, who after Socrates' death, traveled to various cities, but ultimately founded a school of philosophy in his native Cyrene on the coast of Africa. Antisthenes stayed on in Athens and reportedly lectured at the gymnasium which was called Cynosarges (dogfish). Antisthenes was apparently impressed by Socrates' asceticism; his motto was, "I do not possess in order not to be possessed." Like Socrates, he was determined not to acquire money or property. It is said that he dressed so poorly that Socrates once teased him, "I can see your vanity, Antisthenes, through the holes in your cloak." It is to Antisthenes that some trace the cynic philosophy.[19]

Those who pass judgment on men will say that Socrates fared less well with the handsome Alcibiades. The two men had great affection for each other, clearly surpassing that which usually exists between teacher and student. But Alcibiades became the gay, aristocratic, ambitious, pleasure-seeking military genius, whose inconstant loyalty contributed to the defeat of Athens by Lysander and the Spartans; and Alcibiades met his melancholy end even before Socrates came to trial, a circumstance which may have been remembered by many jurors. Betrayals are seldom loved by posterity. Thus, the name Alcibiades has been joined with that of Judas and others who could not summon the devotion needed to fulfill the trust they were given.

Those who study teaching and take interest in the effects a man such as Socrates has upon his students would quickly discover that an extraordinary portion of the students of Socrates became men of profound consequence. There is a lesson there for teachers, should any care to discover how this came to be.

Plato Emerges

Plato was born to a family of the old Athenian aristocracy. It is said that on his mother's side he was related to Solon. On his father's side the pedigree has been traced to the early kings of Athens. All of his life he seemed interested in becoming a politician. His writings give frequent testimony to his having heard a call to the life of the statesman. However, at the turn of the Fourth Century Athens was briefly ruled by that oligarchy of aristocrats that has since come to be called The Thirty Tyrants. A number of these were kinsmen of Plato; and, apparently, this fact made a home town political career impossible for him. Moreover, the execution of Socrates discouraged him with Athenian life, and afterward he left Athens for twelve years, not returning until 387 B.C. While he was away, he studied in Egypt, and like Pythagoras before him, was exposed to the mathematics, science, and history of the priestly colleges.

Plato's predisposition to advise politicians and engage in the business of government never left him. Consequently, his life, during this twelve-year sojourn was not uneventful. At one point, after a sharp and somewhat acrimonious exchange with Dionysius of Syracuse—a vain and rather impetuous king—Plato was denounced and reputedly warranted to slavery. According to this account he was soon ransomed by friends and returned to Athens, whereupon they helped establish him as the head of a school which may have been conceived as an institute for government. It was located in a rustic grove dedicated as a sanctuary to a military hero named *Akademos*. Thus the school itself came to be called the Academy. By the Fourth Century the Sanctuary of *Akademos* or *Hekademos* was a well known religious shrine. It evidently dated back to Mycenean times. There was a temple to Athena and a consecrated enclosure with twelve sacred olive trees grown from cuttings from the sacred tree which, according to myth, Athena, the patroness of Athens, planted on the Acropolis. Oil from these trees was given to winners at the Panathenian Games. There also was an altar to Prometheus where pilgrims to the Panathenian games came to light their torches.

In ancient times this Sanctuary was outside of the city walls, beyond the great Dypylon Gate, about two miles along a trail known in antiquity as the Academy Road. Today of course, the site is well within the metropolis. Located in an area of residence and light industry, it is surrounded by a high link fence, unmarked in any way. There is nothing to commemorate its significance. An excavation in 1958 revealed the foundations of a pre-Mycenean building called the *House of Akademos*. A section of wall 130 yards long which may have been the enclosing wall of Plato's school has also been uncovered. But the major portion of the area remains unexcavated. Even so, on a dry summer's afternoon there is the shadow and hush of a haunted past.[20]

On this site was made the first lasting effort to organized education in the western world. Plato continued as head of the school and its most famous teacher until he died in 347 B.C., at the age of eighty. It is ironic that a man such as Plato, who as much as anyone personifies a thinking man in western civilization, probably regarded his life as a failure. He was a school administrator, and as an author he wrote for his students and for a very limited public. Although it underwent a number of transformations, the school he founded lasted about 900 years, well into the Christian era. His writing fell into three major works. One is called *The Dialogues*. These were composed of a number of rather lengthy conversations which frequently pitted Socrates against other personalities of Greek wisdom. The resulting dialectic became an incisive examination of central issues of Greek philosophy. The *Apology* is not in dialogue form, but we can guess that its success helped persuade Plato to continue using Socrates as a central figure in the dialogues which followed. The second major work is called the *Republic*. It opened with a discussion of justice, a large central section pictures the ideal state, and the last part contained much about correct thinking and the possible forms of knowledge. The *Republic* set forth the principal aspects of Plato's thought. The third and longest of Plato's books was probably written when he was advanced in age. It sets forth the final form of his philosophy of politics and education. Because it sets forth a series of precepts for government, this work is called the *Laws*.

In *The Dialogues* Plato reveals a mixed pedagogical style. At times Plato has Socrates using his interrogative method to produce knowledge which Socrates himself apparently knows. At other times, such as in the *Theaetetus*, his method is an open-ended search for truth he seeks but has not found. It is believed the "open-ended" Socrates of the *Theaetetus* is more true to the historical Socrates than the "knowing" Socrates of the *Symposium*. In the *Symposium* the various speakers present their ideas in coherent discourse, and in the *Apology* Plato is presenting human values by exemplifying Socrates in his finest hour. It is reasonable to believe that *The Dialogues* reveal, as much as anything, Plato's mode of teaching. In the parlance of modern education *The Dialogues* might be called "curriculum materials." It is generally believed that Plato prepared them to make some relatively advanced philosophical issues intelligible and interesting to his students.

What else do they reveal of the teacher? Plato writes mostly as a humanist, not as a systematic philosopher. His expression has meter and precision, clarity and strength. His artistry reveals a keen human insight. In spite of the remoteness, austerity, and coldness of the system called formal idealism, we find *The Dialogues* literally "peppered" with warm feelings and good-natured, even jovial exchanges. Consider the humane concerns reflected in the opening passages of the *Theaetetus.*

Euclid: Have you only just arrived from the country, Terpison?

Terpison: No, I came some time ago and I have been in Agora looking for you, and wondering that I could not find you.

Euclid: But I was not in the city.

Terpison: Where then?

Euclid: As I was going down to the harbour I met Theaetetus—he was being carried up to Athens from the army at Corinth.

Terpison: Was he alive or dead?

Euclid: He was scarcely alive, for he was badly wounded, but he was suffering even more from the sickness which has broken out in the army.

Terpison: The dysentery you mean?

Euclid: Yes.

One would not suspect that this common and amiable exchange between old friends is really the introduction to a classic treatment of perhaps the most perplexing question which philosophy can raise: What is knowledge? At the very end he has Socrates say to the deflated Theaetetus:

Socrates: And does not my art show that you have brought forth wind, and that the offspring of your brain are not worth bringing up?
Theaetetus: Very true.

There are key points in *The Dialogues, Republic,* and *Laws,* wherein Plato deals with the metaphysical problems which raged about him. He nailed them down in such a way as to enable us to say that he completed a philosophical system. That is to say, he supplied answers to the ontological, epistemological, and axiological questions which students of philosophy ask. Again it is important to assert that

Plato did not do this by proclaiming, "Now here is my ontology. . . ." In the *Meno* and the *Republic* he offered a view of reality which came coincidental to other interests which he had in view. Those who ask: What does Plato offer as an ontology? can find a partial answer in a section of the *Meno*.

Come Hither Boy!

The scene was in the well-appointed home of Meno, a well-to-do Athenian whom Socrates called "a pretty young gentleman." The dialogue between the two was on the nature of virtue. As the conversation progressed, its subject digressed to a concern about the reality of the soul. Socrates asserted that his beliefs about the soul stemmed from his conviction that the art which men call teaching is simply bringing forth recollections or memories from another existence. He offered to prove his point in a conversation with one of Meno's "numerous attendants." Meno turned to one of them with the summons, "Come hither boy!," and the slave boy came forward.

Socrates then proceeded, by asking a series of questions, to teach the boy the Pythagorean theorem. The questions asked were leading questions, but at no point did Socrates present information. He simply brought the boy to reason. Out of his reasoning came "notions" which described the geometric relationship of the hypotenuse to the two right angle sides of a right triangle. After establishing again that neither Socrates, Meno, nor any other mortal presented this boy with the specific knowledge which he demonstrated in his responses, the two continued their dialogue as follows:

Socrates:	What do you say of him Meno? Were not these answers given out of his head?
Meno:	Yes, they were all his own.
Socrates:	And yet, as we were just now saying, he did not know?
Meno:	True.
Socrates:	But still, he had in him these notions of his— had he not?
Meno:	Yes.
Socrates:	Then he who does not know may still have true notions of that which he does not know?
Meno:	He has.

Socrates: And at the present these notions have been
                stirred up in him, as a dream; but if he were
                frequently asked the same questions, in different
                forms, he would know as well as anyone at last?

Meno: I dare say.

Socrates: Without anyone teaching him he will recover
                his knowledge for himself, if he is only asked
                questions?

Meno: Yes.

Socrates: And this spontaneous recovery of knowledge is
                recollective?

Meno: True.

Socrates: And this knowledge which he now has must he
                not either have acquired or always possessed?

Meno: Yes.

Socrates: But if he always possessed this knowledge he
                would always have known; or if he acquired the
                knowledge he could not have acquired it in this
                life, unless he has been taught geometry; for
                he may be made to do the same with all geometry
                and every other branch of knowledge. Now has
                anyone ever taught him all this? You must know
                about him, if, as you say he was born and bred
                in your house.

Meno: I am certain no one ever did teach him.

Socrates: And yet he has the knowledge?

Meno: The fact, Socrates, is undeniable.

Socrates: But if he did not acquire the knowledge in his
                life then he must have had and learned it at some
                other time?

Meno: Clearly, he must.

Socrates: Which must have been the time when he was not
                a man.

Meno: Yes.

Socrates: And if there have been always true thoughts in
                him, both at the time he was and was not a man,
                which only need to be awakened in him by put-
                ting questions to him, his soul must have always
                possessed this knowledge, for he always either
                was or was not a man?

Meno: Obviously.

Socrates: And if the truth of all things always existed in the
           soul, then the soul is immortal. Wherefore be of
           good cheer and try to recollect what you do not
           know, or rather, what you do not remember.

Meno: I feel, somehow, that I like what you are saying.

Socrates: And, I Meno like what I am saying. . . ."21

The reader should be cautioned at this point not to conclude
that Meno was an intellectual "pushover." His appearance in this
brief section of the dialogues is misleading. It is true that Plato, at
times, makes Socrates sound like a philosophical bully, and his partners
in dialogue seem like puppets. But this is not always true. Some of the
characters in the dialogues give formidable opposition. Even Meno
when stung by the gadfly provides clear and eloquent rebuttal. If at
this point he appears to play "Charlie McCarthy" to Socrates' Bergen,
it is because Plato is making one of the central points of the lesson.

What is the point? Simply this: Man has a soul when he comes
into the world, and the soul is omniscient. It contains within it all
knowledge. Learning is simply recalling to consciousness part of the
knowledge which is inherent in the soul. The teacher is not putting
knowledge into the learner, he is leading it out. Thus, we have one of
the literal meanings for the Latin verb *educare* (to lead out) which
stands as base for the English verb educate.

There are several elements of interest in this for teachers. First
of all, Plato has offered his theory of man—i.e., man has a soul and
his temporal existence is somehow derived out of something far more
fundamental than his life in the sensible world. Now this vision or
theory of man is the basis for his theories of knowledge, of learning,
of teaching, and of education. Thinking is the activity of bringing forth
knowledge from the soul.22 At another point Plato says, "thinking is the
soul talking with itself." The Platonic teacher, therefore, brings the
learner into a world of thought, and the world of thought provides the
learner with whatever knowledge he can have of his sensible world.
Only men who have souls could manifest it, and if men were not
rational then knowledge would be impossible.

Another element of interest which stands forth in the *Meno* is
that it aligns Plato irrevocably with the Pythagorean tradition in philosophy. The postulation of the soul is congenial to metempsychosis.
And even were this not so obvious, Plato's selection of the Pythagorean theorem to demonstrate his doctrine of recollection would cer-

tainly convince us that his philosophical sentiments were made to harmonize with the metaphysics of that remarkable society of scholars which preceded Plato by nearly two centuries. So, in the issue of change versus permanence, Heraclitus versus Parmenides, Plato tended to side with the latter. However, he did not turn his back on change. On the contrary, he seemed to face it head-on. Both in the *Theaetetus* and in the *Republic* he paid his respects to the ever-changing. The brilliance of his philosophy is, in part, reflected in his accommodation to both. His ultimate reality is, of course, a domain of permanence, but he found a way to show how this permanence is manifested in change.

The Ontology of Formal Idealism

How is this done? Like most great theories, it is really quite simple. Plato created a dualism. Or, to say it another way, he created two realities. One is the reality of idea, and the other is the reality of object. The important thing to note first is that the reality of idea is the true reality and the reality of object is an illusion. Ideas have the character of permanence and objects have the characteristic of constant change. To get this clear, we should detach ourselves from this world and sit, as if on a platform in space, and observe a man come into the world of sensible objects.

One of the most inspiring visions in the literature of philosophy is Plato's analogy of the cave.[23] Not only does it reveal the ingenuity of its author in creating a didactical instrument adequate to his purpose; it is also beautiful. The beauty lies in the clarity and symbolism by which this great ontological vision is shown. Plato begins it with the words, "And now, I said, let me show in a figure how far our nature is enlightened or unenlightened: Behold! human beings living in an underground den." He then goes on to describe these humans as prisoners all seated on the floor. Their legs and arms are chained so that they are compelled to face the wall of the cave. The chains are so fixed that they cannot turn their heads.

Above and some distance behind these humans a fire is blazing. Between the backs of the prisoners and the fire there is a raised ledge. Along this ledge there is passing a constant procession of figures such as statues, vessels, animals. These figures are solid and their shadow is cast upon the wall to which the gaze of the prisoners is confined. Thus the humans chained to the floor do not see the fire, neither do they see the figures. All that they see are the shadows that flicker and dance on the wall of the cave.

These shadows that they see make the whole of their sensible world. They have no other. Not having any other they are driven to think these shadows are not shadows but are real objects, and they will behave toward these shadows as if they are the whole of reality. They will give each shadow a name, and form descriptions of their natures. And because the shadows dance and move they will also say that all things move and change. They will say that change is ubiquitous. They do not know that the shadows are illusions and that change, too, is an illusion because they see only the shadows and nothing more. "To them the truth will be literally nothing but the shadows...."

Then Plato wrote, "And now look again, and see what will naturally follow if a prisoner is released and compelled suddenly to stand up, turn his neck round and walk towards the light." Thus the scene is changed. One of the humans is no longer fastened to the floor. As he first sees the light his eyes are blinded. As his eyes become accustomed to the light he begins to observe the objects on the ledge. He is at first perplexed by these objects; then, he begins to realize that these are objects which in his former posture, chained to the floor, he saw only as shadows.

Now he is aware of the upper world as well as the lower world. The body of man is of the lower world and knows only "shadows." But the soul of man can turn about to view the reality of the upper world. Although the body of man is ever chained to its perception of the material world, his soul may be joined to the upper world and may observe that which is ultimately real. The body of man is part of the world of the shadows. It is a thing of both appetite and change, and subject to all the creature cravings of the shadow world. The body that has the experience of its own soul can feel the ecstasy of the ideal. What are these figures on the ledge which are substance for the shadows on the wall? The figures are ideas, perfect forms, true forms; they are truth. The soul can witness truth, and man can know truth through his soul.

There is a perfect man, a perfect woman, a perfect table, a perfect chair. This perfection can only be known as idea. Earlier we suggested that a perfect circle is an idea and can never be other than idea. It does not change, neither do other ideas change. Because men see only dancing, flickering shadows of these ideas, the illusion of change persists. Occasionally one is heard to say, there is a *real* scholar, a *real* poet, or a *real* philosopher. What does this mean? It means that there is incarnated in the shadow world which men see something that resembles in nearly every respect the idea of a scholar, poet, or philosopher, which is never seen by the man chained to the floor except through the eyes of his soul.

Now how can the soul do this? In Book VI of the *Republic,* Plato suggested that man had four faculties: (1) perception of shadows, (2) faith, (3) understanding, and (4) reason. In effect, the lowest of the four faculties is perception of shadows and the highest faculty is reason. In becoming educated a man becomes proficient in the exercise of all of these faculties. Having accomplished these proficiencies he is capable of observing truth. In doing so he is dependent on the mediational function of his soul.

This, as indicated before, is the philosophy called Formal Idealism. As the words *formal* and *idealism* are considered in relation to the analogy of the cave, the word formal is recognized as referring to the forms which appear on the ledge. The shadows of these forms appear in the senses of men. Idealism is taken to imply that the forms are perfect in nature and can be known only as idea. Returning to the analogy, if the man were asked to resume his place as a prisoner chained to the floor, he would then understand that it is only shadows which he sees. He would know that what was formerly thought to be the whole of reality is only a reflection of reality. He would be given to know that many, even most, men never move from their places, never see other than shadows. He would then realize that those who have looked upon the fire should pity those who have not, for they have known the rapture of seeing what is real and therefore have advanced into wisdom. Plato thought that the fire, the source of light, the cause of both being and existence, the illuminator of other ideas, and the ray that produces the shadows which men see in the world of sense is the *idea of the good.* It is the divine, a source that is its own necessity and upon which all else is contingent. The world of the senses —that which we see, hear, touch, taste, and smell—is a world of shadows. The world of ideas, illuminated by the sovereign idea of *the good*, has a higher reality than the world of the senses.

In his own explanation of the analogy Plato makes it clear again that it was not the man of flesh and blood who was released from his chains and turned round to see the source of the shadows. It was the soul of man which performed this feat. The body through its soul can have the perception of truth. If one were to take the "I" from the word *ideal* the word would become *idea.* The philosophy would then be called *formal ideaism,* and this term would have the virtue of being more descriptive of what Plato had in mind. This ontology of ideas is difficult to comprehend. It is understandable that in this modern age, dominated by science and scientific philosophies, Platonism with its quality of mysticism would be more difficult to comprehend than it was in former times when philosophic alternatives were fewer and metaphysical faiths were more respected.

The Platonic idealist, therefore, is obliged to consider the events of the sensible world to be of less import than those of the world of ideas. If, for example, the state of affairs in the sensible world does not conform to idea, the sensible world is out of alignment and its errors should be set right. There is no ground for compromise unless it can be reasoned that a compromise solution is a step in the direction of ideality. Often those who observe others in such a state of mind simply say, "such men are not realistic." In one sense this may be correct, but in a philosophical sense it is not good to describe an idealist as "unrealistic." An idealist thinks ideas are more real than the materialistic sphere of shadows in which men find "practical" problems. Thus, in holding out for the ideal he is being a realist. It is, of course, a subtle point, but one which helps others to be more understanding of a man whose basic reality is idea and not object.[24]

One might then ask: In a world of practical men is idealism of the Platonic sort obsolete? It is true that idealists are commonly thought to be part of the problem and not part of the solution. Idealists, it is often charged, go about creating problems. They will want to implement their idea of justice no matter what powers are vexed or authorities offended by it. They will insist on certain standards of freedom no matter how much pain or inconvenience these standards impose. They have a certain idea of temperance which is in their view true and right, and there is no way of being right or true without conforming to the idea. But there are other ideas such as manhood, womanhood, parenthood, brotherhood, friendship, leadership, etc.[25] All of these and a host of others are ideas that when implemented in the sensible world make a civilization distinctive. Do these ideas stand eternal, not subject to change? Plato thought they did and many people still agree. Idealism of the Platonic sort is far from being obsolete.

The analogy of the cave—vivid, striking, and beautiful—reveals a hypothetical view of man in relation to his soul and to ultimate reality—or, more specifically, to ultimate good. Biblical literature offers at least one illustration which is predicated on a similar ontology. The Old Testament poem called Job depicts a man who had been a good man; but his goodness was challenged by the Devil, so God agreed that it should be tested. During his interval of trial, Job suffered. Even though he raised a number of poignant questions, his faith did not waver. Though counseled by the orthodoxy that his suffering was the result of sin, Job insisted that he did not sin. He believed there must be a deeper reason for what he called the Lord's giving and the Lord's taking away. If we have faith in God, we know that His knowledge goes far beyond the simple good and evil of this life. Later the Lord took Job up and showed him part of creation. Job returned inspired, but not comprehending. "There are things," he said, "too wonderful for me . . . things which I know not."[26]

If the prisoners of the cave, like Job, were to be taken from their chains and brought into the light of full reality perhaps they, like Job, would find it wonderful but incomprehensible. The words which they know could not describe it; the language they use could not encompass it; and they, like Job, would be overwhelmed.

Man's link to the great real world of ideas is his soul. Education, therefore, must be of the soul in order that the soul may do its work properly. It is perhaps for this reason that Plato's academy was openly religious and the curriculum of the school dealt with the four faculties of the soul: reason, understanding, faith, and perception of shadows. As these faculties grew strong in man, he was no longer shackled to his world of shadows. In a sense he was liberated (one basis for the liberal arts) to have some experience in the world of ideas. The Platonist would say that he seeks truth with the eye of mind. The best kind of life is a life of mind. In many languages the words mind and soul are the same thing. In Plato's thesis it is possible to interchange the words mind and soul without altering the meanings.

The Epistemology of Formal Idealism

Many authorities claim that epistemology is the weakest part of formal idealism. Epistemology is the aspect of any philosophical system which answers to the question: How do you know? In the scientific philosophies, epistemology is often strong and ontology is weak. This is very easy to understand. For example, it would be reassuring if one could say that he knows that ultimate reality is, as Plato implied, a world of perfect ideas and if, in response to how one knows this, he could say that he had been there and observed it with his senses and had made a photograph or two, which he then placed before us. Then his descriptions of ultimate reality would be more convincing. We would be even more reassured if the Platonist would create a vast machine which was able to receive electromagnetic signals from this upper world in the way radar signals rebound from the moon. And if these signals could be recorded by instruments, graphed, and studied, we would have an epistemology as strong as the very persuasive epistemologies of modern science.

But we don't have such instruments of detection. Instead, Plato suggests the formation of hypotheses which are subjected to dialectic; if the dialectic is strong and good the ensuing discourse will rise above the hypotheses in the direction of first principles. The test for the truth of any principle conceived in this way is called coherence. Do the elements of reason cohere? To clarify this question we may resort to metaphysical expression. Any series of statements which lead to a true opinion on the nature of an idea is like a chain with many links. Each link in the chain is comparable to each element of the rationale. In the dialogues we find Socrates attacking each link in the chain a speaker has so fashioned. He tries to break each link by showing that it is unbelievable, is not answerable to logic, contradicts prior statements, or contains some other rational flaw. But if his testing fails to break any of the links, then it is probable that the statement is true. If the test breaks one of the links, then the rationale no longer coheres and stands refuted.

Thus a hypothesis serves a different purpose in the epistemology of Formal Idealism than it does in the modern scientific philosophies. In pragmatism, for example, one is led to believe than an hypothesis is either rejected or made tenable by the test of evidence or of subsequent experience. However, to the formal idealist an hypothesis is a beginning place for dialectic. If Plato asks questions such as what is temperance? what is knowledge? what is justice?, the initial answer of the respondent merely serves as a starting point in the dialogue. The rationalization then proceeds from link to link. Hopefully, as each link is secured, the discussion is that much closer to the principle.

In the epistemology of Formal Idealism, sense experience plays only a minor role. The developing rationale does need some raw material to make thoughts communicable. But, as we discovered in the cave, the things of the material world merely suggest to us the ideas of which they are the sensible form. The most important (or most real thing about a table is the *idea* of it. The second most important thing is the object. It is even appropriate to say the table in itself would have no importance at all were it not for the idea and the word.

At no other place in his work does Plato make so direct an attack upon the knowledge problem as in the *Theaetetus*. In the *Theaetetus*, Plato has Socrates raise the question: What is knowledge? After some coaxing Socrates obtains from Theaetetus the response that, "He who knows perceives what he knows, and, as far as I can see at present, knowledge is perception." By his answer Theaetetus displays a certain wariness, and with good reason, for Socrates' reputation as a dialectician was well known to him. Socrates at first tries to assure him by citing a noble precedent for his view. He recalls that Protagoras said, "Man is the measure of all things," and by that Protagoras must have meant that things are what each man perceives them to be. But then he reminds Theaetetus that Protagoras admitted that all things are in motion and also reminds him that in this Protagoras agreed with Parmenides and Empedocles. In this way, Socrates begins to draw Theaetetus out by revealing the very substantial reasoning of the materialists on *change* and *becoming*. After asserting that he along with most of mankind has been charmed by these doctrines, he begins to describe some of the "flaws" in the knowledge claims of the materialists.

Socrates pointed out that pigs had sensation and, therefore, perception. Is a pig the measure of all things? If not, how can we account for that which a pig knows? To put Theaetetus in further difficulty Socrates argued that if all was constantly changing, including man, there could not be an interval of knowing. That is to say, for a thing to be known through perception it would need to hold itself unchanged for a period long enough for evidence to repeat itself. Because nothing in the material world which appears in the senses remains static, it would change to something else even while the perceiver was reporting his perception. Said he, "We cannot say a thing is *thus* and we cannot say that it is *not thus*." The very inadequacy of our language stands as a complaint against assertions that knowledge is perception. In order to speak of the material world which we perceive in the senses we would need words which do not exist. Theaetetus then agreed that perception could not pass for knowledge. Socrates asked again, "What is knowledge?"

This time Theaetetus replied that knowledge is *true opinion*.

Is knowing true opinion? Socrates patiently led Theaetetus to explore the question. He asked: Can there be false opinion? How does a man know that he knows? What is the meaning of knowing? Are things known by the whole or by the part? Is the whole the same as all of the parts? Each question led to new questions, not to a resolution. Does the man who knows differ from the man who has a true opinion? Surely the man who knows has something more than the man who has a true opinion. What more does he have? Socrates could not satisfy himself. He considered evidence, probability, even elementary forms of language analysis, but nothing pleased him. Finally, he considered that true opinion derived from and supported by reason is the best of all the suggestions he could derive from Theaetetus. Still he was not satisfied, and the dialogue concluded with an admission that his quest for the nature of knowledge had failed.

Thus, Plato was compelled to leave his epistemology in a metaphysical state that was somewhat muddled. His case rested on the soul and its faculties—i.e., perception, faith, understanding, and reason. And he seemed to conclude that a knowledge claim could be sustained and judged only by the greatest faculty of the four, reason. To the idealist, pure reason remained as the highest tribunal on knowledge issues until Immanuel Kant in 1781 A.D. established and identified categories of concepts which he asserted that the mind produces from raw precepts which are fed to it by the senses.[27] Although Kant's structure also rests on a metaphysical base it is better organized and, logically, seems far more defensible. However, any complaint about Plato's epistemology must take into account that he was part of a civilization not far removed from primitive animism and the vivid accounts of mythology. In addition, one senses a degree of partisanship in his argument, as if, once having chosen to build his philosophy on the side of spiritual permanence, he was bound to reject even the strong points of the materialists. Actually, that he did so makes it possible for us to say that he created a complete system. Admitting all of the weaknesses of rationalism as a basis for epistemology, we must still admire Plato's dogged insistence on giving credence to reason in a time when both mythology and materialism presented alternatives which were both powerful and convenient.

The Axiology of Formal Idealism

In the analogy of the cave Plato suggested that the light which illuminated the objects in back of the chained figures and which resulted in the shadows being cast upon the wall to be gazed upon by these prisoners was the idea of the good. This light is to the mind of man as the sun is to his physical vision. If there was nothing but darkness man's power of sight would be of no value. It is the light which makes it possible for man to see. It is appropriate to say, therefore, that man's eyes "aspire" to the light. In the domain of mind (or soul) the good performs an office for the mind (or soul) which is analogous to the service which light performs for the eye. The good illuminates ideas and provides the light by which the "eye of the mind" sees whatever it sees.

The Platonic argument which establishes "the good" as the revealing power emanating from ultimate reality is compatible with classical theism. In the book of Genesis, God said: "Let there be light, and there was light." Men cannot abide darkness, either of their physical vision or of their minds. To Plato one important aspect of the good is the idea of number; clearly, this seems to be part of Pythagoras' legacy to Plato. As a mathematician, poet, and philosopher, Plato seemed convinced that knowing a thing by number or proportion was virtue. This light by which mind is illuminated is not the same as the psychologists' notions about intelligence (this, of course, is presumptuous since no reputable psychologist has claimed to know what intelligence is). The Platonist is interested in reasoning which, from examination of *The Dialogues,* we can take to be a patient, deliberative process by which *a priori* statements are interpreted, examined, and refined. The reasoning man is an enlightened man, which is to say that his mind is turning in the direction of the good and is observing what that light reveals to him.

Now some men reason by nature, and these are the better men. Plato observed that such men are fitted to govern and went on to postulate a style of man which he called the "philosopher king."[28] Other men are less inclined to reason. These serve in a middle class and execute the various functions of the state, including its defense. A third class of men have little inclination to rationality. These are best fitted for the menial duties which must be performed. Each of these classes of men can be given appropriate education, and can live harmoniously by fulfilling their natural functions.

Plato, an aristocrat himself, would not, of course, flinch from espousing a philosophy which explains and supports aristocracy. We will see later how these notions tended to institutionalize aristocracy in western civilization. Again, it was European idealists such as Spinoza, Berkeley, and Kant who finally rescued idealism from aristocracy. Kant asserted that the moral force was within every man and made no distinction. He established "the moral force within me" as categorical.[29]

Even though those committed to a democratic way of life might regret the tendency of Platonic axiology to create hierarchy among men, it must be conceded that axiology is one of the strong points of

Formal Idealism. To some extent it redeems the weaknesses of the epistemology. We can think of the good in three ways: (1) the reason which illuminates pure form or ideas, (2) the vision of ideas in themselves, and (3) the quality of beauty they impart to the objects of the perceptive world. To illustrate these three points we might once again contemplate a circle. The first level of abstraction is reached when the mind (or, in Plato's sense, soul) is in a state of readiness to observe the idea of a circle; the second level, when one perceives in his mind the idea in its pure, perfect, and unalloyed form; and the third level, when he appreciates the beauty of the ideal as incarnated in the material world, such as in wheels, coins, platters, etc. Having seen the idealized form in the mind it is possible to have an aesthetic experience when the ideal is represented in material reality.

Thus, beauty is experienced in three ways—the first being entry into the world of thought, the second being observation of ideal forms in the world of thought, and the third being the perceptive experiences of these forms in material reality. The good, therefore, is (1) that which illuminates the ideal, (2) the ideal itself and (3) material forms which approximate the ideal.

In the world of shadows where man has material reality perceived by his senses, there are two groups of ideals represented. One group has a material form and the other a non-material form. They can be called concrete nouns and abstract nouns.[30] Concrete nouns are such things as table, chair, house, tree, etc. Abstract nouns are such things as justice, love, temperance, piety, knowledge, etc. Neither of these classes of nouns in ideal form is part of man's material existence. The best man can sense is an approximation of them and an appreciation of them.

The man who does good in the world is one who idealizes as much as possible the material realities with which he works. A sculptor, for example, who is forming a statute of a man or a woman will tend to idealize the form. An athlete who runs and plays games which involve coordination will be depicted as slender, supple, small-boned, and clean-featured. A warrior, on the other hand, will be idealized as heavily muscled, sturdy, large-boned, and with rough countenance. Other contrasts can be made of such things as race horses and work horses, or apple trees and oak trees. Each of these forms has a perfect expression in ultimate reality where things are permanent, unchanging, and unending, and each has an approximate expression in material reality which is finite, changing, and temporary.

The search for justice and love in the material world is first a search for the ideal of justice by the eye of the mind. Justice exists as an ideal which men of enlightened reason observe (Socrates noted that men do not create ideas, they take notice of them). Having seen the ideal, a man who does good in the world attempts to idealize the relationships among men in accordance with this paradigm of justice. He never achieves perfection bcause perfection does not exist in material reality, but a thing becomes good in the extent to which perfection is approximated. The same is true of other non-material or abstract nouns. Plato thought of man in two ways, the body and the soul. It is possible to idealize the body of man, and much of the art of classical antiquity did just this. But the idea of manhood is something else. It is, like justice, an example of a non-material or abstract noun. What is the ideal soul of a man? It is commonly supposed that in the material world Plato's ideal of manhood was best represented in the soul of Socrates.

It is commonly known that the physical figure of Socrates was far from ideal. His body and countenance were unlike any of the idealized forms of physical men.[31] His soul, however, constituted an ideal of manhood, and, as such, the incarnated man we call Socrates was presented by Plato as a good man—indeed, almost the ultimate of goodness in men. There are other non-material ideals; for example, there is womanhood represented in the Christian imagination as the Virgin Mother.[32] Other examples might be parenthood, brotherhood, friendship, and so on. To the idealist these ideals are the basis for institutional relationships, and they serve as guides to our knowing which is good and which is less good.

The Utopian

Plato's final work was a volume of short books on the morals, customs, and statutes of an ideal state. It is called the *Laws*. It differs from his earlier works in the respect that much of the friendly and cheerful style so evident in such works as the *Parmenides*, the *Sophist*, and the *Meno*, seems absent. One gets the feeling that Plato had begun to take philosophy far more seriously. (What is really reflected is a trend noted in his later work decreasing dialogue and increasing conventional discourse.) On the other hand, this change may have resulted from his coming at last to grips with what many authorities contend was the central ambition of his life—namely, to govern with perfection. Therefore, the points he made were made directly. He did not take chances with implications and inferences.

In depicting his Utopia, Plato put nearly all of his philosophy and many of his prejudices to work. The blend is interesting but not nearly so well acclaimed by modern authorities as the earlier books. Not only does he reassert the human class distinctions set forth in the *Republic*, but he also advocates a kind of benevolent totalitarianism which the modern world has been attempting to destroy during the last two centuries. He instituted quality controls on the human race by, among other things, the abandonment of infant children who were deformed or deranged (reputedly a custom of the Spartans). This rather "hard-boiled" view of life is pervasive in the compendium of prescriptions which Plato left for the state-builders of the future. Plato is the first of the Utopian writers. Others were to follow. Some of them depicted their dream state as a kind of paradise. Others, such as Huxley and Orwell in our own century, cultivated a horror. Plato's Utopia was not the land of the free, nor was he interested in giving man physical contentment or material comfort. The purpose of his state was to nurture the soul in the direction of the good.

The citizen of the ideal state appeared more Spartan than Athenian. Plato's fondness for Spartan customs may have been influenced by the success of Spartan arms and the high prestige which that city state enjoyed during much of Plato's life. His program for educating both boys and girls included rigorous physical activity such as dancing, games, and military exercises. He wanted education to assure that the state would be blessed by great numbers who would be highly patriotic and fearless in its defense.

However, he rose above this barracks style of life in his curriculum for the soul. Here music and the best work of the great poets were of primary importance. The soul must not be neglected. The cultivation of the inner life was to be accompanied by a corresponding devaluation of the material life. The man with a rich inner life tends to be indifferent as to his material life. Justice, he claimed, can give pleasure to those who perceive it. It is unpleasant and gives pain to those who cannot. He asserted that legislators should be motivated by the ideal of justice and not by the creature cravings of men.

Plato made a clear distinction between charm and beauty. The imitative arts may hold charm in that men find pleasure in them. Beauty, however, is determined by the truth it contains. That which holds truth can also give pleasure. Thus, the qualities of beauty and charm can be combined in an object or act. But beauty (or goodness) can stand alone; and when it does, it is of higher worth than mere charm.

Plato was not a prohibitionist, but he had no qualms about legislating for and against drinking. There were times, such as when certain kinds of work were being performed or when a military campaign was being conducted, that drinking was forbidden entirely. Slaves and women, for example, might never drink while in the city. If matters of importance were at hand abstention from wine should be practiced. Excessive drinking at any time was prohibited.

Authority was to be clear. Plato delineated seven kinds of authority to be used in his state: (1) parents over children, (2) noble over ignoble, (3) elder over younger, (4) master over slave, (5) stronger over weaker, (6) wise over ignorant, and (7) winner of the lot over the loser. It is clear from this that Plato was not formulating a scheme for democracy. Everyone was to know where he stood, and the rules governing the relationships were to be clear and perpetuated through the educational function of the state.

The arts were protected but also prescribed. Poetry and tragedy were of a higher order than comedy which could only be performed by hirelings and slaves (another slap at Aristophanes). Poetry should conform to models. Dancing was regulated by the state, and dances were to be approved by the state. The arts obviously were instrumentalities subservient to other purposes such as the development of the soul, the improvement of the body, or the well-being of the state. *Art for art's sake* seems to have had little sympathy from Plato. If he was inclined to encourage creativity (as apparently he was in the *Symposium*) he suppressed this inclination in the *Laws*.

Three subjects were held to be worthy of free men: (1) arithmetic, (1) geometry, and (3) astronomy. In arithmetic men found a divine necessity which was preliminary to higher forms of knowledge. Geometry taught men to know what was mensurable and what was not mensurable. Astronomy, which reveals the organization and the order of the cosmos, established the foundations for piety and a belief in the gods. This Plato held to be essential.

The laws and procedures go on to a host of other matters. Plato's state would be well regulated indeed. He limited the number of homes in his city to 5,040. This number was apparently decided upon because it could be divided evenly by so many other numbers. He ruled that citizens could not possess articles of gold or silver which were not in the form of money, that youth and maidens should be saved from their lusts by an intense program of work and activity, that marriages and funerals should be modest, and that children should be happy, but not indulged in luxury. His laws covered such diverse matters as credit and retail trade, poisoning and witchcraft, abuse and ridicule. He drew distinctions between slaves, and he regulated hunting. As he went on with his Utopia it became clearer and clearer that the citizen in body was an instrumentality of the state, and the state existed to minister to the souls of its citizens. This totalitarian mood and mode required no apology or explanation. Again the important aspect of man was soul. Therefore, it would be an act of wisdom to create a state which would conscript the citizens' bodies and lives into the service of their souls.

Even so one is astounded by the rules which were to govern the religious behavior of the citizens. A belief in the gods was *required*. Piety was considered a *duty* of each citizen. The penalty for impiety was to be death! Is this the same man who wrote the *Apology*? What was it that brought Plato to a repudiation of Socrates? As a dashing young Athenian Plato followed his master. He risked the disapprobation of his family. He defended Socrates and, anguished at his death, authored a searing indictment which put the accusers and jury forever in the disfavor of history. However, approaching his eightieth year, he was indignant about the insolence of youth; be urged the persecution of heretics; and he advocated the law by which Socrates was tried, convicted, and executed. We look in vain for a reason. Were there two Platos? The greatest authorities say no. The *Apology* and the *Laws* were written by the same author but different men. The man who wrote the *Laws* was older, much older. Was he a wiser man? Plato died much honored, but the work of his later years tends to contradict his early liberalism.

Theory of Education

The theory of ideas furnishes Plato a syntax for his discourses on the soul, love, friendship, duty, art, statecraft, and, of course, education. Actually, it seems that very few of his books do not in some way deal with a problem in pedagogy. Socrates belongs almost exclusively to the field of education, and from the perspective of his reflected interests Plato belongs mainly to education and its close relative, political science. Plato thinks government is the key to good living, and his educational prescriptions are central to the achievement of his preferred style of governance.

Plato is not a democrat, but this does not mean that he does not care about the ordinary man. Both his personal and philosophical orientations to statecraft are aristocratic, but he believes that his conceptions of aristocracy are capable of bringing the greatest good to all. He establishes classes of people and advocates certain roles for each class. His psychology of education and plan for schooling supposes that these classes would select themselves and function accordingly. It comes through as an aristocracy of mind more than of birth, but it seems apparent that Plato believes that the most able minds will come from leading families. However, it is equally apparent that he accepts the fact that good minds could come from anywhere. He knows of course that Protagoras and Gorgias, both leading sophists, had humble origins as did many fellow Socratics. He does not gainsay any of them on that basis. Indeed, Socrates himself came from an artisan class.

It is obvious that from the historical Socrates, Plato had taken a conviction that all excellence is reducible to some kind of knowledge. For the leadership of his state Plato purports to develop a group of men who can acquire this knowledge and use it in the art of governing. It is part of his Socratic conviction that no man does wrong on purpose, and no man is willingly ignorant. The Platonic-Socratic doctrine, therefore, rests on the three-fold proposition that (1) goodness is knowledge ,(2) no man sins on purpose, (3) knowing begins with Apollo's Delphic injunction, "Know thyself." From this knowledge-is-virtue premise comes a theory of education and politics.

It is at this point that the alert reader interposes an objection, namely, that Plato seems to presume that the human will is not capable of bringing a man to commit deliberate and premeditative evil. Human wrongdoing was at least as evident in antiquity as it is now. How can Plato be so naive as to think that knowledge can cure wickedness in men? The answer, of course, is that he does not. He accepts it as a problem and resolves the problem by dichotomizing evil. One part can be controlled by knowledge, but the other must be controlled by laws and punishment. The former part is the greater and by far the more general.

As to the latter, Plato offers only a philosophical shrug.[33] Innate wickedness is a perturbation (or disease) of the soul. It is an unfortunate but true circumstance of mortal life that certain men find parts of themselves at variance with other parts. This disharmony or disorder emerges as depravity, cowardice, or sinfulness. Such men are irreparably defective. There is no remedy for them. The state simply must enact laws and punishment. Thus, for a man who is inherently bad there is no alternative except to be forced into a mode of acceptable conduct.

However, innate evil such as this is not the greatest nor is it the most pervasive. The greatest evil comes about through ignorance. It is not so much a disease as it is malformation or misformation. A few men can overcome it on their own, but everyone else needs help. The evil of ignorance is of three kinds (1) lack of true knowledge, (2) having false knowledge, and (3) having erroneous beliefs about what is known.

Education attacks the evil of ignorance on all fronts. It stands as the way of establishing virtue in men and states. For Plato the effort to educate is of utmost importance. As indicated before, he does not approach it through a single treatise. *The Republic, The Laws,* and no less than eight of the dialogues deal directly with one or more of its aspects. Therefore, one cannot go to a single book to discover Plato's psychology of education or his scheme for schooling.

Even though it is expressed metaphorically, and at times vaguely, there is a psychology of education revealed at several points in his work. In some it emerges more stridently and systematically.[34] It is characteristic of Plato in this as in most other matters to record and discuss the principles by revealing the arguments out of which they are derived. The details of application are largely unrecorded. If principles are correctly followed, details will fall properly in place.

The quality we might think of as mind is referred to in Plato by a word which is translated in philosophical literature as the *nous.*[35] It is, by comparison, a more holistic version of man the learner and knower than many more recent theories. It is a much more extensive conception than that of the brain. It involves harmony in the soul, tendency to idealize and order, perceptiveness of abstraction, perseverance or doggedness in pursuit of the true, responsiveness to reason, intuition of that which stands back of sight and sound, and a desire to know for the sake of knowing. A rustic who is willing to follow his betters stands higher with Plato than others of minor accomplishment who equate wisdom with the mental gymnastics often reflected by a capacity to make long speeches which say very little.

In Plato's psychology, human development is a process which has three phases. In the first phase we see the human infant as a soul suddenly possessed of (and by) a material body. Thus, contact between the immortal soul and the material world is beginning. Suddenly the soul is subjected to all of the unreasoned passions or feelings which are generated by a body in a mortal state. In other words, the immortal soul is abruptly required to cope with anger, fear, and new sensations of pain and pleasure. In effect it is a trauma for the soul to be thrown into life, and the effect is chaos. To the infant and child this chaos is inner and accounts for his need of restless movement and his need to be rocked and comforted. It is during childhood that this inner chaos must be mastered. The violence is lifelong, but is more intense in the early years. Reduction of inner chaos comes about through the regulation and mastery of physical desires. The infant and child must be loved, must be allowed to play. Games, poetry, music, dances, all have elements conducive to order which leads to self-mastery and self-knowledge.

The second phase involves coming to terms with the material world. Having overcome the inner confusion of his entry into the world he turns to the world with interest and ambition. His body now copes with the world successfully; indeed, it is a source of enjoyment. Fear is controlled; anger is controlled; and pleasure is sought. He seeks to own things, and he seeks explanations for the world of matter. He acquires beliefs and inspirits the objects of his belief. His health rewards him with self-sufficiency and self-reliance. He loves. But this is not the love of an infant for security and comfort, nor is it yet the love of a philosopher for reason, art, or beauty. It is simply the love of a man who is in the fullness of his material being. His need for order continues but his interest moves in the direction of material accomplishment and success in competition.

The final phase is enjoyed by those who can rise above the second. Evidently not everyone does rise above it, so it is a matter of ability and opportunity as well as simple maturity. Internal harmony between the life of mind (the nous) and the life of matter comes only to the best. Plato calls upon those who stand on the threshold of this to surmount material being and enter into the beneficent state of transcendence between matter and mind or body and soul. Transcendence is that state in which one is conscious of at least a partial reunion with his immortal aspect.[36] This makes a man capable of wisdom; he can perceive excellence. This key point comes out time and again, but never more clearly than in Socrates' debate with Protagoras.[37]

> Socrates: Now I want you to tell me truly whether virtue is one whole, of which justice and temperance and holiness are parts; or whether these are only names of one and the same thing?
>
> Protagoras: There is no difficulty . . . the qualities are all parts of virtue which is one.

Socrates: Are they parts . . . in the same sense that mouth, and nose, eyes and ears are parts of the face, or are they like parts of gold, which differ from the whole and one and another in being only larger or smaller?

Protagoras: They differ Socrates, in the first way. . . .

Protagoras proves to be a difficult opponent, but Socrates finally gets him to admit that qualities such as justice, temperance, and courage are in their ultimate nature very similar if not the same thing, namely, virtue (as a gold ring, a gold locket, and a gold watch are basically gold). He also forces him to accept that if virtue could be taught, as Protagoras and other Sophists frequently claimed, then it must be knowledge of some kind; and Protagoras sullenly, but finally, accepts the alternative that if virtue is not knowledge then it cannot be taught. This, as it turns out, is a decisive point in the Platonic theory of education; namely, the ultimate end of education at its highest level is to be able to perceive the good or virtue in any of the numerous ways that it is formed in the world.

This is what Plato would have the philosopher know. Only a few men have the capacity, and most of them require extensive training in addition to physical maturity. When ultimately one comes to see goodness in friendship, justice, courage, or craftsmanship he is seeing the same thing in different forms. In each case it turns out to be knowledge of the perfection of the particular form in question.

Platonic Curriculum and Pedagogy

Except in very general things like the theory of ideas or forms students have not been able to develop an undisputed statement of Plato's metaphysics. For reasons widely conjectured upon, his middle and some of his later writings show flashes of realism. Some commentators attribute this to his mission as a teacher while others relate the seeming contradictions to his unceasing political interests and aspirations. The "political" model is nowadays often used to explain apparent turns in Plato's thought.[38]

There is no indication, however, that his educational thinking alters from the aristocracy of mind. His educational prescriptions for the young appear to be universal. Education must be home-centered, but tutors and schools are important. In the main the children should have poetic oral language experience, music, gymnastics, art, elementary geometry, and introduction to reading and writing. Plato is somewhat reserved about numbers. Evidently, his Pythagorean inclinations imbue him with a sense of the mystique of numbers. He is, therefore, apprehensive of the indiscriminate use of numbers by the common man. False knowledge (polymathy) is one of the major forms of ignorance and sources of evil.

The young with aptitude and interest should be given opportunity for further training. The second (or secondary) phase of education is directed to the personal and civic functions of the middle citizen—the soldier, merchant, freeholder, etc. He advocates geometry, mathematics, poetry, arithmetic, and art. He insists on music, dance, gymnastics, military training, and a modicum of science. The Athenian citizen-soldier must be alert, courageous, physically fit, obedient, and capable of forbearing the hardships of soldiering. Moderation, however, is cautioned. He is of the opinion that the training of athletes develops lethargic natures. The military, physical, and musical aspects of the educational program should be state-sponsored. He is less clear about the rest.

At the age of twenty those who have distinguished themselves in learning and displayed interest and aptitude for higher study should be greatly honored and encouraged to go on in higher study. Here the quest for Platonic knowledge begins in earnest. Presumably, the sort of educational activity Plato has in mind is that which is characteristic of his own Academy. The student has advanced training in geometry, mathematics, science, and literature. All of these studies will be undertaken in earnest until their relationships become clear. This period lasts ten years, and as in the education of late adolescents this group is watched to see which of its members show potential for leadership.

At the age of thirty, another selection is made. Those not chosen presumably become the lesser statesmen and guardians. Some, of course, will undertake pedagogical responsibilities or enter into high administrative posts. But those selected for further training are destined to become philosophers and to rule. For an interval of five years they are exposed to the study of dialectics. Because dialectics involves a questioning of first principles it is full of danger for any but the most balanced. Many precautions are required. Those who successfully conclude this five years of training are assigned to offices of state. They serve as high state executives for a period of fifteen years. At age fifty they are allowed to retire from active life. Now they are potential sovereigns. Their time is spent in research and teaching. But they must take turns in governing the state. It would not, Plato asserts, be a pleasant task for them and they would undertake it only under a sense of duty. The philosopher-king would be a reluctant king. His education will have brought him to disdain the tinsel glories of court life. Only a reluctant king is fitted for a throne.

Plato's scheme of education and state governance never came to be in Athens or any Greek city of his time. At the time of his death he had no reason to think his theories were of any major consequence to pedagogy or politics. Centuries passed before they were. But there was a power in his thought and a cogency in his expression which kept his theories alive. He had an excellent forum in the Academy, and although it had ups and downs it continued as a prominent school and the works of its founder remained of interest. When the Roman Neo-Platonists began to elaborate on his works, the Christian church was emerging as a force in the world. Through the latter, certain Platonic ideas about education and government were built into the civilization of western Europe. The acceptance was figurative and never literal.

Perhaps the most lingering aspect of his educational theory is the central idea that true knowledge is virtue and is that which defeats evil and reveals the good. There still resides in western man the idea that through the relentless pursuit of true knowledge one can rise above the petty concerns of the daily world and achieve inner harmony of a soul which is at one with ultimate truth. In this there is faith that such a man is good and will be the cause of goodness in others, for the unknowing stand eager to receive his goodness. As Socrates said to Protagoras, ". . . no man voluntarily pursues evil, or that he thinks to be evil."

Notes

1. T. V. Smith, ed., *Philosophers Speak for Themselves* (Chicago: University of Chicago Press, Vol. I, *Thales to Plato*, 1934), p. 15.
2. Will Durant, *The Life of Greece* (New York: Simon and Schuster, Inc., 1939), p. 355.
3. Attributed to *Timon of Phlius*.
4. Jacques Maritain, *An Introduction to Philosophy*, tr. E. I. Watkin (New York: Sheed & Ward, 1959), p. 39.
5. Durant, *op. cit.*, p. 343.
6. *Ibid.*, p. 358.
7. Alban D. Winspear, *The Genesis of Plato's Thought* (New York: Russell and Russell, 1940), p. 139.
8. Maritain, *op. cit.*, p. 49.

9. Durant, *op. cit.*, p. 363.
10. *Ibid.*, p. 565.
11. *The Theaetetus.*
12. *The Symposium.*
13. A Greek historian and general, who in his younger days was a follower of Socrates.
14. *The Apology.*
15. Durant, *op. cit.*, p. 369.
16. *The Crito.*
17. According to Plato's account in the *Phaedo*, Socrates was teaching philosophy until the hour of his death.
18. Durant, *op. cit.*, p. 505.
19. *Ibid.*
20. When this author visited the site in 1969, he was helped over the fence by one Dimetrios Christopholos, a citizen of Athens, who accepted no reward for this help except a promise of this footnote.
21. *The Meno.*
22. G. M. A. Grube, *Plato's Thought* (Boston: Beacon Press, 1966), p. 137.
23. *The Republic*, Book VII.
24. In the medieval controversy, *Realism vs. Nominalism*, the realist point of view is of the Augustinian, Neo-Platonic tradition. In this era the term realism was used to identify those who believed in the reality of idea.
25. The American idealist, Ralph Waldo Emerson, expressed his philosophy through essays on abstract nouns such as these.
26. Job 42:3.
27. Immanuel Kant, *Critique of Pure Reason.*
28. *The Republic*, Book V.
29. Immanuel Kant, *Fundamental Principles of the Metaphysics of Morals.*
30. John A. Stoops, *Religious Values in Education*, (Danville, Ill.: The Interstate Printers & Publishers, Inc., 1967), Chapter VII.
31. *The Symposium.*
32. George Santayana, *The Sense of Beauty* (New York: Dover Publications, Inc., 1955), p. 189.
33. *The Sophist.*
34. *The Timaeus.*
35. G. M. A. Grube, *op. cit.*, or see the works of the Neo-Platonist.
36. See, *Wisdom of Diotima* in *The Symposium.*
37. *The Protagoras.*
38. Winspear, *op. cit.*, Ch. XIII.

Other Reading

Capes, W. W. *University Life in Ancient Athens.* New York: Harper and Bros., 1877.
Dever, James. *Greek Education: Its Principles and Practices.* Cambridge: Harvard University Press, 1912, pp. 1-107.

Diogenes, Laertius. *The Lives and Opinions of Eminent Philosophers*. Tr. C. D. Yonge. London: Bell, 1915.

Dobson, John F. *Ancient Education and Its Meaning to Us*. New York: Longmans Green and Co., 1932. 107 pp.

Gardner, Earnest. *Ancient Athens*. New York: The Macmillan Company, 1902. Chapters I-VI.

Grube, G. M. A. *Plato's Thought*. Boston: The Beacon Press, 1958, pp. 1-51, 216-253.

Hofstodter, Albert, and Richard Kuhns. *Philosophies of Art and Beauty*. New York: Random House Inc., 1964, pp. 1-77.

Horne, Herman H. *Idealism in Education*. New York: The Macmillan Company, 1910.

Jaeger, W. W. *Paidea: The Ideals of Greek Culture*. New York: Oxford University Press, 1939-1944. 3 Volumes.

Jowett, B. *The Dialogues of Plato*. New York: Random House, 1937. 2 Volumes.

Lodge, Rupert. *The Great Thinkers*. New York: Frederick Ungar Publishing Co., 1964, pp. 1-25.

Neff, Fredrick. *Philosophy and American Education*. New York: Center for Applied Research in Education, 1966, pp. 1-21.

Van Hook, LaRue. *Greek Life and Thought*. New York: The Columbia University Press, 1923, pp. 1-156.

Walden, John W. H. *The Universities of Ancient Greece*. New York: Charles Scribner's Sons, 1909. Chapters I-III.

Winspear, Alban D. *The Genesis of Plato's Thought*. New York: Russell & Russell, 1956, pp. 1-217.

CHAPTER IV

Aristotelian Realism

In the classroom Plato reckons
And at the window science beckons.

This line of verse alludes to a vital pedagogical distinction between Plato, founder of the Academy at Athens, and Aristotle, the most famous of his students. The pagans among us can imagine them both, now happily ensconced in the Elysium, whiling away the dreary hours of that sanctuary for immortals by contemplating the work of our modern schools. Plato smiles upon classrooms in which teachers develop each *nous* to recognize first principles and the other forms of knowledge by which excellence is known. At the same time, Aristotle nods approvingly at the teacher who helps students develop habits of controlled, objective observation of the parts of the world and teaches them to reason correctly about the data they have gathered.

Plato and Aristotle

For two decades these two incomparably gifted men were in almost daily contact, Plato as teacher and Aristotle as student. During his years as an Academy philosopher Aristotle was much more of an orthodox Platonist than in his later years. Indeed, the time came when he was critical of certain Platonic doctrines, and he was even more critical of certain other students of Plato who continued at the Academy after Plato's death. Incredible as it may seem, the differences between the Platonism of Plato and the Platonism of Aristotle smoldered almost unnoticed for nearly fourteen hundred years. Then they exploded in the medieval universities as the contest was resumed by partisans of whom Plato would never have dreamed, speaking languages which Aristotle would never have imagined.

But the differences come immediately alive to the reader who spends an hour with each of them. Plato is a stylist who verges constantly on the poetic. He crosses into that domain when his ardor and idea are joined in an intuition of truth. Plato's religious sensibilities

are evident. One quickly by-passes his logic chopping and mathematical mysticism by sensing his basic acceptance of Pythagorean
doctrines on reincarnation and his personal connection to the Orphic
mysteries. His source of knowledge is man himself. He urges introspection. He asserts that man bears truth in his soul, thus the proper
route to knowledge is interior. Little wonder that Augustine valued
Plato's intuition of the inner man, and little wonder that the fifth-
Century Christian church theologized much of Plato's philosophy and
in subsequent years dogmatized its more superficial aspects.

Aristotle is an observer. He arrives at his metaphysical posture
by applying reason to the raw data which appears through the
senses. He does not look inward so much as he looks out; his view of
the universe is that of a bystander whose views of nature and man are
dispassioned and appear to be uncontaminated by prior convictions
about what it is that he is seeing. As Aristotle sweeps along from one
set of observations and self-evident general conditions to the next,
the reader feels his confidence and sense of wonder growing. Aristotle's
objectivity and thoroughness seem at first admirable and later awesome. He does not sparkle or shine; he does not soar or glide; but then,
seldom does he confuse. It is said he writes as a college professor,
building system as he goes. His expressions are not bound up in
vivid metaphors. His point of view compels credence on the grounds
of what the world of matter presents as its causes and consequences.

Aristotle's rare losses of detachment seem to occur only when
he is discussing his predecessors and contemporaries in philosophy.
Lack of objectivity is the more striking in him because it is rare.
However, it must be remembered that he was a Greek, and a vigorous
one at that. In those times the rivalry among philosophers was often
social and political as well as intellectual, and if they were competing
for students the dialectic at times became an exchange of insults. None
of this was lost to the gossips of antiquity who, quite like their modern
kindred, relished each stroke—and doubtless, when recording it, added
blandishments of their own.

Whatever contemporaries made of Platonism and *Peripateticism*
(as Aristotle's doctrines became called), Plato held most of the attention of western Europe during the first millenium of the Christian
era. Some of the books of Aristotle were preserved in the middle east,
and he was well known to the Romans. But for reasons to be discussed later, Aristotle's concealment from western scholars did not
really end until the Tenth and Eleventh Centuries. In the Twelfth
Century he re-emerged on the wings of metaphysical controversy.

In the Thirteenth Century Thomas Aquinas referred to Aristotle as "the philosopher" as if there were no other. And in the Fourteenth Century Geoffrey Chaucer, when introducing "a clerk from Oxford," said:

> For he would rather have at his bed's head
> Some twenty books, all bound in black and read,
> Of Aristotle and his philosophy
> Than rich rocks, fiddle of gay psaltry,
> Yet, and for all he was philosopher,
> He had but little gold in his coffer. . . .[1]

Writing early in the Seventeenth Century Christopher Marlowe went so far as to suggest that one might "live and die in Aristotle's works."[2] And in modern times one such as Jacques Maritain is moved to declare:

"It can be affirmed without hesitation that among philosophers Aristotle holds a position altogether apart: genius, gift, and achievement, all are unique."[3]

Only a formidable presence could achieve such continuing recognition, and modern classroom teachers are obliged to take more than passing notice of it.

It is accepted that Plato teaches every school boy. Plato's curriculum for the *nous* has been passed along by many thousands of hands across twenty-three centuries for daily deliverance in modern classrooms. As Plato sits beside the boy in school, urging his thoughts, ever building intellectual edifices inward and upward, so Aristotle stands by the window beckoning him to look out upon the world, summoning him to walk beneath the trees, urging him to look and see what is happening all around him.

Both are great philosophers. Plato is a mathematician and Aristotle a biologist. Plato finds his ideal government by reflecting on virtue. Aristotle investigates the same subject by examining the constitutions of one hundred and fifty-eight city states. Western man, in modern times, is not closer to choosing between the two than were the Athenians of the last half of the Fourth Century B.C. One who reflects on this begins to sense the kind of dilemma philosophical scholarship offers.

The Life of Aristotle

Aristotle was born in Stagira, a small town in the Province of Thrace located about 250 miles north of Athens (a good day's drive through modern Greece). In 383 B.C., the year of Aristotle's birth, this was at least a week's journey. However, in those times the cultural distance between the Athenians and Thracians was a great deal more. Athens in the Fourth Century, it now appears, was backsliding, but it was still Athens. In the previous century it was the imaginative and enterprising Athenians who twice defeated the massive Persian aggressions; they established an eloquent and exemplary democracy; they built a maritime empire; and they attracted to their city the best of art and philosophy of the ancient world. The Athenian courts achieved new standards of man-to-man justice, and even cosmopolitan Corinth was surpassed by the variety and vitality of Athenian society. There was a revered style of living and being which was ratified by the name "Athenian." Even after twenty centuries it still is.

Militarily, Athens had bowed to Sparta and Sparta to Thebes, but at the time of Aristotle, Athens was still Athens. The cultural distance to Thrace was much more than, say, Manhattan to Main Street. The Athenians viewed the Thracians as little more than barbarians, and to the south of Thrace were the Macedonians who were worse than barbarians. They were ambitious. Aristotle's initial connection to the Macedonian kings was through his father who was a physician to Amyntas, father of Philip, and grandfather of Alexander. Aristotle's later connections to Macedonia were such that he was clearly identified with the politics and policies of both Philip and Alexander.

There was pride in the Macedonian kings. Philip had taken pains to trace his lineage to the House of Argos and had established himself as a member of the Delphic amphictyony. He had even served as president of the Pythian games held high on Mount Parnassus. As guardian of the historic northern invasion routes, Philip was already the *de facto* protector of Greece. The dialect and manners of his people were not nearly so refined as those of the Atticans to the south, but the House of Macedon was moving up.

Even today Macedonia appears to be farm country. It reminds the modern American traveler of rural Pennsylvania with its lakes, gently rolling hills, wooded slopes, and ever present ridges in the distance. A boy growing to manhood in this country, especially one whose family carried a tradition of medical practice, would learn responsiveness to nature and develop a tendency to value in the way nature instructs men to value. Aristotle was orphaned while still young, but his stepfather took foster parentage very seriously, and it is not surprising that such a man who lived among such people was determined that a promising boy in his custody get the best schooling available. Accordingly, at the age of seventeen, Aristotle was sent to Plato's Academy.

Traditional sources hint that his early days in Athens were not trouble-free. In addition to such cultural disadvantages as he might have had, Aristotle was said to be somewhat flamboyant and given to outlandish dress. He even affected a lisp.[4] Evidently, these small eccentricities were soon overlooked, and as his intellectual gifts became recognized he was marked as one of the most brilliant in the school.

He was an excellent student and his reputation across the twenty years of academic residence grew to the point that many apparently expected him to be Plato's successor as head of the Academy. There were also grounds to suppose that he would have welcomed this appointment. However, when Plato died in 347 B.C. Speusippus, Plato's nephew, was chosen. The apparent rejection of Aristotle must have been the subject of considerable gossip. Tradition holds that, disappointed, he left the Academy and Athens. There has been no indication that he ever returned to the school in which he was educated.

The first and most obvious reason advanced is that Aristotle's departure from Platonic doctrines weighted against his appointment. However, this is probably not so. Research has shown that Aristotle at the age of thirty-seven had not departed from Plato's doctrine. On the contrary, at that time he was still considered one of the more conservative Platonists.[5] When he left the city he was in the company of Xenocrates, also a noted conservative. Moreover, Speusippus had strongly criticized Plato's theory of ideas prior to his uncle's death. Therefore, it is unlikely that the choice of Plato's successor was based on loyalty to doctrine. Indeed, it would have been inconsistent with the Socratic freedoms as prized and often encouraged by Plato to punish an academician for independent views.

There are two theories which have been advanced to explain this matter; both are plausible and possibly valid. One relates to the political alliances of the academicians.[6] Many of them served as consultants to governments of the many still-thriving city states. Quite naturally they were not always so "professional" as discretion demands and their alliances tended to be known. Aristotle's closeness to the Macedonians must have weighed against him. Relations between King Philip and many in the Platonic circle were decidedly strained.[7] The other theory relates to property. Although the Academy is properly regarded as situated in the garden *Sanctuary of Akademos*

which was public, the real school was on Plato's property which was
nearby. It was there that the scholars lived, worked, and slept; it
was there that the confidential instruction was imparted, and it was
there that the true fellowship prevailed. The slaves also lived there
and helped carry out the work of publishing.[8] It would not be surprising then, that for the most practical of reasons, the headship of
the school passed along to a member of the family. Were someone
else chosen, the Academy would possibly have been required to move
or acquire the property.

Aristotle and Xenocrates resumed their studies at the cities of
Assos and Atarneus where they placed themselves under the protection
of King Hermias, an ally of Philip. Aristotle married Pythias, niece
and adopted daughter of the king. It was apparently during this interval of great happiness that Aristotle's intrigues in behalf of Philip
became completely open. Hermias was murdered by the Persians,
and Aristotle and his wife fled to Lesbos where she died in childbirth.
Here again the literature is silent on Aristotle the man. But it is
thought that during this time in his life *Eudemian Ethics* was written.
It contains this poignant observation:

> Lovers sometimes, because they cannot endure the
> misery of the objects of their love, destroy both
> themselves and those whom they love. For they
> suffer more from their calamities than their own.[9]

Aristotle soon took up the company of another woman, Herpyllis,
whom he may have married. She was apparently a good sort, and
the two lived together in peace for the remainder of his days.

It was at this point Aristotle was invited to return to Macedonia
to become the "tutor" of Prince Alexander. Often this is described as
an individual arrangement, but this evidently was not the case. It
actually may have been something of a small college at which Aristotle
was head professor and Alexander the head student.[10] The relationship
of the two, however, was close enough to be meaningful to both
in the eventful times ahead. After the assassination of Philip and the
mercurial rise of Macedonia under the young king, Aristotle returned
to Athens; and, with funds probably furnished by Alexander, founded
a school which quickly rivaled and soon overshadowed the Academy.

The quarters of the school were near a large gymnasium consecrated to Apollo Lyceus.[11] The gymnasium possessed a colonnade or
peripatos. Aristotle called his school the Lyceum. He was evidently
given wide privileges in the gymnasium. In the mornings it is said

that he led his closest students on walks under the colonnades expounding on the formative struggles of nature going on in the trees and flowers which surrounded them. This pedestrian habit soon earned the group the name *peripatetics*.[12] In the afternoons, he lectured in the gymnasium. As we know from the will of Theophrastus, whom Aristotle chose to succeed him, the real headquarters of the school was on private land.

Upon the death of Alexander, Aristotle's political fortunes in Athens became ominous. The latent Athenian disapprobation of him in particular and of the Macedonians in general quickly came to the stage of action. Aristotle apparently was a symbol of Macedonian presumptuousness. There are indications that Aristotle had been insensitive (or perhaps indifferent) to the pent-up resentment of many leading Athenians. Perhaps he trusted too much in Alexander's youthfulness. The Athenians interested in promoting his departure were not disposed to use untried methods for ridding themselves of unwanted philosophers; and, accordingly, a scant year after Alexander's death Aristotle was under indictment for offenses against religion.[13] Mindful of the example of Socrates, and still a lover of his adopted city, he took flight reputedly commenting, "Athens must not sin twice against philosophy."

In modern Athens the site of Aristotle's school is now the Queen's Garden. It is a beautiful park. Here and there sculptured pieces of antiquity protrude from the soil. Beneath it may rest the fragments of an illustrious past, but the garden grows on. Somehow it seems fitting that Aristotle's Athenian haunts survive as a garden and not as a ruin.

In 324, a year after he had departed from Athens for Euboea, he died of a respiratory ailment. His will was preserved and gave as much insight of humanity as of his surviving works. He provided well for Pythias, daughter by his first wife, and Nicomachus, a son by his second. Herpyllis, too, was comfortably settled. He asked that the remains of his first wife be laid to rest beside him. This had been Pythias' death wish and his grief-stricken assurance. Thus, the life of antiquity's most famous biologist was crowned by this tender gesture of elegiac sentiment. What kind of man was he?

The Works of Aristotle

The writings of Aristotle are usually classified according to three historical periods. The first of these periods was the interval when he was a student at the Academy; the second period covered was the twelve years of his stay at Assos and Lesbos, and his instructorship at Macedonia; and the third period covers his twelve-year headship of the Lyceum.

The Academy books are said to include the *Eudemus* (on the soul) and *Protripticus* (on the life of the philosopher) and a number of other works in dialogue form. It is possible that the *Organon, Physics,* and *De Anima* were started during the Academy period. It seems clear that these written works which include recognition of Plato's educational doctrine of reminiscence betray no departure from Plato's doctrine.

During his second period his intellectual autonomy apparently was asserted. It appears that during these years the *Metaphysics* and *Eudemian Ethics* were begun. Unquestionably, these works contain original ideas of which there is no trace in Plato. Portions of the *Politics* may also have been written during this time, although this work probably did not mature until his return to Athens. Most significantly, some criticisms of Plato's theory of ideas and of creation were developed. It is also thought that it was during this period that the doctrine of the "unmoved mover" was added.

The final period is notable for its concentration on science. He produced the *Organon* and the *Metaphysics,* the work on *Natural Philosophy, Nicomachean Ethics, Politics, Poetics,* and *Rhetoric.* Despite all of this he wrote much more that is known about but that has been lost. In addition, more may have been written and lost than is known about.

In commenting on the fate of the Aristotelian library, Gomperez points to a paradox recognized by only the most intense students of the philosophical literature of antiquity. Evidently the books most widely read in antiquity are those which have been lost. Those which were more specialized and systematic, the vast portions of which may have been notations for lectures or notes taken by students, are those best known to us. Gomperez observes:

> The Aristotle of the ancients is not our Aristotle, and ours is not theirs. Those of his writings which they read, or read by preference, have not reached us; that which we have was in part entirely unknown to them, in part known in such a way that to make it a basis for judgment about Aristotle's style would never enter their heads . . .[14]

One of his best known works, *The Metaphysics,* was not on a list of Aristotle's work compiled in the Alexandrine period. But the same catalog contains a number of titles which are part of that book. Clearly then, some selecting, organizing, and editing has been done. This is why it is so important to understand the sort of thing that went on in the Lyceum. Aristotle may have spoken from notes which he turned over to literate slaves to set in coherent prose. His students may have had manuscript writers do the same thing from notes which they recorded. Other possibilities exist. Manuscript production was one of the daily industries of the school. Surely a goodly part of what we have was written by the philosopher. But we are certain that much of it was fashioned into language by others.

What sort of a man was he? It seems clear that we cannot draw conclusions by examining the style of his written work. The ancients speak of its richness, coloring, force, and grace. Our Aristotle was not theirs. Our Aristotle is the logician, observer, analyzer, cataloger, and expositer. We have the professor. Perhaps the ancients had the poet.

The Ontology of Aristotle

Thus the only Aristotle we are privileged to know is he who has arrived through his textbooks and the meager records on him and other notables of that time which have been preserved. His books do yield a powerful philosophical system which must be studied by educators. This system is of interest for its own sake. But it has been more meaningful for educators when it is recognized that for over seven hundred years Aristotle's ideas have been widely applied in the educational institutions of Europe and America, and continue today as the source of educational theories which are as modern as any.

In his metaphysics Aristotle seems to put the concepts of Plato to work in a different way. The job they do in his hands is different. Aristotle is bound to explain the *operation* of the world. Those who argue that Aristotle simply Platonizes do less than justice to the contrast between Aristotle's unity of matter and form and the complete disjunction of the two which Plato describes in the *Republic*. Aristotle evidently finds the hypothesis of Platonic dualism an inadequate base for explanations about how the world functions. To put it in more modern terms, Plato's model seems to contradict that which is going on in the world.

Believing that metaphysics should explain and not proclaim, Aristotle does not build an edifice of thought concerning the ultimate status of particular things. Instead he draws attention to the two self-evident aspects of all of the particular things of the world, namely, they have matter and they have form.

His *realism* comes to flower by his use of the little Greek word "*qua*" (in so far as). His metaphysics is an investigation of being *qua* being. By this he means that metaphysics should be a science of sensible objects and this is as far as their being goes. Thus he turns aside from the notion that sensible objects have either a transcendent quality or an ultimate mathematical reality. He thereby removes mathematics from the ontological throne where Plato had installed it and puts it to work describing three-dimensional objects. The quarrel between theoretical and applied mathematics probably dates from the invention of the first number. Plato belongs to the theory side of this timeless issue and Aristotle to the applied side.

So when a man observes an object, he observes all that there is of that object. But it is important to note that the object is in motion. Therefore, being *qua* being includes becoming. What is the direction of the movement? What is it that an object is becoming? At the risk of oversimplification the reader is invited to think of the object constantly becoming itself. Pray, what would that be?

Aristotle indicates that all objects are composed of prime matter. Matter without form is nothing more than potential. This is called the principle of potentiality. We do not find matter in an unformed state. We can take the stuffing out of a pillow, and the moment it is on its own it takes on a form. However, we can think of stuff *qua* stuff. When we contemplate matter as sheer matter or prime matter we contemplate pure potential.

Form is a property of all things. More than this, it is an active property. All things are in a state of forming. A boy is becoming a man, an acorn a tree, a bud a rose, an egg a chick, etc. Form then includes act. Hence, form is called the principle of actuality.[15] We do not see form apart from matter, but we can abstract it. The form of an oak tree is not a static thing, as Plato appears to suggest. It is not an innate idea. In Aristotle, form in an oak tree is a principle of action. And when the principle of actuality goes to work on potentiality the object begins to emerge.

Every American schoolboy is familiar with the riddle: "What comes first, the chicken or the egg?" To make his metaphysics clear, Aristotle had to take a position on a matter such as this. What comes first is a principle of action which might be called egg chickenness (or chicken eggness?). When one sees an egg or chicken he knows that the actuality or active plan of the chicken-egg cycle is there in the egg (or chicken). Also when one looks at an acorn he recognizes that the principle of an oak tree is there at work. Aristotle said: "It is plain that the actual is prior to the potential."[16] Thus an object is conceived as potentiality responding to a principle of actuality.

Movement in the world is not random. It is directed, purposeful. Indeed, all independent motion can be shown to be related. The potential (that-which-moves) and the actual (that-which-authors-movement) are never apart. The essence of a pig is not the raw material of the pig alone, neither is the idea of pighood separate and apart from the class of animals that resemble it. The essence of a pig is found in the actual and potential together becoming a pigness. Now when we know an object we simply discover its essence. A bush has a bushness about it, a tree a treeness, a horse a horseness, and on and on. Each of these things, therefore, includes its own universal. The universal does not come first as a drawing on a drawing board. It does not come after as the name of things or as intellectual concepts of what exists in the world. The universal is *in the thing* actively working itself out.

If the actual comes first, then what is the source of actuality? If Aristotle had managed to avoid this question his system could have remained relatively independent of metaphysics. The matter (potentiality) and form (actuality) hypothesis is a useful syntax for the discipline of biology. It simply suggests that matter is actualized by certain rules or principles. The world seems to operate in obedience to these principles. Taken together actuality and potentiality can stand as a basis for a reliable body of knowledge capable of indefinite extension. As such, it satisfies all conditions for justified knowledge except the persistent *desideratum* which in his day was the first business of philosophy. Why is there act? Aristotle may have devised a satisfactory model for the description of motion. But why is there motion?

Aristotle's effort to answer this, as reported in several of the extant works, is commonly referred to as the *theory of causes*. The epistemological aspect of this theory will be discussed later. Here it is appropriate to deal with his assertion that motion is *caused*. We may add to the ontological status of every object the fact that it was and continues to be caused. It is impossible to think of an uncaused movement. Causes are principles. Thus actualization is conceived of as cause. He said, "It is the cause that is sought in all questions."[17]

In the *Physics* Aristotle admitted that the modes of causes are many in number.[18] One cause may be the cause of another and so on. However, when causes are traced regressively, that is to say this caused that, and that was caused by this, and so on, the regress becomes infinite. At this, the mind boggles. He declared, "The infinite, as infinite, is unknowable."[19] It is "devoid of parts and indivisible."[20]

Now Aristotle is clearly standing on Platonic grounds. In the introductory sentences of Book XII of the *Metaphysics* he is forced to say there is something else besides plants and animals. This "something" causes movement but it is not moved. *It is an unmoved mover*. Thus, Aristotle resorts to the unmoved mover, but he is unwilling to remain vague. Not only does he wish to be more explicit, but also chides Plato and others for their unwillingness to be more explicit.[21] He indicates that the first mover is pure actuality and is "free of matter."[22] It must actually *be*. It necessarily exists, and because it is its own necessity it is, by definition, good.

On such a first principle the heavens and the natural world depend. Aristotle writes of the unmoved mover as analogical to mind:

> . . . the mind thinks of itself when it takes on the nature of an object of thought. It becomes an object of thought when it is perceiving and thinking, and then thought and object are the same. For that which is thought and essence is the mind. And when it possesses in itself these things, it is actual and active. And actuality rather than potentiality seems to be the divine feature in thought, and the act of contemplation is what is most of all pleasant and best. If then God is always happy in that happy state in which we sometimes are, this is wonderful still. And God is in that happier state.[23]

Pure actuality, the source of motion, is pure thinking which is of itself. This seems to be Aristotle's intuition of God. God is thought and thought is God. God is an eternal consciousness, an intellectual perception, which stands apart from matter and motion but which causes the latter in the former. This "divine mind" is *actual thinking whose object is simply itself*. It is aware of itself and generates its own standards. God's life is a thinking of thinking. The thinking and the object of his thinking are one and the same.

As one might expect, this leaves much to be explained and interpreted, and interpretations and explanations vary. Schafer makes an interesting distinction between God *as a creator* and Aristotle's *unmoved mover*:

> In the philosophical system of Aristotle, God is not the creator of the universe but the cause of its motion, the creator is a dreamer, and the dreamer is a dissatisfied personality, a soul that yearns for something that he is not, an unhappy being that seeks for happiness—in short an imperfect creature

> which aims at perfection. But (Aristotle's) God is perfect and
> since he is perfect he can not be dissatisfied or unhappy. He is,
> therefore, not the maker but the mover of the universe.[24]

In the end analysis, Aristotle's ontology stands on the threshold of
theology (if not in the vestibule). In any event some theologians have
applied it to theism and put it to work in explanations of God. Neither
Christian nor Jew can reproach the other for borrowing from Aristotle.

Aristotle did not heal the breach between matter and idea which
Plato exposed. His actuality of mind as the source of all motion is at
least as remote from the world of objects as Plato's forms.[25] If Aristotle
wished to be more explicit, he succeeded only in raising a different
variety of questions. However, in full retrospect, Aristotle was simply
placing a theological capstone on his metaphysics. The greatest historical significance is in the extent to which he succeeded in giving better
rational foundations to the earlier theological postures of Parmenides,
Xenophanes and the earlier Ionians. In this he may have succeeded to
an extent greater than any before him. The Orphic theogonies were
still deeply rooted,[26] and it is speculated that even Plato was influenced
by pagan pluralism. The Athenians, lovers of Dionysus, would not appreciate Aristotle's theism. Certainly he was more specifically at variance with the long-standing religious attitudes of his fellow townsmen
than was Socrates whom they prosecuted on that charge.

Aristotle's ontology is rightly characterized as a species of Platonism. It is a reorganization of Platonic ideas which include a revised
and very much improved account of the reality of matter. More specifically, he relocated the universal. In Aristotle the form is not static and
not separate from matter. By having form active in matter Aristotle
nearly escaped producing a Platonized ontology, but he is retained
with the Platonic school by his institution of the "third substance,"
the *unmoved mover,* which can be described as "a thinking about
thinking that is going on," and which emanates in such a way as to
activate form which in turn works itself on matter.

The Epistemology of Aristotle

Aristotle's approach to knowledge is through causes. It is not
without Platonic overtones in its general aspects but as it proceeds to
knowledge *qua* knowledge it is increasingly emancipated until Aristotle shows the way for a science which is free of poetic sentiments. For
students of education who are seeking an understanding of the implications of his epistemology for that field, Aristotle's way of knowing

the specific is central. Yet one cannot be true to Aristotle's way of knowing without revealing its more grandiose aspects.

Cause exists in four senses:

> (1) In one sense, that from which as *present material* something is made; as for instance the bronze of a statue or the silver of a cup, and the types of things that comprise these. (2) In another sense, the *form* or pattern, that is the essential formula, and the types of things comprising this, and the parts of the formula. For instance the ratio 2:1 and number in general are causes of the musical octave. (3) That by which a change is begun or stopped. For instance, the adviser is the cause of the act, the father of the child, and in general the maker is a cause of that which is made and the one who makes a change of the change. (4) Again, it means the final end, that is, that for the sake of which something else is. For instance, health is an end in walking. For why does one walk? . . .[27]

The four causes in the above are called (1) material, (2) formal, (3) efficient, and (4) final. The study of an object must include an investigation of the material that composes it; the shape which it has taken; the immediate agency which produced it; and, finally, the purpose it holds in a world which at the ultimate level is its own purpose. Obviously, the final cause takes contemplation of any object to the sublime levels of metaphysics. One can understand easily enough the purpose of the road is the transportation of people between its terminal points or points in between. But what is the purpose of the road in the universe? This is very hard to say, and, if sensing this aspect of "cause" is required for one fully to know the road, then full knowledge of the road, or anything like it, is probably impossible.

When the final cause is restricted to the purposes implicit in the efficient cause, then the four causes constitute a basis for unrestricted scientific knowledge. For instance if we are willing to know an atom bomb by (1) what (material) it is made of, (2) the various formulae (formal) which make it up including those which define its shape, (3) who (efficient) made it, and (4) why (final) they made it, then we have knowledge which is attainable, reliable, and shareable. However, Aristotle is also right that we are bound to inquire what purpose a thing (especially an atom bomb) has in the totality of all things. He is probably also right in his suggestion that this (final) aspect of cause will reveal the unity of all objects. But from the perspective of twenty-three centuries we are compelled to note that this aspect of cause is still speculative, unreliable, and not shareable.

Nevertheless it is clear that "cause" is the form in which warrantable knowledge must appear. Now we turn to the methods by which cause is discovered, and here we detect a sharp break with Plato dramatized in Aristotle's own words:

> Farewell to the ideas for they are inane figments and
> even if they were, they are irrelevant. For demonstrations
> concern things which first fall under the senses.[28]

The analytics of the *Organon* have as their aim an exploration first of the general and then of the specific ways the mind works in order to obtain scientific knowledge. It contains six treatises which include *Categories, Interpretation, Prior Analytics, Posterior Analytics, The Topics,* and *The Sophisticated Refutation.* A detailed account of how each of these treatises consummates in a general method for producing and verifying knowledge is beyond the scope of this chapter. However the distinctive highlights are of relevance.

The major thrust of the *Organon* is scientific demonstration. Such a demonstration reveals that certain things being given, something else necessarily follows. Scientific proof, to Aristotle, involves necessary conclusions derived necessarily from premises which themselves involve true and necessary matters. The external form of this is called a *syllogism.* Now if one examines the nature of the predications within a successful syllogism he can see the extent to which Aristotle's obsession with cause pervades the knowledge method itself.

With characteristic thoroughness, Aristotle defines the schemata of syllogistic argumentation. He describes in detail the three forms by which a perfect syllogism can be consummated and he indicates ways in which imperfect syllogisms can be used to support particular conclusions. His definitions of major premises, minor premises, subjects, predicates, categories, and universals, and their proper, improper, and syllogistic relationships are better reserved to discourses on logic. The central point here is that this elaborate discipline of logic works upon *that which is observed.* It does not yield anything *per se.*

Aristotle remains Platonic to the extent that he still gives reasoning the major role in knowledge making. But he is a realist in the extent to which he is willing to use sense data, carefully observed and classified, as subject matter for syllogistical operations. He deserves recognition for his painstaking refinement of logical methods and for the rigor and clarity with which he illustrated its potential fallacies. His major contribution is his method by which he made sense data subject to rational procedures. Thus, a man can begin the route to knowledge by observing what is going on outside of him. In intellectual history, this tradition is called *peripateticism*. His work is an advance over the Ionians and other Sixth-Century Greek materialists in that it is more rigorous. Furthermore, he demonstrated his methods in his studies of plants, animals, heavenly bodies, and the geology of the earth. By these methods he formulated rationale and methods through which separate academic disciplines were later authorized. Aristotle was not a specialist, but he helped found specialties.

What separates him from modern science? Aristotelianism relies too much on the test of logic. It goes too far with the assumption that the world is logical. Such an assumption is valid if one believes, as Aristotle evidently did, that the final cause is mind. Modern science reduces the role of logic to the production of hypotheses to be tested experimentally or operationally. It is not that Aristotle was inclined to accept appearances as a basis for knowing; his trouble was that his realism stopped too soon and became Platonic. Aristotle began the knowing process by observing the world, but his knowledge was warranted by the test of reason. On the other hand, modern science demands that the final test be experimental or operational. When the product of our reason (a hypothesis) *corresponds* to that which goes on in the world then the hypothesis is warranted as knowledge. Diagrammatically, the epistemological differences between orthodox Platonism, Aristotelian realism, and modern science can be shown as follows:

Orthodox Platonism:

    Reason—observation—knowledge

Aristotelian realism:

    Observation—reason—knowledge

Modern science:

    Observation—reason—experimental—knowledge
              or operational
              test

The Axiology of Aristotle

Even at the time Aristotle taught in Athens there were heated differences among philosophers regarding the good. Several schools in addition to the Lyceum and the old Academy were already in being or soon to start. Elements of cynicism, stoicism, and Epicurean hedonism seemed to be afoot in the city. Nearly all of these new offspring were originated by offspring of the group of students who followed Socrates. Men were constructing philosophical models which were continued as life styles through the Middle Ages and into modern times. One who taught philosophy in Athens in those days would certainly be called upon to make his own ethical pronouncements. Aristotle did so and at great length.

The *Eudemian Ethics* and *Nicomachean Ethics* are his two great philosophical tracts in the field of ethics that have survived. The first is presumably named for a man who was one of his favorite students and possibly the compiler of the work. The second is presumably named for his son Nicomachus who may have published it with the assistance of Theophrastus.[29] Of the two, the *Nicomachean Ethics* is more respected by modern scholarship on the grounds of authenticity, coherence, and scope. It is a work of ten books and one hundred thirty-three chapters.

Aristotle puts his Platonic skills to work in a calm analysis of the human character of man on earth. At the very outset he informs his reader that the good in human terms is easily identified *as happiness*. Unlike some who later were also to put forward happiness as a moral standard, Aristotle believes that happiness is in need of definition and all men need to know how happiness can be achieved. Bridging from his original comments in *The Metaphysics* he now proposes that man is most happy when he is performing the functions for which nature designed him. In the case of man this unique function is the activity of the soul in obedience to reason. The virtues, therefore, that lead to happiness are the states of character which are determined by the operation of reason. Reason, then, is the vital power which separates man from other creatures. A reasoning man is turning in the direction of happiness and, therefore, toward the good.

Aristotle turns to a rational examination of external goods, friendship, wealth, power, beauty, nobility, and children. All of these, he finds, may be instrumental to happiness, but none of them *per se* constitute sufficient grounds for happiness. Indeed, excesses of anything are to be avoided. Moderation is one of the key virtues. Many commentators have pointed out that Aristotle urges moderation in all things except moderation itself. Aristotle, it is said, urges "moderation to excess." Therefore, on matters of prodigality, wealth, exercise, diet, etc., he espouses a doctrine of the mean. Any of them may be necessary or instrumental but none of them alone is broad enough to stand as the general purpose for life. Man is meant to be happy. Happiness requires no further justification. It alone serves no other purpose than itself. Said he, "happiness is something final and self-sufficient, being the end of all action."[30]

Nicomachean Ethics is probably the most widely read of Aristotle's works. There is no doubt that it is the most widely quoted. The sections of particular interest to teachers are those which deal with the learning of those virtues which are instrumental to happiness. In Book II, for example, he proclaims that moral virtues can be best acquired by practice and habit. In regard to this he says:

> But the virtues we get by first practicing them, as we do in the arts. For it is by doing what we ought to do when we study the arts that we learn the arts themselves; we become builders by building and harpists by playing the harp. Similarly, it is by doing just acts that we become just, by doing temperate acts that we become temperate, by doing brave acts that we become brave.[31]

The argument that we "learn to do by doing" is a familiar one to students of education. In modern times it has been associated with the pedagogical prescriptions of John Dewey. Aristotle's advice, however, relates to the formation of good moral habits. This does not cohere with the moral pedagogy of modern experimentalists. For them, learning to do relates to social participation in the solution of moral problems.

Entering into the problem of beauty, Aristotle continues to assert the preeminence of purpose. Portions of *The Metaphysics, Poetics,* and *Rhetoric* reveal his aesthetic theory as consistent with his ontology. His commentaries are devoted mainly to identifying the function which each art form purports to fulfill. Once the function is understood the standard of beauty follows. Beauty in the case of the human body relates to the functions to be performed at certain ages:

> Beauty is different according to the several ages. The beauty of youth is having a body useful in enduring toils, whether those of the course or of personal exertion. . . . But the beauty of life's prime is the fitness adapted to the fatigues of war with an aspect looked upon with pleasure tempered with awe. That of the old consists in the body being capable of the fatigues which it needs must undergo. . . .[32]

Art has to do with creation, and the function of art is to imitate nature. But in doing so there is an emphasis on form. Thus, Aristotle is still Platonist in the respect that he is urging the art of the kind called classic described as the harmonious blend of form and matter in which form is the dominant aspect. As we apply his point of view to selected issues we find that he would be less a critic of Praxiteles who made marble look alive, than some of the more conservative Platonists. On the other hand he would resist the more vivid realism which began to appear in the art of Attica in the final years of his stay in Athens and which tended to dominate Hellenistic art in the two centuries subsequent to his death.

The Poetics in its original form was a much longer and more varied work than that which has come to us. Apparently the original treatise contained another major section devoted to comedy. It attempts to examine the essence of poetry and the proper functions of each of the different species of that art. Perhaps the most vivid aspect of this work is Aristotle's analysis of the tragedy. To him the tragic hero is one who falls from a high state of renown, honor, and property through some error. It is essential that the denouement not come as a consequence of vice or depravity, because the hero must not lose the sympathy of his audience. The tragedy has six distinctive parts from which it derives quality. These are fable (plot), character, diction, thought, spectacle, and harmony. Tragedy initiates a perfect and whole action which at the same time is terrible and piteous. He declared:

> Tragedy is an imitation of illustrious and perfect action, possessing magnitude, in pleasing language, using separately the several species of imitation in its parts, by men acting, and not through narration, through pity and fear effecting a purification from such like passions.[33]

Thus, the function of tragedy is to achieve a catharsis on the part of the audience. It is a high experience which cleanses through fear, pity, and awe. This function places tragedy foremost among the forms of drama. If the play does its work, the audience will be temporarily purged of the iniquities which build constantly within the human spirit. The playgoer resumes his life saddened and more reflective. He is humbled by the immensity of things. And for a while he is a better man. But reservoirs soon begin again to accumulate vile passions and errant desires. Man stands again at the threshold of sin. Another catharsis is needed. And he returns to the tragedy. Anyone who has seen a contemporary Greek audience at The Antigone or *The Electra* and has sensed their personal denouement knows immediately what Aristotle means.

In regard to government, a field in which we must regard Aristotle as expert, he favors broadest possible base. Aristotle is a democrat and *this separates him* from Plato and the more conservative Platonists. He believes that people should share in the management of public affairs and that they should elect their officials. However, he recommends that some selectivity should be exercised in determining who is permitted to be in the electorate.[34] The conditions which obtain from a democratic government and laws are more likely to be consistent with human happiness than those which develop in an oligarchy or monarchy. "Officers should be elected by all out of all. All should rule over each and each in his turn over all."[35]

Aristotle, therefore, saw education as producing good in a different way than Plato who looked upon ignorance as a disease of the soul. Aristotle saw ignorance as a problem for the state, and he urged that a state develop unity and community through the education of its citizens.[36] In this connection he made a declaration which in retrospect a democratic America regards as prophetic to its own aspirations:

> It is evident that laws should be laid down concerning
> education and that it should be public.[37]

Implications for Education

Aristotle's realism begins with matter and moves upward, escalated by form. It is consummated in mind. It begins as a philosophy of material and concludes as a philosophy of mind. The unmistakable signs of hierarchy are there. Centuries later these are made even more explicit in the work of Aquinas. But Aristotle leaves no question that it is a man's function to think, and that thinking brings him to harmony with the cosmic ultimate which is thought.

Aristotle makes a number of observations which result in a pedagogy differing from that of Plato. One of these distinctions is that he trained students to observe and classify objects. Knowing began by examining the relevant state of affairs in the world. Rather than poeticizing that which appears in the senses, Aristotle wants students to see sense data objectively. Mathematics was taught as a method of describing objects and becomes an abstract expression of observed forms. In his hands numbers lost some of the mystique they seemed to have for Plato.

Another distinction is that students were given the opportunity to observe nature. They learned systems of classification and the proper names of all things. Further scientific training of students emphasized logic with particular emphasis on reasoning to causes. Knowledge statements were liberally peppered with statements such as "necessary," "self-evident," "therefore," and "accordingly." Aristotle did not use the experimental method on evidence or use statistical tests for significance.

Aristotle's prescribed school for children is characterized by habit formation. Punctuality, posture, dress, modes of speech and greeting, grammar, etc., are ritualized. Reason is the object, and animal passions and pleasures must be sublimated or controlled. Children are required to speak, eat, walk, and think in preconceived patterns. Knowledge is presented systematically. The curriculum is organized from the specific to the universal, from the particular to the general. Induction is the rule in reasoning.

Nature, to Aristotle, is the foundation of our biological activities. Habit offers a mode for the control of emotional drives. Education begins to come into its own with the cultivation of mind. It is intellect which gives order to chaos and leads to comprehending the totality of life. From the age of seven until puberty the child is given a curriculum of music, gymnastics, reading, writing, and arithmetic. From puberty to age seventeen the curriculum is rhetoric, grammar, literature, geography, instrumental music, and mathematics. For the few who continue beyond the age of twenty-one the program emphasizes biology and the physical sciences, psychology and ethics, rhetoric and philosophy. Such a background makes a universal man.[38]

With his preference for democracy, admiration of the middle class, education for citizenship, prizing of rational excellence, Aristotle is much more at home in modern America and western Europe than is Plato. Even so, there is much that he could not accept. He opposes current efforts to push universal education beyond the age of twenty-one. He believes there are those in every state who are fitted by nature to study and produce knowledge. This is their function, the source of their happiness. The others, fitted by nature for other things, should seek their appropriate function, thus discovering the basis for their own happiness.

Aristotle defends slavery. Slaves, of course, are men of inferior cultures. There is in him a hearty Hellenistic contempt for the rest of the world. He is silent on the desirability of vocational training for slaves and lower working classes. Perhaps this is only a citation of the obvious, but Aristotle began all of his philosophizing by citing the obvious, and he said virtually nothing of this.

He extolled moderation, but men have never been completely happy with moderation. Americans, for example, have nearly deified normalcy in some respects, but in other respects normalcy is the last thing wanted. Aristotle would be dissatisfied with the American obsession with wealth. The profit motive as it works in our modern life he would probably see as good for neither state nor man.

Finally, he would disparage the current feminist drive for equal footing with men in all matters. He respected women, and apparently he dearly loved two of them. But for him the essence of women grew out of the function of womanness. In recognizing women as different Aristotle does not reveal the masculine bigotry of his more conservative colleagues in the Platonic circle. In effect, he again cites the obvious. Men and women are different and the difference should be celebrated and not homogenized. Numerous American women and virtually all American men would applaud him on this. But few women would be congenial with his passage in the *Politics* in which he maintained that "the courage of a man is shown in commanding, and of a woman in obeying.... All classes must be deemed to have their special attributes." So emphatic was Aristotle in recording this passage that he was moved to interrupt it with a quote from Sophocles.[39]

"Silence is a woman's glory."

Notes

1. J. U. Nicholson's modern English translation, *The Prologue.*
2. *The Tragical History of Dr. Faustus.*
3. Jacques Maritain, *An Introduction to Philosophy,* tr. E. I. Watkin (New York: Sheed and Ward, 1959), p. 67.
4. Diogenes Laertius, *Lives of Eminent Philosophers,* tr. R. D. Hicks (New York: G. P. Putnam's Sons, 1925), Vol. I, Book V, pp. 445-455.
5. Theodor Gomperez, *Greek Thinkers Vol. IV* (New York: Charles Scribner's Sons, 1912), p. 20.
6. Werner Jager, *Aristotle.* Cited in Alban D. Winspear, *The Genesis of Plato's Thought* (New York: Russell and Russell, 1940), p. 336.
7. Winspear, *Ibid.,* p. 314.
8. Norman DeWitt, *Epicurus and His Philosophy* (Minneapolis: University of Minnesota Press, 1954), p. 92.
9. *Eudemian Ethics,* Book 7.

10. Gomperez, *op. cit., Vol. IV.,* p. 22.
11. Ernest Gardner, *Ancient Athens* (New York: The Macmillan Co., 1902), p. 528.
12. DeWitt, *loc. cit.*
13. Gomperez, *op. cit., Vol. IV,* p. 24.
14. *Ibid.,* p. 30.
15. *Metaphysics,* Book X.
16. *Metaphysics,* Book IX.
17. *Posterior Analytics,* I.
18. *Physics,* Book II.
19. *Ibid.,* Book I.
20. *Metaphysics,* Book II. Here the infinite seems to resemble Plato's *good.*
21. *Metaphysics,* Book XII.
22. *Ibid.*
23. *Ibid.*
24. Stephen Schafer, *Education and the Philosophies of Matter* (Bethlehem, Pa.: Lehigh University, 1968), p. 8.
25. Rupert Lodge, *The Great Thinkers* (New York: Frederick Ungar Publishing Co., Inc., 1964), p. 53.
26. Werner Jaeger, *The Theology of Early Greek Philosophers* (Oxford: The Clarendon Press, 1947). See ch. IV.
27. *Metaphysics,* Book V, ch. 2.
28. *Posterior Analytics,* Book I.
29. Gomperez, *op. cit.,* p. 240.
30. *Nicomachean Ethics,* Book I, ch. 5.
31. *Ibid.,* Book II, ch. 1.
32. *Rhetoric,* Book I, ch. 5.
33. *Poetics,* Book VI.
34. *Ibid.,* Book IV.
35. *Ibid.,* Book VI.
36. *Ibid.,* Book VII.
37. *Ibid.,* Book II.
38. *Ibid.,* Books VII, VIII.
39. *Ibid.,* Book I.

Other Reading

Allen, D. J. *The Philosophy of Aristotle.* London: Oxford University Press, 1952.

Aristotle. *The Works of Aristotle.* Tr. and ed. W. D. Ross. Oxford: Clarendon Press, 1908-1931. 11 Volumes.

Blakewell, Charles M. *Source Book in Ancient Philosophy.* New York: Charles Scribner's Sons, 1939.

Burnet, J. *Aristotle on Education.* London: Cambridge University Press, 1903, pp. 1-141.

Frankena, William K. *Three Historical Philosophies of Education.* Atlanta: Scott, Foresman & Company, 1965, pp. 15-78.

Freeman, K. J. *The Schools of Hellas*. London: The Macmillan Company, Ltd., 1932.

Gomperez, Theodor. *Greek Thinkers, A History of Ancient Philosophy*. Tr. G. G. Berry, New York: Charles Scribner's Sons, 1912. Volume IV.

Kiernan, Thomas P. *Aristotle Dictionary*. New York: Philosophical Library, 1962, pp. 1-161.

Lodge, Rupert. *The Great Thinkers*. New York: Frederick Ungar Publishing Co., 1964, pp. 30-53.

Maritain, Jacques. *An Introduction to Philosophy*. Tr. E. D. Watkin, New York: Sheed & Ward, 1959. Chapters III, IV.

Marrow, H. I. *A History of Education in Antiquity*. New York: Sheed & Ward, 1956. Chapters II-IV.

Mayer, Fredrick. *A History of Educational Thought*. Columbus: Charles E. Merrill Books, Inc., 1960, pp. 81-104.

Pillsbury, W. B. *The History of Psychology*. New York: W. W. Norton & Company, 1945.

Russell, Bertrand. *A History of Western Philosophy*. New York: Simon and Schuster, Inc., 1945.

Taylor, A. E. *Aristotle*. New York: Dover Publications, Inc., 1955.

Ulich, Robert. *History of Educational Thought*. New York: American Book Company, 1945.

CHAPTER V

The Greco-Roman Schoolmen

The passing of Socrates occurs at the high noon of Greek philosophy. Of course there is brilliant and original speculation in the years which follow. Indeed, the Fourth Century B.C. could be compared to the hottest part of the day. The influences of Plato and Aristotle are colossal in western thought. This justifies their being singled out for the attention of the two previous chapters. But, we are driven to wonder how contemporaries of Plato and Aristotle would react upon knowing the western world had come to reverence them above others. This is a tempting question, for there are reasons to suppose that discerning citizens of the ancient world would be astonished to learn that these two in later times would come to be so exalted.

Certainly there were more colorful philosophers in Athens at the time. Alcibiades, the comely student of Socrates whose wavering loyalties vexed the Athenian effort to ward off the triumph of Sparta was surely a man known to all. Xenophon, another Socratic, was also a military figure of considerable renown. His books were widely read in antiquity. As a man about Athens, Antisthenes was at least as well known as Plato and Aristotle. He was sufficiently close to Socrates as to be among those present at his execution. None of the Platonists were so radical as Crates, the philosopher-poet of Thebes or Eucleides and Stilpo, the skeptics of Megara. If there is truth in legend, Diogenes of Sinope was incontestably the most fabulous character of those times. Later, in the Third Century, there was great public reverence for Zeno of Citium and Epicurus. It is interesting to conjecture that an Athenian who was born in 368 B.C. and who lived as long as seventy years could have known Plato, Aristotle, Diogenes, Zeno, and Epicurus. What would one such as this say of their relative greatness?

Apparently, a philosopher's historical eminence depended as much upon events which follow his life as any which occurred in his time. In some cases philosophers associated with causes which ultimately were lost; in other instances neither the philosopher nor his students wrote at sufficient length for posterity fully to know them; in addition many important books which would have altered impressions or formed different ones were destroyed or distorted. Most of Plato's works were preserved and many of Aristotle's systematic treatises survived; but what is even more important, these works were later seized upon by western institutions which found their rationales suited to new purposes.

Students of education need to recognize that the so-called Cynics, Cyreneans, Stoics, Epicureans, and rhetoricians were highly active in shaping the ethical thought which led to later events. An educator who overlooks them is deprived of important insights. The teaching profession holds custody of the civil forms of the western world and should have some appreciation or understanding of their source. Without such understanding the profession is ill-equipped to assist the oncoming generations in evaluating and transmitting them.

The Cynics

After Socrates and the emergence of the Greek schools of philosophy, the Sophists retired from the more strenuous tasks of philosophy and tended to specialize in rhetoric. Rhetoric, as it turned out, became the big "money maker" of the ancient curriculum. In time, the urban centers of antiquity were visited by a new kind of vagabond who in nearly every visible respect was the opposite of the Sophist. Like the Sophists, these men were controversial. But unlike the Sophists they had no desire to acquire wealth. By some reports they were despised; by others they were honored. Probably, like hippies or hoboes in the modern world, they included many kinds of people, some admirable and others nothing more or less than common criminals.

They called themselves "the dogs," and this reference was specifically to the homeless and unmastered of the canine species. The Grecian Kyon[1] (dog) is the word out of which soon evolved the name Cynic. The origins of the sect have been in dispute.[2] Some reports traced its origins to mythology. These probably were given credence by the air of holiness that certain Cynics managed to effect. The commonly accepted account has named Antisthenes, a student of Socrates, as the founder.[3] However, this has been disputed. It has also been conjectured that Cynicism developed because of the political instability and air of pessimism which followed the Peloponnesian War.[4]

It is said that of all the students of Socrates none exceeded Antisthenes in personal devotion to the master, and none came more to resemble him in both his personal and scholarly style. There is no reason to doubt that the Platonic Socrates is very like the historical Socrates. However, there is one important distinction. The Platonic Socrates occasionally consummated judgment on moral and religious questions whereas it is commonly believed the historical Socrates suspended such judgments. It is thought that Antisthenes remained more true to the *eristic* (style of argument) than did Plato. Antisthenes raised doubts about everything and everyone except those who raised doubts. Possibly this is the way in which he was authentically Cynic. The Cynics of later antiquity questioned all they heard and saw, but they believed themselves above reproach.

Antisthenes' father was Athenian, and his mother was Thracian. He was first educated by Gorgias, the Sophist, and soon developed a following of his own. But after hearing Socrates he stopped teaching and brought his students into the Socratic circle. He was present at the execution of Socrates and afterward resumed his own teaching. Along with Eucleides of Megara, another Socratic, he was constantly at the center of disputes. He is reported to have lectured in the Cynosarges (dogfish) gymnasium near the eastern entrance to the old city. This was probably not one of the better locations. It was reportedly open to aliens and therefore not frequented by the more refined Athenians.

It must be recognized that Antisthenes was not a Cynic in the style by which the sect later came to be known. He owned property and respected laws. The same can be believed of Eucleides and Stilpo. Probably more to the cynic style was their near contemporary Crates of Thebes. Like the others, Crates was devoted to plain living, but his attitude as man, philosopher, and poet was more rebellious. He was openly a sensationalist; he condemned pleasure as a form of slavery, love as a menace to freedom, and desire as a menace to happiness. Crates abandoned property and wealth to become a mendicant teacher. According to Laertius, the woman Hipparchia left a wealthy home, donned a beggar's garb, and went to live with Crates in free love. He sought to dissuade her, but finally they married. The nuptials, we are told, were consummated in public, but their subsequent lives together were models of affection and fidelity.

The central figure in the Cynic tradition is Diogenes of Sinope. His life was so epic-ridden that he comes to us more as a legend than as a man. Apparently, Diogenes was to the Cynic as David Crockett was to the American frontiersman, and the stories of one may be as fanciful as those of the other. Diogenes evidently was exiled from his native city for adulterating the currency. It is characteristic of the conflicting testimony that some say that Antisthenes unwillingly accepted him as a student,[5] while others say that Diogenes could never have met Antisthenes.[6]

His fame as a public figure was based primarily on his biting wit and irrepressible arrogance. Diogenes took every form of vanity as his target. No wonder an anonymous critic of his day said, "Diogenes is Socrates gone mad." When invited to dine with the aging Plato he is supposed to have wiped his feet on a rug saying, "I am stomping on Plato's vanity," to which Plato reportedly replied, "With what vanity of your own, Diogenes?"[7] Diogenes did not often come on the losing end of such an exchange. No one can be certain that Plato so responded, but most of the human race would hope so. Diogenes got wide publicity through an encounter with young King Alexander. Some accounts place the meeting at Athens, but more credible reports place this confrontation on the high eminence above the City of Corinth. Alexander asked Diogenes, who was sunning himself, what he could do for him, and the philosopher reputedly replied, "Stand from between me and the sun." Diogenes got away with it, and this evidently delighted the Athenians whose resentment of the young Macedonian dictator was of a nature as to make such impudence heroic, and Diogenes evidently was not above capitalizing on it. And so his legend grew.

The Diogenes lore includes so many forensic triumphs that we can only assume that the ancient world fell in love with his legend and added to it constantly. He is supposed to have said of another contemporary, "Aristotle breakfasts when it pleases Philip, Diogenes, when it pleases Diogenes." His alleged noonday trip into the Agora with a lighted candle "looking for an honest man" is typical of his reported escapades. In many of his "wisecracks" he refers to himself in the third person. One can easily imagine a pompous high official promenading up the walk to the Theatre of Dionysus, settling himself in one of the high-backed marble chairs, and enjoying the performance, whereupon Diogenes suddenly appears on the hillside above, shouting embarrassing comments at him. All of this would be to the merriment of the common men in the audience. No one, it seems, can do much about such a bantering satirist. Too much of what he says includes grains of truth, and like the most effective of critics, he wants nothing for himself.

Diogenes' fame grew to the point that for some he took on superhuman qualities. One of the major attractions Corinth held for him was the large number of available prostitutes, and he spent a great deal of time with them. He was opposed to marriage. Sexual intercourse was a matter of a man persuading and a woman consenting. He disliked all other human institutions. For him nature was enough for life, but not enough to keep him going indefinitely. He died in Corinth, and tradition holds that for many years afterward a marble statute of a dog adorned his grave near the main city gate. To this day the world cannot decide if he was a saint of uncompromising honesty or simply a crusty exhibitionist. Whichever he was, he was the prototype for a new breed which traversed the world for the next three centuries.

The romantic account of the Cynic who emulated Diogenes reveals him to be a man who dressed only in a double folded cloak, carrying only a staff and a beggar's wallet. The world fed and sheltered the Cynic as if it were his due. To him honesty was not only the best policy, it was the only policy. Like a Hebrew prophet, he would speak when others feared to speak. His poverty was his armor in adversity and his spear in dialectic. He accepted nothing, and therefore had nothing to gain. He rejected morals, laws, institutions, education, property, and family. All of these he denied as obstacles to virtue.

Wherever he went the world honored him and sought his judgment. The lean and haggard Cynic pointing his long, bony finger of accusation at a grasping merchant, an oppressive official, a pretentious priest, or a presumptuous aristocrat was the only form of justice some of the ancients would trust, and it was effective. Even men in high places held him in awe. No one, in those times, could be certain where the power of such a man ended. This, of course, is the romantic view. If we can believe it we find much to honor in the Cynic, and we regret his passing.

But can we believe it? Lucian[8] declares of the Cynics that their "lips water at the sight of a coin, they are dogs for temper, hares for cowardice, apes for imitativeness, asses for lust, cats for thievery, cocks for jealousy." Ordinary people, said he, "are revolted by a philosophy which breeds such brutes." This is harsh, but it is echoed time and again by other writers of antiquity. This version of the Cynics show them to be similar to the modern gypsies who steal, beg, and connive. Instead of offering a dancing bear they entertain others with their impudence, rudeness, and an occasional outburst of practical wisdom. Such accounts as these hold that they were feared and hated, and all manner of invective was directed against them.

The truth we can believe is some place between the two versions.

The Cynics were too ritualized in their dress and manner not to have developed a body of shared assumptions about themselves which were known and widely respected. But for every sincere Cynic there was probably another who was a fraud. There is no reason to doubt the Cynics were obscene and vulgar in manner. Even the best of them were devoted to living according to nature. Thus, every civil law or custom was artificial, unnatural, and—therefore—oppressive. Dogs do not seek privacy for natural functions; neither, then, should men, and the Cynics didn't. Like most sects whose ideals become enshrined they never, even at their best, were as true as they were supposed to have been and many later believed they were. In counseling young Cynics to improve their ways, the Roman Emperor Julian idealized the legendary Diogenes at his repugnant best by saying:

> . . . when Diogenes made unseemly noise or obeyed the call of nature or did anything else of that sort in the market place, as they say he did, he did so because he was trying to trample on the conceit of man . . . and teach them that their practices were far more sordid and unsupportable than his own. . . .

The Cyreneans

With the Cynic firmly in our view we are better able to contemplate his counterpart. We find him in Aristippus who first came to Athens from Cyrene, a city in northern Africa. He, too, was a student of Socrates, but he was reportedly the very first of the Socratic circle to teach for money.[9] For a time after the death of Socrates, he was at Syracuse participating in the court life of King Dionysius. His academic colleague at that time and place was none other than Plato. The account of their shared Syracusean adventures reveals contrast between the personality of Plato and that of Aristippus. One episode reports Plato refusing to join in an effeminate dance at the same time Aristippus joined it with enthusiasm. When Dionysius offered money to the two, Plato refused and Aristippus accepted, but he added his sly comment, "Dionysius offered Aristippus little as he needed much, but offered Plato much who needed little.[10]

If any wit came close to matching Diogenes of Sinope, it was Aristippus. The latter wanted the material life and made no effort to conceal this. When Dionysius asked him why philosophers haunted the doors of the rich, but the rich did not frequent those of the philosophers, he replied, "because philosophers know what they need and the rich do not." When begging a favor for a friend, he fell at the king's feet. When later asked why, he said, "I am not to blame, but Dionysius who has ears in his feet." He bore adversity with grace; and to use a modern parlance, he seemed to be able to "take it or leave it." Once when traveling, his servant complained the money sack was too heavy, to which Aristippus replied, "Pour out what is too much for you and carry what you can."

These exchanges are selected only in part for the human interest. They also help show the contrast between the Cynic and the Cyrenean. The Cynic motto "I do not possess in order to be not possessed" is countered by the Cyrenean, "I possess, but I am not possessed." The Cyrenean was willing to accept whatever life offered and to enjoy it, but the Cyrenean was unwilling to worry that he might lose it. A possession was not harmful to a man if he did not worry about whether he would lose it. This "easy come, easy go" was more than a casual personal attitude. It was an informal expression of a carefully developed hedonism which used human pleasure as a standard for the good. Among other things, the Cyrenean argued that a man should not permit his pride to stand in the way of his pleasure.

When Aristippus finally found his way back to north Africa he organized his school of philosophy. Even though he knelt at the feet of tyrants it seemed that he would come away smiling to himself. He continued to teach a limited materialism which was consistent with the best of Ionian science; but everything, including virtue and philosophy, was to be judged by its capacity to increase human pleasure. One does not sacrifice the material present for a conjectural good. Pleasure, he said, was a kind of gentle motion as opposed to pain which was a more violent movement.[11] He told the world that the greatest legacy he was leaving his daughter Arete was his injunction to set a value on nothing she could do without. She succeeded him as head of the Cyrenean School. She wrote many books, had many distinguished students, and in her own time she was recognized as one of the most gifted women of antiquity. She raised her son as a philosopher. It is of interest to recognize that this is the first time in the history of philosophy that a philosophical tradition was transmitted through a woman.[12]

The Cyrenean influence was a lasting one in that part of the world. Little more is heard of it in Athens, probably because Epicurus was soon to bring his more rigorous hedonism to that city, and through Athens Epicureanism would enter western Europe and live on in the modern western world. One of the central points of this conflict between the Cynic and Cyrenean doctrines of interest to teachers is that Socrates as a teacher had so many different kinds of men around him who were held together by his didactical prowess. When Socrates was gone, and his students dispersed, it was found that Socrates had not given his students a single point of view. There was no Socratic system. His students were disciples of a common spirit and style of inquiry and nothing more. Four who set in motion philosophical traditions which continue to compete for the credence of modern men were Antisthenes, claimed by the Cynics; Plato, claimed by the academics; Aristippus, claimed by the hedonists; and Eucleides, claimed by the Skeptics. In this very striking outcome there is something for all teachers to ponder.

The Epicureans

Epicurus, progenitor of the controversial tradition of ethics which bears his name was by most accounts greatly admired as a man. He was born to one of the Athenian families who colonized the Island of Samos, and evidently he spent his boyhood there.[13] In his eighteenth year he returned to Athens. At that time Xenocrates was at the Academy and Aristotle had just departed for Chalsis on Euboea. Epicurus was a brilliant young man with resolute independence of mind and spirit. He took his military training, as was his duty, and made the rounds of the leading schools of the city; but, he consistently maintained his own intellectual posture so as not to be considered a disciple of anyone. Even as a lad, when a teacher dictated to him the opening line of Hesiod, "First of all there was chaos," Epicurus demanded to know out of what chaos was created.[14] He had an extensive exposure to Platonist teachers, but rejected the theory of ideas and the dialectic. On the other hand, he evidently found geometry to be of value. During his cadetship, Athens must have been in turmoil. This was in 323 B.C., the year Alexander died in Babylon, Diogenes passed away at Corinth, and Aristotle neared his end at Chalcis.

After his ephebic training, Epicurus left Athens to live in Ionia, and study for ten years not far from Ephesus. In the Fourth Century the greatest days of Ephesus had passed. However, the great scholarly traditions of former times were not yet extinct. During this period Epicurus was under the tutelage of Praxiphanes[15] who had studied under Theophrastus, successor to Aristotle. Epicurus also studied with Nausiphanes, a Democritean atomist. These associations are thought important because apparently through them Epicurus formed the doctrines which later became famous in the Garden. Prior to his return to

Athens he had a misadventure in Mytilene where as an upstart philosopher at the mere age of thirty, he attempted to attract students to his new doctrines which, among other things, included an attack on Platonism. Platonists, even in those days, were not above violence, and Epicurus was forced to depart hastily to Lampsacus. During a stay there which lasted four years, he recruited a number of disciples, and in 306 B.C. he moved this group to Athens.

At the time of this second return to Athens, Epicurus was thirty-five years of age. This was a young age to be headmaster of an Athenian school of philosophy. Plato was forty when he began to teach at the Academy; Aristotle was fifty-two when he began to receive pupils in the Lyceum. Philosophy was a way of life for an increasing number of Athenians who by then revered Socrates' notion that a man's purpose in the world was to examine life. Epicurus proffered harsh new insights which clearly challenged the established Platonism which for nearly a century, through the Academy and Lyceum, had been a kind of academic dogma. Some of the guardians of these dogmas had become arrogant and self-righteous. A new school which would incur the wrath of the Platonic establishment would not have a pacific future. The men of the Garden had little peace.

This is probably why Epicurus acquired a private property adequate to his purpose. The use of public places such as the Academy and Lyceum would have been a more distinct challenge than was safe to make (or than Epicurus cared to make). The property was a garden located on the Academy road not far outside the Dypylon Gate.[16] Epicurus also used as part of the school his personal residence within the city walls. As head of the school he chose a title for himself, the translation of which approximates the modern words guide or leader. His disciples were called associate leaders, and instructors he called assistant leaders. The school was also a publishing concern, and the staff must have included a number of literate slaves to serve as secretaries and copyists. One of his innovations was to include women in his circle. Only moderate objections were raised about this until one of them began to publish.[17]

The open love which the students and staff of the school held for Epicurus became legendary. His science was atomistic and consistent with that of both Democritus and the best Ionian traditions. These were put forward with a new clarity and enthusiasm. Greek science, judged by modern standards, probably came to a very high level in the Garden.[18] But it was also in the Garden that Epicurus outlined the ethical doctrines for which he was almost ceaselessly reviled for the next seven centuries. When antiquity was rediscovered by renaissance Europe, cudgels were again taken up against him. The derrogations have been so strong and continuing that even the word Epicureanism has come to have association with gluttony and licentiousness.

However, the careful student notes immediately that this is not justified by the pristine expression of Epicurean doctrine. Epicurus advocates a simple life epitomized by the motto *lathe biosas* (live unobtrusively). Despite charges to the contrary, reputable scholarship shows that his use of pleasure as a moral standard relates to a healthy, balanced mode of life. He teaches that one ought to abstain from those things which result in physical pain or emotional anguish. Thus he advocates neither sobriety nor excess, but moderation. His hedonistic standard is a far-sighted pleasure and not a short-sighted pleasure. It is noteworthy that the Epicurean would take recently recognized hazards of cigaret smoking very seriously. He would also avoid human relations which hold the promise of tension or conflict.

He said, "Nothing satisfies the man who is not satisfied with little. Pleasure relates to matters of satisfaction, understanding, and self-sufficiency."[19] In one of his often quoted fragments he declared, "Unhappiness comes either through fear or through vain and unbridled desire; but if a man curbs these, he can win for himself the blessings of understanding."[20] In another he wrote, "He who least needs tomorrow will most gladly go to meet tomorrow."[21] Thus the secret to pleasure is a learned sensitivity which comes from a careful assessment of those things of greatest worth to man. The Epicurean view is often misunderstood by those who hear quoted that fragment which is erroneously characterized as Epicurus' philosophy of the stomach. "The beginning and the root of all good is the pleasure of the stomach: even wisdom and culture must be referred to this."[22] It is clear, however, that here the word "stomach" refers to inner feeling. The true Epicurean is far more accurately described by another of the master's summary expressions:

> The happy and blessed state belongs not to abundance of riches or dignity of position or any office or power but to freedom from pain and moderation in feelings and an attitude of mind which imposes the limits ordained by nature.[23]

It is difficult in modern times to understand how such a pragmatic or common-sense hedonism could have so irritated the primitive Christian church; but, apparently, it did. Epicureans taught that the way to avoid fear was not to create fear in others. They believed that he who wants nothing cannot suffer from the greed of others. Epicurus guided men to pleasure by teaching them to drive out the devils which torment them from within. The Platonists apparently despised the Epicureans as did the Cynics and later the Stoic Christians. It can be supposed that the Platonists could not detect a commitment to excellence through the pleasure standard. The Cynics and Stoic Christians seem to intuit any form of pleasure as a vanity, a denial of immortal state, and, therefore, entirely the wrong direction for one to take in seeking a moral standard.

Epicurus was well loved. It is said that he wrote over three hundred books. Only fragments survive. What would the modern judgment have been had the whole of his books survived? The sect continued well into the Christian Era, and the life styles associated with the Epicurean ethic survived in Greece much longer. Indeed, many who live today in that part of the world can be called true Epicureans. The hostility of the Roman church prevented the tradition from developing a strong presence in western Europe until the Nineteenth-Century Englishmen, Jeremy Bentham and John Stuart Mill, reintroduced the hedonistic standard. But in modern Greece, the true Epicurean, the man of inner pleasure, is easily found. In a recent American musical comedy[24] about that country, one immediately notes the Cyrenean and Epicurean sentiments in the title of one of its ballads, "Life Is What You Do While You Are Waiting to Die."

The Stoics

It is generally believed that Zeno, the founder of the Stoic school, was of Phoenician parentage. Late in the Fourth Century, while still a relatively young man, he emigrated to Athens from Citium, a well known Cyprian town located on the trade routes of the ancient world. In order to distinguish him from an earlier philosopher of the same name he is usually called Zeno of Citium.

Tradition holds that Zeno encountered a series of misfortunes on his way to Athens which left him nearly destitute. By chance he met the Cynic philosopher-poet Crates of Thebes and soon became one of his students. Being himself now poor, Zeno may have found the straightforward simplicity of the Cynic doctrine much to his liking. But he did not confine his interest to the Cynics. He also spent a period of time at the Academy, and traveled to Megara to hear Stilpo. The Megarians taught a doctrine similar to that of the Cynics, but because theirs did not carry the Cynic obsession for animal simplicity the Megarian school was called Skeptic. Zeno's late education in philosophy, therefore, included elements of the Cynic, Skeptic, and Academic schools. This must have been a contentious exposure, and one having it would be stimulated to either choose one philosophy and follow it or fashion something distinctive of his own.

Zeno happened to be one of those capable of going his own way, and soon he had with him a number of enthusiasts who looked upon him as their teacher. A few of the details about this group are well known. Unlike the garden-bound Epicureans, Zeno's students met in the dust and heat of the center city. The exact site is known; and, at this writing, excavations are underway to discover the remains of the building. It is across the railroad from the area of the Athenian Agora, now uncovered. It was adjacent to the Stoa Attalos which was built later and has now been fully restored (by the American School of Classical Studies). The architectural details of the building are still speculative. However, it is certain that a long porch which opened upon the Agora was prominent in the facade. Porches of this kind may be as many as several hundred feet in length and sixty feet in width. The building above them is supported by fluted columns characteristic of classical architecture. The porch was so prominent an aspect of the building in which Zeno met with his students that the building itself was called *Stoa Poecile* (the painted porch). The students who came to Zeno's lectures were soon called the *Stoics* (the men of the porch). It is widely reported that Zeno taught there forty or more years. Across these four decades the name Stoic became transferred to the doctrines of the school. Tradition holds that death came to him at the base of the steps leading to the porch.

Zeno may have written books; but, if he did, they were not preserved. His philosophy has come to us by indirection. Cleanthes was the second master of the sect, and of all he may have written, only his poem, *Hymn to Zeus*, has survived. But its introductory lines as given in the Adam's translation reveal semblances between Stoic doctrines and later Christian sentiments.

> O God most glorious called by many a name,
> Nature's great king, through endless years the same;
> Omnipotence, who by just decree
> Controllest all, hail, Zeus, for unto thee
> Behooves thy creatures in all lands to call.
> We are thy children, we alone, of all
> On earth's broad ways that wander to and fro,
> Bearing thine image wheresoe'er we go. . . .

From Cleanthes, the leadership of the school passed to Chrysippus (280-205) who organized and systematized the doctrines laid down by Zeno, developed the Stoic metaphysics, and defended the doctrines from the attacks mounted against them by the teachers at the Academy.

One would expect that the attacks of other schools would result in the refinement and purification of Stoic expressions. But such felicity did not occur. Stoicism came across to western Europe with its fallacies well preserved. The primary fallacy stemmed from its effort to combine Ionian metaphysics with a Platonic style of ethics. Although this inconsistency was pointed out numerous times, the tenacity of the Stoic defense only pushed the doctrine toward and ultimately into the murky depths of mysticism. The Stoics could defend their ontology and also defend their axiology, but the two could not be defended on the same grounds. For this reason the Stoic place in the development of western thought is respected more for impact than coherence.

The contradiction within Stoic doctrine is perhaps best summarized by pointing out that Stoic physics is predicated on notions similar to those offered by Heraclitus. Fire is very much at the center of things. The motion within and about things is in some way a movement to and from fire, a warming, or a cooling. Even the soul which animates the body is corporeal.[25] It, too, is a manifestation of fire as might be energy or heat. Hence, the Stoic metaphysics is monistic, deterministic, and temporal. On the other hand the Stoic offers ethical propositions which posit a supernatural good, free will, and eternal being. These contradictions cannot help but weaken the Stoic philosophy. The Stoic ethic clearly implies the presence of evil and presumes that the human will can (and should) overcome evil. Neither the Stoic monistic ontology nor its dualistic axiology lacks persuasiveness. However, the two pose a paradox which is fatal to any satisfactory effort to convert Stoicism into a coherent system. However, this does not nullify the prospective truth of either. In particular, the Stoic ethic is of great potency.

We must pay attention to the Stoic ethic. It has been highly prominent in the development of the western mind. Very few conversations on ethical matters fail to respect Stoic inferences or fail in some way to acknowledge Stoic influences. By this is meant the basic western predisposition to interpose the human will as the agency which turns a man in the direction of the right, the decent, the good and the true and turns him away from the indecent, the evil, and the false. The Epicurean invokes pleasure as the ultimate moral sanction, but the Stoic insists that any foundation of the good involves a conception of duty. Duty in the Stoic sense means general duties such as those which are consequences of being a man. They also include those duties associated with special responsibilities, e.g., teacher, physician, counselor, etc.

Aurelius is a Stoic; Seneca is a Stoic; but it is Epictetus the Phyrygian-born slave of Nero's freedman Epaphrodorus who casts the Stoic ethic into its renowned expressions of serenity and responsibility. As to serenity, Epictetus points out there are things that "are not ours" and things that "are ours." Death, for example, is not ours. The forces of nature are not ours. These things lie beyond the will and the power of man. As such, the Stoic regards them with resignation. This, in turn, leads to serenity. One is obliged to protect the peace of his soul, but this cannot be done unless one achieves serenity regarding those things which are "not ours." If the storm breaks, if the volcano erupts, if a loved one dies the Stoic remains calm and at peace. Such matters exceed the human will. And if the ultimate misfortune is his, he faces it with equanimity.

Epictetus was lame. Whether this came from birth or from accident is not known. But Celsus the anti-Christian offers this account:

> "When his master was twisting his leg Epictetus only smiled and said calmly, 'You will break it.' And when it was broken he said, 'I told you so!' "[26]

Whatever may have been the case, Epictetus was ultimately given freedom and established a school of philosophy in Rome. He was a vigorous man, and his students followed him about eager to hear his pronouncements. He wrote nothing, but his discourses were recovered from the notes and transcriptions made by his students. There can be no question that he called upon men to face up to the fact that their will is free and to bear this burden of freedom proudly.

Men can do nothing with that which is "not ours" except to accept it bravely as befitting men. However, as to those things which "are ours" Epictetus disparages the Epicurean outlooks, as in Book III of his organized discourses.[27]

> Before God, I ask you, can you
> Imagine a city of Epicureans?

"I shall not marry" (says one)
"Nor shall I," (said another) "for it is wrong to marry."
Yes and if it is wrong to get children and
Wrong to be a citizen.
What is to happen then? Where will your
citizens come from? Who will be governor of the
Ephibi? Who will manage the Gymnasia?

From this examination of the consequences of Epicureanism,
Epictetus moves to forthright ridicule of the Epicurean ethic. Said
he:[28]

What is our nature? To be free, noble, self respecting.
What other animal blushes? What other can have a conception of shame? We must subordinate pleasure to these
principles. . . .

"But I am rich and have need of nothing!"
Why then do you still pretend to be a philosopher?
Gold and silver plate are enough for you: What need have you
of judgments?
"Nay but I also sit as judge over the Greeks."
What! You know how to judge? What made you know
that?
"Caesar wrote me a patent."
Let him write you to judge questions of music: What use
will it be to you? But let that pass. How did you get made a
judge? Whose hand did you kiss? . . . In whose antechamber
did you sleep? To whom did you send gifts? . . .
"Well, but I can put anyone I wish in prison."
As you may a stone!
"But I can cudgel anyone to death I wish."
As you can an ass! This is not governing men. Govern us
as rational creatures by showing us what is expedient, and we
will follow it; show us what is inexpedient and we will turn
away from it. Make us admire and emulate you, as Socrates
bade men do. He was the true ruler of men, for he brought
men to submit to him their will to get and to avoid, their
impulse to act and not act.

"Do this, refrain from this, or I will put you in prison."
This is not how rational beings are ruled. But, do this as Zeus
ordained: if not you will suffer harm. What kind of harm? No
harm but that of failing to do your duty: you will destroy the
trustworthy, self-respecting, well-behaved man in you. Look
not for any greater harm than this!"

Epictetus' life began as a slave, but his is not a servile voice.
The literature of philosophy does not contain a more virile expression.

Thus, did he give the Stoics their enduring answer to the utilitarians, intuitionists, naturalists, theologists, instrumentalists, and existentialists. The fact that man is free enables him to will. This leads him to the acceptance of certain duties such as teacher, father, brother, judge, priest, and philosopher.

Each such duty thrusts upon its holder a moral responsibility. Each moral action must be preceded by a calm examination of that responsibility. Here Epictetus introduces a term to be used again centuries later by the phenomenologist, Husserl. The term is *epoche*. Specifically, it means the Stoic is expected to hold his reactions, impressions, and other human responses in suspension until his duty becomes apparent. He urges that men not be carried away by impressions or by things eminently plausible or attractive. Epoche allows recent events and impressions to order themselves with others of longer standing. The emerging order, pattern, or perspective will make the path of duty self-evident. (Phenomenologists use the term epoche in an attempt to see things as they are, in order to get at the object itself, whereas the Stoic uses it to determine value.)

He asks men to beware of the "seductiveness of things" and "the persuasion of appearances." The ultimate Stoic escapes such things in order to make himself as much as possible like God. In one of his later days, it is said that Epictetus declared:

> And what else can a lame old man like me do but chant the praise of God? If indeed I were a nightingale, I should sing as a nightingale; if a swan, as a swan; but as I am a rational creature I must praise God. This is my task; I do it, and I will not abandon my duty so long as it is given me; and I invite you all to join in this same song.[29]

Thus, to Epictetus the irrevocable duty of man is to be godly. One praises God by being like God.

The Stoic ethic establishes virtue as its own end. Hence the vivid contrast with Epicureanism is easily drawn (but often mistakenly overdrawn). Virtue becomes the cause for which men *deny* pleasure to themselves and others. One subordinates the sensual rewards of the temporal life in order to embrace and win objectives which stand beyond it. Stoicism is a philosophy which brings vitality to the life of the city and is congenial to the survival of the state. It teaches the citizen that his suffering is more meaningful than his *pleasure*. One, therefore, has reason to accept without complaint the calamities of life. It offers men a means of understanding the necessity to endure sickness, pain, abuse, ill-repute—indeed, to be indifferent to all things except the loss of virtue.

Of the many influences present in western thought, Stoicism is perhaps the most easily detected. This is not only because it is one of the strongest influences; Stoicism was (and for the most part still is) woven into the fabric of Christianity and the Christian church, which has been one of the most powerful teaching institutions. Although the ethic of the Stoics brought strength to western institutions, the science of the Stoics hampered the development of knowledge systems in physics and nature. However, perhaps the attribute of Stoicism which is most relevant to the point of this essay is that it brought forward a doctrine of duty and planted its banner in the Christian community which, in turn, lived by many of its tenets, grew strong, and persuaded men to conscript themselves into devoted service of the institutions which shaped the thought of western Europe and America.

The Educational Theorists

Men such as Anaximander, Pythagoras, Parmenides, Democritus, Protagoras, Heraclitus, and Socrates produced the thoughts which gave issue to philosophy. Men such as Plato, Aristotle, Aristippus, Antisthenes, Zeno, and Epicurus resolved the issues into systems, doctrines, and schools which speculated on application to social and political reality or physical and natural reality. These were followed by men who produced further refinements which detailed how education should be accomplished.

It is tempting to call this a decline in philosophy. This was implied by an earlier comment, but calling it a decline is perhaps an oversimplification of what occurred. As Rome grew from a provincial to a cosmopolitan center, human interests seemed to face in another direction. Speculation in metaphysics did not enjoy the vogue that it did in the Fifth Century B.C. The schools of philosophy were defending and dogmatizing, not challenging, the doctrines of their founders. Government to the Romans was a practical art. Its end was allegiance to the state and means to this end were found in the military and administrative technologies. In the days of the Roman Republic this limited range of metaphysical concerns seemed to result in a high level of religious tolerance. In this vein Gibbon said of the Romans:

The various modes of worship, which prevailed in the
Roman world, were considered by the people as equally true;
by the philosophers as equally false; and by the magistrates
as equally useful. And thus tolerance produced not only
mutual indulgence, but even religious concord.[30]

Gibbon points out further that intolerance when it developed
was found not so much in the Romans themselves as in the spirit
of the Christians and Jews, and, to some extent, among the Egyptians.
He declared that:

> . . . a republic of gods of such opposite tempers and in-
> terests, required, in every system, the moderating hand of a
> supreme magistrate, who by the progress of knowledge and
> flattery, was gradually invested with the sublime perfections
> of an Eternal Parent and Omnipotent Monarch.[31]

Greek philosophy, remarkable as it was, had not, even to its
own satisfaction, resolved the issues of spirit and matter. The schoolmen at Athens, when making reference to the gods, still babbled
the idle tales of the poets and the incoherent traditions of the Dorian
or Etruscan cultures. Although they implanted the skeptical or cynical
spirit in mythology the schoolmen often took part in ceremonial
functions, frequented the temples, and condescended to act out one
or another of the various pietous rituals. The Athenian schools gave
laws to the Roman Senate, and these laws provided (wisely or un-
wisely) for a union of secular and ecclesiastical powers.[32] The latter
was used as an aid to govern men and, in the main, was servient to
the various objectives of government. Thus, the philosophical schools
were not serious critics of either the temporal or ecclesiastical power.
Pax Romana became the good, and philosophy seemed enlisted in
its behalf.

Cicero (106-43 B.C.) was one of the great figures in Roman
thought. His eclecticism (a tendency to select from various philosophical alternatives various elements which have appeal) was governed
by an obsession with the practical problem which Rome had set for
itself—namely, to govern.[33] Given this problem, and the great fund
of Greek wisdom, it was possible for Cicero to theorize about education, and he did it very well. Against this background it is easy to
understand why he would postulate *the orator* as the paradigm of
the educational enterprise. The magistrate had to lead his people,
persuade his people, and assure his people. His eloquence, therefore, should be of sufficient power to move them. This being estab-

lished as the object of education, the study of grammar, literature, and philosophy was assigned to subservient applications as appropriate. The language of the orator was required to have an effective syntax; he must have knowledge of the poets; and Cicero believed that the orator must master the dialectical tools. The study of gymnastics and dance enhanced the orator's ability to gesture with manliness and grace.[34]

The reader is asked again to note that none of these studies are pursued for their own sake. To some extent the Ciceronian ideal of an orator becomes something unto itself, but to a larger extent the ideal emerged in response to a practical need. The orator gave the appearance of wisdom without necessarily being wise, the appearance of piety without necessarily being devout, and the appearance of commitment to transcending values without really departing from his own political ends. The Twentieth Century knows him well.

Quintilian (35-95 A.D.) was another voice. In the main he agreed with Cicero. He seems to go further in authoritative discourse about the authentic character of the Roman citizen. Again, he is a man of action, an operator in the world of events and not a speculator on possibilities external to this world.[35] The statesman-orator held a prominent role and rose to the superior stations in Roman life. Philosophy held some importance in the training of the statesman, but it was not to dominate him. Quintilian offered numerous prescriptions for the development of children and young men. His belief in education was very strong. He thought that more could be done with most children than was often supposed. He seemed to think that failure of humans to rise to personal distinction was owing more to lack of "care" than of "promise."

Quintilian was a methodologist. His procedures were strong, but his vision lacked philosophic life. He seems to have found no need to look beyond what he saw in good Roman citizens whose professions were served by their rhetorical skills. Thus, like Cicero, his aims were practical, limited to those needs felt by men in their own time. His *Institutes of the Orator* reveals a style of training comparable to that given to lawyers in modern times. It included logic, history, literature, dialectic, and, of course, public speaking.[36] None of these studies had inherent purpose. The purpose was vocational.

Not all Roman thought was at this level. The Romans were impressed by the Stoics. Perhaps this is because so much of Stoic thought, when incarnated in life, is supportive of the state and of the institutional order. As Durant has pointed out: "Epicurus won the Greeks, Zeno won the aristocracy of Rome; and to the end of pagan history the Stoics ruled the Epicurean, as they always will."[37]

Three recognized champions of Stoicism among the Romans were Seneca, Marcus Aurelius, and the aforementioned Epictetus. The first was a man of wealth who found greater riches in philosophy. The second was an emperor who presided over the last great days before the fall of Rome was manifest. The last was a slave.

Seneca called upon men to give up their wealth and luxury and to win freedom through self-denial. "Man," said he, "was happy in a state of nature." So firmly was he captivated by the example of Antisthenes that he declared that men were enslaved by their possessions. Marcus Aurelius, had he been either a better philosopher or a better ruler, might have averted for a longer time the disasters which befell the magnificent capital of the Empire. Pagan Rome seemed to be losing its belief in itself and no alternative thing in which to believe was on hand to hold the unity and devotion of the citizens. Aurelius' Stoicism comes to us in the form of a collection of meditations, most of them melancholy, some even despairing. In one, he contemplates the conduct of the Romans of the previous century. He wrote:

> Consider, for an example, the times of Vespian. You will see all the same things, people marrying, bringing up children, sick, dying, fighting, feasting, trafficking, farming, flattering, pushing, suspecting, plotting, wishing for someone to die, grumbling about the present, loving, heaping up treasure, coveting the consulship and kingly power. Well, the life of these people is over. Come on next to the time of Trajan. Again, all is the same. Their life too is gone. In like manner survey other epochs of time and other nations, and see how many after mighty efforts fell and were resolved into the elements.[38]

Thus, Aurelius found it good to urge men to look beyond the material world for matters of worth. Said he, "whenever in the morning you rise unwillingly, let this thought be with you: 'I am rising to the work of a human being.'"[39] He thought men should develop those propensities directly within their power—"sincerity, gravity, patience in labor, aversion to pleasure, contentment with your lot and with little, frankness, dislike of superfluity, freedom from pettiness."[40] His personal and social views of life were based on the Stoic faith in life forces which exist outside of those men can see. The lights of men only reveal part of reality. Beyond this light is darkness. However, man's reason tells him that there is order so far as he can see. The faith that order exists beyond is, therefore, a rational faith. Men should live in a manner consistent with their authentic nature. Like the Cynics and Skeptics, who preceded him and who deplored the tendency men have to glamorize themselves, pose, and gather abundance, Aurelius urged men to pursue the ends of virtue. He was never far from Plato, and perhaps it can be said that he reflected Plato's more serious side. However, Stoicism as reflected by Aurelius deals more meaningfully with social problems and does not go so far toward speculations on the nature of the archetypes.

In education the Stoic would not seek for a comfortable learning environment. On the contrary, he might well advocate the reverse. The qualities of man which he aspires to develop do not flourish where creature needs and wants are elevated. The real man is polished by adversity. The school which would bring him out will give its students a few hard knocks.

Neo-Platonism

Neo-Platonism would surely have been counted a minor movement in philosophy were it not for the time it emerged. It came to full flower in the thoughts of Plotinus (203-270 A.D.) in the Third Century, an epoch we now see as the twilight of the great day of the ancient world. In this same century elements of what was to become Christian idealism were coming into view. Neo-Platonism is, therefore, often regarded as a link between the ancient world and the middle ages.[41] As such, it stands as the last great statement of classical philosophy, one which was heard directly by those who were to implant the doctrines of the new age. Opinion differs on the ways in which Plotinus and his followers influenced Christian theology, but there is no question that the influence was very strong. Plotinian views are so close in many respects to those which later were espoused by the Church that the arguments that Plotinus was the real founder of Christian idealism are highly tenable. Indeed, some authorities claim Plotinus anticipated Aquinas more than did Plato or Aristotle.[42]

We have very little information about the origins of Plotinus. He seems never to have mentioned his family. His name, of course, is Roman. It is known that in his late twenties Plotinus journeyed to Egypt, and, while at Alexandria, attended lectures given by Ammonius Saccas. He was so enthralled by this great teacher that he remained with Saccas for nearly eleven years.[43] Shortly after Plotinus reached the age of forty, he returned to Rome where he organized meetings for the purpose of hearing philosophical texts read and giving lectures of his own. As a speaker he was inspired and animated, and soon students and supporters gathered to share and assist in his work. His teaching and writing went on in Rome for twenty-six years until, at the age of sixty-seven, he died from the manifestations of leprosy which was in advanced stages during the last two years of his life.

Plotinus seemed always to despise his body, not because it was necessarily unattractive (there is no reliable modern knowledge of his physical appearance), but because he believed that a man's physical presence was a necessary evil. He opined that the suggestions or demands which it placed upon the soul which animated it were unbeautiful and unbecoming to the soul. Thus, he was careful to bar references to his body in all of his writings and he spurned at least one earnest request that his picture be painted.[44]

Plotinus' ontology postulated an Above-Being which was supreme. He maintained that to the human mind this being was unthinkable, and therefore, ineffable. This is because Above-Being is *one* and the human mind (soul) has difficulty in conceiving one. He also projected non-being, and, like Above-Being, it cannot be thought. Non-Being, he maintained, is completely poor, changing, passive, and deficient. This low level is matter, simply that and nothing more.[45]

Being emanates downward from the Above-Being but is contingent upon non-being. Things between Above-Being and non-being are given the quality of being in various degrees. The quality of being which man possesses is somewhere near the middle of this vertical scale and is called soul. The soul looks upward to Above-Being. Interposed between Above-Being and the soul is something called the spirit world which is composed of true forms. This Plotinus called the *nous*. The sight which the soul has of the *nous* is the sight of reason. The Above-Being by emanating downward instills the various qualities of being to the things of the world. Hence this downward looking becomes the world-soul. On a scale of descending reality there are five principles:

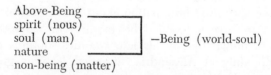

Above-Being
spirit (nous)
soul (man)   —Being (world-soul)
nature
non-being (matter)

The three intermediate principles represent the realms of being.

The Above-Being is motionless and sufficient to itself. The forms of being which exist below the *nous* or spirit world are copies of the archetype or ideas which the spirit world contains. The world-soul which confers being upon the spirit world, the man, and nature, is at rest. However, as individual souls, it inhabits ideas, man, and all of the living things in nature. The individual souls are not at rest but are in motion. Hence, even though they are partly immortal (in the sense that they are derived from that which is eternally at rest) they are also mortal in that their being depends on their animating the husks which have corporeal life.

The *nous* and the world-soul emanate directly from Above-Being. Those levels of being which exist below (man, nature) are active consequences of the *nous* and the world-soul. Again, matter (non-being) is needed. To put it another way, men and all that live in nature take form from the *nous*, take substance from matter, and are brought into being by the world-soul. The souls which men and other living things have are expressions of world-soul but differ from world-soul in that their being contains a mortal aspect.

Why is the descent from Above-Being? Why do we have the *nous*, man, and nature? Plotinus contended that the Above-Being did not will the being of lower levels. These, almost in the Aristotelian sense of an unmoved mover, simply exist because of the nature of the Above-Being.[46] Metaphorically, the sun does not will heat or light; these qualities exist because the sun is of the nature it is. Likewise the *nous* and world-soul are simply unwilled consequences of the Above-Being. In this sense Plotinus believed that we have *emanated* from It and are emanating from It. How shall It be thought? As a source for many rivers which never runs dry? The life of a great tree which pervades the whole and moves the whole while the root and ground are intact? As Plotinus said, the Above-Being is unthinkable, and metaphorical descriptions have the flaw which every metaphor admits by not being the thing to which it is compared. In addition, to think of the *One* it is necessary to take away everything. Thus, any attempt at comparison destroys the thought.[47]

The soul of man, as in the example of Aristophanes' androgynous, is in quest of something. It is not, however, like the split soul which wishes to be reunited or wedded to its other half or mate. The soul of man seeks to *merge* with the world-soul. This merging in Plotinus is the ultimate of love. Like Plato, Plotinus was inclined to depict this desire to merge as the sovereign motivational force in man's life. Out of this he was given clues to the good and the beautiful in life. Unlike

Plato, Plotinus was inclined to think of beauty as immanent rather than transcendental.[48] Although the things in nature are copies of the archetypes, or ideas, they have their own beauty and do not derive all of it from the archetype. The added elements, of course, are process, motion, and the rotary flux of the universe. Plotinus was evidently warmed by the struggle of things to live and survive. In this he seems to have anticipated Schopenhauer. Will in action supplies an aesthetic dimension.

Plotinus, therefore, tends to diminish the stark division which Plato created between spiritual and corporeal reality. His Above-Being resembles, in many ways, Aristotle's unmoved mover. Indeed, with the principle of pure matter at the base of his descending scale, and the *nous* near the top, he created a reasonable facsimile of the matter-form hypothesis. Above it all, however, he placed the Above-Being which is loved but does not love. Things will towards It, but It does not will. In this, therefore, Plotinus differed from the Christians whose doctrines had the quality of love ascending and descending consciously between man and God. Even though Plotinus urges that God is the foundation of authentic life there is no love of God for man, only love of man for God.

This was the mystical, remote, and recondite theory of the Neo-Platonists which was supported by Porphyry, the disciple of Plotinus and Iamblichus. By the time of the Renaissance the Neo-Platonic tradition had acquired such strength that Neo-Platonic humanists such as Marsilino Ficino and Pompanozzi were reinterpreting Plato in the light of Plotinus. In his commentary on the *Symposium* Ficino said of the speech by Phaedrus, "First of all is God, the author of everything who we say as the good itself. He created first the Angelic mind, then the soul of this world, as Plato would have it, and at last the Body of the World."[49] It is surmised that Plato would be very surprised by these words in description of his alleged views.

Neo-Platonism was to live with the growth of Christian idealism. Indeed, it served as a buttress to it by giving philosophic support to church doctrines which called for abstemiousness and mortification of the flesh. There were times when church authority was warmly assured by the standing which Neo-Platonists gave to the spiritual realm. Intended or not, it became a support for the Christianity which was to come. The Latin fathers from Augustine to Anselm quoted Porphyry again and again. The works of medieval Christian scholars contain numerous commentaries on works by the "great" Porphyry. They applaud the metaphysical vision of the Neo-Platonists although they recognize that Porphyry was personally antagonistic to the Christian society.[50] But they pitied him because he lacked the beatific vision furnished by the revelations of Christ. With this vision the Christians made the static, emanational, non-conscious ontology of the Neo-Platonists over into a dynamic, communicating consciousness. All that was required was interposition of faith.

Notes

1. Paul E. Moore, *Hellenistic Philosophies* (Princeton: Princeton University Press, 1923), p. 66.
2. Farrand Sayre, *The Greek Cynics* (Baltimore, Md.: J. H. Furst Co., 1948), pp. 28-49.
3. Moore, *op. cit.*, p. 65.
4. Sayre, *op. cit.*, p. 49.
5. Moore, *op. cit.*, p. 26.
6. Sayre, *op. cit.*, p. 48.
7. Diogenes Laertius, *Lives of Eminent Philosophers*, tr. R. D. Hicks (New York: G. P. Putnam's Sons, 1925), Vol. II, Book VI, p. 29.
8. Sayre, *op. cit.*, p. 2.
9. Moore, *op. cit.*, p. 1.
10. *Ibid.*
11. Theodor Gomperez, *Greek Thinkers Vol. IV* (New York: Charles Scribner's Sons, 1912), p. 218.
12. *Ibid.*, p. 245.
13. Laertius, *op. cit.*, Book X, p. 529.
14. Norman DeWitt, *Epicurus and His Philosophy* (Minneapolis: University of Minnesota Press, 1954), p. 43.
15. *Ibid.*, p. 56.
16. *Ibid.*, p. 92.
17. Leontin, a student and courtesan, wrote a book attacking Theophrastus, head of the Lyceum. Even two and one-half centuries later Cicero viewed this with indignation.
18. Bertrand Russell, *A History of Western Philosophy* (New York: Simon and Schuster, 1945), pp. 246 ff. Russell's account of Epicurean physics is one of the best available.
19. Fragment 60, Whitney Oates ed., *The Stoic and Epicurean Philosophers* (New York: Random House, 1940), p. 51.
20. Fragment, 74, *Ibid.*
21. Fragment 78, *Ibid.*
22. Fragment 59, *Ibid.*
23. Fragment 85, *Ibid.*
24. Zorba the Greek.
25. Moore, *op. cit.*, p. 77.
26. *Ibid.*, p. 94.
27. Oates, *op. cit.*, p. 336.
28. *Ibid.*, p. 337.

29. Moore, *op. cit.*, p. 165.
30. Edward Gibbon, *The Decline and Fall of the Roman Empire* (Philadelphia: Claxton, Remsen and Haffelfinger, 1880), Vol. I., p. 34.
31. *Ibid.*, p. 35.
32. *Ibid.*, p. 37.
33. *Ibid.*
34. H. E. Butler, *The Institutio Oratoria of Quintilianus* (New York: G. P. Putnam's Sons, Inc., 1920), I, p. 61 ff.: IV, pp. 355-409.
35. H. I. Marrow, *A History of Education in Antiquity* (New York: Sheed & Ward, 1956), p. 351.
36. Butler, *loc. cit.*
37. Will Durant, *The Life of Greece* (New York: Simon and Schuster, 1939), p. 656.
38. Marcus Aurelius, *Meditations*, III. Quoted from George Long, tr., *Marcus Aurelius and His Times* (Roslyn, New York: Walter J. Black, Inc., Classics Club Ed., 1945), p. 39.
39. *Ibid.*, p. 44.
40. *Ibid.*, p. 45.
41. T. V. Smith, ed., *Philosophers Speak for Themselves* (Chicago: University of Chicago Press, Vol. II), p. 279.
42. Armond A. Maurer, *Medieval Philosophy* (New York: Random House, Inc., 1962), pp. 190-191.
43. Karl Jaspers, *The Great Philosophers* (New York: Harcourt, Brace & World, Inc., 1966), p. 38.
44. *Ibid.*
45. *Ibid.*, pp. 45-55. Also: Smith, *op. cit.*, p. 279 ff.
46. *Ibid.*, p. 48.
47. *Ibid.*, p. 49-50.
48. *Ibid.*, p. 90.
49. Marsilio Ficino, *Commentary on Plato's Symposium*, included in Albert Hofstodter and Richard Kuhns, *Philosophies of Art and Beauty* (New York: Random House, Inc., 1964), p. 205.
50. St. Augustine, *The City of God, Book X*, tr. Marcus Dods (New York: Random House, Inc., 1950), p. 328.

Other Reading

Armstrong, A. H. *The Cambridge History of Later Greek and Early Medieval Philosophy.* Cambridge: The Cambridge University Press, pp. 53-78, 195-322.

Bowersock, G. W. *Greek Sophists in the Roman Empire.* Oxford: The Clarendon Press, 1969, pp. 18-58.

Butler, H. E. *The Institutio Oratoria of Quintilian.* Cambridge: Harvard University Press. 4 Volumes.

DeWitt. *Epicurus and Philosophy.* Minneapolis: University of Minnesota Press, 1954.

Durant, Will. *The Life of Greece.* New York: Simon and Schuster, Inc., 1939, pp. 482-552.

Eby, Fredrick, and Charles Arrowood. *The History and Philosophy of Education Ancient and Medieval.* New York: Prentice-Hall, 1940. Chapters II-V.

Jaspers, Karl. *The Great Philosophers.* New York: Harcourt, Brace & Co., pp. 5-57.

Moore, Paul E. *Hellenistic Philosophies.* Princeton: Princeton University Press, 1923.

Pates, W. J. *The Stoic and Epicurean Philosophers.* New York: Random House, 1940. 627 pp.

Plotinus, *Enneads.* Revised Henry-Schwyzer text, by A. H. Armstrong. London: Loeb Classical Library, 1966. 2 Volumes.

Russell, Bertrand. *Wisdom of the West.* London: Rathbone Books, Ltd., 1959, pp. 95-125.

Sayre, Farrand. *The Greek Cynics.* Baltimore: J. H. Furst Co., 1948, pp. 1-96.

Vogel, C. J. "On the Neoplatonic Character of Platonism and the Platonic Character of Neoplatonism," *Mind* LXII (1953), pp. 43-64.

Windelband, W. *A History of Philosophy.* Tr. J. H. Tufts. New York: The Macmillan Company, 1938.

CHAPTER VI

Christian Idealism

The Alliance of Faith and Reason

No philosophical treatment of idealism can fail to deal with the presence of Jesus Christ in the world. As a figure, a man, a teacher, he stands at the absolute center of western civilization. The chronometrics of the world's history lead to and from his birth. A significant part of the world's population revere him either as God or one of the aspects of God, and the balance willingly honor his life as among the best and greatest ever lived. He has been called the condescension of God and the exaltation of man. No individual in history was more in harmony with himself, taught with such assurance, and generated greater loyalty. His instructions to man dealt not only with life but also with death. Indeed, for those who follow him, accept him, death becomes an inspiration. Yet, even so, he is a mystery. Critical history cannot approach him. Two thousand years have passed since his brief life. No man has been studied more intently. In some ways we know him intimately, but in other ways we do not know him at all.

In an academic sense he would hardly qualify as a philosopher. His only known teachers were the elders of a synagogue wherein it is presumed he studied the letters and law of the Jewish tradition. It is well known that he never taught these particular things to others. His message to man seems to have been based on his moral insights and the role of love in human relations. His themes were happiness, salvation, and meaning in life. Unlike Socrates and Plato he seemed to believe in democracy. He taught everyone who came to him and he believed everyone could learn from his teaching. His educational goals were of things internal to men and eternal of man, and not of the external and material life. His educational methods were of the existential mode, featured by a personal encounter between learner and teacher. Presumably, he would not have liked the implications of the word "instruction."

His guide was intuition and not cognate knowledge. He seems to have had very little time for the latter. Those whom he chose to be closest to him were not great figures before he knew them. Few of them could read or write. They were simple men—farmers, herdsmen, fishermen—who, like him, had worked with their hands. If he spent much time with any of the men of his day who were scholarly, or noted for wisdom, there is no record to show it. What was his contribution to philosophy? It is difficult to say. Philosophy can no more reach him than history. But this much is clear: he took the various abstract values that had so obsessed the Platonists and the Stoics—such things as love, temperance, justice, wisdom, beauty—, and he made them into a concrete noun which has the name *Christian Life* and is often described as Life-in-Christ.

The timing of his life is an argument for his divinity. Judaism, as a religion, was then bogged down in a legal mire. The best educated of the Jews were absorbed in those days by divisive wrangles over the rules by which the faithful were governed. Rome had established a kind of sovereignty over most of the known world, a circumstance which allowed the freedom of movement so vital to apostolic enterprise. Platonism, Stoicism, and the soon-to-come Neo-Platonism had prepared intellectual grounds which turned out to be highly congenial to Christian sentiments. Philosophy was without vision, the world was without love, and young men were without a cause. The legend of his birth tells that the world was again to be taxed. His parents were on the way homeward to be counted in a census. Organization men, technicians, legalistic scholars, and favor-seeking political kings ruled the provinces, set the human style, and presided over the destinies of men. His coming was well timed, well timed indeed.

His life and sayings are recorded in four biographies which are called Gospels (good news). Biblical scholarship has demonstrated that none of the authors could have known Christ directly. Because he did not associate with men of letters, and he wrote nothing, there are no contemporary written accounts of his life. The earliest Christian documents are the Pauline Epistles, written by a Greek Jew who was himself a Pharisee, but was converted to Christianity after having a vision of Christ while on a trip to the Syrian City of Damascus. Paul and the disciples of Christ undertook their various apostolic missions, usually cooperating, occasionally quarreling, but in every case with an intense zeal and uncompromising commitment which resulted finally in the martyrdom of a significant portion of their number.

The early years of the Christian church have been carefully studied. Even so, there are long periods of silence which must be filled by imagination and fancy. According to legend, Peter traveled to Rome and established a church there. Paul traveled in Greece and Asia Minor, establishing churches, and carrying on extensive correspondence with these churches through letters, a few of which, fortunately, survived. Still other disciples remained in Jerusalem and attempted to perpetuate the society of Christians which had developed before the founder of the faith was crucified.

Paul's new churches were important, and his letters are quite plain in manifestation of the Platonic influences in their early growth. Paul was well trained in philosophy, and his correspondence evidenced his tendency to erect philosophic support for the natural wisdom which came from the lips of Christ. But, inexorably, the center of the movement shifted to Rome; and finally Paul himself went to Rome. Christianity, largely through the work of Paul, had been made a universal religion in the sense that it was not for Jews only. No one is certain about the relations between Paul and Peter. Although Peter is recognized as the progenitor of the Roman church, small clues exist that he lacked administrative insight and that Paul was needed. Whether or not Paul was welcomed by these early Roman Christians can only be conjectured. While in Rome, he continued corresponding with his friends who were responsible for the churches in Greece and Asia Minor. On several occasions he invoked his Stoic precepts against the Epicurean tendencies. This is especially true in the case of the church at Corinth whose congregation exhibited a number of lively propensities (or moral delinquencies) unbecoming to Stoic Christianity. The Macedonian and Asian churches were apparently much better behaved.[1]

Although general persecution of Christians did not get underway until near the close of the First Century, the accepted tradition stands that both Peter and Paul were martyred. In the case of Paul, historical reference to his death is reasonably tenable. Paul had been a Roman citizen, a fact that made travel congenial. His citizenship, however, did not protect him from a government over which the depraved Nero presided. His death, we are informed, occurred about 64 A.D. It is tempting to offer further detail on the life and work of this remarkable man, but such an account is apart from the purpose of this discourse.

The times were not good for academic philosophers. Philosophy went its way, but it laid no hold on men at large. The rich were interested but unmoved. The poor were not touched by it in any way. Christianity, however, had new ideas in abundance, and they appealed to both rich and poor. It was an ecstatic doctrine which foresaw an imminent end to all things temporal and the beginning of the Kingdom of Christ.[2] Perhaps for this reason no literary tradition developed. In the first place, the early Christians were not writers, and in the second place, the world was to end soon and records of that day were probably presumed to be of no value.

The societies of Christians existed in the cities. At first they were tolerated; soon they were suspected; later they were outlawed; and, finally, they were prosecuted (and persecuted). Literally, Christianity as a movement moved underground. Despite this the Christians survived, grew in numbers and even drew inspiration from the martyrdom of their own. In the midst of intellectual and religious poverty, Christianity offered something for which many hungered. Even then there were men who despised a life which had no meaning. The Christian Life at least had meaningful content. Although at no time did the Empire, as such, make what we can judge to be an all-out effort to abolish Christianity, it is clear that the ruling classes were not happy with an extra- or supra-state society in their midst whose fealty was to the spiritual realm and not to the Emperor.[3] On at least ten occasions prior to the Christianization of the Empire, the Christian persecutions mounted to a marked and noted level of intensity. On every such occasion the persecutors finally weakened and Christianity grew. Someone once constructed the metaphor: It (Christianity) was like a nail. The harder it was struck the deeper into the wood it went.

Christian churches were finally established in Greece, Northern Italy, South Africa, Spain, Palestine, and as far to the east as Armenia, Persia, and India. In each of these domains the Christian societies established traditions and developed histories. Because the threads by which western man traces his own civilization run through Rome, the mistake is frequently made of regarding the history of Christendom as the history of the Roman church. Much of the early history of the primitive churches of Christ occurred elsewhere. In the beginning, perhaps the most thriving of these new institutions were those in the east. However, many of these were all but obliterated in the Sixth Century by the rise of Islam and Mohammed's vendetta with Christianity and Christendom. This was not, however, a religious persecution. It was a religious war.

But Rome was, after all, Rome. Until the end of the Third Century A.D., it was the center of the political world. Shortly after the beginning of the Fourth Century there occurred an event which, had it been predicted in the days of Nero or Caligula, would have been called a droll and monstrous fantasy. It was nothing less than the conversion of the Roman Emperor to the Christian faith. There are very good grounds for believing it to be the most colossal event of the first millenium A.D., for, thenceforward, until its demise, the Roman Empire became the protector and patron of the Roman church, and though the secular power of Rome was even then beginning to fade, it was enough to establish the Roman church and the Roman see as the center of the Christian world. The chuch and the state entered into an alliance which was fruitful of both good and evil in the centuries to come.

The title "Papa," a strange mixture of affection, reverence, and awe was in general use elsewhere before it was affixed to the Bishop of Rome. Some church historians trace its origin to the church of Alexandria. It did not have established use in Rome until later. When the Roman church indicates that Peter was the first Pope it means he and a good number of others have been given the title *post facto, post mortem.*

The pattern was set, and although not all of the emperors subsequent to Constantine were Christian, and the power center of the empire and church shifted to Constantinople (Byzantium) and back, Imperial Rome was a thing of the past and Ecclesiastical Rome had taken its place. Under these circumstances the Pope of Rome was an esteemed figure in both the religious and secular affairs of men.

Augustine and the City of God

Early in the Fifth Century the first great philosophic voice of the Christian church was heard. It was the voice of Augustine, Bishop of Hippo (the modern name of the city is Bona). Augustine's early life had been both morally and intellectually disordered.[4] His ventures in philosophy were highly personal and sprang forth in response to the events in the church or in his life which moved him deeply. His ethical and intellectual vagabondage ended with an exposure to the works of the Neo-Platonists, Plotinus, and Porphyry.[5] These philosophies, according to his own account, helped lead to his emancipation from materialistic thought and, ultimately, to his conversion to Christianity.

The Ionians had separated materialistic philosophy from religion. Parmenides had separated idealistic philosophy from religion. However, Augustine brought philosophy and religion back together. He proved to the satisfaction of the church they belonged together; in fact, in his hands they became one. Philosophy (he thought) aimed at happiness, but happiness could not be achieved by philosophy alone. He thought only Christianity could bring true happiness, and the role of philosophy was to explain the faith.

In his treatise, *Against the Academics* (by academics he meant Skeptics), he wrote: "From this moment forward it is my resolve never to depart from the authority of Christ, for I find none that is stronger. However, I must follow after this with the greatest subtlety of reason. For I am so disposed now that I have an unbounded desire to apprehend truth not only by believing it, but also by understanding it."[6] He went on to express confidence that among the Platonists he would not find that which contradicts the teachings of Christianity. In his quest for happiness or wisdom he set two precepts: (1) the authority of Christ and (2) human reason.

Much of Augustine's philosophizing was directed to refuting the position of the Skeptics. He declared that a state of absolute doubt is contradictory. (He who says man can have no absolute knowledge is, in saying this, claiming absolute knowledge.) He conceded that we may be mad, or dreaming, or sustaining illusions, but, he declared, we exist; we know we are living. "We are and we know we are, and we love our being and our knowledge of it."[7] In this he was anticipating the argument of Descartes who offered a similar rebuttal to the Skeptics of the Seventeenth Century. Augustine, twelve hundred years before Descartes was to proclaim, *"Ergo Cogito Sum"*[8] wrote that our certainty of our being and our love of our being is knowledge which does not come to us by way of the senses.

His search for knowledge was internal and personal; and, were it not for his initial submission to authority and its claim to universals, modern existentialists would applaud his method and appreciate his findings. He agreed with Plato and with Plotinus in believing that man had a reasoning soul which occupied an earthly body. The real man, to Augustine, was the soul, and the body it animated was merely an instrument of the soul. The problem of wisdom and happiness, therefore, must be resolved by ministering to the soul and not to the body. The soul and the soul alone arrives at truth, enjoys truth, and brings experience of truth which is happiness.

His doctrine of knowing differed slightly from the Platonic. In Plato's theory (Meno) the soul performed a feat of reminiscence.[9] Augustine seemed to believe that the eye of the soul experienced the light of God and this light illuminated truth. The association of

God and light and identification of God with light were not a contradiction of the Platonic doctrine. The Platonic light was simply
there; it was impersonal; indifferent; Plato's man must experience this
illumination on his own, by his own reason. The Augustinian light
was something which God did for man. It was not done for all equally,
but all share to some extent in the divine illumination. As to the nature
of the truths beheld in this light, Augustine did not go beyond Plato.
His immutable and eternal ideas are just as enticing but just as vague
as those which Plato gave to him.

Augustine draws heavily on the Neo-Platonists for his theory
of creation.[10] His interpretation of Genesis is highly figurative. God,
in creation, developed the seminal principles which have governed
the development of the world. Creation did not produce all things
as now seen. Creation was the implanting of the "seeds of all things."
In other words, God placed the seed of every species in matter, and
each came, responding to the favorable or unfavorable conditions
for its life. This view seemed consistent with Stoic and Neo-Platonic
thinking in every respect but one. Plotinus found the Above-Being
to be indifferent to that which emanated from Him. Creation, to
the Neo-Platonists, was not a conscious act by the Above-Being.
Augustine makes God a conscious progenitor of the world. He knows
He is God and He knows the world because He created it.

Augustine also draws strongly on the Neo-Platonists for his ethical notions. He presents the view that man was formerly one with
God; but, because of original sin, man has fallen away from God.[11]
Love is the force which pulls man (the soul) toward a remerging
with God. However, this is not a natural force which, according to
the Neo-Platonists, is indigenous to the soul. Love was given by
God to man; love is of God, love is God. In giving man love God
gave man a consciousness of God which was also a consciousness
of the good. Man was aware of his conscience. This was his moral
illumination. Men, who feel the love of God inwardly, turn toward
the good.[12]

Augustine's most influential work was one which required thirteen years to complete. According to tradition it was first undertaken
as a defense by Christendom of its newly won recognition as the
religion of the Romans. In the year 410 A.D., the city of Rome was
sacked by the Goths.[13] A great deal of the faultfinding triggered by
this event led to condemnation of the Christians. According to tradition, one heathen historian traced the origin of the calamity to the
abolition of sacrifices by Theodosius and the repeal of the laws of

the ancient faith by those who followed Theodosius to the throne. The point was made that the abandonment of idolatry and ascendency of Christianity were the causes of the misfortunes to which the Empire had fallen.

In 413 A.D., Augustine began to write a reply to this criticism. This furnished him with a theme for the first ten books of a work he called *The City of God*.[14] Before the work was finished he went far beyond his initial purpose, and the final volume came to twenty-two books. They were written slowly and appeared as installments between the years 413 and 426 A.D. His initial treatment demonstrates a powerful mastery of the literatures of both Biblical and pagan antiquity. He reviewed the calamities of the Romans before the time of Christ, showing that their gods had plunged them into vice and corruption. And thus, the fate of Rome was not unique in history. After having reviewed in detail and depth these and numerous related matters, Augustine made the distinction between earthly cities and the heavenly city. He declared that earthly cities are ever destined to perish. He presented the history of the City of God from the times of the prophets to Christ, and indicated that man must choose between the cities. Even though in this life their members are intermingled, the opposition between the cities of the world and the City of God is absolute.[15]

His final book (XXII) gives a vision of the fates of the two cities in eternity. Here Augustine offers specific detail to characteristics of the City of God, even to declaring that "women shall not rise women, but all shall be men, because God made man only of earth and woman of man."[16] He declared that the bodies of men, however disintegrated, shall be entirely reunited. The promise is *oneness with God, fulfillment, and peace.* This dualism between earth and heaven seemed not to be a prescription for the relations between church and state, but implications are inevitable from a document of this power and influence. The effects of it were to appear in the Christian dogma which was rapidly developing. Effects also were soon to be seen in the organization and administration of the church. The soon-to-rise Emperor, Charlemagne, was to adopt it as a base for an earthly paradise, thus joining ranks with the distinguished Utopians of the western spirit.[17]

Augustine, more than any single man, established the cast of medieval thought. It has been said that he "baptized" Plato. He at one point admitted that Plato had accounted for all but the reincarnation. He made no distinction between theology and philosophy. In his own mind he was amending the only defect in Platonic and Neo-Platonic philosophy by delineating the authority of Christ and the prophets on the authentic nature of God. His tributes to his Platonic forebears are exceeded only by his adoration of the divine.

In Book XIX of *The City of God* he wrote:

> In fine, He is the God whom Porphyry, the most learned of philosophers (though the bitterest enemy of the Christians) confesses to be a great God even according to the oracles of those whom he esteems gods.[18]

Even in his final inspiring vision of eternity Augustine made use of the best that went before him. It is a confident and heartwarming account of reality. It offers men something which philosophy alone could not. He ended his great treatise with this charming apology:

> I think I have now, by God's help, discharged my obligation in writing this large work. Let those who think I have said too little, or those who think I have said too much, forgive me; and let those who think I have said just enough join me in giving thanks to God.[19]

Across the past fifteen centuries many have joined St. Augustine in giving thanks. His passing did not signal a vast movement toward philosophy by the great Latin fathers of the emerging church. Augustine did not stimulate his peers to a further pursuit of philosophy. It was not the nature of Christian idealism to raise questions. Christian idealism was designed to settle questions, and it seems that for Christendom the Augustinian vision achieved this result. Augustine, to those who came in his wake, was an authority unlike any authority which had gone before him. The Christian church had its critics and some of them directed their scorn at the works of Augustine. But, unlike Plato and Plotinus, Augustine had no Aristotle or Porphyry to continue his original thinking. Instead he was dogmatized. Perhaps this is the result when reason takes second place to authority; dogma emerges.

The church of the early fathers included men of great faith and missionary zeal. Great figures such as St. Jerome, who seems to have quarreled with Augustine, from his pastorate in Bethlehem composed letters which were transmitted to Christian churches all over Europe and Asia.[20] Not only did they exhort faith in Christ, they kept the personalities of the Christian brotherhood united. The organization of monasticism provided a postal service which served the international relations of the day. The world prestige of the church soared again when Pope Leo (the Great) rode forth from defenseless Rome in the company of secular ambassadors and, exposing himself to mortal danger, took the lead in persuading Atilla (the leader of the Huns and an unpredictable butcherer of men) to turn aside and return to the Danube. In the words of Gibbon:

> The pressing eloquence of Leo, his majestic aspect and sacerdotal robes excited the veneration of Atilla for the spiritual father of the Christians. The apparition of the two apostles, who menaced the barbarian with instant death if he rejected the prayer of their successor, is one of the noblest legends of the ecclesiastical tradition.[21]

In the latter part of the Fifth Century the Germanic tribes from northern Europe continued to ravage the Roman Empire. These northern hordes had beaten down all armed resistance. While overcoming the western part of the Empire they generated deep fears in the eastern half. As this surging tide swept over Europe, the Christian organization was almost the only organization which survived the flood. It remained visible to commemorate what had once been; and Rome, whatever its status under barbarian rule, was still the Pope's see. The popular imagination could not fail to note how strongly the consciousness of the barbarians had been influenced by the spirited majesty of the church. The Pope's court was the only tribunal respected; the Pope's robes still bore the markings of the ancient magistrate, and the Pope's language was still a graceful bastion against the babble of vulgar tongues which was heard in all parts of Europe.

As the power of Empire became less, the power of the church became more. It provided for passage, communication, law, and commerce between state and city, tribe and family. Indeed, as the Sixth, Seventh, and Eighth Centuries passed, it was the only powerful organization in the civilized world. So vast and omnipresent did it become that few among the secular statesmen were left to doubt that, as a society, the church was the City of God about which Augustine so eloquently wrote. With the vision so vividly and materially incarnated who was left to doubt that the philosophy which postulated it was true?

In the interval between the death of Augustine and the Eleventh Century very few philosophized independently of the dogma of the church. Only two will be noted here and only briefly so because neither seriously interrupted or seriously disrupted the steadfast continuance of Augustinian dogma. Both of them were associated with the church. Both offered insightful commentaries on the life of the times, and both put constructions of their own faith upon the work of Plato and the New-Platonists. The first was Boethius who was born in 480, fifty years after the death of Augustine. As a youth, he studied at Athens, and there he encountered the philosophies and the language of the Greeks. He contributed a number of important translations of classical philosophy into Latin and thereby eased the passage of Greek ideas into the Latin world. On his return to Italy he became a consul to Theodoric, King of the Ostrogoths, who was soon to accuse him of treason, imprison him, and execute him.[22] While in prison he wrote prolifically. One of his works, probably the most important, was called *Consolation of Philosophy*. He was honored as a martyr. His small following (Beatus) perpetuated itself across the centuries and was finally confirmed by the church in 1883. The other figure was John Scotus Erigena who was born in Ireland in the Eighth Century. He went to France and became Master of the Palace School of Charles the Bald. In this position and from that forum he wrote and spoke at great length on philosophy and faith; the divisions of nature; and God, creation, and the divine ideas. He seems to have been a creative spirit, and some originality is reflected. But, in the main, it revolved around additional speculative details on the origins of divine ideas which he held to be the creatures of God and advanced the notion, already suggested by the Neo-Platonists, that creation is a continuous process.[23] Neither Boethius nor Erigena suggested a radical departure from the ontology of Augustine and the Platonists. They were, however, landmarks worth noting in developing medieval thought.

On Christmas day of the year 496 A.D., the King of the Franks was baptized. Gregory of Tours compares this event with the conversion of Constantine of Rome over a century before.[24] The Franks were warriors, a rising race, a conquering caste, and a separate nation. The secular power of Europe was gravitating into the hands of the Frankish princes. The alliance between the Franks and the church may have had a sincere moral purpose, but the union of the two offered political advantage to both church and state, and both began to make immediate use of this advantage. Soon Frankish nobility was attracted to the high ranks of the church, and priests and bishops of the church were involved in the perennial maneuvers of great family dynasties to extend the limits of their political control and influence.[25] Reform was needed and, in the fullness of time, great leaders of the church and state emerged to lead it. Ecclesiastics such as Boniface, Chrodegang, and Leo III were successful in restoring the clergy of the church to its spiritual mission, and leaders of state such as Charles Martel, Pippin, and finally Charlemagne gave character to the state which made the union of the two work for the advancement of the institutional order in central Europe. During the reign of Charlemagne the new ideals of church and state found expression, and although the locus of ecclesiastical authority remained in Rome, it was clear that the intellectual vigor of the church was shifting in the direction of Parisian France. Thus, at the close of the Tenth Century the order of things had changed. Cities were developing and new kinds of schools were developing.

The Rise of the Universities

There is no certainty as to why or how the medieval universities came into being. Various accounts are given, but uncertainty is reflected in all of them. Idealists will account for them as the product of man's innate love of order and of institutions which create order. These authorities tend to relate them to the Greek forerunners saying that men will always create such institutions when social stability is sufficiently established to permit institutons devoted to order in knowledge to appear. Realists, on the other hand, indicate these institutions emerged as a response to the sovereign urge in man to know. This view argues that the forces of actualization within man are manifested by an insatiable yearning for knowledge. He has an intelligence which must be fed, and it is inevitable that he will create institutions (feeding stations) wherein he can be fulfilled. Pragmatists, on the other hand, cite social process theories such as *economic determinism* and cite as evidence of this the fact that the early schools were professional in nature. The school at Salerno specialized in medical subjects. At Bologna the specialty was law, and at Paris students and teachers gathered to study religion and philosophy.

The students organized in guilds for protection. Soon teachers did the same. Authority was needed to amalgamate the two. Usually the authority was named by the church. The church authorized degrees and conferred upon students and faculty certain extra-national privileges such as freedom of passage and correspondence. The church was also able to blanket students and faculty with certain intra-national privileges such as immunity from the secular courts. Thus, although the church is not usually cited as the founder of the universities, the universities were sanctioned, authorized, and in some respects sponsored, by the churches. This form of institution spread throughout Europe via the veins and arteries through which the life of the church passed. And, to apply a modern usage, the church authority was occasionally used to "accredit" the emerging institutions.

Most tradition holds that the first to attain the status of *studium generale* was the school at Salerno. This status was commemorated by its having been given Papal authority to award the *Jus Ubique Docendi*[26] which, in effect, was a universal teaching license. Holders of this degree were judged worthy to teach the subject named anywhere in Christendom with the exception of Paris or Bologna where special examinations were still required. This degree is widely regarded as ancestor to the master's degree given in American versions of the university. Teachers will be interested to know that a prominent function of the original universities was the preparation of masters.

The masters were mainly in the arts. Doctors were generally reserved for law, medicine, and theology. Bachelors were simply those eligible to prepare for the master's level. Probably the first of these loosely organized groups of scholars and teachers to accept and use the name and the corporate status of *universitas* was Paris.[27] This did not really occur until the Thirteenth Century. By then a rather elaborate set of traditions and regulations had evolved, and although no one really (either then or now) understood this new creature in the institutional order, there was no question that by the Thirteenth Century the university was in existence.

Anselm and the Ontological Argument for God

Thus the setting of intellectual history between the Tenth and Thirteenth Centuries finds the centers of thought shifting from the church and its monastic orders in the direction of the emerging universities. A new tradition of criticism was unfolding as part of this transformation, and dogma was being questioned. Maimonides had exposed his views; Averroes and Avicenna had arrived from the east; translations of Aristotle were circulating among the masters; and when great leaders of the church arose to speak, questions formed on many lips. The questions begged to be answered, and the consequences of not answering broadened. No longer were there only a few isolated voices who risked martyrdom to raise a challenge. For six centuries men, in general, had been content to establish faith and then summon reason to explain their belief. But in the Eleventh Century men began to demand that faith itself be justified on rational grounds. An Italian monk from the city of Aosta whose name was Anselm responded to the challenge.

Anselm was born in 1033 A.D.; his early schooling was by the Benedictines.[28] In 1059 he left home to study in the French Abbey of Bec where he came under the influence of a renowned teacher whose name was Lanfranc. While at Bec, Anselm wrote most of his books, and in 1078 he became Abbot of the Monastery. Later in 1093 he was named Archbishop of Canterbury and became one of a long line of great figures to occupy that post. During his tenure at Canterbury, Anselm was under the necessity of preserving the rights of the church against encroachment by the monarchy.[29] He was not driven to the lengths of Becket who was later a martyr for this same cause, but his courage and steadfastness were sternly tested. He was twice driven into exile, but the disputes were resolved and he died in Canterbury in 1109 at the age of seventy-five.

Although his administrative distinctions have given him a position of note in history, Anselm is best known to the modern age as a Christian philosopher whose thoughts had originality, depth, and clarity. Like Augustine he was convinced that there are two sources of knowledge; namely, faith and reason. He also believed that faith must be the starting point in the search for truth. In his second major work he makes this point with unmistakable clarity: "For I do not understand in order that I may believe, but I believe in order that I may understand. For I also believe this, that unless I believe, I shall not understand.[30] In this way Anselm clearly extended the tradition of Christian idealism which consistently maintained that philosophers, acting without belief, cannot attain knowledge. On the other hand, with faith or belief in the given or revealed word of the scriptures, philosophy can demonstrate truth, explain reality, and establish knowledge.

But the times were not well suited for systems which rested on faith alone. The tendency to inquire, the habit of skepticism, the mood of criticism, and the proclivity to doubt which emanates from and surrounds vital and growing educational endeavors brought forth questions, raised issues, and weakened faith. Men once again could ask: "But suppose these beliefs are false?" A new spirit appeared in the life of mind. Christian idealism needed another dimension. Even the monks of Bec may have felt this lack when they approached Anselm with a request that he write out a model meditation on God, in which everything would be proved by reason with nothing depending on the authority of scripture. Anselm's first attempt to furnish a model appeared in a booklet which has come to be called the *Monologium.* Making note of the request put to him he said:

> Certain brethren have often and earnestly entreated me to put in writing some thoughts that I had offered them in conversation, regarding meditation on the Being of God, and on some other topics connected with this subject under the form of a meditation on these themes. It is in accordance with their wish, rather than with my ability, that they have prescribed such a form for the writing of this meditation; in order that nothing in Scripture should be urged on authority of Scripture itself, but that whatever the conclusion of independent investigation should declare to be true, should in an unadorned style, with common proofs and with simple argument, be briefly enforced by the cogency of reason, and plainly expounded in the light of truth.[31]

One cannot imagine the Bishop of Hippo so responding to such a request. We must doubt that the Augustine of 410 A.D. would undertake to submit God's being to the test of reason alone; no, he would probably have attacked by declaring the question itself betrays absence of faith. But there were new schools; these were new men; and the church was a vast institution with deep interests in nearly every aspect of secular life; and Christ was five centuries further removed in the lives and times of the monks at Bec.

The first rational proof Anselm offered on the Being of God took the following form:[32]

1) Our senses and our reason make us aware of a great number of good things.
2) Are these good things good through some one thing, or each good through something different and peculiar to itself? Clearly the former.
3) It is the former because it is absolutely certain that if a number of things are said to possess an attribute in greater, less, or equal degree they are said to possess it in some one thing that is understood to be the same in all.
4) Therefore, all true goods have the character of goodness through the same being through which all goods exist.
5) This being is not good through something else, it is good through itself. Hence, it alone is supremely good, unsurpassed, and the most excellent of all beings. It is God.

Using the same form of argument, replacing the idea of good

with the ideas of being and of perfection, Anselm proves the reality of God. In the *Monologium* Anselm arrives at an ontological position similar to that of Plato and the Neo-Platonists, but the route taken is even more pure in reason because he does not posit a soul. This is not to say that Anselm, in any sense, denies soul. He simply does not use it in his argument. In this way he responds fully to the challenge because one can accept the argument without first placing faith in the idea of the soul.

The next effort which Anselm made presumably was inspired by a self-urging to create a simpler argument. It appears in his second great work which is called the *Proslogium*. In his introductory remarks Anselm indicates that the improved argument came to him suddenly after long meditation and prayer. Therefore, he urges the reader to use a similar means to prepare his mind for the meditation. Said he:

> Up now, slight man! Flee, for a little while, thy oc-
> cupations; hide thyself, for a time, from thy disturbing
> thoughts. Cast aside now, thy burdensome cares, and put away
> thy toilsome business. Yield room for some little time to God;
> and rest for a little time in Him. Enter the inner chamber of
> thy mind, shut out thoughts save that of God, and such as
> can aid thee in seeking Him; close thy door and seek Him.[33]

Now it is evident that this meditative effort is not going to take the non-humane form used in the first model of the *Monologium*. Here, Anselm is asking his reader to take the "interior" route rather than the "antiseptic" path of pure logic. He begins by thanking God for creating man in His image, and says to God, as if in prayer, that the image is clouded by the doubt of sins and worn away by corruption. Then he repeats again the sovereign assumption of the Christian idealist, "Unless I believe, I shall not understand."[34]

Anselm then declares: "*We believe that God is a being than which none greater can be thought.*"[35] Referring to the Skeptics he said that some have denied God's existence. This is not new, for in Psalms 13:1, "The fool has said in his heart: There is no God." But, Anselm continues, when the fool hears the words, "a being than which none greater can be thought," the fool understands them. Therefore, such a being exists in his intellect, even though the fool thinks it has no reality.[36]

Now the crux of the argument follows:[37]

> 1) Even the fool can think of a being than which none
> greater can be thought.

2) It is greater to exist in reality than in intellect alone.
3) Therefore, it would be contradictory to say that the being than which none greater can be thought could exist in intellect alone; a being greater than this could always be conceived existing in reality.
4) Thus, there can be no question that there exists in the intellect *and in reality* something than which a greater cannot be thought.

This, as one might expect, did not pass unchallenged. A Benedictine monk from Marmoutier (Tours) named Gaunilon wrote a response which he called "In Defense of the Fool."[38] His objections were twofold: Firstly, he denies he has in his mind the idea of a being than which none greater can be thought; he does not know the reality of God because, as Anselm admits, there is no other reality like him. Here Gaunilon is on the same ground as Plotinus in the Neo-Platonic suggestion that the Above-Being was unthinkable and ineffable. Secondly, Gaunilon asserted that even if God appeared in the intellect there is no reason to believe that He must exist in reality. It is possible to think of a gold mountain or an enchanted island, but this does not warrant a conclusion that such things exist.

Anselm answered these criticisms categorically. He asserted, of course, that Gaunilon did not understand him.[39] Anselm declared that, to arrive intellectually at the "being" than which none greater can be thought, "one simply ascends the hierarchy of goods (as suggested in the *Monologium*). As to the second complaint, Anselm declared that we can reason from existence in intellect to existence in reality in one case only. For there is only one being which cannot be thought *not to be.* This is the being "than which none greater can be thought."

The proof has been attacked by thinkers subsequent to Gaunilon. Centuries later Locke declared: "I think this I may say, that it is an ill way of establishing truth and silencing atheists."[40] Leibnitz referred to it as "an imperfect demonstration." Kant rejected it by saying that the "real does not contain more than the possible."[41] In Muller's translation of the *Critique of Pure Reason* Kant is found saying: "A hundred real dollars do not contain a penny more than a hundred possible dollars."[42]

But Anselm has strong support arrayed in his behalf. Descartes was to construct a similar proof of God's existence. Hegel found of Anselm's argument "the content is indeed right but the form faulty."[43] Spinoza, using a similar (ontological) approach, reasoned, "If then no cause or reason can be given which prevents the existence of God, or which destroys his existence, we must necessarily conclude that he does exist."[44] Anselm's proof was also affirmed by the Franciscans, Duns Scotus and Bonaventura.[45]

Anselm did not confine his thinking and writing to his ontological argument. Nor was his dispute with Gaunilon the only encounter. His philosophical life was as stormy as was his career as a Bishop. He took occasion to denounce Roscellinus who is recognized as an early figure in a philosophical movement called *nominalism*. This movement was just beginning in the life of Anselm, and he condemned it as heretical. However, he did not vanquish it, and *nominalism* survived both Anselm and his protests. It became a great force in philosophy, and its traditions still flourish.

Anselm found it incredible, however, that men could think of universals simply as words. His point of view was *Universale ante rem* (the universal is before the thing). The nominalist doctrine has been sloganized as *Universale post rem* (the universal is after the thing). Paradoxically, the philosophy of Anselm, in his time, was called *realism* (because of his arguments for the *a priori* reality of universals). Students of philosophy have come to refer to the Anselm-Roscellinus dispute as the realist-nominalist controversy. Actually, the doctrine of universals implicit in the tradition of philosophical realism holds that *universale in re* (the universals are in the thing).[46]

One of the students of Roscellinus was a brilliant young scholar named Abelard. He and numerous others carried on the critical spirit which challenged Anselm and which increasingly became characteristic of medieval scholars. Anselm died before the disputes among the Chrsitian idealists, the nominalists, and the Neo-Aristotelians reached a climax at the University of Paris and other centers of learning.[47] In the Thirteenth Century these disputes grew so intense that the very highest circles in the church government were called upon to intervene, first by one side and then by the other. Before it ended, the idea of academic freedom for the academic profession was given its first test in European institutions; and, finally, no less than the Pope himself summoned Christendom's leading scholars to the task of finding grounds on which the differences could be reduced or resolved.[48]

An English philosopher named Alexander of Hales followed Anselm by a century. He was already a professor of theology at Paris when he joined the Franciscan order. He continued until his death to teach as a Franciscan. One who came to study under him was a young Italian named John Fidanza.[49] He entered the Franciscan order in 1238 and came to teach at The University from 1248 to

1255. Ultimately he became Minister General of the Franciscans. Throughout his life as a teacher and cleric he was known as Bonaventura. In 1273 he was made a Cardinal. His death occurred in 1274, the same year as that of Aquinas, the Dominican with whose philosophy Bonaventura had substantial differences. Bonaventura returned Christian Idealism to the general Augustinian line. There were several exceptions, the most notable being his inclination to bring God into the domain of ideas rather than as a Being apart from it. This doctrine became known as exemplarism and assigned God to a role as exemplar or model for all creatures.[50]

So Christian Idealism did not end with Anselm. Neither did it fail to influence the new philosophies. It was the conservative position which was held in the schools of theology and which was most frequently attacked by the Masters of Arts. It lived and prospered among the Benedictines and the Franciscan orders and experienced a revival in the protestant reformation. Christian Idealism has been a vivid aspect of the protestant dogma. Both the Swiss and German versions of the reformation were influenced by it, but probably the former more than the latter, although no one rejected the medieval synthesis of Aquinas more firmly than Martin Luther, who once declared "faith alone justifies us."

Thus, it is not difficult to buttress a claim that Christian Idealism was a powerful force in protestantism, and it has never ceased to be strongly represented in the general community of the Roman Catholic Church. Certainly it has been a vital force in American thought and American ethics. But this particular species of idealism did not reach the American mind unmingled with other theories of mind which came to flower in and subsequent to the European renaissance. The American student of education must also examine these if he would know his people and their view of life.

Education and Christian Idealism

A modern student of education has little difficulty in imagining the goal and manner of education in the style of the Christian idealist. The schools were geared to build faith in the holy word, develop meditative dispositions, depreciate the flesh, and build the Christian character. These aims were sought by the Christian humanists, of whose number Erasmus became the most noted and perhaps the most typical.[51] The philosophical justification was to align the reality of each individual self to the spiritual reality which surrounds the world and contains the organization and order which should characterize the world and all of its people.

At times practices are better described by those who criticize them. In any case, by reading the criticism one gets a fuller and richer picture of the real thing. Christian humanism did not have a more able or incisive critic than Rabelais.[52] Here was the Diogenes of the renaissance! A Rotterdam monk who turned physician, he covered the educational practices of the Christian humanists with a withering and unrelenting satire, and those who wonder if the spirit of the Cynic still lived are invited to read Rabelais' account of the Education of Gargantua which follows:

The Education of Gargantua[53]

"Gargantua awakened then about four o'clock in the morning. Whilst they were rubbing him, there was read unto him some chapter of the Holy Scripture, aloud and clearly with a pronunciation fit for the matter, and hereunto was appointed a young page born in Basche named Anagnostes. According to the purpose and argument of that lesson, he often gave himself to revere, adore, pray, and send up his supplications to that good God whose word did show His majesty and marvellous judgments. Then his master repeated what had been read, expounding unto him the most obscure and difficult points. They then considered the face of the sky, if it was such as they had observed it the night before, and into what signs the sun was entering, as also the moon for that day. This done he was appareled, combed, curled, trimmed, and perfumed during which time they repeated to him the lessons of the day before. He himself said them by heart, and upon them grounded the practical cases concerning the estate of man, which he would prosecute sometimes two or three hours, but ordinarily they ceased as soon as he was fully clothed. Then for three good hours there was reading. This done, they went forth, still conferring on the substance of the reading, and disported themselves at ball, tennis, or the "pile trigone," gallantly exercising their bodies as before they had done their minds. All their play was but in liberty for they left off when they pleased, and that was commonly when they did sweat or were otherwise weary. Then they were very well dried and rubbed, shifted their shirts, and, walking soberly, went to see if dinner was ready.... At the beginning of the meal there was read some pleasant history of ancient prowess, until he had taken his wine. Then, if they thought that good, they continued reading, or began to discourse merrily together speaking first of the virtue, propriety, efficacy, and nature of all that was served in at the table; of bread, of wine, of water, of salt, of flesh, fish, roots, herbs, and of their dressing. By means whereof, he learned in a little time all the passages on these subjects to be found in Pliny, Athenaeus, Dioscorides, Julius, Pollux, Galen, Porphyrius, Oppion, Polybuis, Heliodorus, Aristotle, OElian, and others."

"Whilst they talked of these things, they caused the very books to be brought to the table, and so well and perfectly did he in his memory retain the things above said, that there was not a physician who knew so much as he did. Afterwards they conferred on the lessons read in the morning, and ending their repast with some conserve of quince, he washed his hands and eyes with fair fresh water and gave thanks unto God in some fine canticle made in praise of the divine munificence. This done they brought in cards, not to play, but to learn a thousand pretty tricks and new inventions which were all grounded in arithmetic. By this means he fell in love with the numerical science."

This Rabelaisian account of Gargantua's day continues—Gargantua's afternoon with reading, singing, changing clothes, being rubbed, praying, giving thanks, playing the flute, repeating passages that were read, giving thanks again, getting rubbed again, changing clothes, and coming to dinner. At dinner there is profitable discourse and visits from learned men who had visited strange countries. As for the evening, the account resumes, and once again Rabelais speaks for himself:

"At full night they went to the most open place of the house to see the full face of the sky, and there beheld the comets, if any were, as likewise the figures, situations, aspects, opposition, and conjunctions of the stars. Then with his master briefly did he recapitulate, and after the manner of the Pythagoreans recite that which he had read, seen, learned, done, and understood in the course of that day. Then they prayed unto God the Creator, falling down before Him, and strengthening their faith towards Him, and glorifying Him for His boundless bounty; and, giving thanks unto Him for the time which was past they recommended themselves to His divine clemency for the future. Which being done they entered upon their repose."

As for the idealism of the East, from which source Christian theology owed much of its content, and from which source medieval Christian education gained part of its method, it was not spared from the even more rapacious thrusts of Europe's greatest satirist, the Seventeenth Century Voltaire. In a tale called Barabec, Voltaire dispatched all kinds of mystical asceticism in characteristic style:[54]

Omni: Is there a chance that I may ascend to the Nineteenth Heaven?

Brahmin: It depends on what kind of life you lead.

Omni: I try to be a good citizen, a good husband, a good father: I sometimes lend money without interest to the rich; I give to the poor; I preserve peace among my neighbors.

Brahmin: But, do you occasionally stick pins in your behind?

Omni: Never, reverend father.

Brahmin: I am sorry, you will never attain to the Nineteenth Heaven.

Notes

1. The first letter of Paul to the Corinthians was apparently a rebuke to the congregation for excessive, indeed licentious, parties after celebration of the rite of the Last Supper.
2. Harry E. Fosdick, *A Guide to Understanding the Bible* (New York: Harper and Bros., 1938), p. 51 ff.
3. Justin Martyn, *The First Apology* issued by The Classics Club, *Marcus Aurelius and His Times* (Roslyn, N.Y.: Walter J. Black, Inc., 1945), pp. 259-292.
4. St. Augustine, *Confessions*, tr. E. B. Pusey (Mount Vernon: Peter Pauper Press, 1969), Books I-VI.
5. *Ibid.*, p. 3.
6. Armond A. Maurer, *Medieval Philosophy* (New York: Random House, Inc., 1962), p. 4.
7. St. Augustine, *The City of God*, Book XI, tr. Marcus Dods (New York: Random House, Inc., 1950), p. 372.
8. René Descartes, *Discourse on Method*, tr. John Veitch (LaSalle, Ill.: The Open Court Publishing Co., 1945), p. 35.
9. *The Meno*.
10. St. Augustine, *op. cit.*, pp. 345-379.
11. *Ibid.*, pp. 459-463.
12. Maurer, *op. cit.*, p. 9.
13. *Ibid.*, p. 19.
14. *Ibid.*
15. *Ibid.*
16. St. Augustine, *op. cit.*, p. 839 ff.
17. H. G. Good, *A History of Western Education* (New York: The Macmillan Company, 1960), p. 73.

18. St. Augustine, *op. cit.*, p. 201.
19. *Ibid.*, p. 867.
20. George T. Stokes, *Ireland and the Celtic Church* (London: Hodder and Stoughton, 1888), pp. 170-172.
21. Edward Gibbon, *The Decline and Fall of the Roman Empire* (Philadelphia: Claxton, Remsen, and Haffelfinger, 1880), Vol. I, p. 34.
22. Maurer, *op. cit.*, p. 386.
23. *Ibid.*, p. 39.
24. S. Baring Gould, *The Church in Germany* (London: Weltes Gardner, Darton and Co., 1891), ch. 3.
25. *Ibid.*
26. James Mulhern, *A History of Education* (New York: The Ronald Press Co., 1959), p. 281.
27. Herman Shapiro, ed., *Medieval Philosophy* (New York: Random House, Inc., The Modern Library Edition, 1964), p. 222.
28. Maurer, *op. cit.*, p. 390
29. *Ibid.*
30. St. Anselm, *Proslogium,* tr. Sidney N. Deane, *St. Anselm* (LaSalle, Ill.: Open Court Publishing Co., 1948), p. 7.
31. St. Anselm, *Monologium,* tr. Sidney N. Deane, *op. cit.*, p. 35.
32. *Ibid.*, pp. 35-63.
33. St. Anselm, *Proslogium, op. cit.*, p. 3.
34. *Ibid.*, p. 7.
35. *Ibid.*
36. *Ibid.*, p. 8.
37. *Ibid.*, p. 7-25.
38. Gaunilon, *In Behalf of the Fool,* tr. Sidney Deane (LaSalle, Ill.: Open Court Publishing Co., 1948), pp. 145-153.
39. St. Anselm, *Apologeticus,* tr. Sidney N. Deane (LaSalle, Ill.: Open Court Publishing Co., 1948), pp. 153-170.
40. John Locke, *An Essay Concerning Human Understanding* (London: Ward, Lock & Company), p. 529 ff.
41. Jaspers, *The Great Philosophers* (New York: Harcourt, Brace & World, Inc., 1966), p. 106.
42. *Ibid.*, p. 107.
43. G. W. F. Hegel, *Lectures on the History of Philosophy,* tr. Haldane and Simpson (London: Routeledge and Kegan Paul, 1896), Vol. III, p. 62 ff.
44. Benedict Spinoza, *The Chief Works of Benedict De Spinoza,* tr. R. H. M. Elwes (London: G. Bell and Sons, 1894), Vol. II, p. 51 ff.
45. Jaspers, *op. cit.*, p. 102.
46. Mulhern, *op. cit.*, p. 239.
47. Robert Holmes Beck, *A Social History of Education* (Englewood Cliffs, N. J.: Prentice-Hall, Inc., 1965), pp. 41-43.
48. *Ibid.*, p. 40. See also Herman Shapiro, *op. cit.*, pp. 234-252.
49. Maurer, *op. cit.*, p. 401.
50. *Ibid.*, p. 145.
51. William H. Woodward, *Desiderius Erasmus Concerning the Aim and*

Method of Education (New York: Teachers' College, Columbia, Bureau of Publication, 1964), p. xiii.
In a foreword to this work, Craig R. Thompson declared that the term "Christian humanist" was formerly "possibly clear," but is now "unfortunately ambiguous." This ambiguity apparently stems from a tendency to associate humanism as a counter to "supernaturalism" or "theism."
52. Beck, *op. cit.*, p. 51. See also: Walter Besant, *Readings in Rabelais* (Edin: Wm. Blackwood and Sons, 1883), p. 20.
53. Besant, *op. cit.*, pp. 20-29.
54. Alfred Noyes, *Voltaire.*

Other Reading

Augustine. *The City of God.* Tr. Marcus Dods. New York: Random House, Inc., 1950.
Augustine. *Earlier Writings.* Tr. J. H. S. Burleigh. London: The Westminster Press, 1953.
Baldin, C. S. *Medieval Rhetoric and Poetic.* New York: The Macmillan Company, 1928.
Beck, Robert H. *A Social History of Education.* Englewood Cliffs, N.J.: Prentice-Hall, Inc., 1965. Chapters I-III.
Carr, A. *The Church and the Roman Empire.* New York: Longmans Green and Co., Inc., 1898, pp. 25-96.
Dean, Sidney. *St. Anselm.* LaSalle, Ill.: Open Court Publishing Co., 1948, pp. 3-153.
Hannah, Ian C. *Christian Monasticism, A Great Force in History.* New York: The Macmillan Company, pp. 12-200.
Haskins, C. H. *The Rise of Universities.* New York: Henry Holt and Co., 1923.
Maurer, Armand A. *Medieval Philosophy.* New York: Random House, 1962, pp. 3-122.
Norton, A. O. *Readings in the History of Education: Medieval Universities.* Cambridge, Mass.: Harvard University Press, 1909.
Pope, Mortin. *An Introduction to Early Church History.* London: Macmillan and Co., Ltd., 1919. 163 Pp.
Rabelais, F. *Gargantua and Pantagruel,* ed. D. Douglass. New York: Random House, Inc., 1928. 365 Pp.
Rait, Robert S. *Life in the Medieval University.* New York: Cambridge University Press, 1912. 164 Pp.
Rashdall, H. *The Universities of Europe in the Middle Ages.* Oxford: Clarendon Press, 1936. Volume I, II.
Woodward, William H. *Desiderius Erasmus Concerning Aim and Method in Education.* New York: Teachers College, Columbia University, 1964, pp. 1-101.
_____. *Vittorino Da Feltre and Other Humanist Educators.* New York: Teachers College, Columbia University, 1963, pp. 93-250.

CHAPTER VII

Scholasticism and the Thomistic Synthesis

It is impossible to conceive chaos. One can conceive various stages of tumult, but at the point of chaos all conception must end. Thus the condition of the European world subsequent to the fall of the Roman intellectual order exceeds conception. It was nothing less than chaos, and as to magnitude of disorder there can be nothing more than chaos.

Suddenly a Shapeless World

How can it be described? The dismantlement of the civil forms which occurred in the Fifth and Sixth Centuries generated extreme contradictions. The barbarians were not without organization, unity, or purpose. But like barbarians of all times they turned to the immediate, to the source of sensation; and they turned away from the reflective and the source of idea. Language was vulgarized; manners were derogated. Force and fear, vengeance and ambition, fantasy and illusion became the primary grounds for human action. Sensitivities cultivated by centuries of civilized order were brutalized in less than three generations. The great patterns of thought and language ended in an abyss of absurdities. Virgil, Cicero, Horace, Lucretius, and Platus, the last eloquent voices of antiquity, stood with their kindred at the edge of a thousand-year void waiting until Dante, Petrarch, and their learned contemporaries led them across into the modern world through a renewed self-conscious freedom of the human spirit which has been called renaissance.

Some of that chaotic interval which preceded rebirth can be described by its vivid inconsistencies. Language deteriorated, but an obsession with grammar emerged. Barbarian kings ruled with civility while emperors ruled with barbarity. Diabolical cruelty and lofty sentiments existed side by side as men stopped killing one another in the arena but began burning one another at the stake.

Philosophy moved into the church, theology moved into the government, and republicanism declined. Schools of law emerged as despotism reigned. The clergy prized saintly gentleness and urged unprecedented violence. The church was a refuge for the damned, but, at times, damned refugees. Single works of art included both heavenly vision and hellish imagination, and religious sentiments wavered between blind credulity and heretical disbelief. It is as if a massive fist came crashing down again and again upon the order of the world, continuously shattering its tentative self-notions in such a way as to cause each generation to be less certain of its institutional forms than the preceding.

The great municipal civil schools disappeared and cathedral schools rose in their place. The curriculum based in the quadrivium and trivium turned dogmatic and gave way to historical, philosophical, and moral commentary on scripture. The rich pagan view of life faded, and in its place emerged another which presented man as a servile creature whose God had pronounced upon him a curse of separation. The ancient ideas of political freedom were replaced by new conceptions of class and containment. Few libraries were maintained, and the priceless books of antiquity were discarded or simply rotted on shelves at the neglected centers of learning. Monastic orders developed, and books which bore strongly upon Platonized Christian doctrines were copied in monasteries and nunneries, but many which contradicted or had little apparent relevance to the church doctrine were discontinued and lost. Such philosophy as was preserved endured in the monasteries south of Gaul. The genetic powers of the human race continued to produce men of powerful insight, but in these times such men were ruthlessly suppressed, killed, or banished into the wilderness which surrounded the stage upon which human history was then unfolding. One of these men was the remarkable Fifth-Century author Pseudo-Dionysius who had the good sense to keep his true name from association with the four influential treatises he fashioned. To this day his exact identity is a mystery.[1] A second example was Boethius, a Sixth-Century philosopher of impressive dimensions who was emerging as a profound influence when he was imprisoned and then brutally executed. At the time he was only forty-four, an age when most philosophers begin their greatest work. John Scotus Erigena, a Ninth-Century philosopher, produced some daring thoughts and rose to prominence, but was struck down and reportedly killed either by the hands of his monastic colleagues or by those of his own students.[2]

Foundations for the deadly epidemics to come were laid as mankind learned to live piously in filth. Bathing, which was so thoroughly a part of Greco-Roman life and a matter of pleasure, pride, and comfort even to the common citizen, was discouraged.[3] In a conscious perversion of pagan attitudes St. Jerome argued that garments should be squalid to show the mind is pure. One forbore dirt upon his body to remove pollution from his soul. The pagan overtones of athletic contests served as cause for repudiation of sports of all kinds. Even the games which had avoided violence were to be shunned. The Olympic games finally were abolished in 303 A.D.[4] Physical education, the enactment of laws to preserve and promote health, and, indeed, all concerns for physical well-being of men were reduced to only those matters of sheer necessity; and at times even they were befittingly neglected in the fever of religious passions. The accounts of these times offered praise to men who mortified their own flesh as a repudiation of the pleasures of the mortal state. As if to dramatize this inversion of the personal values of the pagan world, confessions became a literary vogue. The greatest of human achievements was to rise above the flesh and ultimately to repudiate it.

The inversion applied also to arts and letters. The dancing and dramatic arts of former times fell before the flood of Christian asceticism. Christians were urged to have nothing to do with the shamelessness of the theater.[5] In place of secular music the church developed the solemn antiphonal chant which was more consistent with the unwordly procession through mortal life which its doctrine taught as the fundamental human condition. All other music was profane.[6] The ballads of man in love with the world of sounds, sights, and physical passion were silenced and forbidden. The figurative arts returned to formalism. The delicate blend of the abstract and the real which so characterized the painting and statuary of the classical era turned to extreme realism in the hands of the Romans and reverted to extreme formalism in the hands of the Christians. Nowhere was man to tempt himself with the worldly. His principal business was beyond life.

And, of course, government took a similar course. Personal property diminished as a sanction. Large tracts of land came into the possession of church or state, later to be used to reward valorous noblemen who in turn virtually enslaved large groups of peasant serfs who farmed the land in times of peace and rallied to the landlord in times of war. The Augustinian City of God was elevated above the cities of man. Secular government ruled by sanction of the church and the foundations of European aristocracy were found to exist in

Plato. Thus the church baptized both Plato's archetypes and his politics. Justice which in Greco-Roman times had emerged responsive to philosophically derived standards of equity reverted to judgments by unlettered priests and chieftains and to a bifurcation of secular and ecclesiastical responsibility which, among other things, produced such absurdities as trials by ordeal and combat.

How long was this perturbation? By the Tenth Century new civil forms were apparent. Even across the interval of chaos some institutions survived, and certain interests continued. And in the course of events new forms were established which were not known to the ancient world. One of these was the *guild*. During that interval of chaos men of like interests and skills learned to associate for the purpose of protecting and perpetuating these interests and skills. The guilds, as they came to be called, soon became a viable component of an emerging order. Although the fires of scholarship died down, the coals continued aglow even in the cathedral schools where orthodoxy presided. Before the Tenth Century groups of teachers and scholars gathered in the large urban centers to study the professions of law, medicine, and theology. Within these *studia generales* the scholars formed guilds based upon their fields or the nations from which they came. There were faculty guilds and student guilds, and they became elements around which the universities were later to organize. One cannot put an exact date on the beginning or ending of the chaos, but between the time the former order dissolved and the new emerged there were three to four centuries of darkness. And from the dawn of the Tenth Century, three hundred more years would pass before western man would really learn how to combine the best of the ancient world with the best of the modern. Observers of civilization should pause and reflect upon the possible meaning of this.

The Rise of Scholasticism

What was the status of philosophy as civilization began to emerge from its perturbation? The Christian religion was the leading subject of thought. Its divines had put forward the claim that Christianity was not merely the guide to personal life and the means to reunion with God, but also a philosophy in the widest sense that the term is used—that is, a consistent speculative view of man's condition, nature, and surrounding world. They held, without reservation, that the doctrines of the ancient philosophers had to be corrected to conform to those of revelation. The resultant theology was the only true philosophy.

Thus, in its classic sense, scholastic philosophy is a philosophical doctrine of the ancient world which was amended so as to conform to or be consistent with the Christian theology of the Middle Ages.

Now there was one immediate complication for scholastic philosophy. After revelation, logic was its only science; and there was something deadly about this. The new schoolmen in quest of a philosophical expression of the ultimate truth had overlooked a problem which was well known to the ancients. The conservative schoolmen tended to assume there was a perfect correspondence between a word and the truth of the thing for which the word stands. To make this particular matter worse the impoverished Latin of the early schoolmen had not nearly the precision nor the analytical power of the ancient Greek. Some came to recognize this problem, but others did not. The latter, who were in the flush of anticipatory agreement on universals, had little tolerance for dissent. For example, when the *nominalist* Roscelin argued that something must exist before it is given a name, he was denounced and threatened. But this did not resolve the questions proposed by the nominalists.

We can see the problem more clearly through an example. *Man* is a general term. Now what is the relation between the general term and actual men? What is the relationship between the idea of man and the variety of specimens on earth which answer to that name? The nominalist argues that the word man is simply that used to designate or name a class of creatures and the universal contained by the word came after men. The word merely identifies the group. Therefore, the word *man* refers to a class. The realists, those most devoted to orthodox church doctrine, argued that the word stands for an idea which God had before he created man. This simple disagreement as to what this word stands for can create monstrous problems for a logic chopper who is trying to use the language of revelation in a rational demonstration of revelation's truth. What, for another example, is an angel? Do they have a corporeal being? If so, how big are they? Can all of creation's angels dance on the head of a single pin?

The "realist" schoolmen such as Anselm and William of Champeaux held tenaciously to their conservative Augustinian Platonism, and the church backed them with varied powers. But the challenge of nominalism had shaken the dogmas. Even more significantly, the question had gotten into the *studia generales* and members of the masters' guilds had taken positions. The question also stimulated a new interest in the ancient studies, and this in turn consummated in new challenges to the orthodoxy. By the Twelfth Century the question whether philosophy could be contained within Christian theology was now open, and the schoolmen were taking sides. Indeed, it was becoming a matter of increasing dissension, especially in the study centers of France and Italy. Soon the struggle for the intellectual unity of scholasticism was lost. By the Twelfth Century disputes raged everywhere.

Aristotle soon appeared more distinctive from Plato. This, as it turned out, was one of the unforeseen consequences of the aggression of the Christian princes in Spain and North Africa. The great and fertile plains of Andalusia had become a Moorish paradise, and in the Twelfth Century the Spanish city of Cordova was considered "the Athens of the West." Cordova had a library of 400,000 volumes, 300 mosques, 300 public baths, and twenty-one suburbs. As part of its growth a distinctive architectural style had emerged, and the city was frequented by the greatest of the Judaic and Islamic scholars. It was for a time the home and inspiration of Maimonides whose life as a philosopher and court physician to a great military sovereign, Saladin, so closely paralleled Aristotle's.[7] The Crusades resulted in the recovery by Christendom of more than access to the Holy Land. What counted even more to the bifurcation of scholastic philosophy was the recovery of Aristotle's books which were much better known and preserved by the Arabs than by the Christians.

Of equal import was the notice taken by Italian and Parisian schoolmen of the commentaries on Aristotle by Arabian and Jewish scholars such as Maimonides, Averroes, and Avecenna. These men were physicians, philosophers, and mathematicians. Their work was considered a rich find by every part of the intellectual community except certain professors of theology, especially those at Paris, who still regarded themselves as the guardians of Augustinian truth. As late as 1244 they burned copies of the Talmud "in obedience to a papal mandate."[8]

From the vantage point of their Platonized Augustinian doctrines of revelation the objections of the theological schoolmen to the influence of Jewish and Islamic interpretations of ancient philosophy are clearly understandable. At the first glance, the Arabian Aristotle appears to side with the early nominalists. His science begins in perception and his logic is authorized to operate on data taken in by the senses. Little wonder then that the nominalists argued that their propositions had Aristotelian sanction. In addition, Aristotle's theism was much too specific for the conservative scholastics. Plato's idea of the good was quite manageable in their hands, but the notion that the unmoved mover was "a thinking that is of itself" which is completely happy, never angry, indifferent to man, and not involved in creation could not be made to cohere with the revealed nature of God as defined by sacred literature. None of this, however, was lost upon Abelard, the great Parisian celebrity-scholar of the Twelfth Century whose provocations of the establishment as much as anything set in motion the events which led to the incorporation of the university.

It is appropriate that we consider Abelard's life and works as concomitant with the incorporation called "universitas." No other man better personifies the mighty stirring of the human spirit which marked the Twelfth Century. His erudition was extraordinary for a man of those times. He wrote with power in the vernacular, but he knew Greek and Latin as well. Indeed, his sense of these languages surpassed that of the grammarians of his time. Clearly, Abelard was kindred to Crates of Thebes as a man who transcended time and season. Prior to his studies at the cathedral schools of St. Genevieve and Notre Dame, Abelard fatefully encountered the nominalism of Roscelin. Thus infected by an urgency to disputation, Abelard challenged William of Champeaux, the head of the school at St. Genevieve. He had little trouble in silencing him, and he immediately acquired a large following. The authorities refused to recognize his supremacy and denied him a mastership in the cathedral, whereupon he left Paris and established himself as a master of philosophy in nearby Melun.

His fame spread, and his confidence soared. Soon he returned to Paris and with the righteousness of the self-anointed established his own chair within the precincts of St. Genevieve on the south bank of the Seine. His fame as a teacher continued to spread; he continued to study; and, at last, by popular demand, Abelard was permitted to lecture as a master of theology in the Schools of Notre Dame. Thousands from all parts of Italy, Germany, France, and England came to hear him. Testimony to the greatness of his oratorical prowess is unanimous. A vision of Abelard, a tall, graceful figure standing in master's robes holding the enraptured attention of hundreds seated and standing about him has haunted the imagination of any who study the epic events of western education. No one, it has been said, reasoned more subtly than he, and no one used the dialectical tool with greater address. The ardor of his life, the charm and grace of his person, are revealed in the letters of his beloved Heloise who loved him with an "immoderate love." She remained faithful to their all too brief relationship until both of their lives ended.

The details of their personal tragedy and persecution are recorded in many accounts of human infamy. They need not be detailed here, but they add poignancy to the romance of the university and detract nothing from the greatness of Abelard. He was a human voice which challenged the sanctimonious, sacerdotal pronouncements of the church. In his hands all became smooth, easy, and simple. It is said that he reduced theology to philosophy and morality to humanity.

Tradition holds that twenty of his students became cardinals and more than fifty became bishops. He wrote with clarity, reducing all questions to their logical essentials. To Abelard, reason and not revelation ruled philosophy. As a logician he raised questions which in themselves demanded answers. Prior to Abelard the *docendi* (teaching license) was authorized by ecclesiastical authority. After him masters demanded the privilege of issuing the licenses to teach. They won this privilege in 1200, and at that moment the modern academic profession was born. When the masters earned the right to control admission to their own guild, the university was born, the modern academic profession was founded, and relations between the church and the academic community would never be the same.

Further details on the romance of the medieval university belong in an essay devoted exclusively to that topic.[9] It is important to note here that after the Charter of the University of Paris was issued in the year 1200 A.D. the basic "ground rules" for the intellectual life were changed. A kind of academic freedom had been won. The victory was not yet secure. The Charter of Paris was the first beachhead of academic freedom in the western world. It was not won easily; but, once it was won, the masters found themselves possessed of a responsibility for self-examination. The battles before them were still uphill, but there would be no retreat, and in the retrospect of nearly nine centuries there has been no retreat. The university as an enclave of immunity for the examination of truth had been born. But there were perilous days ahead.

The realist-nominalist controversy was not ended. No resolution of the dramatic dissension among the medieval schoolmen had been achieved. Could free minds, powered by free wills, working together in freedom, reach the higher ground upon which the terrible breach between theology and philosophy could be healed? The fifty-year interval after the year 1200 included many discouraging moments. There was dissent, violence, and dispersion. On one of the latter occasions a sufficient number of masters left the university to establish a new institution at the English market town of Oxford. Many of these never returned and Oxford became a university in its own right. Yet, in 1250 the University of Paris was stronger than ever, although diversity of opinion among the schoolmen was never greater. It appeared that scholastic philosophy as a synthesis of the ancients and the Christian was doomed. But some of the greatest scholars of the Christian era were in residence at Paris during that time, or shortly before or afterward. From Italy there were Bonaventura and Thomas Aquinas, from Germany there was Albert the Great. From England there were Alexander of Hales, Roger Bacon, Duns Scotus, and William of Ockham.

Scholars of medieval philosophy give vivid accounts of the speculations each of these men offered in regard to the issues of their time. These accounts are so colorful in their own right and so greatly imbued with interest that the writer of any account of their presence is greatly tempted to explore details. However, the plan of this chapter is directed toward exposition of the influence of the medieval schoolmen on educational thought and practice. For this reason we must look with special interest upon the life and works of Thomas Aquinas. Of all the medieval schoolmen who struggled at the task, Thomas achieved the synthesis which again placed philosophy and theology in a harmonious relationship. His views were challenged by Bonaventura and Scotus, but Thomas won the verdict of posterity. Thomas fashioned what came to be called the "supreme synthesis." His doctrines soon became identified by the name Thomism, and later the casual student of medieval philosophy came to associate the term scholasticism with Thomism. Thomism is probably one of the most profound and by general agreement the most influential of the several expressions of scholastic philosophy.

We now recognize that Thomas Aquinas through his doctrines has more to say about the operation of modern schools than any of the other schoolmen. This being the case it is desirable that modern educators examine this affable, humble, brilliant Italian philosopher in greater detail. One who works in modern education should know the basic presuppositions of Thomism. More American public educators are Thomistic than anyone suspects. Through Thomas, scholastic philosophy achieved a respectability which has endured. There is no small irony in the fact that of all his contemporaries only his teacher, Albert the Great, appears to have suspected there was such transcending greatness in his work.

The Angelic Doctor

As a hulking youth of eighteen he was so reticent and stolid that his fellow students at the University reportedly nicknamed him "dumb ox."[10] Thomas Aquinas, as a young man, would accept this smilingly. His biographers reveal him to be a man of humble and pacific temperament, almost totally without vanity. Such was the nature of a man later to be a recognized genius in both religion and philosophy. Of all the philosophers of Christendom perhaps only Augustine himself had a greater impact on the Christian church and all that it reaches. He is revered as a man of great piety, immense intellect, and vast learning. His stature as a thinker, teacher, and scholar places him among the greatest minds of all time.

If his fellow students did not suspect this prospect in him, they were not alone. His family wanted him to do other things. As things were in those times St. Thomas was of high birth. He was born to a great Neopolitan feudal family, at the Castle of Roccasecca, halfway between Naples and Rome. Nearby is the town of Aquino and somewhat beyond this is the village Cassino. High on the hill above Cassino is the famous monastery so vivid in the memories of American soldiers whose advance on Rome was blocked by that eminence during the Second World War. Few sensitive men of civil sentiments can forget the heart-wrenching deeds which left Monte Cassino a ruin. Part of the anguish of that necessity grew from remembrance that behind those great walls the five-year-old Thomas of Aquino began his schooling.

Thomas' father, the Count of Aquino, surely had no idea that the Benedictine friars of Monte Cassino would instill in his son the tastes and dispositions of a great theologian and philosopher. There is abundant reason to suppose that the father had something else in mind.[11] The child remained nine years at the Abbey, which included one of the best libraries of those times, and these years within the influence of a Benedictine environment in which "humanism, science, and religion formed an indivisible whole cannot have failed to have left deep traces upon his mind."[12] Perhaps he would have remained longer, but Monte Cassino was called upon to endure wars even in those days, and Emperor Frederick II as part of his continuing contest with the Pope expelled the monks from that sanctuary.

Thomas was fourteen at the time, and he was forthwith sent to the recently founded University at Naples where presumably he was exposed to the Neapolitan version of the "trivium" and "quadrivium." More significantly however, it can be presumed that the scholars at Naples had access to recently translated Greek and Arabic works which were unavailable in cities more responsive to the wishes of the Pope. The Count of Aquino died in 1203, and a few months after his father's passing, Thomas decided to enter the Order of St. Dominic.

The meaning of this decision and its shock to the family is easily inferred. The Dominicans accepted as their special vocation the task of cultivating the sciences and teaching them in public.[13] It was not the Dominican intention to remain within the fortresslike walls of monasteries. This order rose with the medieval university and set for itself the task of serving God by teaching in poverty. But as a group the Dominican friars situated themselves among other teachers. When Thomas took on the Dominican habit, a family hope was evidently crushed. It is believed that his brothers, as did their father before them, aspired to make Thomas the Abbot of Monte Cassino, thus tightening the family's political hold on that particular area. So self-evident was the family opposition to Thomas' association with the Dominicans that the Master-General of the Dominican order sent him away, ultimately assigning him to study at the University of Paris.

During his journey to Paris Thomas was attacked by his brothers and locked up for a year. He reportedly spent this time in study and prayer, and thus reduced his adversaries to disgust and despair. When finally released, he continued to Paris, entered the University in 1245, and three years later commenced six years of graduate study under Albert the Great of Germany. In the final years of their association Thomas assisted Albert in founding a *studium generale* at Cologne. He returned to the University of Paris in 1252 and within four years won the Master of Theology degree and the Licentiate in Theology[14] (doctor of theology).

It is important to consider again what the University of Paris was like during Thomas' student days. As a corporation the university was nearing its fiftieth year of existence although the student nations and scholarly guilds were much older. The Charter of 1200 A.D. was itself a concession to the secular teachers, but the struggle did not end with its enactment. The seculars had won large measures of legal authority, but the religious orders (Franciscan and Dominican) had the support of the church and usually of the municipal officers of the city. On matters of philosophical doctrine the masters of theology invoked Augustinian Platonism as the standard for knowing truth and determining error. The secular teacher, the masters of arts, law, medicine, mathematics and astronomy, etc., tended to advocate the Judaic and Islamic interpretations of Aristotle. Thus when the groups were not quarreling over corporate prerogatives they were at war over doctrine. When the secular teachers called for united action the theologians, particularly the Dominicans, often went their own way. When the masters of arts demanded intellectual freedom the theologians responded, in effect, that no one should be free to err. This struggle went on for decades but it was at its peak in the years Thomas was a student.

His career as a producing scholar had already begun. Even before his terminal degree he was producing commentaries on earlier medieval writers. Before long he turned to Aristotle and authored thirteen commentaries on Aristotle's works.[15] In all, thirty-six books ranging across virtually every contemporary issue in theology or philosophy came from his pen.[16] However, students of education give closest attention to two of his summaries, *Summa Contra Gentiles* (Summary against the Gentiles) and *Summa Theologica* (Summary of Theology). The former is presumed to have been written to assist Christian scholars who were in ideological contention with the Islamic and Judaic traditions then emanating from areas of Spain which had been long under Moorish domination. It includes, among many other things, a demonstration that the Christian faith does rest upon rational foundations and that applications of Aristotelian methods do not necessarily lead to a view of the world which excludes Christianity. The *Summa Theologica* is a book prepared for students. Most of it was composed in Italy and during Thomas' final stay at the University of Paris. He never quite finished it.

To understand the position Thomas was in during his professorial years one should keep in mind three groups. The first was the secular masters, many of whom were Averroists and sympathetic to the new nominalism. Averroism was a philosophical doctrine which interpreted Aristotle as a materialist and Aristotle's theology as depicting an impersonal, indifferent God having no conscious part in the creation of man. Understandably opposition to this was shared by the other two of the three groups, one the Dominican Order and the other the Franciscan Order. The Dominicans, to which Thomas belonged, were more independent than the Franciscans.[17] When the Dominicans appeared in a university they tended to operate as a sub-corporation often voting and acting independently. This, of course, would have irritated the remainder of the masters. The Franciscans tended to be aligned with the more conservative religious elements and the church administration. In respect to theological doctrine the Dominicans apparently were more open-minded toward Aristotelian methods and more tolerant of dissent than Franciscans.[18]

Thomas taught at Paris as a Dominican professor until 1259. He then left Paris and taught at the Papal court until 1268 where he encountered the famous translator, William of Moerbeke. Of all the medieval schoolmen Moerbeke was probably the greatest authority on the languages of the ancient Greeks. He gave Aquinas great assistance and fresh insight into the study of Aristotle. In 1269 Thomas returned to Paris where he remained until 1272. Following this he was sent to Naples to help found a Dominican school. In 1274 he was summoned by Pope Gregory to attend the Council of Lyons which was aimed at resolving differences between the churches of the east and the west. On the way to Lyons he died. He was then only forty-nine years of age.[19]

Thomas was firstly a theologian and secondly a philosopher. His philosophy which is called *Thomism*, far from contradicting his theology, supports and sustains it. Thomism uses Aristotelian methods; and it adopts the Aristotelian doctrines of cause, motion, and hierarchy. It also employs elements of Platonism and Neo-Platonism, and frequently resorts to Augustinian sentiments. However, it is not a patchwork of parts and pieces. It is a highly original synthesis composed by a man of extraordinary mind and spirit who clearly moved the vexing problem of reason versus faith to the higher ground of compatibility. This is why Thomas stands at least a shade taller than the other great men who shared with him that dramatic era when our modern universities came into being.

Thomas may have been somehow destined for this task. He was a Lombard nobleman; and even enclosed in friar's robes, this meant something. Family ties such as his were widely respected. He was physically large and strong, and we are informed his presence was commanding. Yet his disposition was even. Professors of his time often engaged in public disputations with their peers. These confrontations were not taken lightly. Academic careers were often made or broken by such events. A theologian whose doctrines were based on Aristotelian methods would be challenged by both the secular and the religious teachers. As might be expected, Thomas was continually embroiled with the Averroests. He was also challenged by the Franciscans, most notably Bonaventura and John Peckham. He was challenged within his own order by the prominent Dominican Robert Kilwardy.

Again it must be remembered that the master of arts of the Paris faculty had been won over to the realism of Averroes who had interpreted Aristotle as preeminently a materialist. The theologians, particularly the Franciscans, were partisans of the Augustinian interpretations of Plato. Thomas was constantly assaulted on one side by the radical Aristotelians and on the other by the Absolute Augustinians. The Aristotle he discovered and taught was the basis of a new Christian posture. "This is the narrow ridge on which St. Thomas moved with incomparable sureness."[20] He did it so brilliantly and smoothly that we may not fully appreciate the magnitude of the feat.

Thomas' academic life was indeed one of controversy. And in the fullness of time this added to the respect and approbation accorded his person. He never lost his temper even in the most strenuous of debates. In public disputation wherein some exceed the bonds of civility he was humble and considerate. Once at the Paris schools when he was in public debate, John Peckham, the Franciscan, proved to be especially pompous and provocative. According to an eyewitness account, Peckham spoke with "swelling and sounding words and exasperated the said Thomas." But, the account continues, "never did Thomas lose his temper, but always answered the said John with kindness and suavity. And the same thing did the said Thomas in all disputations, however acute and heated they became."[21]

Within a few years after Thomas died the Domincans (much to Peckham's disgust) were pronouncing his opinions as those of the whole order. The Franciscan dissent continued on a milder scale as the issues broadened. Bonaventura continued urging faith, love, and the Augustinian "inner man" as preeminent in the Christian doctrine; but as years wore on the church grew more comfortable with the high place Thomas gave to reason. Thomas was canonized less than fifty years after his death, and for much of the subsequent history of the Roman church his doctrines were strongly sanctioned. His shrine became a pilgrimage and services and hymns were composed in his honor. Across the years leaders of the church have encouraged the application of his doctrines to the problems of a Christian life, and his memory has been exalted by the name "Angelic Doctor."

Thomistic Ontology

So frequently and sharply do specialists in Thomistic philosophy differ on the correct approach to an exposition of Thomistic ontology that a generalist trembles at the prospect. It must be remembered,

some argue, that St. Thomas was first a theologian and then a philosopher. Those who bear this in mind insist that the way to understand
Thomas is to follow the path which he made. Therefore, one begins
with his description of God as a creator. Others point out that the distinctive aspects of Thomas' work are those which build upon Aristotelian outlines; and, accordingly, they urge that the student begin with the
elements of Aristotelian philosophy which appear in Thomistic doctrines. Because one of the foregoing chapters dealt with Aristotle, the
latter of these alternatives is chosen here.

Aquinas borrowed extensively from Aristotle's metaphysics, but
that which he borrowed he quickly transformed. Thomas appeared
willing to accept being *qua* being just about the way Aristotle described it. Matter (potentiality) is becoming formed (actuality).
Matter and form in active combination constitute essence, and all is
moving because intellect (unmoved mover) is thinking, and this
thinking continues as the unmoved source of motion. Aquinas, in addition to this conception, had the benefit of Neo-Platonic explorations of
the "above being" and world soul, relation of thought to object, and
emanational conception of the efficient cause.

It must be remembered that Aristotle takes objects for the most
part as he finds them, and he finds them already in existence. He sees
them simply as prime matter being formed or constantly becoming.
They have no metaphysical status apart from the source of their
motion. But Aquinas, on the other hand, asks how objects come into
being. Aristotle's explanation of cause reveals some confusion between
cause and principle,[22] and it does not explain the *being* of an object as
opposed to its *non-being*.

To state it simply, if less rigorously, Aquinas invoked his faith that
objects had to be created. He accepted the revelational doctrine that
the world was brought into its condition of being from non-being.[23]
Aristotle's being *qua* being neglects to deal with the simple but
massive fact that the world exists, and there is no apparent reason
why it must exist. Except for the act that produced its existence, the
world could very well not exist.

Therefore, the efficient cause is existence itself. Here we have
existence *qua* existence. What is existence? It is God. But contrary to
Aristotle, Aquinas has God as a creator. By thought, God has conceived
essences; however, neither the prime matter nor the form which together compose essence have corporeal reality until God endows it
with existence. God, as creator, brings the world into being from non-
being. Creation is pure act, not a conversion or a production of some-

thing out of something. It is an act of divine will, and God's will is an aspect of His understanding.

Before centering further on the theological premise we must consider the clarification Aquinas made between principle and cause. "A principle deals with the order of one thing to another from which the latter proceeds in any manner whatsoever, whether this procession be one of magnitude, time, motion, simple origin, knowledge or dependence."[24] Cause, on the other hand, implies a certain influx into the being of the thing caused. For example, the father may be the principle of the son in the sense that he is the beginning of the son, but the son is free to go anywhere. However the motion of a baseball bat is the cause of motion in the batted ball. The ball includes the motion but can only go in the direction and at the speed which the cause impelled. God as the cause of the world gives its direction motion and purpose and the world is not free of the act which caused it. This distinction enabled St. Thomas to revise Aristotle's concept of the efficient cause to include the kind of cause by which there is an influx of the causal agent into the world. Thus the world is not indeterminate. It is determined, it has a destiny, and is, therefore, teleological. Here he joins St. Augustine in saying that God is not like someone who builds a house and can then leave it alone. Finite things have a constant existential dependence on the creator.[25]

This, then, enables creation to be explained as simply the influx of existence into essence. Thomas' clarification of principle and cause allows Aristotle's suggestion of hierarchy to become more explicit. All things are brought from non-being into being by adding existence to essence. But existence is the element which determines station in the hierarchy. It may be convenient to think of existence as a variable degree of motion.[26] A stone, for example, has essence but could be said to have little existence and, therefore, little being. A bush with life processes, blossoms, flowers, and the like can be thought of as having more existence and, therefore, higher being. An animal which moves about, seeks food, and builds a shelter is still higher in the hierarchy of existence. Man, because he reasons, is an even higher being. God has infused this much more of existence into man. The angels are above man. Aquinas argued that they have no corporeality and in the hierarchy stand next to God. They are pure spirit and their presence is known not only by revelation but also by reason, "for without them there would be an obvious gap in the plan of creation and the continuity of creatures would be broken."[27] The hierarchy, of course, is consummated by God Who Is. As in Aristotle, God is his own necessity and God is intellect. However, in Aquinas the intellect is also creative, willful, and knowing. But these are not multiple qualities. All that God is or does is encompassed in the word understanding. His act of understanding must be His essence and His existence.

By this remarkable combination of Aristotelian, Platonic, and Augustinian ideas Thomas achieved the higher ground of synthesis. God, however, is necessary to the synthesis, and recognizing that many of his time were disinclined to accept the hypothesis of God's reality on the basis of faith, Aquinas developed five rational proofs of God's reality. These he offered in the same ontological style as the proofs by St. Anselm. At the conclusion of each he declared *and all know this to be God.* These proofs are included in many commentaries and are not, in their nature, of specific interest to teachers.

Ontologically, Thomism is distinguishable from Aristotelianism because objects are metaphysical in that not only do they have essence, they also have existence. It is an existentialist philosophy in the traditional (not modern) sense. Existence combined with essence constitutes being. Because existence is a variable as to species, being is hierarchical, and the lower members of the hierarchy exist for the sake of the higher, e.g., earth for grass, grass for cow, cow for man, man for angels, and angels for God. Many do not recognize how profoundly western man believes in hierarchy until, of course, they reflect on how much pleasure he takes in a good steak, or, for that matter, a hamburger.

Thomistic Epistemology

In a treatise he called *On Spiritual Creatures,*[28] Aquinas presents a history of the knowledge problem. His careful consideration of the issues raised by the philosophers of antiquity reveals his profound grasp of the problem. After consideration of the alternatives he again chose to build from Aristotelian foundations. This is not because he was ignorant of the others; but, again, because the Aristotelian syntax was the correct one for aligning faith and reason as consorts in knowing. As in his ontological propositions he was obliged to "thread the needle" to avoid either Averroest or Augustinian dogmas.

Aquinas believes that men can begin the search for truth with sense knowledge.[29] He recognizes the problems this poses. Things as they appear to our senses do move or change constantly. Men who observe are different and, therefore, will observe differently. Some men are more reliable observers than others. Yet there is stability in the way things change. "The philosopher," as Aquinas customarily referred to Aristotle, shows ways by which essences and principles are recognized. These do not change, they are reliable, and they foretell other changes which will occur. Therefore, even appearances have a kind of truth, and the observer must train himself to recognize it.

Aquinas agreed with the corrections Aristotle proposed for Plato's doctrine of ideas. He agreed that we do not know truth by means of ideas existing apart from the sensible world, but by the illumination of intellect. This is the capacity of our minds to abstract principles from sensible things. Now, is this intellect a single thing in which all men share, or does each man have an intellect of his own? Thomas believed the latter to be true.[30] In this he differed from Averroes, who interpreted Aristotle as having said that all men are, in varying degrees, "tuned in" on a single intelligence. On the contrary, Aquinas asserts that each man has his own agent intellect.[31] His metaphorical description of the individual intellect is that it is "the light created by God in our soul." At this point he stands on Augustinian grounds. Mind perceives matter, but mind is more than matter.

His psychology is mystical but explicit. When something appears in our senses an interior image is formed called a phantasm. It is this that enables us to picture the things which we see. A phantasm is, in effect, a miniature likeness of anything which has appeared in the exterior senses.[32] The agent intellect does its work by abstracting the universal from the phantasm. For example, the eye "sees" a man. The moment this happens a phantasm or image of the man forms in the interior senses. This phantasm combines with a germ of knowledge on the nature of man which pre-exists in the soul. Now as the phantasm combines with this seminal or pre-existing (a priori) principle a *perception* results. A *conception* forms as the intellect detaches the universal from the perception. The germs of knowledge are, in a sense, dormant until stimulated by the phantasm. When the two combine in perception, the universal can be separated in conception. The difficulty in comprehending this, of course, is that no psycho-physiological mechanism exists to explain how the detachment occurs. We are left simply with metaphorical descriptions of how the faculty abstracts the intelligible and proves the sensible.[33] Now if the man the eye has "seen" is conceived as a young, tall, and contented man, then we assume the intellect has abstracted the universal on the nature of man with clarity sufficient to warrant the conception of youngness, tallness, and contentedness. Forming conceptions of this kind is the first task of the intellect. In the Aristotelian sense it is the determination of *essence,* and it is the first of the two basic operations the intellect performs.

The second corresponds to the other constituent of created being, namely, *existence.*[34] The intellectual task which corresponds with existence is that of judgment. If the tall young man in the above example is conceived to exist as perceived, that is a simple judgment. However, when the issue moves to an evaluation of modes of existence—as, for example, whether our man is honest, whether he is a leader, or whether he is strong—the form of judgment is complex and involves interpolation of universals. Here the intellect has moved beyond the simple issue of essence and has ventured upon judgments about modes of existence or being.

The test for truth is correspondence. The intellect is true when it corresponds with that which is. Accordingly, one *knows* when his judgment corresponds with the existential state of affairs being judged. The Thomistic doctrine of knowing, therefore, is consistent with its doctrine of being. The object in a state of being is noted by the exterior senses; the interior senses are activated to a perception and a conception of the essence of the object that emerges. After this a judgment is found as to the mode of its existence. The operation is rational and the test of its outcome is the correspondence of the judgment with what is. If judgment and being correspond, then the intellect is true and knowledge has been achieved.

How does one develop the intellect? The answer to this is the leading issue of Thomistic education. The intellect must be trained in perception, conception, logic, and evaluation. One whose intellect is distinguished by these qualities is well educated. Also of interest is the innate goodness of intellectual activity. This is what man does apart from all other corporeal creatures. It is his genus distinction and his God-like characteristic. Hence, when a trained intellect is intellectualizing properly, it is, by definition, moving toward existence, toward God, and toward the good.[35]

Thomistic Axiology

The key to understanding the Thomistic notion of good is the teleology of the system. One must take notice of the direction in which all things are faced, and toward which all things tend to move. In Thomism all things tend toward God, and God is intellect. The terminology used in discussing the moral standard is again Aristotelian.

Aristotle suggested that the final cause of an object is that for which it exists. In other words the final cause is the purpose of the object. Aquinas presents the final cause of all things as intellect. All things exist in relation to intellect. Therefore, rationalism is exalted as the moral standard.[36]

When this is applied to the commonplace judgments which men and women make in the world it means that the good in almost every case is determined by reasoning. This is because when a man is reasoning he is doing that for which he exists; his use of reason is a turning toward the good, and the valuations he performs which are rational are good. Conversely, valuations which are either irrational or nonrational are a turning away from the good. Thus, in order to achieve the good one turns toward the source of reflection and away from the source of sensation. In this way one keeps aligned with the moral purpose of the universe.

The applications of this to the Christian life are almost self-evident. One constantly evaluates his conduct rationally and makes judgments about it. Confession, which in the Roman church is a more formal activity than in most protestant congregations, has its subject matter in the judgments a reasoning Christian makes about his own personal conduct. In the Thomistic syntax the good really begins prior to the confession and any imposed penance. The good begins when the Christian commences his rational valuation and produces rational judgments about himself.

Now by this Aquinas is not challenging revealed moral commandments. However, when the meaning of such a commandment is not explicit in a given situation, reason is the instrument by which clarity is achieved. And in the commonplace transactions between people, the ethical standards which illuminate the rightness of everyday acts are revealed through reason. As to the protest that motivation dominates reason, the Thomist responds that motives, when subjected to an authentic test of reason, must perforce be revealed as goodness or lack of goodness. A rational man will not accept a motive which is not good. Thus the role of schooling in producing rational men looms larger and larger as the place of reason becomes preeminent.

Is *reason* as proposed by St. Thomas a metaethical standard? This is a debatable point. Reason is *ipso facto* good. Thus it fills one of the basic requirements for a metaethical standard. However, if it could be shown that reason can justify an act which God has revealed to be not good, one must assume that Aquinas, the theologian, would in such a case rule against reason. The fact that Thomas foresaw no logical possibility of such a conflict does not rule it out. Therefore, it can be ruled out only on grounds of faith. That is, faith in the proposition that God is, and God is intellect. Because such faith is necessary, Thomistic reason probably should be considered as a normative standard rather than a metaethical standard.

The Thomistic standard for beauty is not easily identified.[37] Turning to the *Summa Theologica* it is found that Aquinas also relates beatitude to the first cause. Beauty like the good flows from the purpose of all things. Thus, once again, we are compelled to contemplate the nature of God. God is the uncreated creator. Gilson reasons at this point as follows:

> Doubtless the cause or object of beatitude is, as just established, something uncreated. But the essence of beatitude, i.e., the acquisition and enjoyment of man of the last end is something human, and consequently something created . . . this operation belongs to the human intellect to the exclusion of every other power of the soul.[38]

Thus to man the essence of beauty is in and of the creative operation of the human intellect. The speculative human intellect turns toward the source of intellect. Now man in his corporeal state cannot apprehend God. But he hungers for this apprehension. This hunger is also his hunger for beauty. True or ultimate beauty is, therefore, not attainable by man in his mortal state. The closest he can come to true beauty is in those experiences of the speculative intellect which approach the divine.[39]

This leaves the status of the arts entirely in the intellectual domain. Sensual appeal is barred. Appeals to the sense find their response in the bodily will and not in intellectual speculation. A man may be charmed by an appeal to his senses or he may be attracted by an appeal to his animal passions, but sense experience is not an experience in beautitude.[40] Beauty in the lingual, musical, figural, or performed arts can only result if the art in question stirs the individual intellect to a higher point in its unending quest to apprehend the ultimate intellect. Thus the mind of man approaches beauty when it moves creatively toward that one form of being which is uncreated.

Now it is doubted if man can achieve this except possibly in rare cases. There are cases where men are supposed to have had "heavenly visions." Many of these can be and are viewed skeptically by the critical examiner. But even the most dubious of the doubters are moved to wonder at the reported experience of St. Thomas himself. He was a humble man of faith who would not seek to aggrandize himself in the eyes of other men. He was a careful and systematic thinker. Shortly before he died he is said to have been transported to a new dimension of experience which moved him afterward to remark that all he had thought and written before was like so much straw.

Thomism in Education

In considering Thomism in education two preliminary points must be considered. The first is that Aquinas was a teacher himself and a very good one. At the University of Paris he was in open comparison with the very best the world of that time had to offer, and he is reported to have been unsurpassed. Of such a man we can expect that his writings—i.e., the way they are organized and phrased —would reveal much of his theory of education and of his pedagogical methods.

The second point deals with Thomism as a perennial theory of education. The neustic force of the term perennial is such that most of the education profession takes it to mean that all doctrines are settled and the school which adopts them continues in the same way year after year. This view becomes reinforced in those whose casual perusal of Thomistic philosophy brings them face to face with Aquinas' pronouncements about the soul and the characteristics of angels. However, Thomism as it has developed in history is more of an orientation toward philosophical problems rather than something like a programmed computer which turns out pre-set answers to philosophical problems. For example, a modern existentialist may use Thomistic methods in coming to terms with the problems of personal existence. A phenomenologist may report in a Thomistic style the data of consciousness. Analytical philosophers find in Aquinas' work some exemplary approaches to the issues of ambiguity in discourse.

Thomas wrote in the Middle Ages. Since then new scientific, social, and religious traditions have emerged. Aquinas in his day was regarded as an innovator, and it is reasonable to assume that were he with us today he would be an innovator. It is the innovator that is perennial and not the philosophy, and there have been innovators who followed Aquinas in his habits and style of innovation. This is why the Neo-Thomism of today claims to be as modern a philosophy of education as any. If the tradition of perennial innovation remains within Thomism, then Thomism, as a philosophy, will be perennially modern.

The continuing goal of Thomistic education is to train the intellect. This is the fixed star in the perennialist theory. The ecclesiastical Thomist will still insist that this is because God is intellect. The Neo-Thomist may not insist that the term God be used. Nevertheless he will use intellect as the ultimate. Now, how does one train the intellect? Aquinas himself seems to be very close to Augustine on the manner of teaching methods. He tends to substitute interior faculties for Augustine's inner man, and this perhaps accounts for his greater emphasis on logic and systematic exposition than upon internal experiences which are ecstatic or inspirational. Aquinas wants man to be under the control of reason and wants him to put his faith in the notion that this is the way to God.

In later times, Thomistic educators begin placing greater emphasis on habit formation, particularly at elementary school levels. This coheres with that part of Thomistic philosophy which suggests that habit is a vital aspect of learning, and control of sensual or animal tendencies can be achieved by habit. If such tendencies toward reason are habitually engendered, the child is on the correct path to a life of intellect. In terms of specific elementary school practices this advocates school uniforms, physical controls, and drill. At higher levels it advocates faculty disciplines as theoretically given through the study of logic, grammar, geometry, and highly structured programs in literature, physical science, and history.

In more recent years some Thomists, partially under the sway of evolutionary doctrines, have begun to revise educational theories in the direction of an "educational naturalism." Under the slogan that "things work together" they have softened the rigors of habit formation. However, they are saved from becoming outright pragmatists by the central fact that intellect remains the goal of education. However, they do not hold with the same strict definitions of intellect as characterized by Thomistic education in previous centuries. Stemming from Aquinas' assertion that each individual includes an agent intellect there appears to be a growing conviction that individual intellects may exert different tendencies, and this is not to be discouraged. Because such disparate tendencies respond to social and cultural forces, the drill and order of the classroom is softened, the school is more in the world and the school is more open to the world and the problems and aspirations of the people who are in it. Teachers are less severe, and their demands of individual students show a respect for differences. However, intellect remains the goal.

In higher education this trend is reflected in an unstructuring of the curriculum in favor of such innovations as the "great books" programs. Through such programs rudiments of analysis are used to probe the recognized work of civilization's most intellectual representatives. Students explore the best that has been thought and said. This is a concession to freedom, something which Aquinas recognized and appreciated. A change such as this is recognized as being an innovation in the direction of an improved intellectualism. It is clear that these neo-perennialist, Neo-Thomistic educational practices are developed as stronger forms of Thomism rather than as an abandonment of the Thomistic standard.

So Thomism is a perennial philosophy, but not in the sense that the term perennial is commonly used. Aquinas is a philosopher in the tradition of Aristotle. As a schoolman his scholastic philosophy is the middle way between the old way of the Platonistic Franciscans as exemplified by Duns Scotus and the new way of the nominalists such as Roscellinus and Ockham.[41] The de facto connection Thomism has to Catholicism should not obscure its relevance to education in general. Thomism has been and can continue to be a basis for innovation in education. Teachers who feel that philosophical theories must stand upon the changing hypothesis of the physical and social sciences will view Thomism simply as one of several vital traditions in the history of western civilization. But, as Copleston declared:

> . . . to those who think that philosophical reflection is grounded in common experience and that metaphysics has a connection to this experience it (Thomism) can be a source of constant stimulus and inspiration.[42]

Notes

1. Shapiro, Medieval Philosophy (New York: Random House, Inc., The Modern Library Edition, 1964), p. 42.
2. Ibid., p. 85.
3. Thomas Woody, Liberal Education for Free Men (Philadelphia: The University of Pennsylvania Press, 1950), p. 98.
4. Ibid., p. 99.
5. E. Brehaut, An Encyclopedist of the Dark Ages, Isidore of Seville (New York: Columbia University, 1912), p. 261.
6. E. Dickinson, Music in the History of the Western Church (New York: Charles Scribner's Sons, 1925), p. 65.
7. Fred Bratton, Maimonides (Boston: Beacon Press, 1967), p. 4.
8. James Mulhern, A History of Education (New York: The Ronald Press Co., 1946), p. 291.

9. A definitive work is Hastings Rashdall, *The Universities of Europe in the Middle Ages* (Oxford: Clarendon Press, 1936), 3 volumes.
10. Eugene Freidman, Joseph Owens, *The Wisdom and Ideas of St. Thomas Aquinas* (New York: Fawcett World Library, 1968), p. 11.
11. Etienne Gilson, *The Philosophy of St. Thomas Aquinas*, (St. Louis, Mo.: B. Herder Book Co., 1939), p. 2.
12. *Ibid.*
13. *Ibid.*
14. *Ibid.*, p. 5.
15. *Ibid.*, p. 10.
16. *Ibid.*
17. F. C. Copleston, *Aquinas* (Baltimore, Md.: Penguin Books, Inc., 1967), p. 12.
18. T. F. Tout, *The Place of St. Thomas in History*, included in *St. Thomas Aquinas* (Oxford: Basil Blackwell, 1925), p. 13.
19. Fredric K. Copleston, *A History of Philosophy* (London: Burns, Oates, and Washbourne, Ltd., 1954), p. 303.
20. Gilson, *op. cit.*, p. 18.
21. Tout, *op. cit.*, pp. 23, 24.
22. Francis Meehan, *Efficient Causality in Aristotle and St. Thomas* (Washington, D.C.: The Catholic University of America Press, 1940), pp. 170-171.
23. *Summa Theologica*, 1a, 46, 2.
24. *Ibid.*
25. *Summa Contra Gentiles*, III, 65.
26. Stephen Schafer, *Education and the Philosophies of Matter* (Bethlehem, Pa.: Lehigh University, 1968), p. 33.
27. Armand Maurer, *Medieval Philosophy* (New York: Random House, Inc., 1962), p. 175.
28. *De Spiritualibus Creaturis.*
29. *Summa Theologica*, 1a, 1, 9.
30. *Summa Theologica*, 1a, 76, 2.
31. *Ibid.*
32. *Summa Theologica*, 1, 85, 1.
33. *Ibid.*, 1, 84.5.
34. Maurer, *op. cit.*, p. 184.
35. *Summa Theologica*, 1a, 13, 2.
36. *Summa Contra Gentiles*, III, 9.
37. Schafer, *op. cit.*, p. 40.
38. Gilson, *op. cit.*, p. 340.
39. *Summa Theologica*, I. 32, I.
40. *Summa Contra Gentiles*, III, 33.
41. Copleston, *Aquinas, op. cit.*, p. 243-244.
42. *Ibid.*, p. 264.

Other Reading

Abelson, P. *The Seven Liberal Arts.* New York: Teachers College, Columbia University, 1906.

Adler, Mortimer, and Milton Mayer. *The Revolution in Education*. Chicago: The University of Chicago Press, 1958.

Bestor, Arthur. *Educational Wastelands*. Urbana: University of Illinois Press, 1953.

Bratton, Fred G. *Maimonides, Medisert Modernist*. Boston: Beacon Press, 1967, pp. 3-105.

Copleston, Fredrick. *Aquinas*. Baltimore: Penguin Books, Inc., 1967, pp. 17-243.

——————. *A History of Philosophy, Medieval Philosophy*. London: Burns, Oates, and Washbourne, Ltd., 1950, pp. 302-423. Volume II.

Gilson, Etienne. *The Philosophy of St. Thomas Aquinas*. St. Louis: B. Herder Book Co., 1939.

Hampsch, John H. "Integrative Determinants in the Philosophy of Education of St. Thomas Aquinas," *Educational Theory*, IX (January 1956), pp. 31-40.

Hutchins, Robert. *The Conflict in Education in a Democratic Society*. New York: Harper and Bros., 1953.

Maurer, Armand A. *Medieval Philosophy*. New York: Random House, 1962, pp. 137-237.

McCall, Raymond J. "The Autonomy of Education: A Thomistic View," *Educational Theory I* (December 1951), pp. 248-250.

McGuken, William J. *Catholic Education: Its Philosophy, Its Fundamentals, Its Objectives*. New York: The American Press, pp. 1-40.

Meehan, Francis. *Efficient Causality in St. Thomas*. Washington, D.C.: The Catholic University of America Press, 1940. Chapters III-V.

Owens, Joseph. *St. Thomas and the Future of Metaphysics*. Milwaukee: Marquette University Press, 1957, pp. 1-61.

Pace, E. A. "St. Thomas Theory of Education." Catholic University Bulletin, VII (July 1902), pp. 290-303.

Schafer, Stephen. *Education and the Philosophies of Matter*. Bethlehem, Pa.: Lehigh University, 1969.

Woody, Thomas. *Liberal Education for Free Men*. Philadelphia: University of Pennsylvania, 1951, pp. 59-131.

Vout, T. F. *The Place of St. Thomas in History*. Oxford: Basil Blackwell, 1925, pp. 1-33.

CHAPTER VIII

European Idealism

A scheme for exposition of a single tradition in philosophy forces upon the writer certain sorrows. At no other point is the decision that this text will deal only with highlights more difficult than now. For now we must pass over, in relative silence, the later years in medieval philosophy. The new universities attracted thought of all kinds, and philosophy, particularly the various derivatives of Aristotelian realism, enjoyed a vigorous and creative resurgence. Before the Fourteenth Century ended, Thomism—the medieval synthesis, the Truce of God— had become established among schoolmen so strongly that it acquired the name *scholasticism*. During this same period nominalism became a fixture in the English universities. The best of Aristotle survived his interpreters, and in the next two centuries the beginnings of modern science would appear. The writer also experiences regret that the itinerary of a work of this length does not permit a more detailed presentation of significant medieval idealists such as Bonaventura or of renaissance idealists such as Ficino, Pomponozzi, and Nicholas of Cusa. This is especially true of the latter, who was a remarkably original thinker and seems to have been neglected by educational philosophy.

Descartes and the Reality of Self

The intellectual routes from the Middle Ages to the modern mind are too diverse for all to be traced in a single volume the length of this. It is a well conceived custom to begin the tracking of idealism in renaissance Europe with the thinking of René Descartes (1596-1650). Descartes is perhaps better known for his contributions to modern science. However, there are elements in his thought which are recognized to be idealistic. One, to which prior reference was made,[1] is his argument for the existence of God; and the other, to which future reference will frequently be made, was his discovery of self.[2]

It is well for the reader who has just finished pondering Anselm's famous ontological argument to examine a similar argument. But before Descartes' argument for the existence of God can be appreciated in full, it is necessary to examine the argument's first major premise, which sets forth Descartes' *idea of self*. This, in turn, creates interest in Descartes as a man. Descartes was born to a French family of well established means and social connections. He was educated in a Jesuit school and his promise as a scholar was soon evident. Upon leaving school he entered military service and experienced some life as a soldier. Ultimately, however, his personal inheritance made possible the leisure for writing and study.

His discovery of self emerged as the consequence of a personal adventure in reflection. The episode has frequently been recounted, but never better than by Descartes himself who describes the setting.

> I one day formed the resolution of also making of myself an object of study. . . . I was then in Germany to which country I had been attracted by the wars which are not yet at an end. And as I was returning from the coronation of the Emperor to join the Army, the setting in of winter detained me in a quarter where, since I found no society to divert me, while fortunately I had also no cares or passions to trouble me, I remained the whole day shut up in a stove heated room where I had complete leisure to occupy myself with my thoughts.[3]

In the description of his ensuing meditation, Descartes detailed how he began his experiment in doubt.

> It is now several years since I first became aware how many false opinions I had from my childhood been admitting as true, and how doubtful was everything I had since based on them.[4]

As the meditation continued, Descartes attempted to enlarge both the number and the magnitude of his doubts until he succeeded in doubting everything he was ever taught and everything he ever believed about life, its origins, its nature, and its destiny. But there was one doubt which he was unable to form, and that was doubt of his own existence.

He, therefore, could accept as the single certainty upon which to build his thoughts the single but massive fact that he existed. "I am, I exist, how often? As often as I think."[5] Thus the famous Cartesian inference: "*Cogito Ergo Sum* (I think therefore I am)." "What is a thinking thing? It is a thing that affirms, denies, wills, abstains from willing, that also can be aware of images and sensations." "Of this," declared Descartes, "there can be no doubt." Some kind of thinking was being done, some kind of being was doing it, and that being existed. Descartes was excited by this discovery. He was also excited by the utility of doubt. It freed the mind both from prejudice and sensation, and where doubt cannot be made to apply there is a basis for a conclusion of truth.

This assertion of the primacy of self was vital to the ontologies of European idealism. But it was not only the idealists who made use of it. Existentialism and the literature of the inner man were soon to come. The precursors of this rich and varied line of thought also turned to Descartes for the support required to sustain a claim that "existence precedes essence." There can be no question that Descartes' self-encounter while enduring a "snowed-in" delay en route to rejoin his command was a great moment in philosophy for it not only led to his discovery of his *a priori* self, but also led to another rational argument for the existence of God.

One of the needed assumptions in the Cartesian argument for God is that a doubting thing is an imperfect thing. A perfect thing would have perfect knowledge and would be free of doubt. This is the only act of faith that Descartes found necessary to his argument, and even this he did not find to be wholly without reason. Because once his own doubt was confirmed to his satisfaction (which is to say that he could not doubt that he doubted) he was forced to conclude that as an existing thinker he was burdened of doubt and was, therefore, imperfect. He constructed a rationale in his *Meditation III* which is interpreted as follows:

How is it that I can think of a perfect being?[6]

1. I am imperfect, therefore, I cannot be a source of perfection. Imperfection cannot create perfection.
2. I cannot receive the idea of perfection from non-existence or nothing because it is impossible for nothing to be the cause of something.
3. The only remaining alternative is that a perfect being exists and causes within me the idea of perfection.
4. Since the only cause for the idea of a perfect being, and since a perfect being is God, God exists.

Therefore, Descartes reasoned, God exists because I can think him. Although his argument differs in content from that proposed by Anselm, its form is similar and its result is identical. Like the rationalism of Anselm, the Cartesian argument is also recognized as an ontological argument. Having established a spiritual reality Descartes proceeded to establish the real nature of the sensible world. Much of this speculation is in harmony with modern science, hence, it is outside of the subject matter of this text. Idealism as it came to fruition in the European mind was greatly stimulated by the Cartesian experiment in doubt.

Spinoza and the Ubiquity of Thought

Baruch Spinoza (1632-1677) was the son of a family of well-to-do expatriated Portuguese Jews who had moved to Holland to escape religious persecutions stemming from the Spanish Inquisition.[7] He was educated in Jewish schools and displayed early brilliance in firsthand study of the Hebrew Bible, the Talmud, the commentators, and Spanish literature. At the age of fifteen he was considered the most promising young scholar of the synagogue. But this colt was much too lively and his corral much too small. The young man took up the study of Latin. This, in turn, led to further language studies under the free-thinking Van Ende[8] who had descended from Roman Catholic influences. Soon Spinoza was heard making utterances not in conformity with the orthodox reviews which dominated his Jewish community. Things of this sort can slip by and wise authorities exercise restraint. This might have happened in the case of Spinoza were it not for the fact that someone chose to make an issue of it. According to some accounts, his sister, reputedly envious of his heritage, reported his heresy to the authorities of the synagogue. Efforts were made to hold him to the bonds, but Spinoza refused and the anathema of excommunication was pronounced against him. The language of the document was robust and decisive:

> With the judgment of the angels and by the saints we excommunicate, cast off, curse, and anathematize Baruch de Spinoza, with the consent of the elders of all this holy congregation . . . with the anathema wherewith Joshua cursed Jericho, with the curse which Elisha laid upon the children, and with all the curses which are written in the law. Cursed be he by day and cursed be he by night. Cursed be he in sleeping and cursed be he in waking. . . . The Lord shall not pardon him. . . . The Lord shall destroy his name under the sun.[9]

With these good wishes and other felicitations, Spinoza departed the congregation. He raised objections, but the nature of his objections reflected a greater concern for his civil rather than his spiritual status. Ultimately, he went to court and established his rights as a Dutch citizen.[10] It is clear from his subsequent life that neither his family nor his synagogue understood him. Spinoza lived the life of a philosopher. He had none of the acquisitive instincts of the average man.[11] Aside from the possession of his bed he did not contest the loss of his inheritance. He learned to grind lenses, a skill very much in demand, but he did not need to work at it constantly because he was patronized from time to time by wealthy Hollanders who had some appreciation of his philosophical genius. At the end, his only recrimination was to have his family cut out of his will. Said he, "they deserve nothing."[12]

Biographers see in Spinoza generally what they want to see. Some see him as a Jewish liberal courageously striving to open the doors to freedom of thought.[13] Some see him as the precursor of revolution—a symbol of a man who rose above tyranny. Others see him as a cautious philosopher who wanted nothing more than to be left alone to his philosophizing, protecting himself even to the point of not allowing some of his works to reach publication until after he had died.[14] Probably the latter view of a man seeking peace is closer to the truth, for in discussing the postponement of his publications he is quoted as saying: "I believe that each man should live as he sees fit; and let those who will die for their happiness, if only I may be permitted to live for truth."[15] These do not sound like words of a rebel. Rebellionists enjoy the havoc they reap and prefer not to miss any of it.

The ontology of Spinoza comes forth in response to a simple question: "What is?" The answer comes in three parts: substance, attribute, and mode.[16]

To get to the core of the *nature of substance*, Spinoza used a method which was similar to that used by Descartes. We can think that everything in the world might not exist except substance. Substance is the cause of itself. We cannot think of it as not existing. What is it? What is the being of Being? It is not simply idea. It is the overwhelming, all-encompassing thought of God.[17] How do we conclude this? It is impossible to think that substance is anything but a self-subsisting reality. We cannot conceive of it as not existing, and we cannot think that its existence is contingent. Therefore, it must be grounded in itself, and must be its own cause (*causa sui*). Substance is thought.

We know substance by knowing its attributes. This is like saying we know a man by knowing the qualities of his appearance. Substance has two attributes: one is thought, and the other is extension.[18] Our experience of anything is either of the idea of the thing or of the sensation of the thing, or both. Now it is important to note here the departure from Platonic dualism. Idea (or thought) and sensation are simply two attributes of the thought of God. There seems to be no separation here such as Plato made between his ideas and his objects. Moreover, Spinoza asserts that substance not only has these two attributes but has many more which are unknown to man. In sum, man can only know two attributes of substance: thought and extension.

Modes are the individual perishable things themselves. Modes are the trees and bushes, cats and dogs, houses and barns, men and women, which have finite presence and being in the world. Now by following through the continuum of the Spinozan explanation, we can say that all of these modes are God. How can we say this? By tracing backward from the mode. That glass resting on the table is a mode. It has two attributes that men (who themselves are modes) can contemplate; one is its idea and the other is the extension of the idea which in the case of the glass is the material through or by which the idea is expressed to the senses. Both of these attributes are of substance which is thought, and thought is God.

This is a pantheistic vision which draws in some respects from earlier sources, but it is also original. Spinoza returns us to an idea of God which has the impersonal unity of the Neo-Platonists, but it is simpler, clearer, and not burdened by postulations on levels of being. Time, for example, pertains only to finite things, only to modes. The cleavage between man and God is simply the separation of finite and infinite. Mode is subject to determination, to knowledge. The infinite is not. All existing things, however, must be understood as a consequence of one substance which is thought.

Man as a mode, according to Spinoza, can have only two of God's attributes: thought and extension. In order to have understanding of things we do not now understand our minds would have to be higher and more excellent than the human mind. But Spinoza finds men capable of knowledge at three levels: (1) opinion and imagination, (2) true belief (which stems from reason applied to sense data), and (3) clear and distinct knowledge which comes from reason alone.[19] Thus knowledge which is uncontaminated by modal reality is the superior form of knowing. Mathematics and logic might be examples of such knowledge.

In ethics Spinoza uses the language of soul, by which we can assume that he means the attribute of man which is thought. The soul may unify with God and achieve an immortality, or it may unite with body and die with body. At this, the Stoics would applaud, and the Epicurians would lament. Spinoza is clearly in the ethical camp of the Stoics, and he adds, to the satisfaction of Christians, the notion that the unity with God is felt through love. "The human mind cannot be absolutely destroyed by the body. Something remains which is eternal. No other love is eternal but spiritual love."

Spinoza wrote of implications of these notions for both education and government. Like most idealists he foresaw the possibility of Utopia if all men arrived at true belief, clear knowledge, and correct attitudes. In his lifetime he published *Principles of Descartes' Philosophy*, a *Theologico-Political Treatise* (anonymously). Immediately after his death there appeared the *Ethics, Political Treatise, On the Improvement of Understanding, Letters*, and *Compendium on Hebrew Grammar*. In 1852, nearly one and three-quarter centuries after his death, the *Treatise on God and Man and Man's Happiness* was discovered and printed.

Leibnitz and Berkeley—Reason Demands God

Another philosopher, a younger contemporary of Spinoza, contributed to the emerging European secular idealism. His name was Gottfried Wilhelm von Leibnitz (1646-1716). His father was a professor of moral philosophy at the University of Leipzig. He studied and won degrees in law and philosophy at this university, but he did not enter the academic life. Most of his life was spent in government. However, his letters, journals, and articles show him to be one of the most gifted men in European life. His theory of reality is called monadism. The term is taken from the word *monad* which was applied to small, indivisible units of matter into which, Leibnitz asserted, the world is divided. Taken together these units make up the cosmos. Each monad is different in character and is constantly changing. Using this as a starting place Leibnitz constructed an idealistic view of a harmonious universe which displays his great intellectual power.[20] His system does not hold implications for education beyond those developed by Descartes and Spinoza, but it serves to demonstrate how another creative mind in the Seventeenth Century constructed a theory of idealism which stood independent of the earlier ecclesiastical tradition.

George Berkeley (1685-1753) was, in a sense, a reincarnation of the cleric-philosopher of the medieval church. He was Irish, and received his early education in Ireland. Evidently he was a brilliant boy. At the age of fifteen he entered Trinity College at Dublin. Later he became a minister in the Anglican church. In 1734 he was appointed a bishop serving the district of Cloyne in Ireland. He was an active man, a visionary. At one time he attempted to found a college in Bermuda. This project failed. He spent some time in Providence, Rhode Island, but his American dreams bore no fruit and he returned to Ireland to finish out his life.

Berkeley evidently was a man who responded to challenges, and it is reasonable to question whether he would have philosophized at all were it not for two brilliant contemporaries who put forward views of reality which were not to his liking. One of these was Isaac Newton, the other was John Locke. Both advanced realistic notions of the universe wherein God was given a place, but not a necessary place. Berkeley was aroused to respond both as a bishop and as a philosopher. To do this he took Locke's epistemology as his base. He agreed that there is nothing in the mind of man that is not first in the senses.[21] This puts him in tune with the empiricists who enjoyed a rising vogue in the Eighteenth Century. In moving across to form his ontological position Berkeley remained consistent. He declared that in order to be, something must be perceived. Thus the Berkeley dictum: *esse est percepi* (to be is to be perceived). Those things which are not perceived simply cannot exist.

What can this mean? Is it true, for example, that if one leaves a room, and its sights and sounds are no longer seen and heard, that room and its contents cease to exist? The question is interesting. Does the existence of anything depend on perception? Will a tree, if it falls unheard in a forest, make a noise? If I shut my eyes, do all of the things which are sensed by my sight cease to exist until I look at them again?

No, this is not what Berkeley meant. Nothing in the didactics of philosophy has helped more to clear up the possible confusion in understanding Berkeley's ontology than the following oft-quoted limerick by Ronald Knox:

> There once was a man who said "God
> Must think it exceedingly odd
> If he finds that this tree
> Continues to be
> When there's no one about in the Quad."
>
> Dear Sir: Your astonishment's odd
> I am always about in the Quad

> And that's why the tree
> Will continue to be
> Since observed by, yours faithfully, God.[22]

Now God's necessity is clear. Reality is all that which is perceived by God's mind. To be, therefore, is to exist as an idea in the mind of God. All reality, therefore, is mind. Now we note that Berkeley has taken an empirical route to a philosophical position similar to that of Spinoza, but having that momentum he completely passes Spinoza by withdrawing material reality almost completely. It is a remarkable tour which begins with an acceptance of materialism and ends with declaring materialism is impossible alone; its existence is contingent upon mind.

Reality to Berkeley is, therefore, essentially mental and *subjective*. In his *Principles of Human Knowledge*[23] he leads through an analysis of mind and matter to the conclusion that matter is an aspect of mind. Matter is, therefore, spirit. This seems a forthright and appropriate philosophical posture for an Anglican Bishop, but there is in it very little on which to base a science of any kind. The consequences of this to knowledge making and to education would be completely unacceptable to the modern world.

Spiritual (Transcendental) Idealism

In any proper account of the philosophy of Europe, the philosophy of man, or the philosophy of anything, the image of Immanuel Kant (1724-1804) must rise off the printed page and form a vision of greatness. How can he be introduced? Is it enough to say that all of the lines of thought which stem forth from antiquity blur in the Roman interval, become again firm and clear in the medieval university, cross the stormy renaissance intact, and converge at a point we call Immanuel Kant? Is it enough to say that modern philosophies are all lines which extend to the present day, and the point from which they extend is Immanuel Kant? Perhaps it is enough; perhaps it is too much. But consult the modern schools, and which does not acclaim him? The pragmatists give thanks for his notions about the utility of *a priori* synthetic assumptions; existentialists are grateful for his clarification of the uniqueness of individual experience; the modern realists appreciate his unveiling the psychological nature of concepts; language analysts value his methods for determining the meaning of sentences; and idealists applaud his interposing mind between sense and knowing. Kant did not found a philosophical school; he made modern philosophy possible. Is it enough to call him a philosopher's philosopher? Perhaps so.

He appears in this text under a heading called *spiritual idealism*. Was Kant an idealist? He was, but only in the sense that his thought contributed to the thought of the idealists. When one writes of other philosophical traditions, Kant appears, and his prominence as a realist, pragmatist, or existentialist will certainly equal his prominence as an idealist. In the history of philosophy no other man has overarched the field in such a complete way. How did he manage to do this? It happens that his major interest was in the element that all philosophical traditions have in common and, in one way or another, the element upon which they all depend. Kant was interested in the nature of reason itself. It is as simple as that. Because in his hands reason became better known, more clearly understood, and in many respects more central to philosophy, no tradition of thought in which reason played a major role was unaffected by his work.

Kant was born in Königsberg, evidently of Scottish ancestry. The reason for the emigration from Scotland to Prussia is not known.[24] He was the fourth of eleven children. The family was a member of a Pietist sect, a fact which bore heavily upon his early education and aspects of his life and work. The Pietists stressed faith, redemption, and imminent association with God.[25] The school he attended was operated by the sect. His school day began each day at 5:30 A.M. with prayer, and prayer followed each class, every hour.[26] (Shades of Gargantua!) Sunday was given almost entirely to religious devotions. Such was the learning environment of the boy, Immanuel Kant.

In 1740 he entered the University at Königsberg. He was evidently enamored of the university environment. After six years as a student he remained on the fringes of the academic community. In 1755 he was awarded the doctorate; even then, he remained at Königsberg with authorization to function as a *Privatdozent* which meant private teacher. This meant that he could announce lectures and receive in remuneration only such fees as his students wished to pay. Kant remained in that rather difficult status for fifteen years. In the meantime, it is presumed he lived in boarding houses and continued his scholarship. His lectures ranged widely and he remained poor. But, he seems to have been very favorably received by students. Indeed, under those circumstances, one could not have continued in that position and remained solvent, even as an innocent bachelor, if not possessed with didactical skills which appealed to students. In 1770, at the age of forty-six, Kant was offered a professorship in logic and metaphysics.

Until the age of fifty-six Kant's published works had been in geography, physics, and general speculations as to the origins of the earth and heavenly bodies.[27] But his occupation of the chair of logic and metaphysics at Königsberg signaled the start of his first great work in philosophy. It was not to appear until 1781. Although it resulted from thought which covered the previous twelve years of his life, the text was written over a period of four or five months. Kant was in a hurry and was not writing for a wide readership. He called the work *The Critique of Pure Reason*. It is not an easy book to read. Even professional philosophers did not appreciate its meaning at first. Kant was a precise man, and it was his nature to give time and space to definitions, distinctions, and classifications. These were essential to his purpose, but they did not lighten the burdens of the reader.

All of this simply informs the student of education who wishes to sail on the Kantian ocean that he is well advised to seek the help of a pilot; he should equip himself well; and he should allow sufficient time. This text does not propose to be a guide to Kant. Rather than sailing the ocean we are bringing the reader to look at a map of it. In this way the reader can see what professional philosophers who have studied Kant have derived from their own experience with his work; and by examining the maps they have drawn, the reader can quite easily infer implications of the *Critique* for idealistic thought in education. However, the actual experience of Kant is something else.

Kant treats man as a knower, and his treatise is of *what knowledge is* and how it is made. To understand his approach it is important to think that knowledge is a product or an aspect of the knower rather than an aspect of the world. This can seem quite baffling until you stop and imagine an adult human being who suddenly arrives in the world empty of knowledge of any kind, even of primary things. The world would appear to him as chaotic. Indeed, he would have difficulty surviving the shock, but if we can assume something as incredible as knowledgeless man we should have little difficulty in enlarging the dream to include the idea that his system would overcome the shock of being suddenly thrust into a *noumenal* world.

Now the *noumenal* world is the world outside of him, and his sense of sight, sound, smell, etc., are activated by it. These *percepts* are supplied to the mind. There is a temptation at this point to make the analogy mechanical; and, briefly, we succumb. In the mechanical sense, the mind is a concept-making apparatus. The concepts which the mind produces can be called *phenomena*. Therefore, the world which our man begins to know is *phenomenal*. That is to say, he knows the concepts his mind has formed. These are *his*. He made them, and he finds them useful. Taken together they constitute his experience.

Does he ever know the noumenal world outside of himself? No. All knowledge begins with his experience of it. All we can say of this is that sensation of the outer world activates the processes of thought which, in turn, produce perception and conception which is experience. In this way man the knower knows. Moreover, experience is unique to each knower; therefore, knowledge is unique to each individual. Schematically the *a priori* elements in the overview are this:

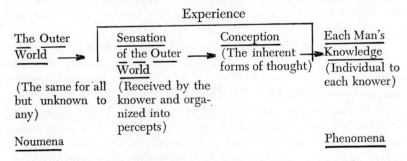

Experience

The Outer World →	Sensation of the Outer World →	Conception (The inherent forms of thought) →	Each Man's Knowledge (Individual to each knower)
(The same for all but unknown to any)	(Received by the knower and organized into percepts)		
Noumena			Phenomena

All of this is preliminary to analysis of how the mind operates on percepts. After intensive analysis Kant produced the following table of categories of pure concepts.[28]

Table of Categories

I
Of Quantity
Unity
Plurality
Totality

II
Of Quality
Reality
Negation
Limitation

III
Of Relation
Inherence and Subsistence
Causality and Dependence
(cause and effect)
Activity and Passivity

IV
Of Modality
Possibility—Impossibility
Existence—Non-existence
Necessity—Contingency

All knowledge that we have as knowers is in the form of ideas. Kant seemed quite willing to allow the world which is outside of our senses to stand as unknowable because the inherent forms of conceptualization limit knowing. Thus such ancient problems as *infinity* and *regression of cause* (when trying to understand the creation of the world) are frustrating because the present forms which thought takes are not adequate to deal with this form of metaphysical question. Cause and effect being an important modality of conception, we are prone to apply it, without realizing whether it is an appropriate or meaningful way to think about the creation of the outer world.

Kant found the realm of analytic knowledge to be much smaller than supposed. There are very few propositions which come to the state of knowledge *by reason alone*.[29] "Analytic" judgments are those in which the connection of the predicate with the subject is through identity (e.g., a = a or (a + b) > a). The categories of understanding referred to previously were derived analytically. Any knowledge which depends partly or wholly upon experience is synthetic.[30] In an analytic statement the predicate can add nothing to the concept of the subject. It merely breaks it up into constituent concepts. On the other hand, if a judgment contains something produced by operations of thought upon sensation (which is to say, experience) the judgment is *synthetic;* e.g., "A body has weight." Now Kant found possible one more form of judgment. He called it the *a priori synthetic judgment*.[31] In this we can make judgments which are not analytic alone because they include things which are known in experience but which are still analytically true because their truth need not be confirmed by experience. He cited as examples the physical principles: action equals reaction; and in changes of matter quantity is unchanged. He declared that such propositions are both necessary *and* synthetic, hence the *a priori synthetic.*

Examples of the three types of judgments follow:

Analytic:	Every square is a rectangle.
Synthetic *a priori:*	Everything that is red is colored.
Synthetic:	There are birds in Florida.

Kant's second great work was the *Critique of Practical Reason,* published in 1788. This work came to have a strong influence on ethical thought. The religious fundamentalists had been losing ground in the face of the philosophy of enlightenment. The *Critique of Pure Reason* did not develop a philosophy of will; and, in addition, it attacked the various ontological arguments for God. Kant was moved to seek rational grounds for morality.[32] His solution was to make one more vast assumption about the spiritual reality of man; namely, that there was a moral force operating within each man. Kant believed that this force was present *a priori*. It was as much a part of man as the thought forms which Kant derived in the *Critique of Pure Reason*. This moral force is absolute; it is its own end. It does not operate to serve other ends such as happiness or comfort. It is a categorical imperative. The categorical imperative was expressed in two ways:[33]

1. Act so that the maxim of your will can always hold good as a principle of universal legislation.
2. So act as to treat humanity, whether in thine own person or in that of any other as an end, never as a means.

In returning then to the question of God, Kant deduced the existence of God from the existence of the moral sense in man. This was the reverse of the traditional formulation which deduces moral maxims from the existence of God.

In the analysis of pure reason Kant dealt with the human intellect, and in practical reason he dealt with the human will. In 1790 he published *Critique of Judgment* in which he dealt with the problem of taste and beauty. In this he formulated certain heuristic principles[34] which lead to the aesthetic judgment. These principles are dependent on the assumption of teleology (or purpose in the universe). Thus, once again, Kant formed a vast intellectual edifice and placed it on the foundation of a human intuition in which he asks man to believe.[35] Thus the source of beauty becomes feeling in experience which is generated by a response to those things appearing in our senses which are representative of the grand purpose of the universe. There are vast implications in this for those who formulate curricula for modern children.

At this point Kant began to encounter difficulties with the state. Frederick the Great, who was a tolerant prince, and who, in his own right, was a renowned philosopher, competent musician, and composer, had died. It was Frederick who offered sanctuary to Rousseau and, although he quarreled philosophically with Voltaire, found in him another kindred spirit. But the enlightenment of France and Germany began to encounter opposition from the clergy. Free thought on religious questions was attacked, and after Frederick few secular leaders found wisdom in supporting political or academic freedom to discuss alternative ideas of God. In 1791 Kant published a small book on religion. Frederick's successor, King Frederick William the III was soon prodded by censors and church authorities on the deviations in Kant's philosophy from the "official line." When, in 1793, Kant published his *Religion Within the Limits of Reason Alone*, the church and state reacted. The king demanded that he explain the "misuse" of philosophy and that he not give further "offense." Kant replied deferentially; unlike Rousseau, he reconciled himself to silence on "sensitive" matters, and until William died in 1797, Kant wrote no more on religion. Soon afterward, however, he resumed his interest in God-ideas and continued to publish in the field. Some of his most direct observations were published posthumously.

By the turn of the century Kant was probably the most influential philosopher in Europe. This influence nowise diminished with his death in 1804. Christianity was deeply divided over his doctrines. His theories opened the way for the German idealism of Fitche, Hegel, and Schopenhauer. Shiller, taken with Kant's theories on aesthetics, discoursed on them, and imbued them with his own literary style. This same trace of transcendentalism came across the seas to England where it turned up in Coleridge and Carlyle, and, finally across to America in Emerson and Thoreau.

Absolute Idealism

The development of European thought on the nature of the mind can be conceived in stages. Descartes took the first step in freeing idealism from its outright dependence on a gnostic faith. His ontological argument, however, was considered to be "thin ice" and although no one broke through it, those who followed Descartes were constantly pointing to flaws. Remarkable as it was, the Cartesian argument simply wasn't enough. Spinoza reformed Plato's dualism into a monism through his notion that thought and extension (the sensible world) were two attributes of substance which he called God. It was an original idea. In it, reality is considered to be one vast mind. Berkeley, dissatisfied with the impersonal nature which this vision ascribed to God, proposed that God made the objective world real by willing it or perceiving it. Berkeley did not restore the Christian form of idealism to vogue in academic philosophy, but he managed firmly to reassert the notion that in God's mind there was a consciousness of Himself (as God) and in addition to a will, God also had a consciousness of objective reality. It was this consciousness, this perception, which gave to the objects of the world their state of being.

Next we find that Kant, responding to the realists and the emerging spirit of science, by-passes all of these outer world speculations to get at man, the knower. The thing we call mind, teaches Kant, separates man, the knower, from the world out there. The noumenal world, the things in themselves, can't be known. What can be known, and vastly improved, is what comes out of the mind. By concentrating within these limits Kant made determinations about the intellect, the will, feelings about the world, etc. He did not deny the realities to which man was exposed and which activated intellect, will, and feeling. His assertion was that all we can know is what man yields from the exposure which becomes experience.

So, according to Kant, mind makes man's reality. But it is the mind of man. Idealism was now *on the ground* where it could be observed. However, it did not stay there. Johan Fitche (1762-1814), who became a disciple of Kant, began to speculate about the universal mind on the other side of the phenomenal (man's) world.[36] In this way he broke the discipline which Kant imposed on himself; and, again, German idealism was off and running with speculation about cosmic reality beyond man. Fitche took his cue from Kant himself who seemed forced to make the assumption of teleology in his *Critique of Judgment* (although the work is so obscure in parts that authorities differ on this point). Shiller (1775-1854) also produced a pantheistic vision which displayed man as the highest expression of the moral purpose of the universe.[37]

Kant terminated his greatest work about the time of the French revolution. There were then alive in Europe various versions of romantic naturalism which were idealized in political ways. The most straightforward personal expression of this was in Jean Jacque Rousseau (1712-1778) who seemed to agree with Kant that man is, by nature, good. Rousseau, however, found his teleology in nature whereas Fitche and Shiller saw teleology delineated in and expressed by the operations of social institutions.

Fitche and Shiller are seen as links between Kant and the next great figure in German idealism, whose work was to formulate a vision of mind as an absolute. His name was George William Friedrich Hegel (1770-1831). He was born into an upper-middle-class family in Stuttgart. He studied in the seminary at the University of Tubingen. After seven years as a private tutor, he became a lecturer at the University of Jena. His tenure there lasted from 1801 to 1805 when his teaching was interrupted by the Napoleonic wars. For a time he edited a newspaper, but, at the same time, he continued his studies and his publications. He was married in 1811, and in 1816 he was appointed to a professorship at Heidelberg. In 1818 he ascended to the Chair of

Philosophy at the University of Berlin, the chair made famous by Fitche, where he remained until the end of his life.[38]

He published four major books in his lifetime:

> *The Phenomenology of Mind*, 1807
> *The Science of Logic*, 1812
> *The Encyclopedia of the Philosophical Sciences*, 1816
> *The Philosophy of Right*, 1820

The main branches of his philosophy were explained in his lectures. A number of notes and transcriptions of these were converted into books published after his death by former students. They include:

> *Lectures on the Philosophy of Religion*, 1832
> *Lectures on the History of Philosophy*, 1833
> *Lectures on Aesthetics*, 1835
> *Lectures on the Philosophy of History*, 1840

It is perhaps unfair to describe one man's philosophy by describing the ways in which it differs from another's. For one thing, it de-emphasizes its originality, and for another, it presupposes a perfect understanding of the work to which the objections are made. However, Hegel is a very difficult philosopher to present. Neither his philosophy nor his style of exposition are amenable to simplification. If one tries to be simple, he soon finds he has departed from Hegel. If one tries to stay with Hegel he soon departs from his readers (or they from him).[39] So it is necessary to lean on others with the hope that those engaged in the study of idealism will sense the direction idealist thought is taking early in the Nineteenth Century, using this as a wedge for prying meaning from texts which are, in places, highly obscure.

Hegel was greatly stimulated by Kant. He was certain that all of philosophy was changed by the intensive work Kant had done in developing the categories of the mind. He believed that philosophers could no longer regard their own manner of thinking with indifference. Now even the style of philosophical discourse had new standards of language; there were new terms, new categories, and new possibilities. But Hegel disagreed (as did the American pragmatist Charles S. Peirce) that a barrier exists between experience and things-in-themselves. He objected to the notion that man was separated from the world-out-there by his mind and its functions. The things-in-themselves could not be conceived as unknown somethings which pumped life into the senses and forced our mental process into producing a phenomenal reality. In this, Hegel thought Kant was dead wrong.

Hegel knew Spinoza's work. It is generally conceded that Kant barely knew it, and he was critical of what little he knew.[40] Hegel's vision was of an uncompromising absolute and this absolute is called mind. One way to imagine it is to sit by a window and look out at the world. All of the things you see are active out there—growing, struggling, moving, surging, competing. Gravity is holding down; life forces are pushing up. Now as you watch this, try to imagine that all of them as they relate together are coming into your mind and there they are being objectified in the form of idea. If you could sit looking at this panorama of life and motion for centuries, the myriad of sights of events and their resolution into other events would form in your mind a running stream of ideas which you might call history. It would not be too difficult to imagine that you are a kind of god and those events out there are extensions of *your own mind* and those "things out there" are elements of your thought and all is operating for the purpose of creating your ideas.

If this much is possible in your imagination, then move one more stage, and imagine that all of the things in the universe (whatever it may be) are elements in the mind of God, and that all of the activity is God thinking, and the resolution of acts in time are ideas. Is it possible, for example, for you to imagine that in World War I, World War II, the Korean War, and the Viet Nam War there were great ideas that "happened"? What would those ideas be? Perhaps it is too soon to say. Was the American Civil War simply the Absolute Mind thinking out its final thoughts on the question of human slavery? Or thinking out certain political relationships between person and property?

Now this is an analogical approach to the absolute mind; and, again, it carries with it all the problems of analogical reasoning. How are we to imagine it? Is the absolute mind a vast and limitless sea? And are each day's events poured into it and sorted out into the great ideas we call history? Is history God's memory? We could use the model of the microcosm and the macrocosm. The atom has been called a microcosmic model of the macrocosmic solar system.[41] Are our own minds on the same scale or on one infinitely larger—microcosmic models of the macrocosmic mind of God? The idea is difficult to grasp. We could try it this way. Imagine that as you go through your day, meeting its challenges, winning some, losing some, you are a tiny part of the macrocosmic mind which is thinking out reality.

This is an ontological vision which carries much of the strength of Spinoza's reality of mind. We see in it much of Kant's view of the mind in process toward objectification of phenomenal world. It gives us a theory that history is what the absolute mind has come to know. It also gives us a basis for theorizing about the good, and we will come to this presently. However, it is first necessary to examine the epistemology of absolute idealism.

The epistemology of Hegel is perhaps the best generally known aspect of his philosophy. The term Hegelian Dialectic is a familiar term. It stems from the idea that there is strife between opposites. We have heard this before. Ionian philosophers, Heraclitus in particular, used it to explain change. Hegel does this, too, but his explanation, though somewhat less poetic, is far more specific.[42] For example, a stone wall needs two things to be erect: (1) gravity and (2) stones. (Try to build anything without gravity!) Now the synthesis of the stones and the gravity is a wall. We can think of the gravity as the thesis, the stone as the antithesis, and the wall as the synthesis. The gravity constantly pulls down on the top stone and the boulders underneath push up. The synthesis remains. Now if we can replace gravity with *idea* and the stones with *nature* we can call the synthesis *object*. Each object, therefore, is a resolution of idea and nature. However, even while the object is forming another idea is working. Thus the object is ever changing.

This becomes more clear in human affairs. For example, farmers have a good year, and more wheat is available than before. The level of consumption acts against the supply inadequately, and the price goes down below the level of government support.

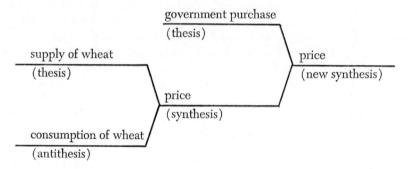

The government is aware that by a counter action it can raise prices to a level which they have come to call parity. Therefore, it purchases wheat to produce a desired synthesis.

Some historians have explained American history using the Hegelian dialectic. For example, we can see the Hamiltonian Federalism versus Jacksonian Democracy.[43] The synthesis of the two was the original idea of American government.

Acting against this synthesis was Jacksonian democracy; so the synthesis became thesis, the Jacksonian ideas antithesis, and a new synthesis was formed only to be challenged by forces emanating from industry, etc. Karl Marx used his own form of the Hegelian dialectic to develop the dialectical materialism so vital to his theories of communism.

At this point we begin to sense the clenched fist in the Hegelian system. It is not that might *makes* right; might *is* right. He believed history to be "the development of spirit in time." He declared:

> A nation is moral, virtuous, vigorous while it is engaged in realizing its grand objects, and defends its work against external violence during the process of giving to its purposes on objective existence.[44]

Hegel believed that in a conflict between nations or individuals the superior principle or spirit will emerge.

On the point of personal identity he turned to the sturdy example across the channel saying:

> Every Englishman will say: we are the men who navigate the seas, and have the commerce of the world, to whom the East Indies belong and their riches, who have a parliament, juries, etc. . . .[45]

Thus, in identifying himself, a man identifies his national spirit and its objects. Hegel went on to point out that men are not free except in their destiny.[46] One achieves freedom through his affiliations, i.e., church, town, and nation. Loyalty and obedience to these entities offer a pathway to self-realization and ultimate freedom. It is little wonder that the architects of the Third Reich found so much in Hegel to draw upon. They misused him. But that always happens to philosophers.

Hegel offered structures which many visiting Americans took home and inserted into American education. In the last part of the Nineteenth Century many American classrooms were dominated by mind-building theories of education. The national spirit was not neglected. Affiliations with churches and other agencies which offer to the individual his self-identification were not neglected. Consider the questionnaires you fill out in the opening sessions of the University. Who are you? You record your name, profession, the schools you attended, the credits you have, the town in which you live, the honors given you (or lack of them), your phone number, and your zip code. That's who you are! If one asks who you are you reply by giving your name, your status as a citizen, perhaps your religious affiliation, your national extraction, your locker number, and your parking place. But is that really who you are?

No one can know what Hegel would say of these matters. He did not philosophize directly about educational practice. But the reader of his philosophy of history cannot escape feeling that he would be pleased to see school open with the Pledge of Allegiance to the flag, an interval of prayer, and an account of the nation's history which emphasized battles, elections, and economic struggles that were won. In Hegel, there is a place for the loser—he produces the winner and, thereby, the loser serves God in his own way.

European idealism did not end with Hegel. One of his contemporaries, who fancied himself a rival, wrote movingly and clearly about the operation of the human will. His name was Schopenhauer. His theory of aesthetics is one of the great works of western philosophy.[47] American education has yet to do much with it. But it is there and waiting. Later Friedrich Froebel (1782-1852), a naturistic idealist almost in the tradition of Rousseau, concentrated specifically on the problems of educating children.[48] His notions of self and its attainment are clearly associated with the philosophy of mind.[49] His educational theories focused mainly upon early childhood education, and his work was well known in America. Because of the Nineteenth-Century German immigration to America and frequent visits abroad by American educators, Froebel's kindergarten arrived in America almost intact. Americans such as Colonel Francis Parker, Elizabeth Peabody, Maria Bolte, and others[50] gave Froebel's theories a brief but authentic life. The American kindergarten has long since been converted to a preparatory school, but at the turn of the Twentieth Century it was an excellent manifestation of naturism as applied to early childhood education.

As for Hegel, he has had representatives in this country. One of the most prominent was William T. Harris, a vigorous man, who served for a time as the United States Commissioner of Education.[51] Hegelian philosophy was highly respected in nearly all American universities in the Nineteenth Century. John Dewey received extensive training in Hegelian philosophy, and although his conversion to experimentalism came early in his career as an educational philosopher,[52] there are in all of his writings elements which seem to cohere with many of Hegel's notions about society. Those who choose to be less than kind frequently point out that Professor Dewey even carried on Hegel's habit of obscurity. Thus, it is possible for scholars to go on for centuries arguing about what he meant, and it is almost impossible for laymen to deal with him at all. But then, as Kant, the man who is alleged to have introduced the tradition of obscurity in German philosophy once remarked, "Everyone doesn't have to read philosophy."

Notes

1. J. Donald Butler, *Four Philosophies and their Practice in Education and Religion* (New York: Harper and Brothers, 1951), p. 127.
2. *Ibid.*, p. 129.
3. René Descartes, *Discourse on Method,* quoted from Monroe C. Beardsly (ed.), *The European Philosophers from Descartes to Nietzsche* (New York: Random House, Inc., The Modern Library Edition, 1960), p. 11.
4. *Ibid.*, p. 28.
5. *Ibid.*
6. *Ibid.*, pp. 40-52.
7. Karl Jaspers, *The Great Philosophers* (New York: Harcourt, Brace & World, Inc., 1966), p. 106.
8. Lewis S. Feuer, *Spinoza and the Rise of Liberalism* (Boston: Beacon Press, 1966 ed.), p. 5.
9. Frederick Pollock, *Spinoza: His Life and Philosophy* (London: Duckworth, Ltd., Second Ed. 1899), pp. 17-18.
10. Jaspers, *op. cit.*, p. 273 ff.
11. *Ibid.*, p. 274.
12. *Ibid.*, p. 273.
13. See: Feuer, *op. cit.*, ch. 2.
14. Jaspers, *op. cit.*, p. 276.
15. *Ibid.*
16. *Ibid.*, p. 279.
17. Benedict de Spinoza, *The Chief Works of Spinoza,* tr. R. H. M. Elwes (London: G. Bell and Sons, 1884), *Ethics,* Part I, Prop. XIV.
18. Butler, *op. cit.*, p. 131.
19. Jaspers, *op. cit.*, pp. 295-298 ff.
20. Gottfried Leibnitz, *The Monadology,* G. Martin Duncan, *The Philosophical Works of Leibnitz* (New Haven: Tuttle, Morehouse and Taylor, 1890), pp. 218-222.
21. Hobert Burns, Charles Brauner, *Philosophy of Education* (New York: The Ronald Press Company, 1962), p. 79.
22. Quoted by Fredrick C. Neff, *Philosophy and American Education* (New York: The Center for Applied Research in Education, 1966), p. 20. Also by Burns, Brauner, *Ibid.*, p. 80.
23. *Ibid.*

24. Will and Auriel Durant, *Rousseau and Revolution* (New York: Simon and Schuster, 1967), p. 531.
25. *Ibid.*
26. *Ibid.*
27. *Ibid.*, 531-534.
28. Immanuel Kant, *Critique of Pure Reason,* tr. Norman K. Smith (London: The Macmillan Company, 1929), Book I, *Analytic of Concepts.*
29. Immanuel Kant, *Critique of Pure Reason,* Monroe Beardsly, ed., *op. cit.,* p. 379. See: *The Distinction Between Analytic and Synthetic Judgments.*
30. *Ibid.*, p. 380.
31. *Ibid.*, p. 381.
32. Immanuel Kant, *Critique of Practical Reason,* Theodore M. Grune, ed., *Kant Selections* (New York: Scribner's Sons, 1929), p. 358.
      See also: Lewis White Beck, A Commentary on Kant's *Critique of Practical Reason* (Chicago: University of Chicago Press, 1960), 306 pp.
33. Immanuel Kant, *Metaphysical Foundations of Morals,* Monroe Beardsly, ed., *op. cit.,* pp. 473, 475.
34. Immanuel Kant, *Critique of Judgment,* tr. J. C. Merideth, (Oxford: The Clarendon Press, 1911), Vol. I, p. 46.
35. Kant, *Ibid.*, p. 117.
36. Durant, *op. cit.*, p. 550.
37. Charles Hartshorne, William Reese, ed., *Philosophers Speak of God* (Chicago: University of Chicago Press, 1953), p. 233.
38. Butler, *op. cit.*, p. 148.
39. *Ibid.*, p. 149.
40. Jaspers, *op. cit.*, p. 387.
41. This form of explanation is adopted by Van Cleve Morris, *Philosophy and the American School* (Boston: Houghton Mifflin Company, 1961), p. 138.
42. Butler, *op. cit.*, p. 152.
43. Morris, *op cit.*, p. 53.
44. G. W. F. Hegel, *Introduction to the Philosophy of History,* quoted in Monroe Beardsly, ed., *The European Philosophers from Descartes to Nietzsche* (New York: Random House, Inc. The Modern Library Ed., 1960), p. 604.
45. Beardsly, *ibid.*, p. 603.
46. *Ibid., The Role of the State,* p. 572.
47. Arthur Schopenhauer, *The World as Will and Idea,* tr. R. B. Holdane and J. Kemp (London: Kegan Paul, Trench, Trubner & Co., Ltd. 1896, Fourth Ed.).
48. Ernest E. Bayles and Bruce Hood, *Growth of American Educational Thought and Practice* (New York: Harper & Row Publishers, 1966), pp. 164-172 ff.
49. *Ibid.*, p. 171.
50. *Ibid.*, pp. 177-178.
51. Butler, *op. cit.*, p. 159.
52. *Ibid.*, p. 417.

Other Reading

Berkeley, George. *The Works of George Berkeley*. Ed. G. Sampson. London: George Bell and Sons, 1897-1898. 3 Vols.

Butler, Donald J. *Four Philosophies and Their Practice in Religion and Education*. New York: Harper and Bros., 1951; pp. 121-161.

Descartes, René. *Discourse on Method*. Tr. John Veitch. LaSalle, Ill.: Open Court Publishing Co., 1945. Part I.

Durant, Will. *Rousseau and Revolution*. New York: Simon and Schuster, Inc., 1967, pp. 531-551.

Feuer, Lewis Samuel. *Spinoza and the Rise of Liberalism*. Boston: Beacon Press, 1964, pp. 1-199.

Hegel, G. W. F. *The Philosophy of History*. Tr. J. Sibree. New York: The Colonial Press, 1899.

Hegel, G. W. F. *Selections*. Ed. J. Lowenberg. New York: Charles Scribner's Sons, 1929.

Jaspers, Karl. *The Great Philosophers*. New York: Harcourt, Brace & World, Inc., pp. 270-308, 311-390.

Kant, Immanuel. *The Critique of Pure Reason*. Tr. J. M. D. Meiklejohn. New York: The Colonial Press, 1900.

_____. *The Critique of Practical Reason*. Tr. L. W. Beck. Chicago: University of Chicago Press, 1949.

_____. *Fundamental Principles of the Metaphysics of Ethics*. Tr. Otto Manthey-Zorn. New York: Appleton-Century-Crofts, Inc., 1938.

Krieger, Leonard. *The German Idea of Freedom*. Boston: Beacon Press, pp. 81-261.

Milton, John. *Of Education*. Incl. in *The Prose of John Milton*. Ed. J. Max Patrick. Garden City, N.Y.: Doubleday and Company, Inc., 1967, pp. 219-243.

Pollock, Fredrick. *Spinoza: His Life and Philosophy*. London: Duckworth, 1899, pp. 1-76.

Schopenhauer, Arthur. *The World as Will and Idea*. Tr. R. B. Haldane and J. Kemp. London: Kegan Paul, Trench, Treeber and Co., 1869.

Spinoza, Benedict. *The Chief Works of Spinoza*. Tr. R. H. M. Elwes. London: G. Bell and Sons., 1884. Part I.

Weidman, Franz. *Hegel*. New York: Western Publishing Co., Inc., pp. 9-122.

Woodward, William. *Studies in Education During the Age of the Renaissance*. London: Cambridge University Press, 1906.

CHAPTER IX

Idealism and the American Mind

A well known American folk tale is based on a supposition that one kind of animal can live in a briar patch while another would be torn to pieces by his effort to pass through it. Brother rabbit, it has been said, can go places and do things that brother fox can not. Brother rabbit was born in a briar patch. In a similar sense a student of American letters is probably much better equipped to explore and analyze the American mind than any other kind of scholar. This style of humanist with his mercurial insights, erudite language, and free-wheeling propensity to combine them in vivid blends, is able to illustrate by color and shadow, by suggestion and innuendo. The picture he makes contains light and dark tones; it contains hint and highlight, fact and fancy. It is judged as composition is judged, whole to part and part to whole. It is criticized as art is criticized, by the aesthetic response it evokes in the reader. Numerous students of American letters have given vivid and stirring pictures of the American mind.[1]

On the other hand, the educational philosopher with the ponderous machinery of his discipline finds the tracking of American ideas or the American spirit a little like going through a briar patch, and he is of a species not at ease in this kind of thicket. Because his methods are generally derived from the world of academic philosophy, the educational philosopher seeks firm and clear distinctions. His figures are geometric in that there is a sharp edge which separates being from non-being. If his distinctions blur into shades or shadows then he has failed, for his delineations must be more precise.

There are several reasons for these difficulties. Americans have not been so devoted to academic philosophy as were their forebears in Greece and Europe. Americans have been action people. Their ideas have been sung in the poetry and prose of the various literary genre and have been reflected in popular attitudes about government, property, religion, and people. Americans have been very eloquent in these expressions. The world in general has been quick to take note of them. Indeed, the utterances of America's savants are well known abroad, and in some cases they seem more revered abroad than in America.

Late in the Nineteenth Century American philosophy produced American pragmatism. This can be called a school of academic philosophy. However, because it tends to deny rather than affirm the reality of mind it is not included in this exposition of idealism. We cannot find a long and illustrious tradition of American academic philosophy which is in the tradition of idealism. To be sure there have been a number of distinguished American philosophers who are regarded as idealists, and there is some originality in their thinking, but even this stands on old-world foundations. Both James and Dewey, who are commonly considered pragmatic philosophers, brought some of their speculations into a compatibility with certain aspects of Hegel's absolute idealism. But the distinction which philosophy gives to James and Dewey rests upon grounds other than idealism. American philosophy in the idealistic tradition can take pride in Josiah Royce (1855-1916) and several of his students, including William Hocking, Mary Calkins, and Herman Horne.[2] There have been other Americans such as William Harris (1835-1909), George Howison (1834-1916) and Bowden Parker Bowne (1847-1910) who were idealists of note.[3] But all of these had studied in Germany and distinguished themselves as expositors and analysts of standing traditions, not as originators of new traditions.

However, there has been philosophic originality in America. We have the *philosophy-in-action* of such men as Edwards, Franklin, Jefferson, Samuel Adams, Paine, Jackson, Marshall, and Dickinson, who pitted their will against an unbroken wilderness and carved out a geosocial reality through which several idealistic traditions now flow in a manner unlike anything before it. It is well that Americans pay attention to their own ideas as well as the ideas which preceded America in time. However, older ideas are also implicit in American life and are not easily extracted and examined by those who have them and feel deeply about them. This is another barb in an already thorny problem. One finds it very hard to locate where a European thought leaves off and an American innovation begins.

American government is designed, in part, for these ideas to contend with each other. American social and religious institutions are designed to express certain believed ideas in service or in worship. And the most influential American literature is in the popular rather than academic form. Much of the popular literature reflects various idealistic postures.[4] These are among reasons the American mind is more readily revealed by students of government, of society, and of letters than by one who goes into the "briar patch" with the philosopher's questions: what is real? how do we know? and what is good? Americans answer these questions in their deeds, their aspirations, and their stories. Recently there have developed in certain leading universities certain groups of scholars devoted to *American studies*. The quest of such inquiry is to divine the American mind, to establish the American metaphysics. By training, these scholars are mainly historians, political scientists, or students of literature. They are not philosophers in a formal sense. Given the nature and the area of the quest, this is probably as it should be.

Can philosophy deal with the American mind? Perhaps not yet. The American mind (if such a thing can be imagined) is still forming itself. The completion date may be far off. Even after this, philosophy will need distance and time for its caricature. One day American civilization will be recorded along with Babylon, Greece, and Rome, and the scholars of that future epoch will name some American and say he was the Plato, the Aurelius, the Anselm, or Aquinas of his age. He caught its spirit and came to symbolize it. He recorded what it was that Americans believed.

Therefore, this brief attempt at analysis of the American mind bears a severe limitation. How can we understand our own incomplete lives? How can we understand our incomplete nationhood? We can answer these questions by saying there can now be no full understanding of American life or land, but we can also say that the questions about them were honestly open and remained so. Nowhere in history do we find a people so disposed to self-criticism and even self-rebuke. To some extent order has been achieved in America, but this order is not serene; on the contrary, it is an order founded and fostered by dialectic. Some say it is founded and operated by law, but this cannot be so. Of far greater importance than law are the generative beliefs and processes by which law is made. Americans refer to these beliefs and processes as democracy. This may be the very best word to identify the dynamics of American life, but it may be that future students of America will want to use a word like *ideocracy*. Emerson pointed out that "republics abound in young civilians who believe that laws make the city . . . that any measure though it were absurd, may be imposed upon a people, if only you can get sufficient voices to make it a law." He went on to point out that such foolish laws are as ropes of sand which perish in the twisting. Said he "they only who build on ideas, build for eternity; and that form of government which prevails is the expression of what cultivation exists in the population which permits it. The law is only a memorandum."[5] This argument is persuasive.

Although in these times there can be no closure on the American mind there can be examination of the "cultivation" of ideas which it seems to contain. Such an examination is relevant to any who take responsible roles in the institutional order, whether the institution be of philanthropy, education, religion, or law. Many will not understand the phrase "building for eternity." Not being an academic philosopher Emerson seemed under no obligation to make it clear. We are not entitled to believe that any civilization in the usual sense of the term can be "eternal." However, each civilization has been marked by thematic principles, and these have been found to endure in subsequent civilizations. This we may think of as the eternity of ideas such as the idea of soul which may have originated in Persia and was formalized by the Pythagoreans, systemized by Plato, clarified by the Neo-Platonists, and functionalized by the Christians. Ideas do have an immortality which is, at least, suggestive of eternity.

Thus, we can now ask the questions: What philosophies of mind are cultivated within the American mentality? What is their source? And in what ways are they original? In asking this question the reader is reminded again that the so-called philosophies of mind (those which fall within the categories of idealism) by no means encompass all of the philosophical systems which are possible. Excluded from such a consideration are the philosophies of matter (realism), the philosophies of process (pragmatism), and the philosophies which elevate the reality of self (existentialism). What remains which can be called idealism? Quite a lot remains. American literature and lore offer abundant witness to the spiritual base of the American mentality. Numerous classification systems are possible. Those chosen for this exposition are Christian idealism, formal idealism, physiocratic idealism, transcendental idealism, and absolute idealism.

Christian Idealism

The full force of renaissance did not arrive in England until the reign of Elizabeth.[6] It is true that earlier Englishmen had risen to distinction. The Tudor period has seen Sir Thomas More and Colet, but the circumstances which leavened the discovery and creativity of the English renaissance did not emerge until Elizabeth ascended the throne. The reason for this is probably best summed up by the statement that during the forty-five years of her rule (1558-1603), Elizabeth governed well.

Always herself in the danger of the scaffold, she presided in a brutal age when force was appreciated and used. Although at times she seemed coarse and heartless, by the standards of her age she was a moderate among monarchs who were inclined to sever troublesome heads wherever they found them. In person she was jealous, capricious, demanding, and often ungrateful. All of this is revealed in the melancholy episode of Essex. He in his chagrin and frustration reputedly snarled, "Her words are as crooked as her carcass." She, on her part, remained remorseful but resolute till the axe fell on his proud neck. She was, after all, a woman.

She was exceedingly well educated, shrewd, and capable. She chose and trusted good ministers. She loved England and viewed it with a sense of destiny unmatched by her predecessors, and England prospered at home and abroad. Although, in her time, England performed great feats of arms, the age of Elizabeth was a time of relative peace. As might be expected, therefore, among the upper classes there was intellectual ferment. It was a great age of literature. Shakespeare was writing plays and Bacon was lighting the way to a new science.

But renaissance did not penetrate far below the upper stations of English life. The issue of burning interest among the burghers and the yeomen was reformation. During the Sixteenth Century Tyndale completed an English translation of the Bible, a work in which he persisted despite the opposition of secular and ecclesiastical authority. In 1536 he was seized, imprisoned, and condemned to death. As he was burned at the stake he reportedly cried, "Lord, open the King of England's eyes."

The eyes that were opened were those of a queen and not of a king. Elizabeth's religious policy was to ventilate religious dissent. She was formally excommunicated by Rome, but the record is clear. She tried to find a basis for Puritan, Presbyterian, Anglican, and Roman Catholic to exist together. Only when representatives of the latter attempted to overthrow her did she intervene, legislate, and prosecute. On the other extreme, the separatists and Puritans influenced by both Swiss and German reformation agitated against the established church. After Elizabeth there was economic decline and added social unrest. The extreme elements of the protestant movement could not be reconciled to the established church or the estab-

lished order. The ideas of colonization were implanted in English policy during the age of Elizabeth. Although she established no colonies in
the new world, she established a foreign policy which made this inevitable. Thus colonial policy was a happy solution to a nation badly
strained by economic reversals and religious dissent. The Jamestown
enterprise and the New England enterprise responded to those conditions.

The New England Puritans were always a divided group.[7] Within
it was a Presbyterian element which loved the mother church and
mourned its failures and the militant separatist element which took
the extreme view of the Calvinistic "universal priesthood of believers."
Puritanism in America was a complicated problem. The group contained its own liberals and conservatives. But the central point is that its
philosophical orientation reveals few renaissance influences. The Puritans were *Christian idealists* in the tradition of Augustine and Anselm.
There is the same reliance on faith; however, the Christian idealism
of the Puritan tended to be less tempered by the reason which was
thought so vital by their European forebears. The Puritan Christian
idealism was based on faith as explained and justified by scripture with
special reference to Hebraic scripture. The issues were not of a
philosophic order in the usual sense. The issues were of the governance
of the church. The Congregationalists were advocates of lay control,
and the Presbyterians worked for control by the clergy.

These internecine conflicts among the Puritans would tempt any
ideologist. However, because they did not involve philosophical issues
at an ontological level we must pass the details. But it was inevitable
that the issues of church government fought for by John Cotton, the
Mathers, and John Eliot and approved by such figures as Thomas
Hooker, Roger Williams, and John Wise would sooner or later awaken
one of the New England intellects to philosophy. It did not happen
until the end of the Seventeenth Century. Congregationalism had held
its own, but the new sources of dissent plagued the Presbyterian
zealots.[8] Calvinism was losing the battle in the old world. John
Locke and other materialists were finding credence in the new world.
Presbyterian Calvinism in New England needed a new champion and
in the first quarter of the Eighteenth Century Jonathan Edwards
stepped forward to fill this role.

Not only did Edwards assume the role of defender, but he seemed
to relish it, especially in his later years.[9] This, in retrospect, seems unfortunate for philosophy, and certainly it was not fortunate for Calvinism because once determined on this course, he illuminated the

landscape of hell in a manner unprecedented before and unequaled since. His polemics finally placed him into confrontation with the social movement and humane mood of his time. New Englanders seemed to have grown tired of hearing that they were fallen and evil by nature. As Americans entered the second century of their colonial life they seemed not convinced that this made sense.[10] At the end Edwards was dismissed from his parish and became a symbol for all that which liberals were opposing. He tried so hard to save the old church but actually seemed to do more to hasten its end by personifying its incongruity with the emerging New England. Indeed, his imprecatory conduct hastened a new Congregationalism. This is the first part of the double irony that was the life of Jonathan Edwards.

The second irony is far greater than the first because little doubt stands today that Edwards had a natural power to philosophize which was unrivaled in his time. In the early and middle years of his ministry Edwards, the philosopher, struggled against Edwards, the authoritarian Puritan mystic. Before the latter won, the former demonstrated an extraordinary promise which, alas, was never fully realized. The source of his inspiration cannot be determined. Despite their brief exposure to Elizabethan England this small segment of people entering into a second century of relative isolation on the edge of a vast wilderness remained intellectually and morally akin to their ancestors of the Middle Ages. It cannot, therefore, be astonishing that the first great philosophical mind which arose in their midst was closer to Plotinus than Descartes, more attuned to Augustine than to Locke. He was closer to Anselm than his English contemporary, the Anglican Bishop George Berkeley. It is in the philosophy of Edwards that we find New England Calvinism at its best; the tragedy for him and for Calvinism is that he did not realize this. In a sermon in 1734 he expounded the thesis that "There is such a thing as a spiritual and divine light immediately imparted to the soul by God, of a different nature from that obtained by natural means."[11] He went on to speak of emanation as a divine principle, comparing beauty and God to light and sun. However, later he came to say that this beatific harmony was broken by original sin. From this point onward, his dogma ruled his reason. Finally, all gravitated to the grotesque vision of pessimistic determinism and the horrors which awaited the unconverted sinner.[12]

But for an interval, brief and fleeting, we saw a return of Plotinus and a promise of Emerson. Speculation on this early colonial philosopher has found reason to regret the absence of the philosophical spirit and intellectual stimulation which undoubtedly kept men of this stature in Greece and in medieval and renaissance Europe from wasting their genius on extreme mysticism and decadent institutions.[13] Whereas Berkeley mingled with leaders of thought in London, Edwards was sent to a frontier mission to lecture Indians on the non-freedom of the will. Isolated in Massachusetts, cut off from parturient interaction with other men of thought, misguided into a style of fire-and-brimstone, fear-mongering evangelism, his mind never really escaped the prison of fear and dogma.[14]

But the link of the Puritan thought to the Christian idealism of the Middle Ages seems clear. The obsession of Puritan leaders with the issue whether the church should rule and who should rule the church overshadowed their more abstract reflections. However, the consciousness that ultimate reality is a spiritual configuration governed by a living God with an active will, Who is conscious of man, Who judges man, and Who knows He is God, is in the foundation of Puritan values. There is also the assumption that man is inherently fallen and, therefore, in sin. This is amended by a clear and straightforward assumption that the church is God's institution given earthly presence for the purpose of offering man an opportunity to return to a condition of grace. These are orthodox elements taken almost intact from the Christian beliefs of the Middle Ages. As the first tradition of idealism to sustain itself in the continent of North America it continues to obtrude upon the value structure of American society and the consciences of individual minds, even in the Twentieth Century.

Physiocratic Idealism

How far is it from Eighteenth-Century New England to Eighteenth-Century France? The distance in milieu is difficult to imagine. Eighteenth-Century France is called the Age of Enlightenment. Some even call it the Century of Philosophy. It began in inquiry, moved to criticism, and ended in revolution. It produced Voltaire and Rousseau. The former reflected the spirit of the age; the latter belongs to all ages. Perhaps the best that can be said of this time is that it made Voltaire and Rousseau possible, but just barely so. Liberal as it was, tolerant as it became, and value as it did the reasoning observer, the philosophy of enlightenment was not big enough to include Rousseau. He was apart from it, though a product of it.

What is it that happened to philosophy? It became part of the knowledge systems. No longer was it separate from science, history, jurisprudence, and politics.[15] It was no longer a detached part of the intellect, isolated from practical inquiry. It became an active force within knowledge systems. It contributed syntax to knowledge systems, giving those systems direction, meaning, and application to the life of the state. It was undeniably one of the most powerful movements within the French enlightenment, and it manifested in the collective views of Gournay, Quesnay, Mirabeau, and Pierre S. DuPont, the latter of a town called Nemours. DuPont summarized the views of the school in a monograph called *Physiocratie* (1768). The name, taken from the Greek "let nature" (physis) "rule" (kratein). The most direct application of the philosophy was to the emerging discipline of economics, and is recognized immediately by its most enduring slogan *"laissez faire"* (Gournay's motto, "let him do").

Despite its emphasis on nature and free economics, it is considered idealism. This stems from its primary emphasis on a belief that all of nature responds to a body of natural laws which are permanent, are true, and are *a priori*. Man, if he is free to operate according to his *a priori* acquisitive and competitive nature, will produce more things of higher quality and greater variety than when operating within a system of restraints.[16] This philosophy's vision of man as a producer disdains luxury and excessive wealth as degenerating forces. The highest expression of man is of man the producer. In this state he is closest to the ideal which is incarnated in his nature.

The doctrine as applied to economics is reflected in Quesnay and Adam Smith[17]; as applied to politics it is reflected in the writings of Condorcet[18] who deduced the doctrine of *inalienable rights* as expressed in his *Tableau of the Progress of the Human Mind*. As applied to capitalistic free enterprise it was reflected in the American innovations of Pierre Samuel DuPont himself, who invented the term. DuPont served the French government as an inspector of manufacturers; he left the government in 1776, but in 1783 he returned to assist in the negotiations which resulted in England's recognition of American independence. Having opposed England in certain elements of the revolution, he exiled himself to America in 1799.[19] Subsequently, this remarkable philosopher-industrialist founded the industrial American enterprise which began as a powder mill on the banks of the Brandywine near the city of Wilmington, Delaware.

It would be a mistake, however, to assume that physiocratic ideals governed the development of American industry or even the development of that particular "blue chip" which was founded over a century and a half ago by DuPont. Clearly, American industry has sought the protection of, as well as freedom from, American government. Its traditional uses of American labor have assigned little or no value to the natural or spiritual fulfillment of man. Great American industrial leaders have accumulated wealth and indulged in luxuries. All of these tendencies are denials of the physiocratic ideals. This is not to condemn the American industrial enterprise. It simply emphasizes that the physiocratic ideals in American life are elsewhere.

Specifically, they are in the political writings of Thomas Paine, the agrarian democracy of Thomas Jefferson, the agrarian economics of John Taylor, and the American applications of such European educators and educational theorists as Rousseau, Pestalozzi, and Froebel. Physiocratic ideals were integrated with the methodology of American democracy by Jefferson. In this blend physiocratic idealism achieved a higher expression than in France itself where it remained attached to the feudal order. Jefferson, inspired by Condorcet and Paine, came forward with a vision of man possessed with rights which were natural to his being. Any control placed upon him diminishes him and deprives him from fulfillment. Such control as cannot be avoided should be vested in government which is local and responsive to expressions of his will.

Both Jefferson and Taylor seemed satisfied that man's social destiny was directed and measured by his economic development. Thus, the planter should be free to buy and sell to all the world the produce of his soil, hand, and heart. This placed them in sharp contrast with the industrial leaders who demanded that government invoke its power to tax and tariff as a means of fostering a national economy. In contrast to physiocratic economics, industry has argued with conviction that governmental regulations which are good for American industry are good for American life.

In education, Pestalozzians and Froebelians brought the educational ideas of those pioneers to this continent and put them to practice on a scale far greater than in Europe. The Pestalozzian mode was instituted in Oswego, New York, under the leadership of Edward Sheldon.[20] The Oswego movement not only manifested in the public school but led to the establishment of a normal school as well.[21] Even earlier in the Nineteenth Century other Pestalozzian styles of schools were established in Philadelphia, in Louisville, Kentucky, and in New Harmony, Indiana.[22] By all standards of magnitude the strongest Pestalozzian expression in the American curriculum was reflected in the early industrial arts movement.[23] However, as this movement progressed, industrial arts became a school subject rather than a method or an application of a free-growth learning theory.[24]

Froebel turned his attention to early childhood education and developed his kindergarten on the developmental potential of *guided play*. Here, given freedom and opportunity, the child unfolds (as perhaps a rosebud unfolds) in the direction of the ideal which is shaped within nature's grand design. The kindergarten flourished in the United States. Its pioneers include such notables as Elizabeth Peabody, Mrs. Carl Schwiz, Marie Bolte, and Colonel Parker. The Froebelian influence can still be seen in the American kindergarten. But, as often happens, this institution seems to have become something else.

The force of that which we call physiocratic idealism is still present in the American mind. It has been superseded in economic thought and remains an object of sentimental rhetoric in the political sphere. Recently a new stamp (40¢) was struck commemorating the melancholy Thomas Paine. Celebrated in early life, his views soon became much too liberal for a young nation confronted by its own responsibility. Now America is acknowledging its debt. However, physiocratic ideals have been preserved in education and may, in present times, be experiencing a renaissance. As educators speak of "individualizing" instruction and "ungrading" the school, one feels the convictions of Rousseau, Pestalozzi, and Froebel are still alive and vital. Indeed, they seem now to be spreading. As to the rest of contemporary life, the word freedom has lost the associations given it by the physiocratic philosophers. It was a great and very romantic movement which began by a belief in the existence of ideals which were in some way imbued in man and nature. For a time there were men willing to give this belief social, economic, or political reality. But the agrarian mentality of the Virginia squires passed with the last generation and States' rights became a lost cause. Only in education does the authentic physiocratic spirit survive.

Formal Idealism

The plantation mentality of rural Virginia differed from the plantation mentality of the Deep South. The physiocratic democracy in Jefferson's idealism was a vastly different thing from the aristocracy which was imbedded in the idealism of John Calhoun and the circle of Charleston or Carolinian intellectuals of the first half of the Nineteenth Century. Students of American history who have been particularly attendant to the antecedent events of the American Civil War are increasingly in accord that it was the arrogance and intransigence of the northern abolitionists which welded the Virginians and Carolinians into the same confederacy. There is ample evidence that slavery "that peculiar southern institution" was not sustained by the Virginia intellectuals. Many of them freed their own slaves, and others had avowed their intention to do so. They were restrained, in some cases, by a growing resentment of abolitionist propaganda, but it is doubted that they would have seceded or have gone to war over slavery alone. Physiocratic democracy gave ideology to state sovereignty but not to human slavery. Located between the hostile extremes Virginia could not be neutral in armed conflict. Given her strong military traditions and numerous "fire eaters," Virginia would not be disposed to neutrality.

It remains a matter of debate whether Virginia could have given leadership in a search for diplomatic solutions. Some assert political fumbling in the north made this impossible. Others say that Calhoun, for all of his hostility, was a statesman who had the confidence of the Deep South and could better than hold his own against the northern intellectuals in Congress and elsewhere. After Calhoun passed away, his brilliant advocacy was not replaced, and the Deep South, no longer confident of its strong representation in the government, turned at last to those who for some time had argued the path of secession and armed resistance. These questions will forever be issues in historical analysis, and there are many now who are fond of demonstrating that the American Civil War was caused by inept men, fought by inept generals, and followed by inept government. The whole story, as told today, often becomes a salute to the human spirit which we are asked to believe overcame one blunder after another. It is an improbable tale which has a Colonel Lee of the United States Army, who reputedly opposed slavery, capturing and court-martialing one John Brown, who also opposed slavery. The hanging of John Brown was attended by a devout Presbyterian mathematics teacher named Thomas Jackson who brought to those present a corps of military cadets over which he presided. Jackson, it seems, would have been at home in Seventeenth Century New England and would have approved the sermons of Jonathan Edwards.

Before the tale ends, Jackson died of wounds, but not before he had won acclaim as America's greatest military tactician, and Lee surrendered a southern army to a northern army whose officers were unheard of when the conflict began. In the Deep South other northern armies had been ravaging a great culture, punishing it for what was believed to be an arrogant and unwarranted insurrection and a capricious indifference to human dignity and human suffering.

Those who assert that such a war could have been avoided by reasonable men do not understand the nature of idealism. Once men accept a set of metaphysical assumptions as true, their reason, no matter how vigorous or valid, turns them in a path which is different from that of other men with other assumptions. The American Civil War was inevitable because the ideological range was too great to be spanned by the statesmanship of the times. Compromise can be readily negotiated on empirical concerns. But men find extreme difficulty in negotiating their metaphysical assumptions. The conflict was between the materialism and transcendental idealism of the North and the formal idealism of the Deep South. The physiocratic idealists of Virginia had some things in common with both North and South. But when the balance was tested, Virginia was compelled by her geography and commitment to local sovereignty to join the Confederacy. Once war begins, ideological or metaphysical objectives are displaced by the necessity of winning.

Charleston intellectuals in the first half of the Nineteenth Century developed as much as America ever had of an aristocracy. The model, of course, was the style of Greek democracy advocated by Plato in the *Republic*. In addition to John Calhoun and his political disciples were writers such as Hugh Legare, William Crofts, and Gilmore Simms. Alexander Stephens, the great Georgia intellectual who served as vice president of the Confederacy, was well established as a southern liberal and believer in Jeffersonian agrarianism.[25] The South Carolina philosophy of government contained the classical elements of the Greek republic. It imposed itself easily on the southern mind and soon became the southern ideology. It was impossible for any to resist. Stephens was unable to do so. He joined his friend Bob Toombs of the Calhoun circle and joined Plato in his views on slavery. He admitted that at the time of the Constitution many statesmen held the view that enslavement of the African was in violation of the laws of nature. But, said Stephens:[26]

> Those ideas, however, were fundamentally wrong. They rested on the assumption of the equality of the races. This was an error. Our new government is founded on exactly the opposite idea; its foundations are laid; its cornerstone rests upon the great truth that the negro is not equal to the white man; that slavery-subordination to the superior race is his natural and normal condition. . . .

Jefferson's aristocracy (if we can presume such a term) was, according to Jefferson, an aristocracy of talent which emerges in freedom. The aristocracy of the Deep South was based upon ontological suppositions which were as old as philosophy itself. Plato, particularly in his later years, would have approved of them. Each great plantation was a community, ruled by a well educated gentry whose duty it was to institute such humane laws as to assure the good life of all concerned.[27] There was much in common between the Platonic idea of a city-state and the Carolinian idea of a plantation. There is much in common between the Platonic idea of a philosopher king and the Carolinian idea of a plantation master. The latter was bred and nurtured to responsibility and correct sentiment. Nothing can be more certain than the fact that many, probably most, plantation masters were exemplary in this respect. Alexander Stephens himself was considered a model.[28] His pronouncement of the inferiority of the negro in the context of his philosophy was not a repudiation or a denouncement of the negro. Rather, it was an acknowledgment of responsibility for him, a responsibility which he took very seriously in his personal affairs.

As the ontological suppositions which supported this idyllic life settled deeply within the people of the South, understanding between the Deep South and the North virtually disappeared. Secession was inevitable, and war was its consequence. War did not destroy the formal idealism of the Deep South, but the social, political, and economic aftermath of the war made its prewar institutional reality impossible. Gradually a new institution, segregation, emerged. For nearly ninety years it was legal. For the past two decades it has been illegal, but *de facto*. Segregation no longer stands on idealistic foundations and is certainly not confined to the South. From the confusion which appears in contemporary discourse we can be assured that *de facto* segregation is not yet understood by its Twentieth-Century practitioners. However, it is clear that the ideological conflicts of the Nineteenth Century have evidently given America a long and ulcerous aftermath. *De facto* segregation is one unhealed irritation which continues to be nettled and chafed by certain cultural circumstances in the urban life of modern America.

Transcendental Idealism

An explanation of American transcendental idealism could have any one of a number of starting points. Three have been selected for this explanation. The first of these three points is the Unitarian movement, the second is the philosophy of Immanuel Kant, and the third is Daniel Webster. Each of these offers has something vital to contribute to an understanding of transcendentalism in America. The Unitarian movement's contribution was its dramatizing the unbinding of the puritan moral conscience, which it seems for two centuries had been leashed by Calvinistic dogmas and the Yankee reverence for property. When it came unbound, it came with a roar, and the great pens of New England, dripping with polemic, anguished over man's heartlessness to man, not only in New England but everywhere. Immanuel Kant produced a metaphysical vision which was made to order for an intellectual revolt against human tyranny of any kind, real or imagined. Kant supplied the initial shot for the transcendental cannon, and after the first great fusillade, ammunition fashioned by Fitch, Shelling, Hegel, Wordsworth, and Coleridge was used to continue the bombardment. Webster became a human symbol of all which transcendentalism disapproved. Understanding Webster, therefore, is a way of understanding the transcendentalist. In his person he represented all that transcendental idealists thought America could have been and failed to be.

The Unitarian movement had as one of its curious aspects the formation of a new style of liberal congregationalism which finally incorporated as a new protestant denomination. But the Unitarian movement is seen as much more than simply the emergence of a new church. Forces grew in the New England mind which were generated by or parallel to those associated with the John Locke and the French romantics. The American political and military efforts to achieve independence from England joined cause with the anti-Trinitarianism which was challenging orthodox Calvinism in the Congregational churches of New England. In the period from 1750 to 1775 the persons who were urging political independence were also pushing back at the Calvinistic grip which encased and retained the church. These were the theological liberals of New England.[29]

King's Chapel, the oldest Episcopal chapel in New England, was the first to become openly Unitarian. Without the war it might not have happened. But the church had lost its rector and many of its leading families in the departure of leading Tory families in 1776.[30] Mr. James Freeman, a graduate of Harvard, became lay minister. His style of discussion-leading free inquiry was appreciated by the remaining congregation. Finally, reference to the Trinity was struck from the order of worship.[31] Freeman was chosen pastor, and in 1785 King's Chapel became the first American Unitarian church. This astonishing development soon led to others as Unitarian sentiment continued to build in the Congregationalist churches. By the turn of the century the issue was heated to the point that battle lines were drawn. Harvard College could not remain neutral. In 1805 Henry Ware, an avowed and active Unitarian, was appointed to the Hollis Chair of Theology at Harvard. The existing grounds of compromise were thus washed away; the breech was open.

In 1808 Andover Theological Seminary was founded in the interests of traditional Trinitarianism. This was mainly a reaction to Harvard's apostasy. The orthodox line at Andover was protected by a requirement that at stated intervals each professor sign a statement of the seminary creed.[32] *The Panoplist*, edited by Jeremiah Evarts, was launched in another spirited effort to retain popular support for the orthodoxy. But New Englanders were evidently weary of mechanical explanations of God's reality and of hearing that they, their children, and all of their fellow townsmen, were inherently evil. The spell of Edwards had been broken, and the Unitarian movement grew.

Congregations were divided, but the bonds of property and the Yankee respect for those bonds held them together. For a time the storm centered on the pulpit as congregations fought among themselves to have clergy favorable to one or the other side of the issue. However, the conflict moved to the courts when the Unitarian denomination became a formal reality. This reality is dated from the celebrated ordination sermon preached by William Ellery Channing, the recognized leader of the American Unitarians. From this time forward liberal factions in the churches of New England began to establish control.

This came as a consequence of an 1820 decision by the Supreme Court of the State of Massachusetts which gave the Unitarians in Dedham, Massachusetts, a large share of the church property in dispute.[33] With the legal position clear that the "majority of communicants" would control matters relating to church property some of the orthodoxy and their ministers were forced to leave and establish new churches of their own. Thus, in a number of New England towns the *First* Congregationalist church became the Unitarian and the *Second* Congregationalist church became Trinitarian. It is easy to imagine the bitterness this sort of thing created. The reminiscences of Oliver W. Holmes (Sr.) vividly depict his iron-willed clergyman father leading his Trinitarian congregation into a new church. Others did the same, and the traditional church carried on and grew in strength under the driving passion of such pastors as Lyman Beecher of the Hanover Street Church.

The subsequent history of the Unitarian church, though interesting, is of minor relevance here. In New England, because of the legal consequences of the rules of the Congregationalist polity, the Unitarians held possession of church properties, many of which dated from the dawn of American colonial life. Although open, unrestrained, and undogmatic, the New England Unitarians are still culturally part of an older heritage. This generates a stability which tends to belie the radical theological stance of earlier days. Unitarian churches other than in New England tend to draw membership from the disaffected or free-thinking members of the community.[34] It has become a haven for those who wish to come to terms with ultimate reality in their own way. To be this, as a church, the church must be a denial; it must deny everything and affirm nothing except a kind of humanistic faith in humanity. The Unitarian church does assert this with something approaching the regularity and intensity of dogma.

This humanism has been considered by critics of Unitarianism as a pale and vague substitute for all that Unitarianism denies. The denials are so systematic that Unitarian churches have been accused of taking perverse pleasure in conducting services in the style of town meetings. Charles G. Finney, the eminent Nineteenth-Century revivalist, spoke of the Boston Unitarians:[35]

> The mass of people in Boston are more unsettled in their religious convictions than in any other place I have labored in, notwithstanding their intelligence; for they are surely an intelligent people on all questions except religion. It is extremely difficult to make religious truths lodge in their minds, because the influence of Unitarian teaching has been to lead them to call in question all the principal doctrines of the Bible. Their system is one of denial. Their theology is negative. They deny almost everything, and affirm almost nothing. In such a field error finds the ears of the people open; and the most irrational views on religious subjects come to be held by a great many people.

Finney's complaint serves to illustrate the distance between the Trinitarian and Unitarian worlds. In the Trinitarian world Sunday service was a time to bring forth the ancient fears and to offer the time-honored answers of assurance. In the Unitarian world Sunday service brought forth the ancient questions and the communicants departed with whatever answers, fears, or doubts their own moral and intellectual power produced.

The Unitarian movement was more than a struggle over reforms in the church and clergy. With metaphysics at last unbridled, Nineteenth-Century America became marked by various adventures in Utopianism and perfectionism. Very prominent among these was the extraordinary venture of John Humphrey Noyes (1811-1866), who even though enrolled at Andover heard "inner voices" which suggested he transfer to Yale.[36] Later, his continued consultation with the inner voice and his radical and passionate preaching in Massachusetts and Vermont led to the establishment of a Christian-communist community at Oneida, New York, which experimented with a complex marriage. In effect, every man in the community was married to every woman. Their lives were, nonetheless, structured and regulated. Partners in physical love or procreation applied for and were granted authorization. Children belonged to the community. The design of the structure was to allow the power of human love (physical and spiritual) to motivate and rule human relationships.

Another great movement was personified by the life and work of Mary Baker Eddy (1821-1910), the founder of Christian Science. This movement, composed of strong-willed people who were also possessed of uncommon literary power, developed upon belief that the problems (physical, mental, and spiritual) of men are best resolved in absolute faith. The first sentence of her famous *Science and Health* reads, "The prayer that reforms the sinner and heals the sick is an absolute faith that all things are possible in God."[37] The effort by the orthodoxy to parry the thrust of Harvard with the blade of Andover was not lost on other Christian congregations. One after the other church denominations founded colleges, endowed theological chairs, and developed preparatory schools. Other adventures in Utopianism such as the effort at communal living at Brook Farm were tried. In the Nineteenth Century American religious life took on all these galvanic new dimensions which included scholasticism, social experimentalism, and finally, abolitionism.

Abolitionism came late to New England, but it was in New England that its flamboyance and exuberance and pitiless invective reached a climax. The social conscience of New England had at last become a formidable thing. Indeed, it seemed to shake the world itself. Not all of the abolitionist incendiaries were New Englanders, but New England furnished the intellectual bastions from which a drum-fire of social criticism and appeals for social reforms was heard. By conventional standards of self-interest, the abolitionists were not self-interested. They were attacking property, and property returned the attacks in kind. They did not win honor, power, wealth, or social respect. They were an ill-assorted lot who, but for their mutual distress over human slavery, would not have gotten on well together. William L. Garrison, Samuel J. May, Edmund Quincy, Jonathan Sewall, Theodore Parker, Lydia Child, Wendel Phillips, Thomas Higginson, Henry Beecher, and James Lowell (in his younger days) were joined by heroic personalities from the Middle States such as Lewis Tappan, Gerrit Smith, and Lucretia Mott. They, along with others, developed and hewed to a hard line which eliminated any continuing possibility for a rapprochement with human slavery.

Taken as a whole the Unitarian movement describes the American mind as a young colt, free, for the first time, in his new pasture. As such colts do, he really kicked up his heels. The hobbles, strictures, and shackles of old-world prescriptions, the old reverence for property, and Christendom's view of man as an incarnate evil were questioned. American men were at last free to discover themselves and their new world. The day when their first great transcendental visions would turn into portentious responsibility was far distant. It would come, but until it did, there was a moment of exuberance. A new colt was showing itself in a big, bright, new pasture, and the diverse, pluralistic American mind was showing itself to a world that could not fail to be astonished and captivated by its performance.

A young colt will be aimless for a while, but soon he acquires a direction and a bearing. Those first frenzied moments of freedom do pass; his ecstasy does not continue or he would tear himself asunder. As a new colt needs and acquires direction and bearing, this new cast of American mind needed and acquired a philosophy. One was at hand. It was perfectly suited. To find its origin we turn back again to the Old World, to the diminutive man who looms so large in modern philosophy, the savant of Königsberg, Immanuel Kant. This new cast of the American mind needed a moral purpose not founded on formal God-dominated philosophical structures. This base had to be wholly rational; it could not wear the aspects of rejected dogmas. No better base could be found than that which was suggested by the man who depicted the inspiration of his own private conscience thus: "Two things fill the mind with ever new and increasing admiration and awe . . . the starry heavens above and the moral law within."[38] A moral consciousness was the obsessive quality of the Unitarian movement, and long after it surpassed being simply church reform it continued on a broader scale to be a profound inner search as man continued to examine *himself* for the ethic of the new world.

The orthodox had taught that all men are inherently bad and that the rules, dogmas, and strictures work together in ways to make them good. The Unitarians, Utopians, and perfectionists were arguing that all men are inherently good and that rules, dogmas, and strictures obscure and frustrate their goodness and work together in ways to develop mistrust, envy, greed, and the other vipers which poison the humanism of man. Could there be a moral philosophy for man which did not install new vipers in his bosom? What better prospect could there be than one which established the categorical imperative to *act so that the maxim of the will can always hold good as a principle of universal legislation,* or in its second formulation, *so act as to treat humanity, whether in thine own person or in that of any other, in every case as an end, never only as a means.* This moral imperative, formulated in Kant's *Critique of Practical Reason,* further extended in his *Religion Within the Limits of Reason Alone,* and embellished by his disciple Fitche, was tailor-made for the newly emerged intellectual forces in America.

The transcendentalism of Kant was first communicated to the English-speaking world through the poems and essays of English authors such as Carlyle, Wordsworth, and Coleridge. But the American appetite for spiritual idealism was just as great as Britain's, and throughout the Nineteenth Century a steady procession of American intellectuals found their way to the great capitals of European learning. More than a few of them returned deeply imbued with the German Idealism, most of which was based on Kantian metaphysics. While it is true that many of the same Americans were more strongly impressed by the modifications of Hegel, there can be no mistaking the prominence of the Kantian moral imperative in the mainstream of American transcendentalism, particularly of that stem which came to such vivid flower in the Concord School which centered on Ralph Waldo Emerson and included such prominent figures as Thoreau, Fuller, W. E. Channing, and Bronson Alcott.

American transcendentalists seem to have been less influenced by Kant's ontology which restricts experience to the phenomenological world or by his views on the nature of aesthetic judgments. In these matters the American transcendentalists apparently turned to older traditions such as those espoused by Plato, the Stoics, and especially Plotinus. They also turned to the pantheism of Spinoza and to the absolutism of Hegel. But there cannot at any point be a dismissal of Kant. Even as Kant was being hounded for his radical religious views by Frederick William II and was ending his scholarly days with a series of cautious expressions on the nature of God, forces in American life were then mounting which would make the fresh and robust philosophy of the *Critiques* a world-wide crusade against enslaved bodies, regimented spirits, and fear-mongering religions. Many years, numerous struggles, and the emergence of new ways and worlds have brought men to the second half of the Twentieth Century, but this crusade still moves on.

We can trace the origins of American transcendentalism to the Unitarian movement, and its intellectual bearing and direction to the moral vision of Kant. But we can understand transcendentalists better as men by observing how they interacted with the man who symbolized their greatest frustration, Daniel Webster. Daniel Webster was a sound political scholar and was something of a creative thinker. As a member of the American Whig party he was never burdened by a single, consistent ideology which had to be carried through the various political wars. The Whigs were usually in the position of gathering together the various factions of dissent inspired by the affirmative political principles of Jefferson and Jackson. Intellectually, Webster was a realist of the Locke, Burke, Hamilton, and Adams tradition. He would, therefore, respect property and come to its defense. He was also a lawyer and a politician, and as his standing in both professions advanced, his clients and patrons were increasingly men of influence. He worked for them and used his very considerable powers in their behalf.

Even as a young man his speeches were recognized for their intellectual and rhetorical virtuosity. He was possessed of a prodigious memory. His powers of eloquence were of such magnitude that any of his utterances which extended beyond a few sentences were regarded as events worth noting. It is little wonder that the transcendentalists and assorted radicals fulminated against him. It is easy to forgive an oaf for his oafishness, but Webster was not an oaf. He understood freedom, he loved the land. He had no personal hatred of Jacksonian Democracy or of Adam Smith and *laissez faire*. Possibly he would have come to terms with the transcendentalists and they with him, had it not been for the issue of slavery and its extension. This became the crux of the problem, the bitter and undissolvable pill, and those on both sides who had to swallow it are shown to us more clearly because of their performances.

Arrayed against Webster was a formidable group of American writers which included no less than Emerson, Channing, Parker, Garrison, Philips, Higginson, Harriet Beecher Stowe, and others. Webster, Calhoun, and Clay emerged as the three titans in the struggle over the American constitution. With each compromise new layers of scorn were heaped upon Webster. As Webster summoned and consecrated his powers to a defense of the Union, the howl of his transcendental constituents grew in fury and intensity. Finally, they began to discredit his earlier triumphs, attributing bad motives and even lack of originality to his defense in the celebrated Dartmouth College case which he argued before the Supreme Court in 1818.[39] Whittier's wrath was exposed in *Ichabod*. Emerson terminated a commentary on Webster's role in the *Fugitive Slave Law* with the memorable and incisive metaphor, "All the drops of his blood have eyes that look downward."

But the student of Webster finds him no friend of slavery. He was a practical realist working along the only lines open to him for abolition. The formidable men of the Concord school, all men of peace, harboring an intense aversion to violence of any kind, were openly advocating a course which they knew could only be won by invoking the most fearsome bloodbath in the history of the continent. The New England transcendentalists were men of ideas, not men of responsibility. They knew and, by their silence, approved of John Brown's grim enterprises in Kansas and of his insurrectional aims at Harper's Ferry. Ever far from the scenes of physical combat, the New England transcendentalists despised the fight with Mexico, rebuked one national leader after another, and arrayed their eloquent words to battle the institutions devoted to freedom and order. Men who carried the burdens of state and the responsibility for order largely ignored them. For this they deserve praise.

This is not to say the transcendentalists did not affect the men of their times. However, they speak even more strongly to the men of the second part of the Twentieth Century who are urged by many in our own times to regard these noisy and, at times, incoherent philosophers as national heroes. They had little stomach for personal heroism, and perhaps, this is to praise them. They did well what they could do and that was to reflect deeply and sincerely from a position which assumed man's inherent goodness. They gave America something to think about; this is to honor them. If tempted to heroics, they resisted successfully. Emerson was more than once importuned to join the skirmish. But he recorded in his journal: [40]

> I walked at night, and bemoaned myself because I had not thrown myself into this deplorable question of slavery, which seems to want nothing so much as a few assured voices. But then in hours of sanity, I recover myself, and say, "God must govern his own world; and knows his own way out of this pit without my desertion of my post which has none to guard it

but me. I have quite other slaves to free than those negroes,
to wit, imprisoned spirits, imprisoned thoughts, far back in the
brain of man,—far retired in the heaven of invention, and
which, important to the republic of Man, have no other watch-
man, or lover, or defender, but I."

Emerson, the transcendentalist, attempted to solace his manly
conscience by discovering that there was a God, who governed the
world and who knew how to get out of the "pit" of slavery on his
own, but who had somehow, either by neglect or deliberate appropriation, left all "imprisoned thoughts" and "imprisoned spirits" for poor
Emerson to uncork on his own. However, Emerson as a philosopher is
not renowned for his logic, so he bravely remained in Concord and
philosophy gained. Indeed, Webster, the man of the world, loved
good wine, good food, good land, good livestock, and the good life
in general, and he indulged in them during his hours away from the
responsibilities of state he carried. Portraitures of Emerson reveal
his narrow figure, deep-set intelligent eyes, sharp features, and serious
countenance. There were things that Emerson liked too, and he did not
leave them. Can Emerson in justice criticize Webster? The judgment
of history will be close.

Perspective is needed. Much is made over Thoreau's going to
jail for one night over non-payment of a poll tax during the Mexican
War. His few hours in "the brig" are often used to give additional
moral credence to his brilliant essay on civil disobedience which soon
followed. Time and a good deal of unintentional amplification have
made this seem more than it was. If most accounts of Thoreau's life
merit belief, then he, too, was more inclined to stage a personal retreat
from the onerous demands of the social participation than from a direct
and bold confrontation with the realities of social justice. We see no
indication in advance of the incident that he took extra pains to draw
attention to his self-willed imprisonment. He did not avail himself
of many other opportunities to go to jail. Undoubtedly, his fellow
townsmen would have had no reluctance in obliging him if he did. In
his essay we find him in a high spirit of self-justification. Neither
Thoreau nor Emerson had the vanity or the pretentious advocacy
needed for planned martyrdom. Both were excellent and highly original
philosophers. Their works are well worth the time one needs to study
them properly. However, they were not statesmen. They did not have
the ability nor the temperament for administrative tasks. Social conscience and moral insight are one thing. Social responsibility and moral
duty are quite another. America can be proud of her Emersons, but

she owes her existence to her Websters. This is a thesis which young readers might ponder.

The transcendentalist movement included many vivid personalities. It is difficult to pass any of them without comment. From the militant Unitarian parson, Theodore Parker, who established a conception of evolutionary theism, to Margaret Fuller, the impulsive feminist, there was a range of vigorous and strong-willed Americans unmatched by any group of history. Parker, for example, was described by one of his biographers as "the best working plan of an American yet produced." In his time his moral commitments and abrupt manners made him loved and hated. Said he: "I have had to arm myself. I have written my sermons with a pistol in my desk, loaded with a cap on the nipple, and ready for action."[41] He was equal to his moment in history. Margaret Fuller, as another example, was a valiant non-conformist in the best tradition. A brilliant writer and conversationalist, she stood bravely against the array of stupid inhibitions which were the plight of women in her day. Her life stands as inspiration to the literature of independence and courage.

The extreme liberal wing of the transcendentalist movement was located in the Concord literary circle which gathered around Emerson and was so prominently associated with the transcendentalist journal called The Dial. Of this group, philosophy must take particular notice of two. The first is Emerson himself and the second is Henry Thoreau. The two men not only shared the same interval of time, but the latter spent part of his life in a hut located on the property of the former. There was no question of discipleship or even of undying friendship. It is hard to imagine them as kindred spirits. Each is a special case. What did they share besides time and property? Simply a belief that there are ideas in the mind which are laws in man and nature. They believed that God and nature are brought together in men. They accepted soul as the cause and not the consequence of life. They were also joined by their common mistrust of society and its processes. Indeed, they loved and revered the transcendental in man and came to despise and reject all which distorted or suppressed it. They raised polemics against property, government, trade, slavery, and urban life. They wanted men close to the land, close to nature.

Emerson (1803-1882) had a satisfying but undistinguished career at Harvard. He taught briefly and then entered the ministry. Unhappy with the requirements which sacramental dogma forced upon him, he resigned his pastorate and sailed for Europe where he visited Carlyle, Coleridge, and several other leading figures. It was the first and most momentous of three trips, for it was upon his first return to New England that his rich outpouring of lectures and essays commenced and began to attract notice. Among his best works are his two volumes of *Essays* wherein he displayed his fascination with abstract nouns, e.g., *Friendship, Politics, Self-Reliance, Intellect,* and the *Over-Soul.* Another highly regarded book contains his impressions of the English people which he published in a volume called *English Traits.*

Emerson as a philosopher was not a logician or system builder.[42] He was a passionate and eloquent intuitionist. His essays are characterized by epigrammatic or highly metaphorical expressions put forward in units of thought having a piquancy and ardor which catapult the reader into his own reflections. His poetic prose is, therefore, almost too rich to follow, and the reader is frequently called upon to suppress his imagination in order to track the coherence of Emersonian discourse. He believed "in the divine sufficiency of the individual." In this he never faltered and never compromised. Emerson also sustained the transcendentalists' posture of ultimate optimism and ultimate good. He believed evil is not in nature and no evil by nature is created. Such evil as exists stems from the works of men. No American has written more inspiringly about the idea of man.

It is difficult to associate Emerson with a standing philosophical tradition. He has been called an arch-Platonist,[43] but despite his preoccupation with the abstract noun he certainly is not a Platonist of the classical mode. Of all the philosophers of antiquity, he seems more in harmony with Plotinus. His magnificent vision of the *Over-Soul* matches clearly the cosmic arrangement taught by the Neo-Platonists. His view of man expressed in *Circles* evidences an attraction to Indian literature and philosophy. His conception of nature as a manifestation of spirit could be a derivation from Spinoza with a brush of Hegel. However, it is difficult, even dangerous, to develop these associations. Emerson's philosophizing was as free and as original as his unrestrained intuition. He seemed to feel no obligation to be consistent, logical, or academic. For this reason the dominion of literature acclaims him more openly than do the more skeptical domains of philosophy. Philosophy wants more than eloquence in its sentences. On the other hand, literature wants more than didactics in its poetry. Emerson's philosophic efforts, therefore, may belong to literature, and his deliberate poetic efforts are handed off to philosophy.

However, as in any original thinker, his thoughts and expressions concern us deeply. Our efforts to lodge him in academic categories are useful only to the extent that such efforts help us better to understand his thoughts. We turn to Emerson constantly for that phrase which so embraces and envelops an idea that it leaves it with nothing to be added. Some claim he said a great deal; others argue that he said very little; but all will agree that whatever he said he said about as well as a man could say it.

Thoreau (1818-1862) was more rhapsodical than Emerson. His attachments to nature and idea were of Sapphic intensity. Where Emerson's prose moved upward into metaphorical abstractions, Thoreau's headed out-of-doors across meadows, lakes, and along wooded trails. He constantly congratulated nature for being what it was. He found a kind of truth in the trail, in the fragrance of summer flowers, and in the undefiled autumn landscape. His first book, *A Week on the Concord and Merrimac Rivers,* was published in 1849. His most famous book, *Walden,* was issued five years later.

The most dramatic interval in his life came in 1845. During that year he built a cabin at Walden Pond on property owned by Emerson. He lived in this cabin for two years, two months, and two days. Contrary to what is commonly believed, he was not a hermit. He traveled to town to see a friend, and numerous visitors came to see him. But he did manage to form a powerful liaison with nature, and the spell was never broken.

Thoreau was a student of Greek philosophy, and his mastery of this field can quickly be detected in his writing. During most of his adult years he kept a Journal which is increasingly regarded as his greatest work. He took interest in economics, politics, and religion and became an unrelenting critic of the contemporary social enterprises in these fields. His fellow townsmen regarded him as a "queer bird." Prior to his death from tuberculosis in 1862 he enjoyed a formidable reputation as a naturalist. His standing as a philosopher did not emerge until several decades after his death. Although many "social action" liberals of the Twentieth Century have taken him aboard as the founder of their cause, we find little in their cause and in his to justify such a match. Thoreau was distrustful of society and wanted nothing so much as to have a life which was free of its strictures. He is much closer to the physiocratic ideals of Jefferson than was Emerson. Only his firm panentheism holds him in the transcendentalist category. His mode of life is kindred to the lives of Hipponax, Heraclitus, Antisthenes, Diogenes, Zeno, Plotinus, Spinoza and Rousseau. They did not philosophize alike on most matters, but each of them, in one way or another, dramatized his break from the common lot of men. Their genius could not be brought to compromise with the ways of men. The miracle of western man is that he has learned to tolerate such dissent. It wasn't easy. Thoreau did not have the applause which came to Emerson. But men of this nature do not need applause.

Absolute Idealism

It has been established that the idealism of Hegel differed significantly from that of Kant. Hegel had clearer access to the philosophy of Spinoza and seems to have been more deeply impressed by Spinoza. In addition, Hegel originated his own notions of the way forces interact dialectically, and Hegel added to Kant's philosophy of individual spirit the suggestion that the identity of the individual is divined through the successively larger strata of social reality to which he belongs. This gives a man a real stake in his country. In a sense, his nation stands as a measure of who and what he is. Its principles become his standard of value, and his realization of self is accomplished mainly through his participation as a citizen in its affairs and through his loyalty and sacrifice to its ideals. In this vision a man's spiritual self merges with the spirit of the socal realities which go ever outward until it becomes the all-encompassing absolute which is God.

Immediately after the American Civil War there was a strong sense of unionhood and nationhood. In the eyes of many Americans the war was a contest in which these ideals had been fought for and won. The consciousness of this great struggle was prominent in the mind and mood of the people. The national government had been tested in the dialectic of insurrection and battle. It came through as the *superior principle.* A great new industrial empire was building in the north, the western frontier was alive with expansive enterprise, and the south was grudgingly fitting itself into a national scheme, not agreeing might was right, but recognizing, after all, that might was might.

The times were ripe for absolute idealism, and in the sixty years which followed the American Civil War, absolute idealism tended to dominate the philosophical posture of the American people. But it was implanted in American life several decades before 1860. Many of the German scholars who came to America, such as Frederick

Rauch (1806-1841) who served for five years as president of Franklin and Marshall College, Francis Lieber (1800-1872) who became a professor of history at Columbia, and Carl Follen (1796-1840) who taught German at Harvard, are a few of the several who brought Hegelian themes to American classrooms. In addition, numerous Americans traveled and studied abroad. They returned deeply influenced by Hegelian thought. Foremost among these were Edward Everett, George Ticknor, George Bancroft, G. Stanley Hall, Arthur Tappan, Horace Mann, Henry Bernard, Jared Sparks, William T. Harris, and Henry W. Longfellow.

This list is only partial, but even as far as it goes it demonstrates the high level of exposure which German idealism was given before, during, and immediately after the American Civil War. There is no question that at the outset of the war the great day of the *liberal* transcendentalists was passing. If for no other reason, its anti-government, anti-society attitudes lost credence during the great wartime invocation of national concern, and the even greater postwar growth of national identity. The scepter of influence in New England passed to the Boston Brahmins who were bound to liberal transcendentalism by concession to the preeminence of man's spiritual nature but who saw that this spiritual nature was integral with a social absolute rather than infinite alone of itself. Of the group, of course, were such notables as Ticknor, Everett, Lowell, and O. W. Holmes, Sr. The Emersonian circle recognized this Boston branch of idealism for what it was and cared little for it. But as the Nineteenth Century entered its second half it was the absolutists and not the transcendentalists who were in ascendancy.

Certainly the eye of the education student must fall with interest on Horace Mann. He was an educational theorist who had deep commitments and brilliant qualities of leadership. He was not a professional philosopher, but his theories were heavily influenced by an overriding social concern which was clearly consistent with the emerging absolute idealism in America. In his *Twelfth Annual Report*[44] he delivered his vision of an inspired public education. He began it by saying:

> Without undervaluing any other human agency, it may safely be affirmed that the common school . . . may be the most effective and benignant of all the forces of civilization.

He concluded this preamble by saying in part:

> I proceed, then, in endeavoring to show how the true
> business of the classroom connects itself, and becomes iden-
> tical, with the great interests of society. . . .

There is no question that Mann's philosophical orientation was in the direction of the absolute. He informed property owners who had no children that the "state" is a collective person and that its property must bear the cost of saving youth from poverty and crime and of preparing them for the discharge of their "social duties."[45]

Edward Everett is another great figure whose name must catch the eye of teachers. Noted as an eloquent speaker, Everett served as President of Harvard University during a decisive period of its development. Most commentaries on his place in American life and letters depict him as the "other man" who spoke at the dedication of the National Cemetery at Gettysburg. If we were to seek a single occasion which reflected a turn of the American mind toward absolutism we would probably do no better than to choose the order of exercises at Gettysburg on November 19, 1863. In response to a suggestion by Governor Curtin of Pennsylvania the eighteen states which were joined in defense of the Union had, in the summer of 1863, following the three days of carnage in early July, joined in resolve to establish a national cemetery at Gettysburg in order that their respective soldiers who mingled and fell together in defense of the Union might be "honorably interred." The national character which was given the cemetery was a symbolic gesture not lost upon those who took part in the decision and the subsequent arrangements.[46]

After a military procession from the town to the cemetery, prayer, and music by the Marion Band, Everett stepped forward and, as befitting a Massachusetts man, offered a deferential and open-hearted tribute to the beauty of Pennsylvania in late autumn. He then related in some detail the sequence of events during the three days of battle which occurred slightly more than four months before. Every state, corps, regiment, and nearly every officer of general rank was singled out for praise. Everett, the historian, then took command of the war itself, and with great care he linked the southern cause to the tradition of *rebellion* rather than that of armed conflict between two nations, each having equal claim to sovereignty. America was America, it was not a collection of states and colonies, sects and cults, merged so the whole may serve the several individual interests. As he approached the end of his second hour at the rostrum, Everett turned to the President and said:[47]

The people of loyal America will never ask you, sir, to take to your confidence or admit again to a share in the government the hard-hearted men whose cruel lust for power has brought this desolating war upon the land . . . they may live in safe obscurity beneath the shelter of the government they sought to overthrow, or they may fly to the governments of Europe. . . . There let them stay. The humblest dead soldier that lays dead and stiff in his grave before us, is an object of envy beneath the clods that cover him, in comparison with the living man, I care not with what trumpetry credentials he may be furnished, who is willing to grovel at the foot of a foreign throne for assistance in compassing the ruin of his country.

Everett went on briefly citing "the bonds that unite us as one people." He warmed to his description of America and he declared the bonds of union to be of "perennial force and energy." Entering his final soaring paragraph, he declared:[48]

And now, friends, fellow citizens of Gettysburg and Pennsylvania, and you from remoter states, let me again, as we part, invoke your benediction on these honored graves. You feel, though the occasion is mournful, that it is good to be here. You feel that it was greatly auspicious for the cause of the country, that the men of the East and men of the West, the men of nineteen sister states, stood side by side on the perilous ridges of the battle. You now feel it is a new bond of union, that they shall lie side by side, till the clarion, louder than that which marshalled them to combat, shall awake their slumbers. God bless the Union; it is dearer to us for the blood of brave men which has been shed in its defense . . . and down to the last period of recorded time, in the glorious annals of our common country, there will be no brighter page than that which relates *The Battles of Gettysburg*.

Everett was followed on the program by a hymn composed for the occasion and sung by the crowd. And then the President came forward to speak. His few words took no more than two minutes. Whatever manner of philosopher he may have been previously in his life, the President was at that moment a Hegelian idealist. His opening sentence referred to a nation founded on the proposition of equality. Then he went on to suggest that the idea was now being tested in the way that such ideas are tested, by war. The idea of Gettysburg was already "hallowed" and "consecrated" by the struggle and by the sacrifice. But at that moment the test was not over; there was "a great task remaining before us. . . ." He appealed that from "these honored dead we take increased devotion—that we here highly resolve that the dead shall not have died in vain. . . ."

That afternoon at Gettysburg was a great moment for sentiments consistent with Hegelian metaphysics. Americans now belonged to the land. As the President solemnly noted, "the brave men, living and dead, have consecrated it far beyond our poor power to add or detract." The sentiment runs true: men who give themselves to a land then belong to the land. Robert Frost in modern times sang of this in his imaginative and strangely moving *Gift Outright*. Americans in the tradition of absolute idealism take self-identity from the nation. Were he not followed at Gettysburg by the President of the United States, who then and there presented the English language with its greatest ode to democratic government, Everett's words would have been better "noted" and "long remembered." This memorable confrontation of Everett's eloquence and Lincoln's poetry vividly dramatized how poetry will always dominate eloquence. However, eloquence is something with which to reckon, and Everett was a very eloquent man.

Of all the absolutists, none represents a more lasting influence on the American mind than George Bancroft (1800-1891). Caught up in the nationalistic spirit of the late Nineteenth Century he wrote a ten-volume *History of the United States*. He revised it twice, the final revision containing a volume on the *History of the Formation of the Constitution*. His metaphysical style has often been compared to a long "Fourth of July oration." However, he reflected a deep and abiding faith in the American spirit and the American idea with particular reference to the Jacksonian fashion. His influence in the writing of history was at its peak at the time the American public school was forming. Bancroft's style of history was, therefore, etched deeply on the American history which was taught to the generations of America in the late Nineteenth and early Twentieth Centuries. The modern modes of historical criticism find much fault in this kind and form of historical research and writing. However, even today, it is not entirely out of vogue. Many Americans have a view of their country which Bancroft and his kindred produced. They still conceive of western civilization as a long struggle culminated by the great success we call America. Whether one likes it or not depends on the definition of history he accepts and the uses of history which he approves.

Unquestionably the public school leader who did as much as any to implant the notions of absolute idealism was William T. Harris

(1835-1909). No student of American education can overlook him. He came from Connecticut to the public schools of St. Louis where he began employment as a teacher of shorthand. In slightly more than ten years he became the superintendent of schools. He also came to be prominent in the St. Louis philosophical society and was attracted to Hegelian philosophy through influences he encountered there which included an association with the native German philosopher, Henry Brokmeyer (1828-1906). An articulate, driving man with deep internal commitments, Harris soon became a national figure in education. He was associated with the establishment and served as editor of the *Journal of Speculative Philosophy* which catered markedly to Hegelian views. In 1880 he left St. Louis and joined with Bronson Alcott in an effort to formalize the Concord School of Philosophy.[49] The effort they made seems reminiscent of the effort by medieval philosophers to synthesize Plato and Aristotle. Transcendentalism and absolutism of that day had some things in common. Perhaps grounds could have been found to lead transcendentalists to a greater acceptance of the requirements which social order places upon individuals. Perhaps, at the same time, Hegelians could have been persuaded that a man is free by nature and not by association with other men in a state. But neither of these things happened, and in 1887, after seven years of relative freedom from heavy administrative burdens, Harris accepted appointment as United States Commissioner of Education. He held this position until his death which occurred twenty-two years later.[50]

During the period, Harris was a leading influence in American thought and practice on education; many of the formative decisions which shaped the educational patterns of the Twentieth Century were made. Among them, of course, was the establishment of graded schools; the conversion and relegation of Pestalozzian ideas to shop *courses*, home economics *courses*, and "extracurricular activities"; the Committee of Ten and the movement to general school standards. And, of course, during this period the national flag, the King James Bible, and the portraits of men who symbolized nationhood were also implanted as standard aspects of the public school classroom. It would be absurd to suggest that all of these things are traceable to Harris himself. However, every one of them is clearly a manifestation of an American philosophy of education which during this era guided on Hegelian metaphysics, and Harris was the leading American Hegelian figure of the time. He is one of the few men who could walk simultaneously on both sides of the street, the side called philosophy and the side called administration. One gave him power and the other purpose. As a consequence, he became a leader in the "St. Louis School," which in turn gave the nation other leaders. He helped found the first great American Journal of Philosophy; he guided the development of a city school system; he held the national commissionership; and he was a popular lecturer.

Hegel did not have his way at every point. Even Harris found it possible to accept the psychology of learning that the American followers of Herbart brought to the attention of American educators. Herbart's great moments on this continent were short-lived. Further evidence that the Hegelian "mind-builders" could tolerate other interpretations is found in their acceptance of the Froebelian kindergarten movement. It seems ironic that Harris and other idealists could accept Froebel's naturistic "unfolding child" and the methodology of play. The irony rests in the subsequent failure of the kindergarten to retain its Froebelian character during an era when educational psychology and experimentalism emerged. The irony is explained by the emergence of standardized testing which had the effect of converting many American educators from "mind-builders" to "headhunters."

Other idealists or educational administrators who moved in the tradition of absolute idealism included such great figures as George Elliot, President of Harvard, who gave leadership to the Committee of Ten and Nicholas Butler, the powerful, brilliant, and dedicated President of Columbia University. Among the philosophers whose teaching and writing contributed to this particular expression of the American mind were Borden Parker Bowne (1847-1910) of Boston University; George H. Howison (1834-1916), who was originally a member of the St. Louis School, studied for a time in Germany, and became professor of philosophy at the University of California; and James E. Creighton (1861-1924), professor at Cornell and prominent in the establishment of the *Philosophical Review*.[51]

Josiah Royce of Harvard (1855-1916), who was mentioned before, was strongly influenced by Hegelian thought, but seems to have oriented his philosophy on a much broader base. He is considered by many as America's outstanding idealist. His work was more academically based than others who were directly or professionally connected to educational practice. But several of his students performed notably in the field of educational philosophy. Of particular renown in education was Herman H. Horne of New York University whose texts in the field of educational philosophy are becoming recognized as the classic statements of American idealism in education.[52] Mary Calkins of Wellesley[53] and William Hocking of Harvard[54] are also widely recognized.

Finally, reference must be made to John Dewey (1859-1952), the Vermonter, who took his secondary and collegiate training in his home town of Burlington. After he was graduated from the University of Vermont in 1879 he taught for two years in the high school at Oil City, Pennsylvania. He returned briefly to Vermont and then in 1882 resumed formal training in philosophy at Johns Hopkins in Baltimore. He completed the Ph.D. in 1884. While at Johns Hopkins, Dewey studied under George S. Morris (1840-1889). Graduate study was still a very new undertaking in America and Johns Hopkins was a new and experimental enterprise. Many professors were coming and going. Evidently G. Stanley Hall, the experimental psychologist, was also present at the time Dewey was there and may have influenced Dewey's thought. Thus Dewey was exposed to the metaphysical idealism of Morris and the experimentalism of Hall. It is not clear whether the contest for Dewey's mind was settled on ideological grounds or simply by the circumstances of life. Morris departed Johns Hopkins for the University of Michigan and Dewey accompanied him to become an instructor in his Department of Philosophy. To all the world, Dewey at this stage of his career was an idealist whose metaphysical posture was outlined on Hegel. Thus, in 1884 Dewey is found to have been moving in the mainstream of American idealism.[55]

However, Dewey had listened to Hall, his dissertation was on Kant, and he was acquainted with the logic of the American pragmatist, Charles Sanders Peirce. Dewey's tenure at Michigan extended to 1894. It was interrupted only by a one-year lectureship at the University of Minnesota. Dewey left Michigan to assume the Head of the Department of Education and Philosophy at the University of Chicago. There are numerous indications that he never ceased to be a vigorous and wide-ranging student of philosophy. A new body of thought seemed ever to be forming in his mind. Some students of Dewey assert that by 1892 he had come to think that the doctrine of the Universal-Self was superfluous, or at the very least, irrelevant. There seems little question that shortly before or shortly after his arrival at Chicago Dewey had pushed aside the major trappings of the absolutist and turned his back upon the metaphysics of his mentor, George Sylvester Morris.[56]

Students of education are fond of believing that this change was, if not instigated, at least confirmed by Dewey's experimentalist approach to curriculum and method in education, as reflected in his organization of a laboratory school at the University of Chicago. Contemporary accounts differ on how well the effort was received in the university and by the profession. But a fuse was lighted, and from that time onward the name and ideas of John Dewey were in the middle of nearly every conversation or statement of opinion about American education.

In apparently rejecting Hegelianism, Dewey stepped aside from the ontological approach to education and embraced the experimentalist epistemology. The ultimate effect of this was the development of his own "tough-minded" form of American pragmatism. With this epistemological focus he worked out a series of statements on American education.

In 1905 he left Chicago to become a professor at Teachers College, Columbia. He remained there as a distinguished professor until he retired in 1930. However, he was not one to remain within the academic enclosure of a university. Indeed, he set the style for a modern professor by lending his name and support to a host of social and professional enterprises. As a writer he was very productive, and his disciples are legion. It seems clear that after he arrived at Columbia he became even more strongly impressed by the philosophical-psychological speculations of William James. Among his many books are *School and Society, Interest and Effort in Education, The Quest for Certainty, Education and the Common Faith,* and *The Problems of Man.*

Having made so clear-cut a conversion from the tradition of absolute mind to the traditions of pragmatism one may wonder at this exposition of Dewey in a chapter devoted to idealism. Indeed, most of Dewey's devoted followers would protest his appearance in this kind of context. The protest would be well-founded. He is more appropriately famed as a *philosopher of process* than as a *philosopher of mind.* However, Dewey did not abandon metaphysics. He postulated society in place of the Universal-Self. His pragmatism constantly leans against the reality of society. Now it may be argued that the conception of Universal-Self is a metaphysical idea and the modern conceptions of society are not metaphysical. But as the argument proceeds those who argue for the reality of society make it sound more and more like a *creature* with processes, needs, and wants the like of which other creatures have. They suggest that there are social problems which *a society* has, and these problems, like raw and bleeding wounds, must be ministered to in order that the men who draw their selfhood from this afflicted society can be better men.

So in Dewey it seems the Universal-Self is demoted into being simply society. But the society can produce values; it can establish the standards of taste, it can identify the good, it becomes the arbitrator of justice. Is this abandonment of the absolute? It appears not to be so. Certainly Dewey's vision of society is more believable and more apparent than Hegel's relatively more grandiose and obscure notions. But in many ways it is not so complete or so satisfying to the inner man which constantly cries out for a complete answer to the great questions regarding the wholeness and relatedness of the entire cosmic order. Dewey, therefore, seems to have kept a streak of absolute idealism in his philosophizing. It is disguised by the word society, but it is there. And when Dewey uses the word society it seems to take on the qualities of the infinite and is by no means wholly devoid of spiritual subject matter. This brilliant and incomparable American philosopher is not, by any standard, a champion of American idealism, but he is subject to interpretation as an idealist in the tradition of the absolute. This explains his inclusion on these pages.

Summary

The American mind is still an ideological battleground. Certainly the philosophies of matter and of process are in the center. Usually they are found at work trying to solve the problems and create peace. The two remaining philosophies of mind, transcendentalism on the liberal side and absolutism on the conservative side, are usually found at work creating the problems which the philosophers of matter and process want to solve. The extreme left is epitomized by the socialist movement which wants nothing so much as to free men from the oppressive needs of the appetite in order that he can rise to his authentic stature as a man. Society and its institutions—political, educational, and philanthropical—have value in the extent to which they make this emergent man possible. It is said of socialists that they love the idea of humanity but despise people. The absolute is epitomized by the extreme right which feels the necessity of the nation, the state, the community, to give personal self-identity to the man. From the Civil War veterans who "waved the bloody shirt" to the militant John Birch and Neo-Nazi groups, the lines are reasonably clear.

In their idealism the American people are pulled toward the

right or left. Presumably all can locate themselves somewhere in this ideological spectrum which depicts *individual man* on one end and *nation*, or the idea of nation, on the other. It matters little that philosophers of matter and process argue that this dichotomy is not real and not the correct form of the problem; this is the way it seems, and much of the American dialectic operates as if the dichotomy were real. And so the national conversation about such things as Freedom, Justice, Temperance, Duty, etc., goes on. To transcendentalists they mean one thing; to absolutists they mean something else altogether. Under such conditions it cannot be said that the American mind is threatened by serenity and American life is in danger of becoming tranquil. Americans are not sedate; they love the clash of ideas. Like the Greeks of the Fifth Century B.C., they relish the forum. It is difficult to escape the notion that man in this American theater is ascending to a new philosophical summit. Just as the issues of change and permanence were the rock and flint for Hellenistic thought, the issues of man and society are driving the American mind to the formulation of a new synthesis which, though perhaps far off, must come.

Notes

1. A general discussion of how certain historians have attempted similar caricatures is included in William H. Dray, *Philosophy of History* (Englewood Cliffs, N. J.: Prentice-Hall, Inc., 1964), ch. 5. Dray makes particular reference to F. H. Underhill, "Arnold Toynbee: Metahistorian," *Canadian Historical Review*, XXXII No. 3 (September 1951), pp. 201-219, and Christopher Dawson, "The Problem of Metahistory," *History Today*, I, No. 6, (June 1951), pp. 9-11.
2. J. Donald Butler, *Four Philosophies and Their Practice in Education and Religion* (New York: Harper's and Brother's Publishers, 1951), pp. 159, 160.
3. *Ibid.*
4. One of the best known epitomizations of American ideas in literature is Vernon Louis Parrington, *Main Currents in American Thought* (New York: Harcourt, Brace and Co., 1958). An effort which makes special reference to educational ideas is Maxine Greene, *The Public School and the Private Vision*, (New York: Random House, Inc., 1965).
5. Ralph Waldo Emerson, "Politics" from *Essays by Ralph Waldo Emerson* (New York: Thomas Y. Crowell Company, 1926, 1961), p. 403.
6. Dorothy Mills, *Renaissance and Reformation Times* (New York: G. P. Putnam's Sons, 1939), p. 293.
7. William Sweet, *The Story of Religion in America* (New York: Harper and Bros., 1950), pp. 45-65.

8. Adam L. Jones, *Early American Philosophers* (New York: Columbia University Contributions to Philosophy, Psychology, and Education), Vol. 11, no. 4, ch. 4. Edward's noted sermon, *Sinners in the Hands of an Angry God*, (1741) is especially awesome to modern-day readers. It is a proclamation on the necessity of salvation.

9. *Ibid.*

10. Parrington, *op. cit.*, pp. 160-163.

11. *Ibid.*, p. 158.

12. Sweet, *op. cit.*, pp. 136-137.

13. Parrington, *op. cit.*, p. 162.

14. *Ibid.*

15. Ernst Cassirer, *The Philosophy of the Enlightenment* (Boston: Beacon Press, 1965), pp. 4-5.

16. Will and Ariel Durant, *Rousseau and Revolution* (New York: Simon and Schuster, 1967), p. 72.

17. *Ibid.*, p. 769.

18. Charles A. Beard, *The Economic Origins of Jeffersonian Democracy* (New York: The Macmillan Company, 1915), ch. XII.

19. Durant, *op. cit.*, p. 75.

20. Earnest Bayles and Bruce Hood, *Growth of American Educational Thought and Practice* (New York: Harper & Row, Publishers, 1966), p. 141.

21. *Ibid.*

22. *Ibid.*

23. John S. Brubacher, *A History of the Problems of Education* (New York: McGraw-Hill Book Company, Inc., 1947), p. 285.

24. Charles A. Bennett, *A History of Manual and Industrial Education, 1870 to 1915* (Peoria, Ill.: The Manual Arts Press, 1937), pp. 453-455.

25. Parrington, *op. cit.*, pp. 82-93.

26. *Ibid.*, p. 91.

27. Francis Pendleton Gaines, *The Southern Plantation* (New York: Columbia University Press, 1924), ch. III.

28. Parrington, *op. cit.*, p. 91.

29. Sweet, *op. cit.*, p. 240.

30. *Ibid.*

31. *Ibid.*

32. *Ibid.*

33. *Ibid.*, p. 242.

34. Willard Sperry, *Religion in America* (New York: The Macmillan Company, 1947), p. 89.

35. Jan Karel Baalen, *The Chaos of Cults* (Grand Rapids, Michigan: Wm. B. Eerdmans Publishing Co., 1946), p. 213.

36. Carl Carmer, *Listen for a Lonesome Drum* (New York: Farrar and Rinehart, Inc., 1936), p. 144.

37. The Christian Science textbook, *Science and Health*, was first published in 1875 and has gone through many editions.

38. See ch. VII.

39. Parrington, *op. cit.*, p. 39.

40. *Journals*, Vol. VIII, p. 316.
41. Quoted by Parrington, *op. cit.*, p. 415, from *Additional Speeches*, Vol. I, pp. 13-15.
42. See: Emerson, *Emerson's Essays, op. cit.*, p. viii. The association of Emerson with Platonism is by Irwin Edman in his *Introduction* which fronts the volume.
43. *Ibid.*
44. *The Twelfth Annual Report* was the last of his tenure as secretary to the Board of Education of Massachusetts. Many consider it his fullest statement on education. The quotations are from the introduction.
45. James Mulhern, *A History of Education* (New York: The Ronald Press Co., 1946), p. 508.
46. Report of a Select Committee of the House of Representatives of the Commonwealth of Pennsylvania, *Soldiers' National Cemetery at Gettysburg* (Harrisburg: Singerly and Meyers, State Printers, 1864), pp. 67-73.
47. *Ibid.*, p. 106.
48. *Ibid.*, p. 106-107.
49. Butler, *op. cit.*, p. 159.
50. *Ibid.*
51. *Ibid.*, p. 160.
52. Herman H. Horne, *Philosophy of Education* (New York: The Macmillan Company, 1927).
53. Mary W. Calkins, *The Persistent Problems of Philosophy* (New York: The Macmillan Company, 1917).
54. William E. Hocking, *Types of Philosophy* (New York: Charles Scribner's Sons, 1929).
55. M. H. Thomas, *A Bibliography of John Dewey, 1882-1939* (New York: Columbia University Press, 1939).
56. Butler, *op. cit.*, p. 419.

Other Reading

Arrowood, C. F. *Thomas Jefferson and Education in a Republic.* New York: McGraw-Hill Book Company, 1930.
Beard, Charles A. *The Economic Origins of Jeffersonian Democracy.* New York: The Macmillan Company, 1915. Chapter XII.
————, and Mary R. *The American Spirit.* New York: The Macmillan Company, 1942. Chapters V-VII.
Beck, Robert H. *A Social History of Education.* Englewood Cliffs, N. J.: Prentice-Hall, Inc., 1965, pp. 71-107.
Brubacher, John. *A History of the Problems of Education.* New York: McGraw-Hill Book Company, 1947, pp. 23-134.
Cash, W. J. *The Mind of the South.* New York: Albert A. Knopf, Inc., 1941.
Cassirer, Ernst. *The Philosophy of Enlightenment.* Boston: Beacon Press, 1951, pp. 134-273.
Cremin, Laurence A. *The Transformation of the School.* New York: Alfred A. Knopf, 1962. Chapters III-VIII.

Curti, Merle. *The Growth of American Thought* (3rd ed.) New York: Harper & Row, Publishers, 1964. Chapters III-XV.

Edwards, Newton, and Herman Richy. *The School in the American Social Order.* Boston: Houghton Mifflin Company, 1947. Chapters VI-XX.

Emerson, Ralph W. *Essays.* Boston: Houghton Mifflin Company, 1883.

French, William. *America's Educational Tradition, an Interpretive History.* Boston: D. C. Heath & Company, 1964. 402 pp.

Gaines, Francis P. *The Southern Plantation.* New York: The Columbia University Press, 1924. Chapters I-III.

Greene, Maxine. *The Public School and the Private Vision.* New York: Random House, Inc., 1965, pp. 9-45, 75-139.

Mayer, Fredrick. *American Ideas and Education.* Columbus, Ohio: Charles E. Merrill Books, Inc. Parts IV, V, VI.

Mulhern, James. *A History of Secondary Education in Pennsylvania.* Philadelphia: The Science Press Printing Co., 1933, pp. 3-25, 145-175, 439-474.

Nef, John. *The United States and Civilization.* Chicago: University of Chicago Press, 1942.

Parrington, V. L. *Main Currents in American Thought.* New York: Harcourt, Brace and Co., 1958. Vols. I-III.

Persons, Stow. *American Minds: A History of Ideas.* New York: Holt, Rinehart & Winston, 1948.

Santayana, George. *Character and Opinion in the United States.* New York: Charles Scribner's Sons, 1920.

Schneider, Herbert W. *A History of American Philosophy.* New York: Columbia University, 1946. Chapters III-VIII.

Stoops, John A. *The Education of Inner Man.* Danville, Ill.: The Interstate Printers & Publishers, Inc., 1969, pp. 5-98.

Sweet, W. W. *The Story of Religion in America.* New York: Harper and Bros., 1950. Chapters III-XX.

Twing, Charles F. *A History of Higher Education in America.* New York: D. Appleton and Co., 1906, Chapters I-VI.

Walquist, John T. *The Philosophy of American Education.* New York: The Ronald Press Company. Chapters V-VIII.

Woody, T. *Early Quaker Education in Pennsylvania.* New York: Teacher's College, Columbia University, 1920.

CHAPTER X

Realism and Pragmatism: The Empirical Traditions in Education

One grim and uncongenial winter day of the year 1626, a sixty-six-year-old Englishman was riding in the country. During this journey an hypothesis occurred to him which needed testing. So he stopped his carriage at a farmhouse and purchased a freshly killed and dressed chicken which he then stuffed with snow to observe the effects of cold upon putrefaction. Inversely, while so doing he took a severe chill of his own and repaired to a nearby house of a friend wherein he died. The irony of this event was consummated by later recognition that his death, the death of Francis Bacon, occurred while he was in the midst of an experiment.

The New Science

It was to men of the Seventeenth Century that Bacon proposed methods whereby men could verify rational speculations. Born in 1561, he was educated at Trinity College, Cambridge, where evidently he received such a massive dose of scholasticism that his taste for university studies vanished. Universities have often "flunked" students, but Bacon "flunked" the university. He left Cambridge and began the career which landed him in the intrigues of Elizabethan court life, administrative positions during the reign of King James, and a seat in the House of Commons. He endured a charge of bribery which led to his exile from court. However, indications abound that the matter was greatly inflated; the king advised that he not contest the matter; and Bacon, in his later years, was not greatly concerned with his career in government or what opinions the chicanerous court politicians had of him. As a public administrator he emerged from a bloody and tempestuous era of English politics with his head intact; and this, in itself, must be counted a significant political achievement. Moreover, he was then ready to turn exclusively to the work which had filled many of his leisure hours since departure from the university. This work and not his career as a public servant is what the world now honors.

Bacon continues an enigma to modern scholars. This man among all of his time was aware of the moribund state of English scholarship; yet, unaccountably, he chose to spend much of his life fawning over the lords and monarchs of the English court. He was displaced in time, living among men who had no appreciation of his extraordinary vision. In his spare time he began writing *The Great Instauration*. In its preface he recorded that:

> . . . it must be plainly avowed that wisdom which we have derived principally from the Greeks is but like the boyhood of knowledge, and has the characteristic property of boys: it can talk but it cannot generate; for it is fruitful of controversies, but barren of works. So that the state of learning as it now is, appears to be represented to the life in the old fable of Scylla, who had the head and face of a virgin but whose womb was hung round with barking monsters, from which she could not be delivered. . . .[1]

Bacon made two points which helped open the way for modern science. The first dealt with restricting the role of logic in making knowledge. In all of the scholastic philosophies reason was sovereign. The test of logic as designed by Aristotle was used to determine the worth of any proposition. The dogmatists clung to this idea with a zeal such as to menace challengers. Men had been burned at the stake for submitting doubts to the world about Aristotelian methods. Even in the Seventeenth Century it was still an act of courage for Bacon to note that:

> . . . logic though it be very properly applied to civil business and to those arts which rest in discourse and opinion, is not nearly subtle enough to deal with nature; and in offering at what it cannot master, has done more to establish and perpetuate error than to open the way to truth. . . .[2]

Incredible as it now seems, this was such a novel view that Bacon probably left this world not knowing how right he was.

The second point validated the experimental method. It was not enough to discontinue logic as a method for the determination of natural truth. Something had to be used in its place. Sheer sense perception was no more to be trusted than logic. Bacon indicated that the senses fail in two ways: at times they yield no information and at other times they give false information. Moreover, he went on to say that when the senses do apprehend a thing, such apprehensions are not to be relied upon because, "sense has reference always to a man, not to the universe; and it is a great error to assert that the sense is the measure of things."[3]

Bacon, therefore, accepted neither the Socratic nor the Protagorean version of man as the measure of all things. He allowed, however, that the senses could be used in knowing, but they needed to be used in specific ways and under specific controls. His solution was the experiment; said he:

> . . . I have sought on all sides . . . to provide helps for the sense . . . and this I endeavor to accomplish not so much by instruments as by experiments. For the subtlety of experiments is far greater than sense itself.[4]

He went on to propose that "the office of the sense shall only be to judge of the experiment, and the experiment itself shall judge of the thing."[5]

It boggles the imagination to think what the world would be today had this Baconian insight occurred to Aristotle who brought science to a plateau upon which it remained for nineteen centuries. Bacon's innocent-sounding proposal for the *experimental method* was the herald cry of a new age. The bond to the methods of Greek science was broken and modern science entered upon its ascendancy.

Bacon was not alone. Although the Seventeenth Century was not marked by great technological advances, it was the century of the new science. As it unfolded Descartes erected philosophical defenses of perception which enabled men to live in comfort with their embryonic scientific methods. During the Seventeenth Century Spinoza developed a liberal idealism which encouraged acceptance of scientific truth. Hobbes and Locke established premises for the empirical study of man. John Amos Comenius, the renowned educator and Moravian Bishop, offered a theory of mind and matter which attributed a passive state to the former and an active state to the latter; and before the Seventeenth Century ended Isaac Newton was fashioning his mechanical vision of the universe which was to become the source of countless hypotheses, including his own central theory of gravitation. We must look upon the scientific men of that age with admiration. Science was not achieved easily. After that brief period of unfulfilled promise in pagan antiquity many tried to take progress in hand, but it was not securely held until the Seventeenth

Century. It was not easy for the Greeks to resist the lure of the mystical and hue to the rational, and it was a struggle for the fathers of modern science to subordinate the rational to the newer mode of knowing. But in the Seventeenth Century men acquired science. Its three-hundred-year tenure between then and now has been but a drop in that vast ocean of the past. The attainment of science was a colossal event in the history of this planet, and on the scale of cosmic time it happened just a moment ago.

New traditions of realism soon appeared, and as the new science gained strength and academic respectability other men of philosophical insight broke from the dogma-bound scholastic doctrines, and a rash of new theories about the reality of nature appeared. No classification scheme has seemed adequate for organizing them. *Ecclesiastical realism* which emerged in the Jesuit schools was simply a trimming of the Thomistic sails to the elemental changes wrought by the experimental method. Because Thomism is discussed elsewhere in this text it has not been included here. *Physical realism* or the realism of material science, which was the greatest and most immediate beneficiary of the new methods, broke sharply from metaphysically oriented natural philosophy and by combining theoretical mathematics with rapidly developing techniques for measurement and experimentation organized its separate disciplines of chemistry, physics, and biology. Each one of these soon had rigorous standards of investigation and description of its own. These fields, which in time were to create "an explosion of knowledge," began to work new influences upon the organizations and attitudes of the academic profession. Their influence on educational philosophy, however, was indirect and came more as a consequence of massive technological effects rather than of doctrinal or ideological inferences. For this reason physical realism will not be described here.

Empirical Realism (Mechanistic)

The one new tradition in realism which produced immediate changes in educational theory has been called *empirical realism*. This is because the philosophers of this tradition turned immediately to the problems of human sensation, understanding, and association. The empirical method is one which accepts experience and not reasoning *per se* as the basis for knowledge. Empiricism as a word is derived from the Greek *en peira* which means "in trial." Empirical realism ultimately produced other new academic disciplines called social sciences, which included psychology, anthropology, economics, and political science. However, as will be shown, there have been sharp doctrinal differences among empirical realists. These differences resulted in pronounced divisions within the oldest of the social science disciplines and in some cases these dissensions could not be resolved without creating new fields such as sociology, social relations, government, and international relations. Another notable development was the movement of history from the humanistic dominions of arts and letters into the social sciences. Finally, because empirical realism focused so strongly upon the question of learning and the nature of social enterprise, a strenuous effort was made to include the study of education as one of the social sciences. This, however, did not happen.

Some of the most important differences among the empirical realists emerged even before the end of the Seventeenth Century. The first of the line was Thomas Hobbes (1588-1679), a younger contemporary of Bacon and sometime acquaintance of the brilliant Italian physicist and astronomer, Galileo. Hobbes, an Oxonian, was as remorseful as Bacon about the state of learning in the universities. On one of the early pages of the *Leviathan*, his greatest work, he chastized the universities for teaching the scholastic doctrine that each object in the world put out its own essence to be perceived. As he put it he doubted "that the thing seen sendeth forth on every side a *visible species* . . . a visible show, apparition, or aspect or being seen; the receiving whereof into the eye is seeing."[6] And with equal ardor he denounced the parallel doctrine that "the thing heard" sent forth "an audible species." He concluded this criticism of these long-standing academic dogmas with this sardonic observation:

> I say not this as disproving the use of universities; but . . .
> I must let you see on all occasions by the way, what things
> would be amended in them; amongst which the frequency of
> insignificant speech is one.[7]

In his effort to describe sensation, emotion, understanding, imagination—indeed all the sanctuaries of human thought and decision—, Hobbes attempted to apply Galileo's theories of motion. By so doing, he constructed the first mechanical vision of man.[8] Hobbes saw man as composed of moving parts and this was justification for a mechanistic psychology which viewed sensation simply as a meeting place of moving parts. The nature of this motion, he thought, was deducible from the general theory of mechanics. The Hobbesian psychology, therefore, purported to become a part-by-part analysis of the human physiology. Thus, Hobbes' empiricism presented a mechanical explanation of human experience. As did most of the philosophers of his time, he went on to extend his theory to an explanation of nature, human society, government, the rights of sovereigns, and the Kingdom of Heaven.

Hobbes called the operation of a set of parts within the human physiology which led, for example, to specific kinds of understandings, by the word *faculty*. He believed that by speech and method the faculties of the mind may be improved.[9] Hobbes hoped his physiological theory would lead to a deduction of ethical truths, and these in turn by education and discipline could be inculcated into the faculties of men. The implications of this mechanical hypothesis for ethics, psychology, and pedagogy are self-evident. Although in retrospect they may seem naive in certain aspects, the fundamentals of this version of empirical realism survive in modern behaviorism.

Empirical Realism (Naturalistic)

A second and strikingly different version of empirical realism was offered by John Locke (1632-1704). He was educated at Westminster School and Christ Church College at Oxford. Locke was a man of great versatility. He was a physician, philosopher, and educator, but he also served the House of Shaftesbury as a confidential secretary. Poor health and political estrangement from the English throne combined to enforce an extended exile in Europe during which time he wrote the philosophical works for which he was later renowned. The two which have been very relevant to education were *Essay Concerning Human Understanding* and *Some Thoughts Concerning Education*. Both of these works defined an empirical realism which has stood as an interesting contrast to that of Hobbes.

Instead of depicting the mind as a complex of moving parts organized mechanically into faculties, Locke offered an organic, naturalistic conception. He preferred to imagine the mind as a "white paper, void of characters."[10] Some philosophers refer to this as the *tabula rasa* (or clean slate). It is an unformed something to which experience gives definition. Said Locke:

> . . . how comes it to be furnished? Whence comes it by
> that vast store, which the busy and boundless fancy of man has
> painted on it with almost endless variety? Whence has it all of
> the materials of reason and knowledge. To this I answer in one
> word, from experience. . . .[11]

To his physician's eye the mind is implanted in the body and is an organic part of the body. He seemed to regard it as integral to sensation. His central point was that the mind has no innate ideas which lie dormant within it. He went to great length in demonstrating the mind's flexibility and malleability.

Probably the next most widely recognized part of his philosophy came to be his description of the objects of the world. Locke reasoned that an object can be understood in terms of three qualities.[12] These qualities are as aspects of our experience with objects as they are encountered in their actual state. In examining these qualities it is important to remember that the objects have qualities and when perceived in the mind these qualities become ideas.

The first of the three qualities are the *primary qualities*. These are characteristics which are utterly inseparable from the body of the object. Locke described primary qualities by use of the words solidity, extension, figure, and mobility. If he were writing in modern times he might have substituted the words "mass" and "density" for the first two of the four. These primary qualities produce what he termed simple ideas in men—namely, solidity, extension, motion, etc. No matter what is done to an object it will retain these qualities. The illustration of a candle is used.[13] Even if the candle is melted and its shape thereby changed, the wax has solidity, weight, figure, and it can be moved.

The next of the three qualities are called the *secondary qualities*. These are more easily defined by example. The surface of an object may be such that when light is reflected from it a sensation of green appears in the eye. Color is not a primary quality of the object. Yet we are bound to associate the object with that color the senses apprehend. Other secondary qualities include such things as texture, taste, smell, pain, etc. Accordingly, secondary qualities are distinguishable from primary in that primary qualities are in the object exactly as they appear in the senses and secondary qualities are different in the senses than they are in the object. The objective reality of secondary qualities differs from that which the senses report.

The third of the three qualities which Locke ascribed to objects have been called *tertiary qualities*. These are the characteristics of an object which produce motion or change in other objects. A burning object such as the sun is an example of an object which includes this quality; a magnet may be another. This type quality may be considered as the power an object has as a consequence of the particular constitution of its primary qualities.

Having shown that mind is possessed of no *a priori* ideas, having determined that the objects of the world possess in themselves certain qualities, and having indicated that these qualities are the source of the idea the mind forms of them, Locke proceeded to elaborate on the characteristics of human understanding which are derivable from these premises. Man is part of the world which he observes and he has a special way of understanding and interpreting that which he observes. It is what we have come to call a naturalistic view and Locke puts it to work in developing his ideas about education.

His treatise *Some Thoughts Concerning Education* began as a series of letters advising a friend of his by the name of Edward Clarke on the upbringing of the latter's children. The letters attracted some favorable attention and under this encouragement Locke put them together as a book. As such it was not so systematic as his other works; it was pervaded by down-to-earth suggestions on the what and how of nurturing children. He begins with a quotation taken from the Roman poet Juvenal, "a sound mind in a sound body," and proceeds from there to a common-sense doctrine of educational naturalism. He urges schooling based on healthy, active children having ample time for play, learning skills when ready and motivated, and participating in activities designed to inculcate habits of gentility. Punishment should be moderate but consistent in the early years, but this should be supplanted by love and confidence as the child matures.

He opposes the teaching of rules as standards of conduct. As he puts it, rules "will be always slipping out of their memories."[14] Instead of this he would have children practice the "same action done over and over again until they have got the habit of doing it well."[15] But he cautioned that men "even from our cradles, love liberty, and have an aversion to many things, for no other reason, but because they are enjoining us." He urged discipline in moderation and that the most be made of the natural drives and inclinations of the child. Near the end of the work, he again counsels the educator to use common sense by quoting Juvenal: "If there is good sense, no heavenly power is lacking."

Empirical Realism (Skeptical-Perceptual)

David Hume (1711-1776), a Scotsman educated at Edinburgh,

was the first to bring these new empirical schools under strong critical scrutiny. For this reason his contributions have generally been viewed as negative.[16] In his first work called A *Treatise on Human Nature* he offered views on generalizations about empirical phenomena which come as a consequence of induction. The unassailability of his assertions has been reflected in Bertrand Russell's well known quip that "You can do two things with Hume's arguments, accept them or ignore them."

Perhaps an example is the best way of describing Hume's claim that there can be no logical demonstration for the validity of inductive inference. If, for example, a man were hanging onto a building ledge high above the street, you might call to him saying, "Don't let go or you will fall." He, along with the rest of the world, should accept that as a perfectly true statement. However, suppose to the astonishment of all he called back saying, "You cannot demonstrate that logically; and even if I did let go, and then fell as you have asserted, it would not establish the validity of your statement for all cases such as mine." One hearing such a response from such a ledge-hanger would be tempted to ask, "Is your name David Hume?" He is the only man in the history of philosophy (or anything else) who might make so preposterous a response.

Yet he is perfectly right. There is no logic which will validate any empirical cause or rule. Neither can logic be used *a posteriori* to demonstrate or validate a general statement about experience, for any such demonstration would presuppose the very principle which it is to demonstrate.[17] This did not seem to bother Hume so much as it has others who have seemed to wish that it could be done. Hume simply pointed out that we have to supply belief that the experience of the world is habitual and we can make predictions on the basis of those habits which we believe. Hence, if one said to the ledge-hanger, "Don't let go because I believe you will fall," and he replied, "So do I," Hume would be content with the exchange. Now, of course, to all practical ends men of the world would be content to allow that a fall from the ledge to the ground would be lawful even though the lawfulness of the event cannot be induced from observation of all of the previous events of its kind. However, this is an extreme example, and in order to prevent this account from picturing Hume as silly, we can offer an illustration not involving such probable events as falling bodies. Let us suppose a social scientist finds a pair of short-legged trousers in the locker room and is, therefore, prepared to declare, on the strength of logic, that they were left behind by a short-legged boy who departed the premises without trousers. Again, he may be perfectly right, but it can also be demonstrated logically that the trousers in question may have belonged to the younger brother of a tall, absent-minded boy who purported to leave the trousers off at the cleaners but forgot them in the locker room. Induction provides only hypotheses about experience; it cannot verify. If the scientist wants to assert as a rule that all short-legged trousers which reach the locker room are worn to that place and only by short-legged boys, his rule can stand only as an act of faith. Far from verifying this rule, logic demonstrates that countless other possibilities are open.

The second article of Hume's skepticism is probably more relevant in modern times than it was in his own. Briefly stated it means that "is" cannot be made to be "ought." One cannot determine the good simply by examining any set of conditions. Hume's position which nowadays is called the autonomy of ethics follows:

> In every system of morality which I have hitherto met with, I have always remarked that the author proceeds for some time in the ordinary way of reasoning and establishes the being of God, or makes observations concerning human affairs; when, of a sudden I am surprised to find, that instead of the usual copulation of propositions, *is* and *is not*, I meet with no proposition that is not connected with an *ought* or *ought not*. This change is imperceptible; but is however of the last consequence. For this *ought* and *ought not* expresses some new relation or affirmation, it is necessary that it should be observed and explained; and at the same time that a reason should be given for what seems altogether inconceivable, how this new relation can be a deduction from others, which are entirely different from it.[18]

As summarized, this means no moral rule or judgment can be deduced from sets of premises which do not, in themselves, contain moral rules or judgments.[19] Therefore, ethical rules are also justified only by faith.

Hume's skepticism led him to think that the only way to conceive of the self was as a center or locus of perceptions. Here again he is in contention with Locke's intuition of "self." For he indicates that "When I turn my reflection on *myself*, I can never perceive this *self* without some one or more perceptions. 'Tis the composition of these, therefore, which forms the self."[20] This "I perceive, therefore, I am" conception of self suggests that the self cannot be intuited, but what is even more difficult the perceptions are unsharable.

Thus, at the end it appears that Hume left the world with no hope for a system of empirically based knowledge. The content of his philosophy would indeed be judged negative were it not for three subsequent developments.[21] The first of the three was the use of his insight on the nature of perception as the foundation of *associative psychology*, which made use of whatever perceptual introspection seemed to reveal. This later was attractive to men such as James Mill, John Stuart Mill, Bain, Huxley, Stout, and Ward. The second development was that he became the prototype for a style of social scientist who questions constantly and will not be appeased by prestige, appearances, conventions, or soothing voices. This skepticism is a style of doubting rather than knowing, but its usefulness has been demonstrated time and again. The third development was through a single source. In the end, it could be shown as the most important. One day Immanuel Kant picked up the *Treatise* and began to read it; and, as Kant later put it, "Hume awakened me from my dogmatic slumbers."[22]

Empirical Realism (Positivistic)

Hume is frequently identified as the originator of the positivistic tradition in empirical realism. This is true in the sense that certain species of the modern positivists frequently resort to Hume for standards of criticism. The term positivism, however, was given its primary associations by the French philosopher, Auguste Comte (1798-1857). His doctrines are variously termed *Supernatural Humanism* and *Classical Positivism*. He is also widely recognized as the founder of sociology as an academic discipline.

According to Comte, knowledge has progressed through three developmental states. The earliest is the *theological* stage which characterizes the knowledge of primitive people. The syntax of all such knowledge is supplied by their belief in gods. Events are explained by the intercession of specified deities. The second stage is the *metaphysical*. Under the spell of metaphysics men explain the events of the world in terms of impersonal laws or causes. Scientific principles take the place of gods as controlling forces. The god of light is replaced by principles of illumination, and the god of thunder is replaced by the physical theories of sound, etc.

Now we note that Comte stands on the same ground as Hume insofar as he indicates such laws or principles as acts of faith disguised as renderings of logic. It follows then that the third, final, and most advanced stage is *positivistic*. Positivistic phenomena are never explained spiritually or in terms of natural laws or principles. Judgments are based upon observation of events which are verified by sense experience. His metaphysics, therefore, is negative in the sense that he denies any special status to spiritual realities such as God (in the conventional sense), soul, mortality, moral value, beauty, truth, and the abstract nouns such as justice, friendship, etc. Positivism can be traced through men such as Herbert Spencer, Charles Saunders Peirce, Ernst Mach, and to the Vienna circle which became recognized in 1924. The current variant forms of positivism include logical empiricism, logical atomism, and the various analytic schools.

Comte viewed mathematics as the basis of knowledge and constructed a hierarchy of knowledge with sociology at the top. In his view sociological knowledge was the end of knowing. His religious views supported this in that he came to regard humanity *qua* humanity as divine. Thus, sociological knowledge stood where theological knowledge did in primitive people and metaphysical speculations do in less scientific people. Sociology, as a discipline, is now more than a century old, but in comparison to other disciplines it is still one of the youngest of fields. In a comparatively short time it has come to a widespread acceptance in the academic world.

Natural Realism (Theory)

A full account of Nineteenth- and Twentieth-Century empirical realism is beyond the plan of this chapter. Reference to Jeremy Bentham and John Stuart Mill is made elsewhere in this text. Certainly the commentaries of Alfred N. Whitehead, Bertrand Russell, and George Santayana are of interest to students of education. The celebrated theories of Charles Darwin which have transformed the social, psychological, and biological sciences have also influenced practices in education. Herbert Spencer's elaboration of Hobbesian psychomechanics is of high significance in an age when men are producing machines which perform thoughtlike operations. Each of these men offered original dimensions of empiricism, which, in one way or another, extended from the earlier works by Hobbes, Locke, Hume, or Comte.

We have called the Seventeenth Century the century of science. By the same authority we can call the Eighteenth Century the century of philosophy. It began with Locke and ended with Kant. Between them occurred that season of wonder called French enlightenment. The Europe of that era was peppered with exciting intellectuals such as mathematicians Leibnitz, Laplace, and Newton. Literary figures such as Voltaire, Boswell, and Goethe gave new vitality to the languages of Central Europe. Music offered greatness in Bach, Mozart, and Beethoven. In history Gibbon composed a pedimental account of the decline and fall of Rome, and Adam Smith composed a persuasive theory of economics. It was also in the Eighteenth Century that Frederick William II, King of Prussia, became Europe's lonely model of the philosopher king. This was the epoch in which began the political and intellectual revolutions of the modern world. At its end the western monarchies were either overthrown or weakened, and metaphysics was likewise dethroned and put to work as a source of assumptions on which new value and knowledge systems might stand. It was the men of the Eighteenth Century who ordained that governments would serve and not rule, and the philosophers of that time ordained that ontology thenceforward was subordinate to epistemology.

The man whose spiritual and intellectual qualities most exemplify this age of creativity, revolution, and reform was probably the French music copier, literary light, educational theorist, and philosopher Jean Jacques Rousseau (1712-1778). What a commentary on man in society his life became! His mother died at his birth, and his father soon abandoned him. He had oddities in his nature which he frankly admitted.[23] He was branded a heretic, was charged with crimes, fathered illegitimate children,[24] and was suspected of insanity. His manners were as abominable as he was unpredictable. He repaid the magnanimity of those who conceded to his genius with resentment and gratuitous contempt. Even Voltaire, a discerning patron of the talented, was reduced to exasperation. Rousseau was a man who would not meliorate and could not compromise.

But after he died, Rousseau became the ideologist of the French Revolution, an influence on Kant and Schopenhauer, a theme for Schiller and Goethe, a force in the socialism of Marx, and a continuing inspiration for the Swiss schoolmaster Johann Pestalozzi. During the fifty years which followed his death Rousseau was a symbol of the tormented man of nature long suppressed by a hierarchy of customs, manners, laws, and conventions. Few lines in the literature of man are so stirring as the opening sentence of his *The Social Contract:* "Man is born free, and he is everywhere in chains."

But *The Social Contract* is not simply a polemic against the established order. In the early pages Rousseau orients his arguments upon human nature and human experience, and reasons onward from those premises. As he puts it, he reasons "from the actual to the possible." Rousseau does not develop a fully conceptualized operational government. Instead, he demonstrates the principles from which an operational government should be derived. In the course of this he displays an admirable grasp of the history of government as illuminated by theorists from Plato to Machiavelli. The note which differs is the grounding of reason upon human experience and the rededication of government to the service of man's freedom.

Rousseau insists that in order to secure personal freedom individual men must enter into a social contract.[25] It is through the contract that institutions which guarantee the natural rights of man can arise. He demonstrates the right of the strongest, as manifested by monarch and special ruling classes, to be unnatural and alien to freedom.[26] The treatise displays throughout, the basis for naturalistic politics. Rousseau does not offer a utopia. He pays respect to the Spartans and Romans of the republican period. Consistent with this he stops short of a full endorsement of democracy. He declared, "If there were a nation of Gods, it would govern itself democratically. A government so perfect is not suited to men."[27] He placed his emphasis on the standards by which good government can be recognized.

> When, therefore, one asks what in absolute terms is the best government, one is asking a question which is unanswerable because it is indiscriminate . . . there are as many good answers as there are possible combinations in the absolute and realistic positions of people. But if it is asked by what signs can one tell whether a given people is well or badly governed, that is another matter; and the question of fact can be answered. . . .[28]

This is what makes *The Social Contract* so devastating. Rousseau shows the people a basis for discontent without endangering his thesis by offering specific counterproposals. Had he advocated specific forms of government, his critics would have an easier time.

The Social Contract offers several innovations in political thought. Rousseau shows the sovereign to be an "artificial person" standing for the collected people in covenant[29]; he declares that the act of sovereignty is a declaration of the will of the people, and, therefore, it constitutes law. The chagrin with which these views were received by the established authorities resulted in the banning of the book in some places, its burning in others, and numerous warrants for the arrest of its author.

In May, 1762, only eleven months after publication of *The Social Contract*, and before the fulminations subsided, Rousseau published *Emile*. The furor over this book, when added to the furor over the other, resulted finally in the necessity of his flight to the Swiss city of Berne; and when expelled from there he repaired to nearby Neufchatel, which at that time in history was under the jurisdiction of King Frederick II of Prussia. King Frederick was himself a philosopher and appreciated Rousseau, although he disagreed with him. From that time onward, Rousseau was an outcast. He lived for a time in England under the hospitality of David Hume whom he soon accused of plotting against him. Rousseau's parting letters left Hume bewildered and disillusioned and convinced the English-speaking world that Rousseau was insane. His vagabond life ended at his death which occurred near Paris in 1778. But shortly thereafter his spirit began to work its influence upon the great events of the world.

Emile had simply added to Rousseau's indictment of the prevailing political arrangements a chastisement of the modes of education then in vogue. Because these were mainly dictated by the church, *Emile* was regarded as an attack upon Christendom. The response of the church was a classic case of overreaction as council after council and prelate after prelate denounced his work and proclaimed both it and him heretical.

What was the thesis of *Emile?* Still influenced by the empiricism of Locke and holding to his custom of powerful beginnings, Rousseau penned as the opening sentence of *Emile*, "All things are good as they come out of the hands of the creator, but everything degenerates in the hands of men." He rejects methods of training children by unnatural means. He depicts this as training obedient marionettes for a decadent society. Rousseau maintains such schooling stunts the robust growth which nature promises and results in the child's becoming a conforming mediocrity crammed full of the fears which his religious teaching breeds into him. He would avoid education in the dogmas of the church in the early years. He would not tell Emile about these things until he was in his adolescent years.

Rousseau indicates that learning is natural. All a child does in natural experience is the work of nature, the sovereign educator. Tutors must be guided by nature. He said, "Our pedantic mania for instructing constantly leads us to teach children what they can learn far better for themselves and to lose sight of what we alone can teach them."[30] A teacher must, therefore, ally himself with nature and not suppress nature. His education of Emile shows a reverence for childhood and a passionate determination to keep it free from the corruptions and pollutions of an artificial pedagogy which would mutilate the child's developing nature and deny it fulfillment.

Nature and not man sets the goal of education. "... the vocation common to all is the state of manhood; and whoever is well trained for that cannot fulfill badly any vocation which depends on it."[31] He divided the education of Emile into three stages and the curriculum of each stage is dominated by what is natural for his age. On questions of morals he cautioned against preaching. His method is love, kindness, and above all else example! example! He turns to the education of women, and with the skill of an accomplished novelist he introduces Sophie. Emile becomes enamored by Sophie, they marry, and the book ends by all singing praises of Emile's upbringing.

The book is a classic of both sentiment and language. Its arguments are strengthened by the eloquence of passages such as:

> Oh men be humane! It is your highest duty; to be humane to all conditions of men, to every age, to everything not alien to mankind. What higher wisdom is there for you than humanity? Love childhood; encourage its sports, its pleasures, its loveable instincts. . . . Do you know, you fathers, the moment death awaits your children? Do not store up for yourselves remorse, by taking from them the brief moments nature has given them. As soon as they can appreciate the delights of existence, let them enjoy it. At whatever hour God may call them, let them not be without having tasted life at all.[32]

All of this would be received in modern times with better grace had it not come from a man who abandoned his five illegitimate children to an orphanage.[33] But considering the problems which Rousseau may have recognized in himself, as a father, his children may actually have benefitted from this apparent callousness.

Natural Realism (Practice)

Johann Heinrich Pestalozzi, born in Zurich in 1746, lived much of his life near the places Rousseau knew as a boy and in which he spent part of his exile. While at the University of Zurich, he read the newly published *Emile*. After leaving the university, he took up farming. He invested heavily both his and his wife's resources in the development of a tract of land near Zurich and in building an imposing house which was called *Neuhof* (new home). But his agricultural venture failed, and all was soon lost except the house and a few of the surrounding acres.

When his son Jacobli reached the age of five, Pestalozzi's thoughts turned back to *Emile*. In time these reflections became a resolve that he would convert his Neuhof into an orphanage. When it became operational, this institution accommodated about eighty children. With support from the nearby cities of Zurich, Berne, and Basel he developed a curriculum centered upon gardening, farming, and housework. Instruction in language arts, morals, manners, and scriptures grew out of the work the children performed. His educational method led from the hand to the head and to the heart.

Convinced of his success and encouraged by friends Pestalozzi began to write of his pedagogy. After a number of systematic efforts failed to attract notice, in 1781 he put in popular form his well known *Leonard and Gertrude*. This book was published by one of his friends and gained him wide recognition. However, his genius as a teacher was offset by his helplessness as a business man, and his school was constantly on the edge of bankruptcy. Later, the devastation of the Napoleonic wars caused Pestalozzi's skill and interest in the education of orphans to be in great demand. As armies and governments followed one upon the other, Pestalozzi was given new responsibilities at various locations. He continued teaching until the age of seventy-nine. Two years later in 1827 while still writing and planning for another school, he died.

His most famous book on method, *How Gertrude Teaches Her Children*, revealed his bond to Locke and Rousseau. And a partial listing of visitors to a demonstration and teacher training institute he operated at Yverdon included celebrities Friedrich Froebel and Johann Herbart, both of whom later became strong influences on American education, the former through the kindergarten movement and the latter through his educational psychology. Of these two Froebel emerged more strongly committed to the Pestallozian mode of pedagogy.

Pestalozzian influences in education reached America as early as 1818 and were instituted with high favor at various locations. Both Horace Mann and Henry Barnard spoke highly of naturalistic methods. However, the Hegelian influences and special interpretations of Herbartian psychological methods in the latter part of the Nineteenth Century won the competition for the teaching methodology of American classrooms. In addition, Nineteenth-Century America was rural. It was difficult to convince American farmers there was educational value in farm work. So American education, for a time, lost sight of *Emile*, and education in the Pestalozzian mode became associated with "progressive" education.

Late in the Nineteenth Century Froebel's kindergarten was instituted in America. It lasted awhile and then vanished. The name kindergarten was retained to identify that which goes on before children enter the first grade. By some inversion which the histories of education will one day explain, this "kindergarten" became a preparatory school. Nowadays, to start another turn of the wheel, argument for nursery schools has been heard which exalts the Froebelian doctrine of play for the "unfolding" of children. It seems that *Emile* has survived in educational theory for those under five. How long this will last no one can say. The day when America will no longer tolerate illiterate infants may soon be upon us.

Herbartian Pedagogy

Johann Friedrich Herbart (1776-1841) is our Nineteenth-Century German model of an educational philosopher. He was a successor to Kant at the University of Köningsburg where he taught both philosophy and pedagogy. It is difficult to estimate the extent to which he may have been influenced by Pestalozzi, Kant, and his popular contemporary Hegel because Herbart is original. The combination of his theory of mind and pedagogical procedures combines in what we recognize today as the beginning of educational psychology.

There is no question that he was impressed by the work of Pestalozzi because his doctrines emphasize the many-sidedness of human interests. He opposed the theory of mental faculties which was variously expressed by the ecclesiastical and the Hobbesian realists. At the same time he repudiated Rousseau's extreme naturalism with its unremitting demand for revolt against traditional morality and culture. While wishing to broaden the structure of school curricula and to develop extracurricular activities, Herbart would not concede that nature itself was the curriculum and mankind's greatest tutor.

Herbart's theory of mind and education focuses upon the "apperceptive mass." He indicates that body and soul exist at birth but mind does not. Instead, mind develops in educational experience. To understand what mind is, it is necessary to clarify the nature of idea. Herbart is a modified Platonist to the extent that he believes that ideas are particles of "soul stuff" which reside in both the consciousness and the subconsciousness. As a consequence of experience ideas pass from the subconscious to the conscious and back again. The passage is continuous, but as this transmigration goes on the ideas group themselves into apperceptive masses. That is to say, they group themselves according to similarities which exist between them. The development of these masses is what we call mind. When apperceptive masses exist in the consciousness they take in new ideas which are similar to them.

Herbart sees *mind building* rather than *mind training* as the object of education. This building of the apperceptive masses is, in reality, the building of a cultured, moral, religious, and informed man. The end of education is the building of lifelong traits and interests. The "cycle" which produces these apperceptive masses begins with interest or motivation; but there must be content, and this is drawn from the natural sciences, social sciences, and historical studies. Logical studies such as mathematics and grammars are included, but their merit is utilitarian rather than intrinsic. Or, in other words, they are included for content value rather than a supposed capacity to train or discipline mental faculties.

He organized pedagogy into five steps, and these became the theme of many courses in pedagogy in teacher training institutions in the United States. They were usually designated *The Five Steps in Recitation,* and they were regarded as essential steps in the teaching-learning process:

1. *Preparation,* the development of student interest.
2. *Presentation,* exposition of the new idea.
3. *Association,* showing its relationship to ideas already acquired.
4. *Generalization,* the forming of a general idea or concept.
5. *Application,* the use of acquired ideas in solving problems.

The impact of this pedagogical outline on American educators of the last half of the Nineteenth Century was astounding. Men such as Charles DeGarmo of New York, Charles McMurry of Illinois, and his brother Frank of Teachers College Columbia studied under disciples of Herbart at the University of Jena. They published books on teaching methods and in 1892 with the help of others founded the National Herbartian Society. Their influence coincided with one of the great eras of standardization in American schools; and, consequently,

for over six decades school text books reflected the influence of Herbartian style of "lesson planning." Even in the so-called curriculum
development era which began in the middle 1930's, the unit planning
which teachers and specialists performed still reflected Herbartian influence. The wholesale belief by Americans of the late Nineteenth
Century and early Twentieth Century in Herbartian lesson planning
was reflected in the insistence of many parents and conservative educators that this was the way to teach.

The diminishment of Herbartian influences coincided with the
rise of educational theories founded on American pragmatism as in-
doctrined by its leading expositors William James and John Dewey. As
early as 1902 the name of the National Herbartian Society was changed
to the National Society for the Study of Education.

Today Herbart's name is seldom heard in educational meetings.
Young teachers hear it in association with old-fashioned ideas. Mind
building is generally rejected as a pedagogy of days gone by. Yet there
are still a few veterans, nearly all retired, who remember it as the
latest thing. In the blush of their youth Herbartian pedagogy was a
brave new method.

The American Pragmatists

In 1924 an event occurred which has come to be of permanent
interest to students of philosophy. Alfred North Whitehead came to
America. Although it is true that he was nearing the age of retirement
at the University of London, he had much yet to do. His acceptance of
Harvard's invitation was in the spirit of a young man looking forward
to a long-hoped-for opportunity.[34] Whatever may have been the problems of American institutions, they posed no obstacles to a free philosophical spirit who wished to range across the often formidable boundaries and prerogatives of academic disciplines. Whitehead wanted this
freedom. But, of even greater importance to Whitehead, the Americans were doing decisive things in philosophy, and Whitehead, ever
the clear-sighted observer, saw this and rejoiced in the opportunity to
participate. Although his original contract was for five years, he continued active teaching at Harvard for thirteen years and lived ten
years beyond his retirement there. His death occurred in 1947. During
this time, American philosophers had an incomparable opportunity to
see themselves through the eyes of one who had reached the summits
abroad. The picture Whitehead mirrored back was gratifying. White-

head was convinced that an exciting new era of philosophy was coming to flower in the American universities. Moreover, his own metaphysics of process was in harmony with this innovation, and possibly because of this the most comprehensive aspects of his own speculative philosophy came to fruition during these American years.

In 1936, he wrote to his American colleague, Charles Hartshorne, expressing belief that the founders of the "American Renaissance" were Charles Peirce and William James. He went on to point out that of the two James was the analog to Plato and Peirce to Aristotle.[35] He admitted that the time order did not correspond and the analogy should not be pressed too far, but the very strength of such a tribute did not fail to bring Americans at last to the stage of self-recognition.

This self-recognition offered a sharp contrast to the standing tendency of American philosophers to remain deferential to German philosophers. During the latter two-thirds of the Nineteenth Century and the first two decades of the Twentieth, boatloads of scholars from the "New World" crossed the Atlantic to hear the disciples of Hegel, Fitche, Kant, and Herbart. There was a transplantation of German idealism which even as late as the 1920's still flourished within American institutions, but Whitehead took little notice of this. His offhand remarks were treasured in the memories of those who knew him. In one observation about the futility of the absolute he said, "Hang it all! *Here we are*. We don't go behind that; we begin with it."[36]

As had many other men of genius, Charles Sanders Peirce (1839-1914) made his way through life misunderstood, unrecognized, and frequently at odds with the world around him. His life was almost constantly afflicted by financial, marital, and professional problems. It is a figurative truth that no American university of his time stood tall enough to perceive his significance. This is an old story. The western world was also unkind to Boethius, Bacon, Spinoza, Rousseau, and numerous others. America's treatment of Peirce was well within the standards the western world has established for men of unusual insight.

His father was a mathematician on the Harvard faculty, and he filled his son's childhood life with exercises in logic, studies in chemistry, and a thorough reading of Kant's *Critique of Pure Reason*. Despite all this (or perhaps because of it), Peirce was undistinguished as a Harvard undergraduate, finishing seventy-first of the ninety-one in his graduating class. It has been speculated that his mind was too independent for the university undergraduate curriculum of his time. However, his record as a graduate student in chemistry was distinguished.

His only notable academic appointment was a five-year lecture-ship at Johns Hopkins University. He was considered an able expositor. His failure to continue in academic life has been attributed to such things as marital instability, failure to keep regular hours, and in-ability to work congenially with others. Aside from association with a group of brilliant Americans who formed a "metaphysical club" at Cambridge, Massachusetts, in the early 1870's, Peirce had no notable association with a learned society. Most of his working life was given to service in the United States Coast and Geodetic Survey. He wrote numerous articles in his spare time. William James was one of the few who recognized his originality and turned his own considerable gifts to the popularization of Peirce's ideas, the most notable of which was a method of knowing, which Peirce called *pragmatism*.[37] James and John Dewey continued to develop this method in ways not en-tirely to the satisfaction of Peirce. He felt sufficiently strong about the distinctiveness of his own ideas as to later reidentify them by the name *pragmaticism*, a word which he declared ugly enough to be safe from kidnappers.[38]

Ironically, because James and Dewey were better known in the academic world, and because James, in particular, referred to Peirce as the source of most of his empirical ideas, and because he made no effort at a compendious expression of his philosophy, Peirce in many commentaries stands as the archenemy of metaphysics and repudiator of abstract values. Those who try to understand the full force of his work will quickly perceive that neither of these things is true. When viewed on his own, apart from his better known associates, he is seen as America's most original philosopher.

It is difficult to discuss his work in ordinary language and remain true to his rigor. On the metaphysical side Peirce surprisingly reveals a tendency toward absolute idealism. When discoursing on absolute idealism writers of ordinary talent must usually choose between clarity and distortion. When one tries to be completely true he becomes obscure. When one tries to clarify, he distorts. In this explanation the path of clarity is chosen, and the risk of distortion accepted. If the result is obscurity, then it won't matter.

In his notion of the absolute Peirce depicted three attributes which (as here understood) are the universe of feeling, the universe of action, and the universe of thought. He broke sharply with Hegel who seemed to assert that the absolute was the universe of thought alone.[39] By assigning to the absolute these distinctive attributes, Peirce saw the possibility of philosophizing in each and dealing with the metaphysical problems appropriate to each. The thrust of his own philosophical work was in the universe of action.

He proposed that our conception of things be fashioned from practical effects. His words were that we consider "what effects, which might have practical bearing, we conceive the object of our conception to have." Then, said he, "Our conception of those effects is the whole of the object."[40] Using this method men can refine out from the metaphysics of action "a precious essence" which makes us able to think more clearly about what is going on. We could say it this way: Our school policies, techniques, and resources are the *effects that have a practical bearing on our conception of them.* Our conception is formed by noting how the performance of these things registers upon the problem we are attempting to solve, and estimates of their value are made accordingly. Now, if we wish to state this even more clearly, and correspondingly be more indifferent to Peirce's standard of rigor, we could say "a conception of a thing is understood as its practical effects."

This epistemology of practical effects has acquired a number of variant expressions over the past seventy years. Philosophers drawn to the reality of process and scholars in the social sciences look upon it as powerful method. Ofttimes its applications appear so down-to-earth that laymen do not think of pragmatism as philosophy; indeed, they often consider it an alternative to philosophy. Peirce, the hero of common sense and practical wisdom, seemed to have little of his own. He took his inheritance, settled in Milford, Pennsylvania, and tried to support himself by his writing. His home included an attic wherein he could work undisturbed. Impoverished in his later days, it is reported that he evaded creditors by retreating up the ladder to his study and frustrated their pursuit by pulling it aloft behind him. In 1914 he died of cancer.

William James (1842-1910), the erudite complement to Peirce, escaped the personal fate of the latter. As a member of a brilliant family which appreciated both the pain and potency of genius he was supported in the trials of adolescence and young adulthood by generosity and understanding. James did not set out to be a philosopher, but his was not an intellect to be contained by a single specialty. He proceeded from medicine to psychology, and the latter led him directly into philosophy. Had he not followed this academic route he would probably have reached philosophical inquiry on account of considerations within his personal life. One of these, of course, was the stimulation of a gifted family. His sister, Alice, had literary gifts comparable to his own, and his brother, Henry, wrote novels like a philosopher. Probably an even greater motivation was a continuing struggle to bring the religious gnosticism of his early personal development to terms with the consequences of his scientific inquiry. It is now clear that his conflict created a deep personal crisis during which suicide was an oft-considered resolution. Again, he was well supported by his family and especially by an understanding wife.[41]

The combination of his version of Peirce's pragmatic method, his interpretations of psychology, and his continuing interest in religion resulted in a philosophical outlook which James called radical empiricism. But it was hard for a man of his breadth of insight and power of language to remain as a part of a single tradition. To be sure, he escaped rationalism, but in such varied philosophic postures as have been found in *Principles of Psychology, Pluralistic Universe, Talks to Teachers, Will to Believe, The Varieties of Religious Experience,* and *Pragmatism* students of philosophy were given material which will be reexamined and reinterpreted for years to come. As his fame grew he was invited to lecture in most of the prestigious forums of the western world, and this continued to broaden his already wide range of intellectual associations. He was a gregarious man with marked social grace. During the final years of his life, his fame assured, he was unfailingly cheerful. The rhythmic melancholy of his younger days was rarely in evidence.

William James added significantly to the unfolding American intellectual tradition. He broadened the applications of Peirce's doctrines. For him pragmatism was a theory of truth rather than just a theory of meaning. As he pointed out:

> What we say about reality thus depends on the perspective into which we throw it. The *that* of it is its own; but the *what* depends on the *which* and the *which* depends on *us.* . . . A sensation is rather like a client who has given his case to a lawyer and then has passively to listen in the courtroom to whatever account of his affairs, pleasant or unpleasant, the lawyer finds it most expedient to give.[42]

James taught that *if theories work they are true.*[43] Thus his pragmatism appears again and again even in his speculations about the divine. A man is entitled to any religious posture which unifies his experience, gives tentative meaning to what lies in his senses, and galvanizes him onward in quest of new facts. Religious experience comes from the fact that the conscious person is continuous with a wider self through which saving experiences come.[44] The world of our present consciousness is only one out of many worlds of consciousness that exist. At some point on the boundary of our consciousness it becomes continuous with other worlds, and higher energies filter in. As James put it he can, as a scientist, imagine that his own conscious world of sensation is all there is, but when he does this he hears an inward monitor whispering the word "bosh!"[45]

James seemed to feel something is there which man makes use of in coming to terms with the deeper side of experience. He termed this the "over belief" in order that it be distinguished from the world of shareable scientific knowledge.

James indicates that most interesting and valuable things about a man are usually his over beliefs. This rich vein of religious thought along with that later developed by Whitehead has yet to be mined. Educators and students of religion will one day turn to these and other notions to discover ways that organized education can deal with values.

Pragmatism and Education

The life and works of John Dewey are discussed elsewhere in this text. Although he was strongly influenced by James and applied pragmatic methods to his study of educational problems, Dewey belongs in an even broader context because his works were in two fields. From the time he assumed his professorship at Columbia he was offered the forums of both philosophy and education. In regard to education, he quickly became an international celebrity, and he was given occasion to consult in the development of the educational systems of Turkey, Mexico, and the Soviet Union. He also lectured in Europe and the Orient. Dewey saw relationship between schools and something he came to call society. The tie was such that reform in one became reform in the other. The impact of his doctrines upon American scholarship has been extensive. In a sense he was Charles Peirce with a social mission, and he was William James without a tendency to mystical speculation or overstatement.

Dewey termed his pragmatic method experimentalism. It was ready-made for education because it was, after all, how men learn. Experimentalism offers its epistemological premise as a basis for curriculum and method in the teaching-learning transaction. Reflective thinking, instead of leading from *a priori* principles, begins in a world that is *indeterminate*. In short, there is nothing present but a felt need.

The felt need may be a yearning, a discomfort, a feeling of tension or of loss, and this sets the knowing process in motion.

The next step is critical. It is the intellectualization of the problem. Many accounts of pragmatic reflection show the problem as given. It is not. The problem is in fact a statement of a need. Such a statement is not easily developed. In social situations it is especially difficult. When one formulates a problem he formulates implicitly the sort of solution which will resolve it. For example, a man in search of something will have to define the something.

The third step is a search for possible solutions. The mind goes to work forming hypotheses. These are examined rationally, and one is chosen for trial by action. The others are held in reserve, awaiting the results of the pragmatic test. The test cannot fail to produce knowledge. The practical effects of the test will be understood in the light of the problem. Success, failure, or ambiguity is a possible outcome, and, whether one or another, it can be counted as asserted knowledge. Knowledge gained in this way is not a truth in the traditional sense. Instead, the assertability of knowledge is either warranted or not by the evidence of the test.

Now the process, as it goes on, is not always this formal or orderly. In some cases, the examination of hypotheses results in a redefinition of the problem. In other cases the study of hypotheses results in a determination to go on living with the need. For example, a family may decide they need a swimming pool in the back yard. The members decide how big it should be and find a location, but when the hypotheses reveal cost, maintenance, and responsibility, the chosen hypothesis may be to forget about the pool and live with the need. All of this activity produced knowledge which was assertable and warranted by evidence. The family may know in this way it would rather not have a pool.

Pragmatists (or experimentalists) accept this kind of problem solving as central to curriculum and method. Rather than run children through a maze of pre-set experiences, they would have them work experimentally learning by problem defining, and by building, examining, and testing hypotheses. This, as they view it, develops a scientific habit of mind. This is as much of an external goal as educational pragmatists will consent that education as a general enterprise can have.

In order to get fuller comprehension as to what pragmatism (experimentalism) implies for schools it is necessary to deal with those aspects of this philosophy which might be termed ontological or axiological. Many will argue that pragmatism does not have an ontology or axiology in the traditional sense. However, the literature of pragmatism does contain speculation on the ultimate nature of process and offers theories of valuation. Ontological expressions can be *verbial* as well as *nominal*, and ontological elements can be *active* as well as *substantive*. This being the case it is proper to say that the ontology of pragmatism is process.

When process is viewed as ontology then it is easy to see why process becomes its own end. Or to say it differently, *process is product, and product is process*. Such an idea, as Dewey admitted, is difficult for the western mind to comprehend. This is because since the time of Plato and Aristotle we have been intellectually conditioned by means-ends thinking. In this traditional style of thought processes are regarded as means adopted to achieve some end. But in the pragmatist's world there are no ultimate ends. The pragmatic world is indeterminate. Men and women have needs which they feel, and for them the meeting of these needs becomes "ends-in-view." All of this is process, and process produces its own artifacts. The sovereign example of an artifact of process is that of man himself who emerged as a consequence (simply that and nothing more) of the process of evolution. Man was not created by a creator, and process is not understood as having a beginning. One way of saying it is that man is one of the more recent and most complex manifestations of mammalian epoch. His special distinction is that within him a special characteristic called intelligence has commenced to evolve, and it has evolved to the point where he (and of all other manifestations of process, only he) can see something of the process. And, as Whitehead remarked: "*Here we are*. We don't go behind that; we begin with it."

There are no ultimate ends. There are simply ends-in-view. In valuation (instrumentalism) there is no ultimate good. The good is good-for-an-end-in-view. When pragmatism deals with "man" as a plural noun, the word society comes into use. In fact, most pragmatic thought since William James usually deals with man as a "social-vocal organism." In pragmatic theory human society is also a manifestation of process. Some theorists suggest that society has processes. Those who oppose them on this, claim these theories become aberrations by being drawn to metaphorical extremities which depict society as some sort of creature. For example, "soft minded" social theorists may *rationalize* a utopia and attempt to put "social processes" to work in behalf of their dreams. This admixture of Platonism and pragmatism is really an effort to intrude upon process and carve out a "niche of greatness" for a special social era or entity. Those in opposition to this argue neorationalism of this kind may have a place in existentialism, but rationalization and pragmatism tend to be mutually exclusive.

In conservative pragmatic theory, society is not an end or a means; it is a word for process. *Society is process.* Society is an action that is constantly occurring. Grammatically, therefore, society is not a noun; it is a verb. Thus, when a pragmatist suggests that educators prepare children for society, they mean prepare them for intelligent, scientifically minded participation in an action-that-is-going-on. There are no absolutes, no fixed ends, and no transcending moral propositions. This is a "tough minded" ontology. Scientifically minded citizens will, in communion, articulate a consciousness of social needs which through social action become articulated as ends-in-view. These, so to speak, become community values. The community made them, and the community can change them. No one needs to go to war or to kill anyone else. There are procedures whereby changes in values are effected. When these procedures are controlled by scientific intelligence, change can be both orderly and felicitous. Each individual enlists his trained intelligence in the process. If he can overcome passion and prejudice and, what may be even more important, learn not to be condescending, he can place his faith in the belief that each outcome of social action simply results in a reformulation of the problem as the action then moves forward to another stage. Nothing, therefore, is ever won or ever lost. Instead, process moves in one direction and then another.

Likewise, social consensus never forms; instead it is constantly forming; first it is this and later it is that. There is no direction, no ultimate determination, only the higher ground of intelligence-in-action as seen from the perspective of evolution. The human race solves its problems. First it was survival by technology, more recently it has become survival from technology, and values have been changing accordingly. Men, once proud of their factories and cities, proud of their large families and appropriated resources, proud of their abilities to disembowel the earth and pollute its waters, are now calling all of these into question; this is not a re-evaluation. The valuation has simply been a continuing thing. The articulated values of today differ from those of yesteryear because there has been an altered sense of social need. Cursing the past is part of it; this is how most of it sounds; but it is unintelligent behavior to regret the past. The "good" of the past was for the past only. One cannot expect the good of the past to be good for now, and one must not anticipate that the good of now will be that of any time in the future.

Finally, the ontological vision yielded by application of pragmatic epistemologies is a *pluralism* and its axiological counterpart is a *relativism*. In the course of a single day a social man may enter a number of realities. He goes to work, takes part in the processes there; he goes to a restaurant, and takes part in those procedures. He may go to a baseball game where three strikes are "out"; where thirty-five-year-old players are "old"; where he drinks beer straight from the bottle; and where he may share his sentiments with thousands so long as his outcries do not violate the boundaries of oral language conventionalities. On the other hand, he may go to a theater and enter agreeably into that universe of expectations. These are different realities and the standards of conduct are relative to each. What is acceptable as good in one ontology is totally repugnant in another.

The pragmatist finds it neither an intrusion on freedom nor a compromise of integrity for an individual to adapt to social expectations. The kind of war whoop that delights a football crowd is out of place in a lecture hall (even if it comes from the lecturer). Pragmatism simply asks the man-in-society to face up to this pluralism and relativism and to adjust accordingly.

Whitehead speaks of "trained intelligence"[46] and the experimentalists of the "scientific habit of mind." This is as far as pragmatism will go in articulating an external goal for education. Dewey announced in the first article of his *Pedagogic Creed* that "All education proceeds by participation in the social consciousness of the race." He went on to observe that "This process begins unconsciously almost at birth, and it is continually shaping the individual's powers, saturating his consciousness, forming his habits, training his ideas, and arousing his emotions." It is in this way that each individual inherits the "funded capital of civilization."[47]

Dewey argued that education has two sides, psychological and sociological, "And neither can be subordinated to the other."[48] Because education is a social process a school "is simply that form of community life in which all those agencies are concentrated that will be most effective in bringing the child to share in the inherited resources of the race, and to use his own power for social ends."[49] As thus understood, education is a process of living and not preparation for living. Selection of school activities and experiences, therefore, should be based on psychological and sociological considerations instead of logical (or traditional ontological) propositions. The school has a central role in social progress because "education is the fundamental method of social progress and reform." A school does not communicate knowledge in the traditional sense. The school is a procession from traditional social values to social emergent values. The older members of the school environment (school board, administration, older teachers) tend to reflect the former, and the younger members (younger teachers and students) tend to reflect the latter. Each is examining the other but as change continues, and the older depart and the younger become older, that which was at one time emergent becomes tradition and new emergent values are registered on the continuum.

As Dewey stated, "Education must be viewed as a continuing reconstruction of experience; the process and the goals of education are one and the same thing.[50] This puts all of the slogans of pragmatic education in a more meaningful light. When a teacher in the experimentalist tradition declares that he teaches "children and not subjects," he is saying that he is bringing the child into a conscious participation in processes which have names, such as individual reflection, society, nature, culture, and valuation. These are not understood as ends (or abstract nouns). They are actions going on. By teaching children as they participate in these processes which can be summarized by the terms "experience" or "life," the children inherit all that processes have yielded from the past, develop their own powers, and continue to keep this "ongoing change" under the control of an evolving human intelligence. Thus, do we "teach children and not subjects."

For more than half a century pragmatic interpretations of educational theory have been made by a number of distinguished American educators. A partial listing of the more noted of these includes John Childs, William Kilpatrick, George Counts, Sidney Hook, Ernest Bayles, Theodore Brameld, and Boyd Bode. As one might expect, men of such vigorous scholarship do not agree in all respects. Indeed, any representation of pragmatism in educational theory which comes out as a "party line" would be misleading. Reconstructionism, experimentalism, socialization, life adjustment, social humanism, individualism—these are variant doctrines of pragmatic thought about the curriculum or methods.

There has been disagreement among the pragmatists as to how central the school is to social reform (or progress). However, there is no mistaking the great influence pragmatism has had on the view laymen have on the role of school in society. Since 1950, the schools have been considered as a powerful instrument to achieve long-range social objectives. The most notable among these are racial integration, secularization, and the elimination of poverty. American schools are now in the midst of these struggles because elements of the public who have embraced these ends-in-view sense the school is what certain pragmatic theorists claim it to be, namely, the place where society reconstructs or reconstitutes itself.

Modern Empirical Realism

It is important to note that the empirical tradition which is traceable to Hobbes, proceeds through Herbart and Spencer, and is reflected in the work of Thorndike, Tyler, and other notable figures of the American testing movement is still very much in evidence. This early tradition which gives objective reality to the world and vaunts the scientist as an objective observer certainly lives on. Experimental psychology is not to be confused with "experimentalism." Clinical psychology embraces certain pragmatic traditions, but some schools of social science avoid pragmatism almost entirely, or simply accept it in the Peircean sense that pragmatism (pragmaticism) is simply a method of conceptualizing. Many social scientists, for example, are unwilling to assume that education has no external goals. Holding to the view that educational enterprises have objectives they make the claim, "Tell us what they are, and we will measure them." Once measures are devised (or divined), researchers can examine effectiveness of school procedures. Able students are identified and a host of techniques can be used to discover, diagnose, and remedy the deficient. On this tradition the medical model is applied, and the testing and diagnostic field is becoming so large as to be considered a growth industry. With data processing now available one receives his S.A.T. score as part of his cosmic identity (along with such things as name, baptismal, and I.Q.).

This tradition continues undergirded by the faith that such things are "out there" and should be identified and measured. No effort will be made here to further delineate the various empirical schools which exist within this broad and still flourishing tradition. But the students should be generally alert to the strident conflicts which now rage in the social sciences and especially alert to the way these differences are reflected in the applied field of educational research.

Measurement is apparently here to stay. However, the meaning of that which is measured and the uses measures can be given continue a matter of wide conjecture. Each year it becomes increasingly clear that standard measures are being used in ways that trouble even the manufacturers and merchandisers of tests. One can assume, therefore, that this tradition of empiricism will be critically reviewed in the years to come. Philosophy of social science is fast becoming a professional specialty; the passages of Hobbes' *Leviathan* are again quoted widely; the skeptical canons of David Hume are more frequently invoked; and the naturalism of Locke, Rousseau, and the Pestalozzians lives on.

Notes

1. Francis Bacon, *The Great Instauration*, The Preface.
2. *Ibid.*
3. *Ibid.*
4. *Ibid.*
5. *Ibid.*
6. Thomas Hobbes, *Leviathan*, ch. I.
7. *Ibid.*
8. R. S. Peters, H. Tafiel, *That Behaviorism Can't Account for Thinking*, included in Leonard Krimerman, *The Nature and Scope of Social Science* (New York: Appleton-Century-Crofts, 1969), p. 219.
9. Hobbes, *op. cit.*, ch. VI.
10. John Locke, *An Essay Concerning Human Understanding*, Book II.
11. *Ibid.*
12. *Ibid.*, ch. VII.
13. Donald Butler, *Four Philosophies and Their Practice in Religion and Education* (New York: Harper and Bros., 1951), pp. 288-289.
14. John Locke, *Some Thoughts Concerning Education*, ed. Peter Gay, *John Locke on Education* (New York: Teachers College, Columbia University, 1964), p. 42.
15. *Ibid.*
16. Rupert Lodge, *The Great Thinkers* (London: Routledge and Kegan Paul Ltd., 1949), p. 223.
17. Hans Reichenbach, *Experience and Prediction* (Chicago: The University of Chicago Press, Phoenix, ed. 1961), p. 342.
18. David Hume, *A Treatise of Human Nature*, Book III, Part 1, Sect. 2.
19. R. S. Peters, Ethics and Education (Atlanta, Georgia: Scott, Foresman & Company, 1966), p. 27.
20. Hume, *op. cit.*, Part IV, Appendix.
21. Lodge, *op. cit.*, p. 240.
22. *Ibid.*
23. Rousseau, *Confessions*, Books I-III.
24. *Ibid.*, Book VII.
25. Rousseau, *The Social Contract*, Book I, ch. 6.
26. *Ibid.*, Book I, ch. 3, 4 and Book III, ch. 6.
27. *Ibid.*, Book III, ch. 4.

28. *Ibid.*, Book III, ch. 9.
29. Rousseau, *Emile*, Book I, ch. 7.
30. *Ibid.*, Book II.
31. *Ibid.*, Book I.
32. *Ibid.*, Book II.
33. Rousseau, *Confessions*, Book VII.
34. William Ernest Hocking, *Whitehead as I Knew Him,* included in George L. Kline, *Alfred North Whitehead, Essays on His Philosophy* (Englewood Cliffs: Prentice-Hall, Inc., 1963), pp. 7-17.
35. Kline, *op. cit.,* pp. 198-199.
36. Hocking, *op. cit.,* p. 8.
37. Robert L. Leight, *Education and the Philosophies of Process* (Bethlehem, Pa.: Lehigh University, 1968), p. 13.
38. *Monist,* April 1906, p. 166. Also Charles Hartshorne and Paul Weiss, *Collected Papers of Charles Sanders Peirce,* Vol. V., para. 414.
39. Justus Bachler, ed., *Philosophical Writings of Peirce* (New York: Dover Publications, 1955), pp. 259-260.
40. This statement at times has been called awkward and bewildering. But Peirce insisted he chose each word with care, emphasizing that it dealt with concepts, not with things, and that it was a principle of method rather than a proposition in metaphysics. The statement first appeared in *Popular Science Monthly,* January 1878, p. 293, in an article, "How to Make Our Ideas Clear."
41. Leight, *op. cit.,* p. 18.
42. William James, *Pragmatism,* cited in John McDermott, *The Writings of William James* (New York: Random House, Inc., 1968), p. 452.
43. *Ibid.,* p. 453.
44. William James, *Varieties of Religious Experience,* cited in John McDermott, *The Writings of William James* (New York: Random House, Inc., 1968), p. 779.
45. *Ibid.,* p. 782.
46. Alfred N. Whitehead, *The Aims of Education and Other Essays* (New York: The Macmillan Company, Free Press Ed. 1967), p. 14.
47. John Dewey, *My Pedagogical Creed,* Article I.
48. *Ibid.*
49. *Ibid.,* Article II.
50. *Ibid.,* Article III.

Other Reading

Ayer, A. J. *The Origins of Pragmatism.* San Francisco: Freeman, Cooper and Co., 1968.
Bacon, Francis. *The Great Instauration.* Included in E. A. Brutt. *The English Philosophers from Bacon to Mill.* New York: Random House, Inc., The Modern Library, n.d.
Bayles, Ernest. *Pragmatism in Education.* New York: Harper & Row, Publishers, 1966.

——————— and Bruce L. Hood. *Growth of Educational Thought and Practice.* New York: Harper & Row, Publishers, 1966. Chapters III-XII.

Bode, Boyd H. *Modern Educational Theories.* New York: Macmillan Co., 1927. Chapters XIII-XV.

Brameld, Theodore. *Education for the Emerging Age: Newer Ends and Stronger Means.* New York: Harper & Row, Publishers, 1965.

———————. *Toward a Reconstructed Philosophy of Education.* New York: The Dryden Press, 1956.

Breed, Frederick S. *Education and the New Realism.* New York: The Macmillan Company, 1939.

Broudy, Harry S. *Building a Philosophy of Education.* Englewood Cliffs, N. J.: Prentice-Hall, Inc., 1961.

Childs, John L. *American Pragmatism and Education.* New York: Henry Holt and Company, 1956.

———————. *Education and Morals.* New York: Appleton-Century-Crofts.

———————. *Education and the Philosophy of Experimentalism.* New York: The Century Company, 1931.

Comenius, John A. *The Great Didactic.* Tr. and ed. by M. W. Keatings. London: Adam and Charles Black, 1907.

Counts, George S. *Dare the School Build a New Social Order?* New York: The John Day Company, Inc., 1932.

Dewey, John. *A Common Faith.* New Haven, Conn: Yale University Press, 1934.

———————. *Art as Experience.* New York: Minton-Balch Co., 1934.

———————. *Democracy and Education.* New York: Macmillan Company, 1920.

———————. *Experience and Education.* Tiffin, Ohio: Kappa Delta Pi, 1938.

———————. *How We Think: A Restatement of the Relation of Reflective Thinking on the Educative Process.* New York: D. C. Heath & Company, 1933.

———————. *The Philosophy of John Dewey.* Ed. Joseph Ratner. New York: Holt and Company, 1928.

———————. *The Problems of Men.* New York: Philosophical Library, 1946.

———————. *The Quest for Certainty.* New York: Minton-Balch and Company, 1929.

———————. *Reconstructionism in Philosophy.* Boston: Beacon Press, 1949.

———————. *The School and Society,* rev. ed. Chicago: The University of Chicago Press, 1930.

Gay, Peter. *John Locke on Education.* New York: Teachers College, Columbia University, 1964, p. 176.

Herbart, J. F. *Science and Education.* Tr. H. M. and E. F. Felkin. Boston: D. C. Heath & Company, 1897.

Hobbes, Thomas. *The English Works of Thomas Hobbes.* London: John Bohn, 1899.

James, William. *The Meaning of Truth.* New York: Longmans, Green and Company, 1909.

———————. *Pragmatism.* Boston: Longmans, Green and Company, 1907.

—————. *Talks to Teachers*. New York: Holt, Rinehart & Winston, 1900. Chapters V-IX.

—————. *The Varieties of Religious Experience*. New York: Longmans, Green and Company, 1916.

Kline, George L. *Alfred North Whitehead: Essays on His Philosophy*. Englewood Cliffs, N. J.: Prentice-Hall, Inc., 1963, pp. 7-17, 53-158.

Komisar, Paul B. and C. J. B. Macmillan. *Psychological Concepts in Education*. Chicago: Rand McNally & Co., 1967, p. 249.

Locke, John. *Essay Concerning Human Understanding*. Philadelphia: Troutman and Hayes, 1853.

—————. *Some Thoughts Concerning Education*. Cambridge: Cambridge University Press, 1934.

Lodge, Rupert. *The Great Thinkers*. New York: Frederick Ungar Publishing Co., Inc., 1964. Chapters VII, IX, XI.

Mandelbaum, M. *The Problem of Historical Knowledge: An Answer to Relativism*. New York: Liveright Publishing Corp., 1938. Chapters III, IV.

Muirhead, J. H. "Peirce's Place in American Philosophy," *Philosophical Review* XXXVI (1928), pp. 460-481.

Nagel, E. "Charles S. Peirce, Pioneer of Modern Empiricism," *Philosophy of Science*, VII (1940), pp. 69-80.

Peirce, Charles S. *Collected Papers of Charles Saunders Peirce*. Ed. Charles Hartshorne and P. Weiss. Cambridge, Mass.: Harvard University Press, 1931-1935.

Rousseau, Jean J. *Confessions*. New York: Random House, Inc., The Modern Library Ed., n.d. Books I-XII.

Rusk, Robert R. *Doctrines of the Great Educators*. New York: St. Martin's Press, Inc., 1965. Chapters V-XIII.

Spencer, Herbert. *Herbert Spencer on Education*. New York: Teachers College Press, Columbia University, 1966.

Thompson, Manley. *The Pragmatic Philosophy of C. S. Peirce*. Chicago: University of Chicago Press, 1953. Chapters IV, V, VI.

Wierner, Norbert. *Cybernetics: Or Control and Communications in the Animal and Machine*. New York: John Wiley, 1948.

CHAPTER XI

Mind and the Phenomenological Method

The mind is still a mystery. No one has explained it to the satisfaction of all philosophers. The only acceptable statement which is offered about the mind as a category of philosophical inquiry is that it consists of a group of unresolved issues. If by some miracle all of these issues could be settled, then the study of progressive philosophy would be reduced to the size of a course in, say, driver education. Most of the vast body of philosophical literature which has been accumulating since the days of Socrates would be deposited in the documentary storage bins visited only by historians. Only a small portion of this literature would continue to circulate and only a part of that would continue relevant. In addition, a number of branches of philosophy and several academic disciplines would vanish along with most of the world's religious organizations.

This is because most of the world's literature, many branches of philosophy, and nearly all of the academic disciplines take validation from one or more of the contemporary theories about the nature of mind. Each academic discipline, for example, is sustained by some kind of standard for knowledge; and this standard, in turn, rests upon some theory about what the mind is or how it works. For example, much of mathematics is built upon a faith in the axiomatic method, and this in turn relies upon a belief that rational or logical truth is an inexorable process and property of mind. History offers a different case. Some historians sense there is a correspondence between social processes and mental processes. This encourages them to organize history in accordance with a theory of mind; and, in their hands, the human past becomes rational. Some students of language assume that discourse originates in thought. Then they follow this by assuming that thought has logic; and, therefore, the grammar of discourse is logical. Others say language is simply communication, mind has no special status over and above other organic components, and, therefore, the grammar of discourse need not be logical.

Not only are each of the academic disciplines dependent on a theory of mind, but as each discipline develops it sends its own probe back into the question. Psychology, sociology, economics, education, and all the rest in one way or another ask the question: what is mind? When this happens it becomes apparent that a critical method of history can be used to dispute any written history[1]; a coherent philosophy of mathematics can be used to refute any mathematics[2]; and a philosophy of religion can be written which would challenge any established mode of piety.[3] As one might expect, the same can be done to any established theory of education.

Not only is the mind the grand enigma of philosophy; it is a mystery to all of scholarship. No one can really say what effects an undisputed theory of mind would have upon the academic world. However, if the nature of the mind were suddenly revealed in a way such as none could dispute, one could reliably expect that vast portions of the academic world would vanish. Indeed, if it would be discovered that the truth about mind would be something distinctly different from any of the theories currently recognized, virtually all of the present academic world would dissolve and disappear. The presence of mental theory in the realms of knowledge is that pervasive, ubiquitous, and crucial.

It is a safe wager that this great enigma is nowhere near revelation. The student of education may then ask: Why go further? Why read of disputes? Is there not enough of certitude to know? Why regenerate ancient quarrels when there are deeds in the world which cry out to be done?

There are at least three points to be made in response to these questions. The first of the three is that educators must understand knowledge problems. In one way or another schooling involves knowledge. Very often classroom teachers are unaware that the information they confidently dispense, often with a sense of high righteousness, may itself have "feet of clay." The second point to be made is that efforts are underway to construct philosophical methods which do not depend on a theory of mind. These efforts may not succeed, but a teacher would profit from understanding what it is that positivists, pragmatists, radical empiricists, and phenomenologists are trying to do. The third point is that the institutions in which teachers work have purposes. The purposes may be implied or covert, but they are there. Most institutions of education are oriented to one or several theories of mind. For these reasons it is not possible for philosophers of education to be indifferent to the metaphysics of mind.

No matter how sophisticated teaching technologies become, the educational philosopher is bound to ask in every case why they should be used at all. No matter how multiformal the order of educational institutions becomes, the educational philosopher is bound to examine each form[4] and depict, however he can, ways by which educators can understand more clearly what is before them. Such tasks as these do not require an ultimate solution to the nature of mind, and they may not require dogmatic adherence to any of the alternative theories, but they do require consideration of prevailing views which are thought meritorious.

Indeed, nearly every form of schooling seeks to accomplish something that is mental. One may reasonably conclude, therefore, that schools are as various as are acceptable theories of mind, and those who wish to understand schools must explore at least the most widely recognized among the modern alternatives.

The Mystique of Mind

Magicians are clever men. Seemingly they produce something out of nothing. A typical magician will hold aloft a box which is apparently empty; in fact, he goes to great lengths in demonstrating its apparent emptiness. Then he will close the box, clap his hands, open it again, and pull forth a living, flapping rooster. This done, he reverses the performance, and when the box is opened again, the rooster is gone and once again the box is apparently empty. To appearances the rooster is materialized out of nothing and is then dematerialized back to nothing. The rooster comes to be and then ceases to be, but for a moment it is there and as full of life as any rooster one might find in any American barnyard.

In these days no one really believes the magician "made" and then "unmade" a rooster. Everyone knows that somewhere the rooster was cleverly concealed, then cleverly revealed, and then just as cleverly reconcealed. We applaud the performer for this cleverness. Oftentimes, after such performances, children gather around the "wizard" and ask him to explain his tricks. Occasionally he does this. A modern magician can explain his "magical events." So if one seeks to know about these things he consults a magician or a book about magic.

Men are producers of mental events. This is to say, they are conscious sources of thoughts or ideas. They know, feel, and will. Men are aware; they form abstraction, symbolize, and use language. They apparently hold in common a special capacity, process, or property called reason. They remember events and predict events. They feel dissatisfaction, form hypotheses, and evaluate effects. They offer definitions, discuss feelings, express anxieties. These are but some of the many ways mental events are noticed. To all appearances mental events, like the magician's rooster, come out of nothingness and, similarly, they return to nothingness. Like the rooster, no one doubts that they exist. Now a magician can explain his magical event. Why not ask a man to explain his mental event?

This is the point at which the analogy dissolves. Man can not explain his own magic. If he is the source of mental events he has never managed fully to comprehend how he produces them. On the other hand, if he is not the source, but something of a medium, then he has never managed fully to comprehend what the source is, how he receives the signals, or how he converts these signals into the phenomena called mental events. There are numerous theories about how this happens, and they contend with each other for the favor of academic opinion. None of them has achieved a clear supremacy; most of them have devoted advocates in modern edification. The best that can be said of any one of them, therefore, is that it offers a plausible explanation of how mental events occur.

In western civilization the oldest and still highly influential is Platonic *idealism*. This would include theories of philosophers such as Plato, Zeno, Plotinus, Augustine, and Aquinas. In each of these cases something we can call mind is above and beyond man. His physical and personal attributes are effects, extensions, emanations, or reflections of these. Within this body of theories there are various opinions as to free will, the qualities of the good, and the properties of the divine.

Another popular theory is called *interactionism*.[5] This includes some of the modified forms of Platonic idealism and teleological forms of materialism. Included are philosophers such as Aristotle, Epicurus, and especially Descartes. These theories suggest that there is something above or around man. We can call this something mind (or spirit), and man reacts to its activities. In addition, however, these theories allow that man is something on his own. He can push back. His daily activities register on the mind or spirit which surrounds him and he is a partner with whatever else there is in working out the reality of the world. Many interactionists develop theories of mind-body dualism. There are many strong points in these arguments, but there are a number of problems as well. Cartesian man tends to be divided. Traditional literature based on this view dwells on the soul and such things as will or destiny. But much recent speculation tends to discount this as "ghost in the machine" mythology.[6]

Interactionism allows for *psychokinesis*.[7] This term refers to beliefs that mental events have a special force of their own and can bring about physical events. Hence we can consider the commonly called "special messages from the beyond." Many men are willing to bet their lives on a belief that they have received such "messages." It also enables us to consider forms of extrasensory communication between human beings. Modern men of science have been uncongenial to evidence of telepathy, but men of science bring an admitted prejudice against such data. Even so, a goodly portion of the human race are not willing to agree that their hunches or suspicions are merely the force of perceived events on experience. Many people think there is something more. Intuition holds a dominant place in the life and works of nearly everyone, including many scientists.

The term *epiphenomenalism*[8] relates to any belief or set of beliefs which holds that mental events or mental states exist but must first of all be brain events or brain states. As we have seen, this point of view had its first modern expression in Hobbes' *Leviathan*. This, of course, is the position held today by many behaviorists. It does not necessarily deny that there is a surrounding world of the spirit, mind, or soul. However, it does maintain that such things, even if they do exist, do not produce mental events. Epiphenomenates argue that mental events come from the functions of the human brain and from those alone.

Considerable support for epiphenomenalism comes from recent research with drugs and brain surgery. It has been demonstrated that by stimulating certain regions of the brain, memories are sharpened, forgotten things recalled, hallucinations are created, the capacity for falsehood is diminished, and so on. All of this tends to be very convincing, but there are still a few problems. The brain in this theory still remains something of a "black box"; percepts go in, and concepts apparently come out. What really goes on in the box? How does a brain event become a mental event? Is there a lapse of time between the two? Reason is obviously coherent. Therefore, how does a mental event when turned back upon the brain (which allegedly produced it) stimulate a brain event which results in a mental event coherent with those events which have gone before? In questions such as these, epiphenomenalist theories form their own mystique and fail to remove the mystique from the mind. Possibly more research will eliminate the puzzle.

Another class of theories might be called radical (or skeptical) empiricism. These views have in common the suggestion that mental events are simply perceptions of physical activity.[9] This doctrine is traceable to the skeptical realism of David Hume, and those who now hold this view insist that it confuses the issue to think of mental events as having any kind of independent reality. Thought can be considered as perceived brain activity. Analogically, a sight event does not give the thing seen another reality. Why should a brain event, when perceived in whatever way it is perceived, have a second and additional reality called a mental event? The solution, argue such theorists, lies in understanding how brain events are perceived.

But a satisfactory explanation for this has not yet been produced. Even an acceptable schema of the psychophysical operations would then have to deal with the matter of the consciousness and its cognates (superconsciousness and subconsciousness); beyond these problems is the issue of language and symbol, and beyond this lie the problems of concept formation, clarification, and retention.

So when men form thoughts they are indeed makers of "a magic" that they cannot explain. The best they can do is shape some kind of belief about what happens. Plato's world of ideas and Descartes' mind-body dualism are not so fashionable as once they were, but the fact is that there are no facts which disprove these or prove any of the more recent notions. However, this does not mean that philosophizing is useless or that philosophers must sit back and wait until someone gets a bright idea which will pull it all together. That may happen some day; but, meanwhile, there is plenty to do.

Phenomenology

For example, we could go to work on what we are given. We could simply describe, analyze, and report the data of consciousness. This would enable us not to worry about the truth or falsity of these stated theories. If methods can be developed whereby the phenomena experienced within consciousness could be accurately noted, a basis for reliable knowledge will exist. The philosopher would not then need to reflect on *how* he got the concept of the pencil in his hand. He begins by recognizing *that* he has the concept; in effect, it has already been presented to him, and his task is to find a means of describing it. This effort to avoid the mystique of mind is *phenomenology*.[10]

The term phenomenon has wide currency in the English language. One who attempts to understand the term as it is applied in phenomenology must consider its history. Prior to Immanuel Kant the term phenomenon related to illusions of one kind or another. But in his famous *Critiques* Kant establishes a much broader meaning for the term. It is recalled that Kant separated the noumena from the phenomena. He reasons that the noumena are those which exist on the "other side" of the mind. All men have of the noumena is what the mind presents, and the mind presents concepts. Therefore, men do not perceive the noumena; they conceive the noumena. The work of the mind, therefore, is to receive percepts of the noumena, convert them to concepts, and present them into the consciousness of men. Now concepts which appear in the consciousness of men are called phenomena. They may be illusions, but they are all we have. Men may live in a universe of noumena, but they can know only phenomena.

German philosophers of the next generation, and most notably Hegel, offer an alternative understanding for the term phenomena. In his first major work, *Phenomenology of the Spirit,* Hegel attempts to show the development of mind (or spirit) through various levels at which it perceives itself as *phenomenon* until it reaches the level of complete development where it apprehends itself as *noumenon.* In Hegel, therefore, the science of phenomenology is the endeavor of the mind to know itself through the study of phenomena. Or, in other words, to discover the mind by examining the ways in which it presents itself to the consciousness.

In the middle of the Nineteenth Century the definition of phenomenon was widened by various usages until it became almost a synonym for "fact." One would use the term in reporting whatever he observed. In this way phenomenology became regarded as a kind of science of description. And phenomenological studies were undertaken of a number of subjects, including such problems as moral consciousness. At the turn of the century Charles Sanders Peirce used the term in regard to all kinds of descriptive studies, including not only all that is observed but also whatever is before the mind.[11]

Thus the term became so broad as to be almost without meaning until it was taken over by the German philosopher, Edmund Husserl (1859-1938). In his hands phenomenology was developed as a method, or a way of doing philosophy. In the interval since 1900 the phenomenological method has attained wide credence. Today those in philosophy who refer to themselves as phenomenologists usually believe the phenomenological method is the only correct method of philosophizing. Numbered among these may be such noted existentialists as Martin

Heidegger and Martin Buber. Jean-Paul Sartre gave his general work *Being and Nothingness* the subtitle *An Essay on Phenomenological Ontology.* Sartre did not discuss the details of his phenomenological method. On the whole, it can be said that most philosophers accept the phenomenological method as a method of description, but issues develop over the extent to which the phenomenological method can be used in analytical or valuative enterprises.

The Phenomenological Method

Husserl owes much to the works of his teacher, Franz Brentano. Brentano was not a phenomenologist, but his studies on inner perception as a source of intuition and infallible self-knowledge helped prepare the way for Husserl's work.[12] Brentano noted that we are not only conscious, we are conscious of things. In other words, we are conscious *about* things. Some have argued that his *aboutness* is not an adequate or appropriate basis for the study of consciousness; but, again, it is not consciousness itself which the phenomenologist wants to take in hand but the things which appear in consciousness.

This particular way of looking at objects is dramatized by the slogan *"Zu Den Sachen!"* When this is translated literally it means "to the things!" Here "things" are taken to include the widest possible range of objects. However there is a psychological force in the slogan which does not come across in translation. It has been suggested that if one would add the exhortation "get down to business" the full polemical force of the slogan would emerge.[13] Thus "to the things" becomes the proper way of doing philosophy by men who are serious about it.

Husserl proceeded to develop explicit methods to accomplish this. As early as 1905 his ideas attracted attention in German philosophical circles and his point of view began to win acceptance. The movement was spread by activities of Husserl's students at the University of Gottingen. A number of these came to the United States during the Second World War. Meanwhile, the phenomenological method continued to influence the works of European existentialists such as Heidegger and Sartre. Aspects of phenomenological method offered epistemological premises which many existentialists accepted and used in their work.

In addition, the phenomenological method was applied to a number of disciplines. Max Schaler, a well known phenomenologist, used the method in anthropology; Rudolf Otto applied it in his studies of religion; Karl Mannheim used it in sociology; Victor Frankl used phenomenology in his approaches to psychiatry. Probably the most significant influence of phenomenology currently in American schools appears via Carl Rogers' applications of phenomenology to theories of personality.[14] The effect of this particular thought upon curriculum and counseling seems to be growing each year.

To understand the method we must recall again that Kant informs us that the noumena or things-in-themselves exist. This existence, however, is not knowable as such. What is knowable is the phenomena (of the noumena) which are rendered into the personal consciousness by the work of the mind. Husserl stands on these same grounds in approaching the first aspect of his method. His first step forward in developing the method is to declare that we can *bracket out* any thought about the actual existence of the object and deal with the phenomenon the mind renders *as if the phenomenon is the thing.*

Now this introduces the phenomenological method as essentially a method of reduction. In this regard it is similar to Descartes' experiment in doubt. Only what is immediately and imminently apparent to the consciousness may be considered. The rest is bracketed out. Bracketing as he uses the term is similar to the practices of mathematicians who "bracket" certain mathematical expressions in order that they can deal with them independently of the general expression in which they are contained. Any judgment concerning that which is bracketed out must be suspended. This suspension of judgment Husserl called *epoche*. Husserl evidently appropriated this term from ancient philosophy, although he gives the term a different meaning from that which was applied in antiquity. He demanded we count as knowledge only that of which there is complete certainty. Phenomenological reduction, therefore, restricts our knowing to the pure data of consciousness. This intuition of the object, the phenomenon itself, is the only indubitable datum.

Recently Professor Nancy Larrick at Lehigh University prepared an anthology of children's poems which she called *Green Is Like a Meadow of Grass*.[15] This title was taken from a line in one of the poems written by one of the children. As such it constitutes *a private ostensive definition of green.* An ostensive definition is one given by pointing to something.[16] A private ostensive definition occurs when one points to a commonly known thing to explain his consciousness of a phenomenon. Recently a lady employer who was seeking to fill a clerical position declared that she was seeking "a woman and not a girl." When the person she addressed replied that help was needed in understanding that particular distinction, the response was made by referring to persons known to both, as follows: "Well, Grace is a woman and Ellen is a girl." Thus understanding was achieved without stating a plenary definition of either womanhood or girlhood. This is how ostensive definitions work. But in *Green Is Like a Meadow of Grass* the ostensive definition is private. One may hear a child say this and respond by agreeing that is just what green is. To the child, however, this intuition of green represented in the private ostensive definition is self-evident, certain, and, therefore, apodictic. It stands above scientific theories about green (the length of light waves and the like). Such matters have no meaning for the child; therefore, they are suspended (*epoche*).

The next stage of reduction is called eidetic. Husserl evidently resorted to Plato for this term. Knowing how Plato attempted to move every conversation in the direction of "first principles" helps us to understand eidetic reduction. We might, for example, ask the child if there are not other green things. The child might respond by naming other things. After discussion and analysis the child may make a more general statement about green. This statement would be at a higher level of abstraction. The higher abstraction is made possible by (1) an enlarged consciousness of green and (2) application of rational powers. However, the abstraction still originates in the feeling and intuitions of the child. The child must acquire it, and he is the only one who can have it. Therefore, his knowledge of green is *personal* and continues so, even as higher abstractions are attained. Even while his schooling advances and the abstraction grows as elements are removed from *epoche* and added to the concept, the concept is still *personal*. At this point Husserl's doctrine of intentionality is invoked.[17] This means that thinking of any kind about the data of pure consciousness involves a personal *act* (doubting, affirming, denying, willing, refusing, feeling, imagining, valuing, etc.). The implications for this on American education are resounding and if this point of view occurs to and is accepted by a sufficient number of American schoolmen our schools will be drastically transformed.

One can start out by saying ostensively of happiness that happiness is "a warm puppy." But as his personal notion of happiness grows he will make use of the world of ideas. He will want to encounter all the best that has been thought and said about the subject. But every thought he brings to the subject is borne on the wings of a personal intention or act.[18] The final stage of reduction occurs when the person (phenomenological ego) attempts to correlate his phenomenon with the actual thing. Happiness as a thing-in-itself does exist—that is, it has a transcending reality which gives its appearance into our consciousness. We began by bracketing out the existence of the real thing, but now we have a personal consciousness about happiness, and we begin to conjecture how that correlates with the real thing. A man can say with absolute certainty that "my idea of happiness is . . . ." This was bracketed in. He can also declare, "In general, happiness in people exists when . . . ." Originally this was bracketed out. By noting the difference, he can gain some estimate of the originality and uniqueness of his person. In this way he may begin to intuit his selfhood.

Returning to the nature of green, the phenomenological ego might begin with green by defining it as "like a meadow of grass." As time goes on the child's notion of and feeling of the phenomenon of green will enlarge and deepen. It is not inappropriate to suggest that the child's cogitation of green becomes enriched as it rises to higher levels of abstraction. Another child writing about green and quoted in the same anthology of children's poetry[19] started with this line: "Green is in summer time trees." This statement is the pure phenomenon as it appears in consciousness. But even more interesting is the movement to abstraction in the line which followed in which she said, "Green is in a sweet mint breeze." The movement to abstraction is occasioned by her *intention* to elaborate. Now we can imagine how the child will later move to even higher levels of abstraction. For example, she may *feel* that green is the earth, the sun, and life; and green is the freshness of the air which gives her breath; and green is the earth telling her that it lives, that she lives, and that all live together; and, finally, that green is the *good in nature*. But as this abstract richness grows the realization also grows that there is something such that when it appears in her consciousness it gives her this green. What is this thing-in-itself that is out there? What is this objective green? It has been bracketed out, held in suspension.

One day the child is taught that this thing that is out there (green-in-itself) is a condition on the surface of certain objects that reflects light of a certain kind and absorbs all others. She is taught that this surface is composed of such things and in such a way that when light strikes it she has the experience of green in her consciousness. Again, as in the case of happiness, she has an opportunity to see the uniqueness and originality of her person. She is aware of the "wonder of wonders"—that she is a being aware of her own subjectivity and that in her subjectivity lies all the reality and meaning that the world can have. These are only the primary distinctions between phenomenology and other methods of philosophy. The central points to bear in mind are: (1) Phenomenological statements are non-empirical in that they do not represent the state of affairs in the world. Phenomenologically, green may be a meadow of grass, but empirically it is not, and the phenomenological ego knows this but holds this knowledge in *epoche*. (2) Phenomenological statements are descriptive. (3) Phenomenological statements describe phenomena. (4) It is important to understand that phenomena are essences. (5) It is also important to understand that these essences are rendered into the consciousness by the mind by a mental activity called intuiting.

Thus, the phenomenological method has a triadic base which Husserl called *Ego, Cogito, Cogitata*. The first element of the triad, the phenomenological ego, is more than consciousness; it is a philosophizing consciousness which constantly reduces things by suspending those things which can be doubted. The second element of the triad, the *cogito*, is thought about the relationship between the subjective understanding of a thing and such objective knowledge as the world has of that thing. Every thought has that which is thought about. Every phenomenon has a noumenon. There are as many thoughts about green as there are people. And yet there is one green. This, of course, is *cogitata*.

Now with particular reference to the last two of these points, the consciousness comes to include a world of intuited essences. In other words each mind creates a world of phenomena and gives it into the consciousness of each person. This is what one has. It is his "life world." In phenomenological writing the term *Lebenswelt* is becoming increasingly known. It, too, represents an important idea for education. The *Lebenswelt* (life world) is the world which encompasses our conscious life. Its essences are determined through phenomenological reduction. Clearly, one does not reach it through scientific interpretation. Science demands that one turn himself completely *off* and become pure objectivity. Phenomenological reduction demands that one turn himself completely *on* and become pure subjectivity. Scientific interpretations, therefore, are held in *epoche* as the *Lebenswelt* develops. Such interpretations play a proper part in self-identity when the person is able to correlate his *Lebenswelt* with the objectivity of the physical world.

What does the "life world" as a philosophical construct offer to the person? Probably the most important offering and by all means the most important for education is the prospect for philosophizing in two worlds. One can philosophize within and about his own "life world"; at the same time he can deal with the "world view" which science develops. The personal "life world" comes from the philosophizing ego. The ego emerges from its culture. It originates, exists for an interval, and then ceases to exist. It deals with problems and decisions. It initiates activities, and it plans, aspires, and creates. It is capable of significance and capable of nonsense.[20] The phenomenologists insist that teachers, for example, should understand that for each child in the room there is a *Lebenswelt*. And the teacher enters into each of these "life worlds" in a way that is peculiar to each of them and unknown to the teacher.

Intentionality

The *Lebenswelt* needs a principle of organization. The life world is not just a jumble of assorted phenomena completely devoid of syntax. It is not, to use William James' wonderful phrase, "a booming, buzzing confusion." The life world is orderly, and the basis of this order exists in Husserl's doctrine of intentionality.

The philosophizing ego is possessed of a will that is constantly a force in the consciousness. A man is always in the act of doing something he intends doing. Thus the term intentional as used in the Husserlian doctrine is meant as a modifier to the word act. One should first understand that the human consciousness is in a continuous state of personal action and then understand that every action is intentional.

For example, I put the food on the table, I open the window, I call to the children. Now in each of these three sentences the agent (I) takes some deliberate action (places, opens, calls) toward something (food, window, children) at some place (table, wherever the window is, wherever the children are). Each intentional act has these four elements: the agent, the act, the object, and the place. Intentionality is, in this sense, grammatical and gives the consciousness, during any given interval, the organization it needs. If one can imagine that all purpose or intentionality would fall away from a person one can immediately sense what a tangled mass the phenomena of his consciousness would suddenly become.

It is important to recognize that consciousness as used here flows to the broadest possible range. It is not restricted to mental events such as thoughts. It includes such physical acts as placing food on the table, because as one performs the act he is conscious of its being performed by himself. It is important to remember that man in a conscious state is never without intention and is always in a state of action. And, finally, it must be remembered that intentionality itself is a phenomenon. In every case a man's purpose is intuited in the same way as are other phenomena. No one else, therefore, can know his intention in the way that he knows it. And so it follows that no one else can understand the organization of another's "life world" as it is understood by the person who lives within it.

Educational Counseling and the Lebenswelt

The *Lebenswelt* tradition in phenomenology, as it relates to the field of educational counseling, is probably best represented in the expressions of Carl Rogers. Rogers seems to rely heavily on the concept of the self "as an explanatory construct." Rogers envisions the end of personality development as a matching of the phenomenal field of experience and the conceptual structure of self. When these entities are in "congruence," the person represents the "maximum in realistically oriented adaptation."[21] This would also mean the person has arrived at a personal value system.

Rogers apparently believes that a person, in the presence of a sympathetic counselor, can develop this ability to come to terms with his immediate problem. At the same time he will develop a more ample life. This style of counseling is often termed "non-directive" and calls for skill in developing "empathy" with the person counseled. In effect, the counselor is expected to enter the phenomenal field of the person counseled and become a part of his life world—indeed, as if he wore the client's skin in place of his own. In fact, it may be appropriate to suggest that he merge with the client in such a way as to be considered a helping agent in the phenomenological field. Needless to say, this requires uncommon personal strengths on the part of the counselor. Above all, the counselor must be able to accompany the client in his effort to work out a hierarchy of personal values. This also means that, while at work, the counselor must put his own values aside. It is no easy thing to become neutral in favor of the client, but this is what is required.

Other counseling theorists have identified their views as phenomenology. However, there is some question whether all such views go as deeply into phenomenological methods as do those of Rogers. Snygg and Coombs, for example, are identified as phenomenologists.[22] However, their orientation to phenomenology seems more constrained. While they agree that the person can know only his phenomenal field they tend to deny the presence of a person with a free will as the self-directed developer of the field. In fact they assert that choice is a "pseudo-concept." Snygg and Coombs make the phenomenal field itself the determinant of behavior.[23] Assuming that all behavior is regular and lawful, they indicate that so-called decisions are simply perceptions in the phenomenal field of those things which appear self-enhancing. The organism (self) then simply takes the action which holds a minimum of disturbance to itself.[24] Thus, they dig into the metaphysics of the pragmatists and empirical realists for such fundamental notions as behavioral laws, need satisfaction, perception, and testing of hypotheses. The Snygg and Coombs view seems to represent a mediation of the non-directive counselors, many of whom are Rogerian phenomenologists, and the clinical counselors, many of whom are partial to measurements and their applications through the problem-oriented medical model of illness, diagnosis, therapy, and cure. Basic to the Snygg and Coombs position is a requirement that the counselor intervene in the development of phenomenological ego by actively seeking to reorganize the phenomenological ego into a more satisfactory accommodation with surrounding reality. In this, the counselor takes upon himself a much more decisive responsibility. Is the counselor justified? Perhaps so, but justification cannot be found in phenomenology itself. The originators of phenomenology were deeply committed to the notion that the self can develop only from within. It is doubtful if phenomenologists who adhere closely to the Husserlian position would have welcomed the metaphysics of the empirical tradition (or of any other tradition) into theories of personal development which are put forward as expressions of the phenomenological method. Husserl was apparently opposed to "psychologism"[25] or the theory that mathematical and logical laws are derived from psychology. Moreover, by withholding intentionality, the phenomenological method is deprived of one of its primary characteristics.

So all that is called phenomenology does not necessarily cohere with the pristine traditions of phenomenology. When all elements are analyzed out of the position held by Snygg and Coombs, the only one that appears consistent with its method is the assertion that man acquires knowledge only from that which appears in his phenomenal field. On the other hand, a number of modern views which are not called phenomenological are consistent with the assumptions offered by Husserl. For example, Michael Polanyi offered a view of personal knowledge which held that men have two kinds of knowledge. The first he called tacit. This knowledge is the same as knowledge possessed by animals. It is pure consciousness. The second he called explicit.[26] Tacit knowledge is acritical; explicit knowledge is man's awareness of what appears in his consciousness. It is manifested in his capacity to conceptualize, evaluate, and articulate. This appears to be similar to the Husserlian stage two, namely, the invocation of personal intentionality. Polanyi went on to assert that all knowledge is personal, that *fact* is inseparable from *value*, and that science cannot be severed from the humanities.

The Body and the Person

Of all the theories of mind only extreme idealism tends to deny the existence of bodies, and only radical empiricism tends to deny the existence of mind. Thus all but a few philosophies of mind accommodate a distinction between body and person. It seems an obvious distinction to make, especially for educators. But in recent years the effects of scientism in teaching, testing, and school administration have brought American schools perilously close to regarding children and youth as bodies. Some of the trends in prospect depict bodies interacting with teaching machines in highly mechanized settings. Even when this is done in the name of individualization of instruction, it is important to note that the individual at the machine is a body, and not a person.

Now the medical profession deals with bodies. The reason for this is perfectly understandable. In cases where problems of the mind directly intervene in the health of the body the medical profession will call upon the profession of psychiatry for assistance. Even here, the medical model of illness, diagnosis, treatment, and cure is often followed. However, the certainty of the relevance of the medical model to problems of mind and the work of teachers and counselors is not considered so great as it formerly was. Its relevance to the work of education is even more dubious. Teachers do not minister to a body but to a person. This concept of person is larger than the concept of body. Of all the theories of mind none gives more stress to this than phenomenology. This calls for the humanization of the curriculum and the establishment of a humane pedagogy.

Children are persons and persons have an aversion to being treated as bodies. It is difficult for adults to understand the impact of inhumane treatment on a child. However, by returning to the example of the medical profession and its practices, recently this author came into possession of an account written by a professor (a humanist) who was convalescing from the effects of surgery. He wrote of his personal perturbation over the clinical spirit of the hierarchy of nursing attendants and of his valiant efforts to bring about humanistic reforms. The account follows:

The Unhygienic Humanist

One distressing aspect of my stay had been an incessant assault on my personal propensities. These young women, unfailingly young and usually attractive, glided noiselessly to my bedside, plunged a thermometer into my mouth, grasped my wrist, and then began a period of uninterrupted gazing at a wrist watch. As the period approached end, I grew in expectation of the sort of civil exchange which occurs between persons who had shared an interval of physical proximity. But, alas, as the instrument was withdrawn from its harbor, I was confronted with questions such as, "Did you wash your legs?" Or more ominously, "Have your bowels moved?" Now the first question was readily answered because it referred to something I might or might not have done, but the second was beyond the reach of personal volition and seemingly placed the two of us in discussion of an event in which neither of us as a person had a part.

Now the rational implications of sudden depersonalization led to a momentary restraint in the dialogue which was grossly misunderstood; as a consequence of the misunderstanding, a team of these enthusiastic feminine prefects appeared with a grotesque plumbing apparatus the chief characteristics of which were an enormous plastic water bag, a generous length of hose, and menacing nozzle (the functional aspects of which were all too apparent). Complying with their insistence that I form a strikingly undignified posture I suddenly found the lower regions of my inner parts being converted into a vast unnatural reservoir not unlike that known in history as the Johnstown Dam. I had known for years about the Johnstown Dam but never until that moment did I ever feel like the Johnstown Dam.

Anyone with an understanding of the inexorable consequences of the hydraulic principles thus employed could predict the practical effects of this kind of abuse. The knowing attendants retreated to a discreet distance, and as I sat listening to the splashing and trumpeting of my aggrieved organs I remorsed over my inability to deal humanely with these people and resolved not to remain defeated.

The next time this particular question was put, the interrogator was thrown back on her humanity by the fullness of my response. Indeed, there was a degree of over-kill as evidenced by the poor girl speeding from the room saying, "I am sorry I asked." Subsequent exchanges were such that I found evidence on the part of the nurses of a deeper appreciation of my personal sensibilities. In fact, in no more than two days the question was abbreviated to "Is everything O.K.?" And my response was shortened to, "Yes, and how are you?" Humanity restored, it seemed that another blow has been struck for the dignity of man.

Implications for Education

This valiant humanist in a hospital bed fought to preserve his person. He was able to do this. But how can a child in the first, second, or third year of his schooling fight to preserve his person? He has his ways, of course, but they don't always work. And children who are unwilling to be appropriated in this way may simply "drop out." This does not mean they remove themselves physically from the classroom. It means intentionality by which their "life world" is organized is directed to other ends than those of the school. Now by one means or another they may be continued in school until they are sixteen years of age. They may even, by forces of their culture, be compelled to stay until they are graduated from high school. But for all practical purposes, they dropped school as a favorable aspect of their life world sometime before "elementary education" ended.

The phenomenologist would have teachers recognize that each child brings his own developing life world to class, and the phenomenologist would hope that teachers would learn to be sensitive to and appreciative of what might be in each of the life worlds before him. The contents of these worlds cannot be known in the empirical sense that things are known, but there is a pedagogical style which stems from a recognition that these worlds do exist, and the education one gets in life is taken on through the phenomena of the life world.

The application of phenomenology to pedagogical practice would demand that the phenomenological ego be nurtured, not suppressed. Thus, at that stage of schooling, the core of the child's activity should be the intensification of consciousness and the encouraging of the child to explore the fullness of his awareness of that which is in his consciousness. Children, then, will become poets; they experience music; and they will use music to denote experience. Dance intensifies the rhythm of nature. Rhythms appear in music, in language, and they have a prominence in the phenomenological ego. Art is a means for recording and bracketing-in that which appears in the stream of our consciousness.

For these reasons the center of the elementary school curriculum could become poetry, art, music, and dance. What then, one might ask, of our traditional skills? The phenomenologist would respond to this with questions of his own. Is there anyone who fears that in the fourteen years that we have available to educate children and youth we shall not have time to teach them to decode the written language, to use the general properties of arithmetic, or to learn to write them down? Why, now that we have before us an unprecedented fourteen years to educate men, must we have elementary schools which have the same curriculum as they did when we had only six or eight years? The time has come when we must develop a philosophy of education which is equal to the opportunity that we of all men in history have before us. Such a philosophy would commit us to a personalized education (not an individualized education).

Phenomenologists would argue that we must not minister to externals alone. Our education is not of the body and the brain: it is education of the person, of the mind. How much more wonderful it is, they say, to be a part of a school where a child is loved, not just taught, where a child is subjectivity and not objectivity, where the relations between child and teacher are in the Buberian sense I-thou rather than I-it.[27] They urge that we turn aside from the medical model; our children are *persons*, not *bodies*. They argue that at last, in the long span of the Christian era we are in a full position to heed the injunctions of the great Latin father, St. Augustine, the first great philosophical voice of the Christian Church, who at one point said, "Concerning universals of which we can have knowledge, we do not listen to anyone speaking and making sounds outside ourselves. We listen to Truth which presides over our minds within us...."[28] And, at another point Augustine stated, "turn not outside of yourselves, truth dwells in the inner man."[29]

Notes

1. For philosophical alternatives consult William H. Dray, *Philosophy of History* (Englewood Cliffs, New Jersey: Prentice-Hall, Inc., 1964).

2. Ernest Nagel and James R. Newman, *Godel's Proof*, contained in James R. Newman, *The World of Mathematics Vol. 3* (New York: Simon and Schuster, Inc., 1956).

3. For philosophical alternatives consult John Hick, *Philosophy of Religion* (Englewood Cliffs, New Jersey: Prentice-Hall, Inc., 1963).

4. Hastings Pashdall, *The Universities of Europe in the Middle Ages, Vol. I* (Oxford, England: The Clarendon Press, MDCCXCV), p. 5.

5. Richard Taylor, *Metaphysics* (Englewood Cliffs, New Jersey: Prentice-Hall, Inc., 1963), pp. 15-21.

6. Gilbert Ryle, *The Concept of Mind* (New York: Barnes & Noble, Inc., 1949), p. 63.

7. Jerome Shaffer, *The Philosophy of Mind* (Englewood Cliffs, New Jersey: Prentice-Hall, Inc., 1968), p. 75.

8. *Ibid.*, p. 68.

9. See Thomas Hobbs, *The Metaphysical System of Hobbs*, collected and edited by Mary W. Calkins (La Salle, Illinois: Open Court Publishing Co., 1948).

10. Shaffer, *op. cit.*, p. 23.

11. R. J. Hirst, "Phenomenology," *Encyclopedia of Philosophy* (New York: Crowell-Collier and Macmillan, Inc., 1967), p. 135.

12. William S. Sahakian, *Outline-History of Philosophy* (New York: Barnes & Noble, Inc., 1968), pp. 328-333.

13. Hirst, *op. cit.*, p. 137.

14. Sahakian, *op. cit.*, p. 328.

15. Nancy Larrick, (anth.) *Green Is Like a Meadow of Grass* (Champaign, Illinois: Garrard Publishing Co., 1968), p. 27.

16. See P. F. Strawson, *Individuals* (London: Methuen and Co., Ltd.).

17. Edmund Husserl, *Ideas*, W. R. B. Gibson, (trans.) (New York: Collier Books, 1962).

18. Edmund Husserl, *Phenomenology and the Crisis of Philosophy*, Quentin Tauer, (trans.) (New York: Harper & Row, Publishers, 1965).

19. Nancy Larrick, *loc. cit.*

20. Marvin Farber, *Phenomenology and Existence* (New York: Harper & Row, Harper Torchbooks, 1967), p. 123.

21. Carl Rogers, *Client-Centered Therapy* (Boston: Houghton Mifflin Company, 1951), p. 532.

22. Carlton E. Beck, *Philosophical Foundations of Guidance* (Englewood Cliffs, N.J.: Prentice-Hall, Inc., 1963), p. 66.

23. *Ibid.*, p. 71.

24. Donald Snygg and A. W. Coombs, *Individual Behavior* (New York: Harper & Row, Publishers, 1949), pp. 14-33.

25. Sahakian, *op. cit.*, p. 333.

26. Michael Polanyi, *The Study of Man* (Chicago: The University of Chicago Press, Phoenix Edition, 1958), pp. 11-39.

27. Martin Buber, *I and Thou*, (trans.) R. G. Smith (Edinburgh: T. and T. Clark, 1937), p. 75.

28. Quoted from *On The Teacher*, (trans.) J. H. S. Burliegh, *Augustine, Earlier Writings* (The Westminister Press, 1953).
29. *De Vera Religione.*

Other Reading

Beck, Carlton E. *Philosophical Foundations of Guidance*. Englewood Cliffs, N.J.: Prentice-Hall, Inc., 1964. Chapters III, IV.
Buber, Martin. *Between Man and Man*. Boston: Beacon Press, 1955.
——————. *I and Thou*. New York: Charles Scribner's Sons, 1958.
Edie, James M. *An Invitation to Phenomenology*. Chicago: Quadrangle Books, Inc., 1965. Parts I, II.
Farber, Marvin. *Phenomenology and Existence*. New York: Harper & Row, Publishers, 1967, pp. 113-195.
Heidigger, Martin. *Existence and Being*. Chicago: Henry Regnery Co., 1949.
Husserl, Edmund. "Phenomenology," *Encyclopedia Britannica*, 14th ed.
Kiner, Edward D. "Some Problems in a Buber Model for Teaching," *Educational Theory* XIX, (Fall 1969), pp. 396-403.
Kuenzli, Alfred, ed. *The Phenomenological Problem*. New York: Harper & Row, 1959.
Lauer, Quentin. *Phenomenology: Its Genesis and Prospect*. New York: Harper & Row, 1958, pp. 185.
Lee, Edward and Maurice Mandelbaum. *Phenomenology and Existentialism*. Baltimore: The Johns Hopkins Press, 1967, pp. 268-272.
Luipjen, William A. *Existential Phenomenology*. Pittsburgh: Duquesne University Press, 1960.
Polanyi, Michael. *The Study of Man*. Chicago: The University of Chicago Press, 1963. Lectures I-III.
Rogers, Carl. *On Becoming a Person*. Boston: Houghton Mifflin Company, 1961.
——————, and Rosalin Dymond, eds. *Psychotherapy and Personality Change*. Chicago: University of Chicago Press, 1954.
——————. *Client Centered Therapy*. Boston: Houghton Mifflin Company, 1951.
——————. *Counseling and Psychotherapy*. Boston: Houghton Mifflin Company, 1951.
Ryle, Gilbert. *The Concept of Mind*. New York: Barnes & Noble, Inc., 1949. Chapters I-IV, VIII.
Shaffer, Jerome. *Philosophy of Mind*. Englewood Cliffs, N.J.: Prentice-Hall, Inc., 1966.
Snygg, Donald and Arthur Coombs. *Individual Behavior*. New York: Harper & Row, 1949.
Wagner, James. "Toward a Heuristic Theory of Instruction: Notes on the Thought of Michael Polanyi." *Educational Theory* (Winter, 1970), pp. 43-45. Vol. 20, No. 1.
Wann, T. W. *Behaviorism and Phenomenology*. Chicago: University of Chicago Press, 1964, pp. 1-78, 109-140.

CHAPTER XII

Existentialism

Some who take up the study of philosophy are partially in hope it will bring a revealing light to shine upon themselves. Along the way, however, it becomes evident that the bulk of academic philosophy does no such thing. Vast portions of the field are given to building ontological systems, and soon it becomes evident that this system building is really the manufacture of books and talk about great houses in which no one really lives. At this point many become discouraged with philosophy, thinking that for all of its promise it offers very little to a man alone in the world burdened with the responsibility to fashion a meaningful existence.

A Contest with the Absurd

Perhaps this is mildly overstated. Few would question that men such as Augustine, Aquinas, or Berkeley, for example, lived happily in accordance with their ontological systems. But in each of these and kindred examples the "system" is dominated by a strongly held religious posture. In each such case the ontological system in question is properly described as that which resulted when the philosopher formed a metaphysical explanation of his religious faith. To be sure, these edifices of thought are worth beholding for their own sake. That they are so pleasing to men of intellect is analogous to enthusiasts of domestic architecture admiring the stately mansions on a winding suburban road by saying, "they are beautiful, but I couldn't live in any of them." And, indeed, the only people who do live in them are those who find some kind of god in the structure. Ordinarily it is not good to press analogies too far, but this one has deeper range than most.

Ever since Parmenides offered the persuasive doctrine, *thought is being*, theologically oriented philosophers in quest of an explanation of being that was consistent with their theology took thought as its own object and thereby intellectualized *being*. Components of being were invented, including potency, act, essence, archetype, cause, principle, substance, extension, relationship, and their cognates. Things like these were arranged in rational structures which conformed to logic. The resulting ontologies were plausible because the identity of thought and being was preserved. Because of this, being continued to be regarded as rational. Irrationality, therefore, was an ontological error and was eliminated in order that ontology would not lose rational status. Of course, all a man needed to do in order to live happily within any rational ontological system was to believe in its god.

But mortal life with its fears, fashions, and fevers is not rational. Life is lived by men with passions in their stomachs. They are creatures of reverie and imagination. There is something in man which rhapsodizes and enspirits. Many philosophers of history insist that any imposition of rational structures on human events results in a distortion of history. Not long ago one of them said, "history is simply one damn thing after another." So this is life; life is not rational. Life is absurd, an absurd and meaningless struggle. As William James once noted, "life may not be a struggle, but it certainly feels like a struggle." A man wants help in his struggle with the absurd, and if none of the theologically ordered ontological systems has won his religious faith, then his contest with the absurd goes on.

This is one reason why many men never cease to be fascinated by the non-systematic or anti-dogmatic philosophers who tease and chide, provoke and attack, dispel illusion, and repudiate rationality. The world continues intrigued and tormented by the Socratic gesture. Even the vaunted smile in recollection of the puppy-dog antics of the Cynics and Skeptics of antiquity. And the modern world continues impressed with the Epicureans of those early times who philosophized about the harmonies a man can achieve within the terminal points of his mortal state.

Antiquity was rich in this kind of thought, but the medieval schoolmen and renaissance philosophers had few to question the ontological system builders. When questions did arise they were not tolerated. The pagans had no priestly class which stood guard over a special truth. But the Middle Ages were not lacking in this. Even though men such as Rabelais or Boccaccio were usually about, the obsession of bishops and princes with ontological ladders which led up to their own eminence and from that on up to God was so overwhelming that the critical spirit so typical of ancient times was ruthlessly subdued. If someone of prominence did seek another outlet it often turned out degenerate. Finally, in the enlightenment of Eighteenth-

Century France, Rousseau and others assailed the oppressions by which institutions abused and distorted the natural man, while in Germany Kant was formulating premises for a Copernican transformation of philosophy. Then, in the first half of the Nineteenth Century, a figure rose and drew across human affairs the kind of line which informed the world another era had begun.

Kierkegaard's Arrow

The source of revolution is not always predictable. Few of his own time would have thought the Danish Christian mystic, Soren Kierkegaard, capable of manufacturing a time bomb set to explode in Europe and America a little more than one hundred years after his birth. One would have expected that a progenitor of general reform would be a leader of men. But Kierkegaard was ebullient, unstable, and unpredictable. He was constantly in a state of emotional or intellectual ferment which, among other things, amplified his personal problems beyond his capacity to deal with them quietly.

He was born in Copenhagen in 1813, and aside from three trips to Berlin he spent his life in that city and its environs. He prepared as a theologian, but never accepted a pastoral responsibility. The major episodes of his personal life were so jarring to him that his books and articles take both starting point and subject matter from the emotional stirrings subsequent upon such events as the conflict and rapprochement with his father; a broken love affair; a general upheaval in his spiritual commitments; and, at the end, a furious quarrel with leaders of the Church of Denmark.[1]

He did not have a following of students. His nature was, in fact, so hypersensitive and uncompromising that nearly all of his social connections seemed ultimately to end in some kind of hurt.[2] Despite the many happy hours he whiled away in gay and intellectual conversation with his friends at taverns and coffee shops, he has been remembered as a lonely man. His books and pamphlets were controversial,[3] but he was not in his lifetime widely read outside of Denmark. His figure was slight, bent by spinal curvature, and his features were sensitive and brooding. At the age of forty-two, health deteriorated, inheritance exhausted, he collapsed on the street and days later died at the hospital to which he had been taken. Kierkegaard was neither a pedagogue nor a systematic philosopher. At his passing he left a city which knew him only as a rebel theologian with an unruly mind. A few suspected there was a great deal more to him than this. In a strange and perverse way Soren Kierkegaard himself was one of the few.[4]

How is it that now, a little more than one hundred years after his passing, we find this human whirlwind of passion and antagonism so close to the center of our modern thought? His flamboyant humor and irony are enough to win him a modest place in literature. His attack upon the church is noteworthy, but the clergy even in his day knew the whip of honest thought. Previous indictments of Christendom had been characterized by the intensity if not the ardor of the Kierkegaardian assault. In retrospect, it appears that Soren's epistemological arrow struck the ontological balloon of European idealism at the moment it was ready to burst. Indeed, the arrow achieved just enough penetration to achieve detonation. Genius requires timing, and it was this superb timing which has raised up Kierkegaard as "the father of existentialism."

Extending the metaphor, his attack upon the church, relevant as it was, turns out to be the bow rather than the arrow. Soren was a reluctant archer. Indeed, it appears that he struggled to come to terms with the church. He had a great personal need of the church. But Christendom's obsession with its own organization and its alliances with power and wealth together with the continuing harlotry of its clergy, when contrasted with the pristine sentiments of New Testament Christianity, became in Kierkegaard's hands the paradox of bow and string. Ultimately it was too much for one of his sensitivity, commitment, and insight. And in the end, the arrow was in flight.

What sort of arrow? Kierkegaard did not question the identity of thought and being; neither did he question the cognates of being as proper objects for thought. But he took the view that no one lives in the ontological systems which come out of rational speculation who is not religious about the object which makes the system operate. Christendom, in his view, had fallen to the point that one had to be either religious about the church *or* about Christ. The two in his view had come to be mutually exclusive. As a Christian, therefore, the former of the two alternatives was out of the question. The men of the new testament dealt with the inward life and not with ontological systems. The apostles of Christ ministered to the inner man.

His first target was Hegel who occupied the prestigious chair of philosophy at the University of Berlin and who died two years before Kierkegaard's first article appeared. Of such metaphysical castle building he declared, "A logical system is possible but a system of existence is impossible."[5] He went on to deride philosophers who presented their ontological systems as real:

> The fact that philosophers talk about reality is often just as deceptive as when a man reads a sign board in front of a shop, "Ironing done here." If he should come with his linen to get it ironed, he would be making a fool of himself, for the signboard itself was for sale.[6]

He likened such ontological systems to reading out of a cookbook "to a man who was hungry."[7]

His fateful confrontation with Christendom was still in the making; the philosophical conflicts bringing it on were stirring in him as early as 1843 when he wrote his first book which he called *Either Or.* At that time he was absorbed in a moral dilemma growing from a marital engagement he avidly sought and then found obliged to break. In *Either Or* Kierkegaard pointed out there were two kinds of men, aesthetical and ethical. Human life thrusts upon each individual the choice of being one or the other. The aesthetical is the man of sensual pleasure who needs and wants the gratification of flesh and appetite. Don Juan is the model. The ethical sees himself associated with that which transcends the flesh. He senses the eternal aspect of his being and lives accordingly. His actions are not dictated by craving senses but by an intuition of the right in regards to his transcendental being. This being acquires a spiritual dimension in the final section of the book which he called "prayer." Presumably, on the grounds of ethical manhood Kierkegaard became aware of his potential inadequacies as a husband and parent; and, therefore, as the ethical man he forced the termination of his romance. Through the subsequent crises of his life Kierkegaard recognized ever more deeply the call of the inner ethical voice. His unremitting stream of books, essays, articles, and pamphlets—some under pseudonyms—reiterates again and again the mounting dread (*angst*) which the aesthetical man feels as his maturing awareness of his ethical nature brings him inexorably to the point of despair. The end of the aesthetical life is inevitably despair. In time, the ethical in Kierkegaard became identical with his inner, personal, and passionate Christian sentiments. He thinks of himself as kindred to the New Testament Christians, on fire with a new vision of life. He first denounces the academization, depersonalization, and rationalization of Christianity.[8] He appeals for the authentic Christian:

> And what does this mean? It means that everyone for himself,

in quiet inwardness before God shall humble himself under what it means to be a Christian. . . .

But the bow and string were now taut. Bishop Mynster, head of the church, although a friend of Kierkegaard's father, tended to keep Soren at a distance. He was aware of the smoldering sentiments in the young philosopher and consoled himself that Kierkegaard was his complement in theology. For his part Kierkegaard looked upon Mynster as a gentlemen of refinement and respected their personal connection. Because of it he refrained from making public pronouncements of his estimate of Mynster as a Christian but in his private journal he fulminated over Mynster's stewardship of the faith. In July of 1854 Mynster died, and Kierkegaard's restraint vanished. When Professor Martinsen who was chosen to succeed Mynster followed the latter's burial with an address in which he called Mynster a "witness to truth," the arrow was dispatched. In a series of letters in a newspaper called *The Fatherland* Kierkegaard expressed himself in this spirit:

> January 29, 1855
>
> . . . the new Bishop by thus canonizing Bishop Mynster, makes the Christian Church from the Christian point of view an impudent indecency.
>
> March 20, 1855
>
> . . . Christianity cannot be well served by calling this sort of thing Christianity . . . .
>
> March 30, 1855
>
> . . . for "Christendom" is the betrayal of Christianity[9]; a Christian world is apostasy from Christianity. . . .

Kierkegaard seemed convinced that all of his life was coming to a purpose in the attack. He spared none of his polemical prowess, striking at professors, philosophers, theologians, clergy, politicians, princes, governments—anyone he found guilty of the distortion and destruction of Christianity. To him Christianity was an individual matter, an inner feeling, a private commitment. The church and all it stood for was worse than nothing; it was an abomination in the air, a prostitution of that in the human spirit which is most dear. The cannonade against Christendom, though polemical in the extreme, was masterfully directed. The shots were not scattered about; each one was carefully aimed at a well surveyed target as the accumulated insights of three decades of spiritual frustration, anger, and torment were combined in obsessive release.

Kierkegaard then had but one year to live, but his pamphlets and articles of that interval placed all of his previous work in a new perspective. Above all other things they made it clear that once again a private, individual man stood before the whole order of institutions and demanded freedom for himself and demanded also that the church, state, and university desist from transgression upon that which he found within himself to be holy. The old order tried to deal with his charges by ignoring them, and Kierkegaard, the Christian, died estranged from the church. But a century later many in the church were ready to end the contest on his terms.

In an essay called *The Present Age* he spoke to his own time about the pervasive effort to subdue the individual, but he also spoke to our times. In the following passage one has only to translate the word public as the word society to make its commentary relevant to the Twentieth Century.

> A public is everything and it is nothing, the most dangerous of all powers and the most insignificant: one can speak to a whole nation in the name of the public, and still the public will be less than a single real man, however unimportant. The qualification "public" is produced by the deceptive juggling of an age of reflection which makes it appear flattering to the individual who in his way can arrogate himself to this monster, in comparison with which concrete realities seem poor. The public is the fairy story of an age of understanding. . . .[10]

Nietzsche's Hammer

It is interesting to compare Kierkegaard with the other celebrity of Nineteenth-Century existentialism, Friedrich Nietzsche. The former was a Christian man who loved the cross, suffering not so much from its burden as from travesty and traduction of its meaning. Nietzsche was a pagan who denounced the aporia suffering not so much from Socratic doubts as from the ensuing constructs of "good" and "evil." Kierkegaard was the son of a successful industrialist; Nietzsche was of the family of a Lutheran minister. Kierkegaard and his father had serious problems; Neitzsche was raised by women; neither had an enduring, uninterrupted friendship. Kierkegaard was a lover of Christ and an apostate of the church. Nietzsche was a lover of the Dionysian and an apostate of European civilization. Both insisted in different ways that the individual must not be dominated by either ontological systems or the institutions by which such systems are enshrined. Kierkegaard found his inspiration in the ethical. Nietzsche found his in the dynamics of nature, of appetite, and of the passions about which men compose music.

To the academic profession, Kierkegaard was a theologian turned essayist and pamphleteer, and Nietzsche was a philologist turned poet and philosopher. Neither as a man could cope satisfactorily with the world into which he was thrust, but both authored philosophical denunciations which would set many worlds spinning in new directions. The Danish theologian and the German philosopher were both controversial in their times, but neither of them was acclaimed. Kierkegaard died with a vision of Christ as his personal savior. Nietzsche, while exalting the unrestricted powers of natural man, grew hopelessly insane and spent the final ten years of his physical life in unremitting silence.

Nietzsche was born in 1844 and endured a boyhood of piety and rigorous study. From the age of four he was brought up by his widowed mother, two aunts, and a grandmother, all respected, God-fearing, upright, and provincial. He went to a prestigious preparatory school and completed his university training at Leipzig. So promising was his academic career that he was appointed a Professor of Philology at Basel even before the awarding of his doctorate. He plunged into teaching and research with particular emphasis on Homeric literature and pre-Socratic philosophy. But two fateful endowments had already commenced to work upon his life, both having their origins early in his days as a university student. The first was his complete break not only with the religious traditions of his own family but also with those of contemporary Germany. In pressing his scholarship of Hellenistic literature and philosophy he soared as freely as any pagan and formed ecstatic bonds with certain pre-Socratic doctrines of the Dionysian mode. The second was a progressive hypertension marked by severe headaches and periods of melancholy. As he matured these physical perturbations came with greater frequency and increasing intensity until late in 1888 when he lost contact with the world. Some describe the symptoms as a classic progression of syphilitic infection, but others find this speculation to be untenable.[11]

His first major book, *The Birth of Tragedy,* was received by most of the academic profession with stunned hostility. Not only was it an immediate challenge to the religious attitudes of the western world, but it also went so far as to attack Socrates and the Socratic heritage of critical scholarship. The academic men of his time, tolerant as they were, must have been unaccustomed to being hit with "both barrels." His approach was to pit the Dionysian tradition in Hellenistic legend against the Apollonian. The outward aim of the book was to show the source of Greek tragedy. Its thesis was that tragedy was a dramatic form originated in the ritual choral dance of the Dionysian cult and that tragedy attempted to blend the two dissimilar modes of life. Apollo, the radiant one, the deity of light, the giver of idea and perfection, is contrasted to Dionysus, the joy and lust which pervades all nature, the intoxications of life, the bond between man and man, man and woman, and man and nature. The purity, the form, the idea are Apollonian. The rhythm, the poetry, the surge of desire and joy are the Dionysian. Whatever the merits of this dichotomous analysis, Nietzsche went on to point out that the Socratics, acting in the Appollonian spirit, and generating a religious commitment to the rational, had destroyed the tragedy in art and suppressed the Dionysian life. Far from freeing man or bringing him to heed Apollo's Delphic injunction "know thyself" the Apollonian influence in western civilization had through the "demon" Socrates made the real man of nature subservient to an imaginary man of idea.

The book pleased some of Nietzsche's friends, most notably the composer, Richard Wagner, but the academic world was appalled by this assault upon its venerable traditions. Although his ten years of teaching at Basel were terminated because of poor health and at the regret of the university, the academic profession never warmed to him. The most meticulous of scholars set about to find technical flaws in his philology as if believing that the thesis would be defeated by incorrect notations.

For one who struck so deeply with his pen Nietzsche was a reasonably compliant citizen. He had, in his way, met his military responsibilities, but he was not a fighter. In person he was well mannered, quiet-spoken, and congenial. His intellectual friendships such as with Wagner tended to be tempestuous, but as a man he offered harm to no one. His physical stature was unimposing. His face was said to be dominated by the intensity of his eyes. On two occasions he made feeble or perhaps furtive attempts to form a marriage, but for all that he exalted in the Dionysiac he did not impress the world as a lover. He freely admitted that his writings were one thing and he was another.

The ten-year interval between his university teaching and the onset of his final illness was very productive despite the rhythmic variations of his health. He had experimented with several styles of writing and found the aphorism very effective. The aphorism is a capsule statement of a general condition. However, for Nietzsche it was a short paragraph having its topical sentence phrased in high polemic and its supporting sentences in explanatory polemics. It is not a style suited for academic analysis or system building, but Nietzsche was trying to do neither. In the introduction to one of his last books, *Twilight of the Idols* (1888), he discussed what he called "philosophizing with a hammer."[12] By this he evidently meant that he used his aphoristic hammer to sound the idols of western civilization as one might sound a tuning fork. But one who reads Nietzsche cannot accept the vision of a small hammer deftly striking a tuning fork.

Each Nietzschean hammer blow was a massive whack upon the structure or foundations of western institutions. And in those last years of productive writing he sent boards and splinters flying at every stroke. He, whose early scholarship was the history of words, now took deeper inspiration from experience of nature. *The Gay Science,* first published early in this period, still reflected the Dionysian spirit, but the author's interest had shifted to man's religious enslavement. In it appears the famous poem about the madman, which stands as his proclamation of the death of God:

> . . . even Gods putrefy. God is dead! God remains dead. How shall we console ourselves, the most murderous of murderers? The holiest and mightiest that the world hitherto possessed has bled to death under our knife—who will wipe the blood from us?[13]

This parable which proclaims the "death of God" features a madman with a lighted lantern at high noon in the market place. The scene is reminiscent of the legendary escapade of Diogenes in the Agora. However, some commentators insist that this central figure is Nietzsche himself and the scoffing unbelieving crowd are his contemporaries before whom he smashes the lantern on the ground, saying "I come too soon."[14]

This is merely a prelude to works such as *Beyond Good and Evil* and *Towards a Genealogy of Morals*. He probably reaches his literary pinnacle in *Thus Spake Zarathustra* in which he tends to abandon his aphoristic style in favor of allegory and parable. A summation of these works is too much for these few paragraphs to encompass. After establishing that man is about to rid himself of the self-imposed neurosis called God, he is prepared to build values based upon life, his own life. His psychology is a predication on the human will which he conceives as a will to power. The emancipated man, no longer diminished by God, can now emerge as a superman. But this can only be as a consequence of his continued nihilism. He must reject all that would dominate him except life itself. In *Zarathustra* he recognizes that the common man will not heed this summons to ultimate greatness. Said Zarathustra, "they do not understand me: I am not the mouth for these ears."[15] Only the uncommon man can lead the way to higher ground. Nietzsche deplores the notion of equality and the homogeneous influence of democracy. His hatred of democracy is reminiscent of Heraclitus of Ephesus who twenty-five centuries before had denounced suppositions about human equality with equal ardor. Democracy is the enemy of the higher man, the superman. Zarathustra sings of the dearness of Life, and he finds Life dearer to him "than all my wisdom had ever been."[16] *The Twilight of the Idols* simply arrays many of his earlier ideas in support of this notion. Nihilism is now in crescendo; Dionysus reigns; and the autonomous man, eagerly embracing life in all its fullness, denying life nothing, and denying all else that would diminish life, stands forth in glory.

Nietzsche, this unhappy man, was deprived of life, the very object of his philosophy. His books assigned an inferior status to women. Their role was to bear the sons of the warriors and tend the kitchen. In *Zarathustra* he proclaims, "thou goest to women? Do not forget thy whip". Of this Bertrand Russell later observed, "nine out of ten women would have got the whip away from him, and he knew it so he kept away from women...." While tormented by his own physical pain and self-doubt, he angered and remorsed over the human race that is and yearned for the human race that might have been:

> I shall not suppress a sigh. There are days when I am haunted by a feeling blacker than the blackest melancholy—*contempt of man*. And so as to leave no doubt as to *what* I despise, *whom* I despise: it is the man of today, the man with whom I am fateful contemporary. . . . I suffocate of his impure breath. . . . I traverse the madhouse world of entire millenia be it called "Christianity", "Christian faith", Christian Church with a gloomy circumspection. . . . Our age *knows*. . . . What was formerly morbid has today become indecent.[17]

There were a few accounts to settle. Nietzsche wrote his version of his friendship and quarrel with Wagner. He completed a compendium of his poems, then January 1889 he collapsed and was heard no more. His mother and then his sister maintained custody of him until he died in 1900. There has been some ugliness about the extent to which his sister may have altered his letters and unpublished notes. Some of this doubt relates to a book called *Will to Power* which appeared later. However, this scandal is primarily of interest to specialists. The student of education attempting to trace the bloodstream of modern ideas will recognize in his incarnation of the Dionysian spirit the signal gun for the commencement of a general critique of man's fumbling efforts to idealize his world and himself into some kind of general ontological system. Nietzsche died at the dawn of a new century not knowing that his provocations together with those of the Danish mystic who preceded him would set the western world into a rage of controversy and bring the individual man to higher levels of awareness.

The Doctrine of Personal Resolve

Often students are heard debating the practical implications of Kierkegaardian or Nietzschean ethical pronouncements. These forensic exercises are interesting but futile. Both men are critics, neither are builders of doctrines. Their arguments are directed against the hypocrisy of institutions and against unrelenting and unwarranted domination of either the inner man or the natural man by rational systems. Both are ethical protests and not ethical programs. For this reason it is useless to ask: Does this mean if "such and such" then Nietzsche would rule "so and so"? Nietzsche does not build a method for normative judgments, and his own life is so unlike his philosophical vision that an adequate basis for inferring a Nietzschean ethic does not exist.

The one major illustration of this in our times was both horrible and ludicrous. Certain theorists who later became part of the Nazi movement in Germany found certain utterances of Nietzsche very much to their liking. His vivid prose on the superman, the elite, the will to power, and the Anti-Christ gave transport to overwrought imaginations within the Nazi cult.[18] Nietzsche was nominated as the "Philosopher of the Third Reich" by men who apparently did not take the trouble to discover that Nietzsche had, among other things, a personal distaste for anti-semitism, no high opinion of the German people, and a contempt for German institutions. Neither Kierkegaard nor Nietzsche developed an existentialism adequate for broad ethical understandings. This was to be the mission of existentialism in the Twentieth Century.

Existentialism and evolution were two vital challenges which Nineteenth-Century scholarship presented to the world. Philosophers of the Twentieth Century were given new material on which to work, and the work has not ended. Those who chose to press the challenge of existentialism found it represented an inversion of traditional methods. To some degree, all traditional systems presumed that men had some prior essence to which existence had been supplied. Even Thomism which gave prior status to existence depicted man a creation of a creator such that aspects of the creator were imbued in the creature. The existentialist inversion of method was rendered by assuming that *existence came first* and that essence developed later.

Now one familiar with the alleged role of genes in shaping human characteristics could object to his assumption as naive. Man as a creature is terribly limited in ways too numerous to mention. Like all of the other inhabitants of nature he is aware of his limits. However, unlike others he is aware that he is aware. This is the key. The moment existential man becomes aware of his awareness he intuits his potential freedom. The freedom is absolute. Camus dramatized this by stating that the choice begins with whether or not to commit suicide.[19] Freedom is that extensive. Using the Cartesian method of reduction, the only thing an individual is not free to do is to deny that he presently exists.

A man sits at the center of his own world, knowing that world through his own existence. He supplies spirit and essence to all that he perceives. One can imagine forty men sitting together in a room. Then there are forty worlds in that room. Each man is at the center of one of the forty, and each man also has a reality in each of the thirty-nine others as all the others have a reality in his. None of these existential worlds are the same; moreover, not one of the men can know another's world in the way he knows it. This is because each existential world is unique. It is unique because its knower is unique. When the knower ceases to exist his existential world disappears with him. Thus *esse es percepi* is used here in a personal way. In order for an object to be, one must perceive it as part of his world. The object has such reality as he endows it with. The pencil in my hand is real only because I perceive it and value it. Now if it bothers me I can put it aside, forget about it, or throw it away. In this way the pencil ceases to exist and I have performed the feat of nihilism. I am free to do this as well.

It is technically correct then for the existentialist to say that all the human history he perceives culminates in his existence. Why not? If his existence ended what would become of the history that he perceives? One can see the basis for Nietzsche's challenge. If the existential man hears the Apollonian injunction "know thyself," he replies to know myself is to know that I am free, the way before me is open, and the world which preceded me and which surrounds me is whatever I resolve that it be because I am the source of its being. Its being is illuminated by my existence. I can make part of it into nothingness, and if I end my own existence then all becomes nothingness.

Now this, of course, is stating the principle, and the moment one recognizes the principle there comes a flood of questions. Civilization has a way of taking possession of a person's existence, even to the point that a man can believe that he has little if any room to express his own resolve. He is loved, managed, and scrubbed in infancy and made to believe in his obligations. He is marched about in school. He goes to work, pays taxes, performs civic duties, and prepares a home so he can beget more humans who do the same. If a promotion is offered him he is obliged to take it. He dresses, acts, and talks to suit the company. He salutes the flag; he bows his head in grace; and he keeps to the right-hand side of the road. How can he understand this principle of freedom for personal resolve as applied to this world of struts and caps; homes and schools; banners, bugles, and standing armies?

Of course this brings to mind the objections of Nietzsche. In order to put together a society which does rational things we endow it with rational structure. Then we insist that the individual members do their duty at every point. This, to the existentialist, unmans man. He cannot reject his own freedom. He cannot become a sheep. For example, Plato's *Republic* was for sheep. The only possible men in that particular social "paradise" were the philosopher kings, and they were so thoroughly under the discipline of reason that it would be unlikely that a purely human response would come from any of them. Plato, who believed reason divine, did not want a human response.

How, then, can the civil man in a civilization recognize and realize his existential state? This is the problem. And the answers which can be developed for it are of colossal importance to education.

If men are free to fashion personal existence and meaning on the basis of personal resolve, then what kind of social arrangement, what kind of education, and what kind of governance will ensue? It would surely be a madcap world if every man were responsible only to himself, and existential man would shortly destroy himself in a welter of conflicting purposes and misunderstandings. How can this doctrine become a basis of order?

Modes of Being

In pursuing this thought it must first be understood that personal existence in its applied state becomes personal being. The most rigorous existentialists insist that such personal being is non-rational, and, therefore, absurd; and any effort to analyze it, perforce, distorts it. Why, they ask, should men simply resume the same ontological games which so far have resulted in nothing but self-distortion and self-denial? They say the best that can be done with personal being is to report it through the figurative, literary, and performing arts. Through such arts one can present being *qua* being which can be shared and, therefore, analyzed. Such analyses can be consumed by persons and add dimensions of meaning to their personal being; but personal being, *per se*, is beyond the reach of philosophy.

On the other hand, there are others who are willing to try to develop a philosophy of being, but in deference to the more rigorous existentialist they suggest that such analyses are in the tradition of phenomenology. This is true of the well known contemporary French philosopher, Jean-Paul Sartre. Using the methods of Husserl, Sartre depicted being at three ontological levels. The first is *being-in-itself.* This level has long been understood in philosophy. It is nothing more or less than objective reality. When a man is asleep and is not dreaming his body is being-in-itself. Life functions are going on, but there is no consciousness. A similar state exists when certain neural functions are impaired to the point that the body goes on living and the body responds to its needs as a body, but there is no awareness. The parlance "like a vegetable" is the symbolic description, but the more accurate simile is "like an animal."

But a man who is awake and aware of his being exists at another ontological level. He is aware of himself, of his needs, of his interests. He has to choose a way to get comfortable, to get understanding or enjoyment, to get on with his personal aspirations. He likes some things and dislikes others on the basis of personal taste or preference. He is aware of his condition, his life. He gives a status to the objects and persons around him. In this state, being-in-itself becomes a nothingness out of which (or through which) the things in the world are known, and a man in such a state of awareness is said to be in a state of *being-for-itself*. To put it another way, a man is in this ontological mode when he is aware of his human state which, of course, transcends the in-itself and all of its limits. Sartre in attempting to achieve clarity borrowed Heidegger's definition that the being-for-itself world is "that in terms of which human reality makes known to itself what it is."[20]

Sartre expanded at length on the organizations which *being-in-itself* assumes. One of these is time. He develops some fascinating notions of the past, present, and future as in the organization of personal being. His examination of the transcendence of the in-itself and for-itself yields a possible outline for a revised knowledge theory. Numerous school curriculum issues of the future lie buried in these speculations.[21]

The third ontological level is the *being-for-others*. One might imagine himself on a street corner wondering if his feet would stop aching or perhaps get worse, or thinking whether he would order lobster or veal cutlet at the restaurant; and as a flow of similar concerns crosses his awareness he stands in a recognized state of *being-for-itself*. Suddenly he notices that a man is staring at him very intently, and just as suddenly his being changes. There is another in his being, and all is altered. To begin with, the other may or may not be welcome. In a sense this staring intruder is attempting to dominate his being. Even if he isn't, it may well seem so, and if it seems so to the existentialist then it is so. Forgotten are the lobster and the aching feet. What could be his interest? Whatever it is, the private *being-for-itself* world is gone and in its place is a *being-for-others*. There are a host of problems at this ontological level. For one, if you enjoy the intrusion you may be a masochist who enjoys the sadism of the staring intruder. However, if sadism is also your nature you may stare back just as intently and perhaps compel the intruder to turn away. Now if you are a sadist you are apt to count this a good thing and feel pleased that it happened.

Sartre's own example of the change from *for-itself* to *for-others* is easily kept in mind. If a man is crouched in a corridor looking through a keyhole at whatever is going on inside a room his major concerns might well be to get the most comfortable posture and the best possible alignment of his eye with the aperture for maximum view. Now suddenly another person appears in the corridor and observes the man peering into the keyhole. The latter then experiences a new kind of discomfort. Whatever his feeling of guilt may have been in his own eyes, it is now something else in the eyes of the other. His transcendence of *in-itself* to *for-itself* is now in turn transcended by the *for-others*. In Sartre's words:

> The for-itself when alone, transcends the world; it is the nothing by which there are things. The other by rising up confers on the for-itself a being-in-itself-in-the-midst-of-the-world as a thing among things.[22]

The act of appropriation (sadism) or being appropriated (masochism) can be interpreted as an interesting way to view teacher-student relations. It has been suggested, for example, that many teachers choose the profession of classroom teaching or administration because of its inherent opportunity to appropriate others. On the other hand, many students get on well in school because they enjoy being appropriated. All this is just fine. But what happens to the student who has appropriational (sadistic) tendencies of his own? The other extreme is the teacher or administrator who hopes to be used by others. His professional methods are based on his being appropriated and he manages his responsibilities from such a posture. But what happens to a student who wants to be appropriated (masochist)? When one examines other well known relationships in education such as student and counselor or doctoral candidate and advisor using this analytical mode, a number of intriguing insights emerge. Whether they have validity or not is a question no one has answered. However, if validity is present one is immediately tempted to suggest that the current styles and modes of American education are such that those who are masochistic in nature stand a better chance for success in school than those of the other extreme.

Existentialist Views

Aside from the asserted primacy and non-rationality of personal existence, existentialists have very little in common. Perhaps two tendencies have appeared. One is existential atheism which is formidably represented by the interpretations of Sarte and Heidegger.

The other is existential theism represented in various ways by such as Marcel, Jaspers, Buber, and numerous theologians such as Barth and Tillich.

The views of Sartre and Heidegger propose that dread of nothingness or non-being is the beginning point in philosophy. Being (the I am) is based on the Cartesian Cogito. The atheism is not militant as in the case of Nietzsche. Instead it takes the view that the existence of God does not matter one way or another.[23] Any explanation of the "why" of personal existence is nonsensical because it is simply beyond sensing. The dread of nothingness is countered only by the prospect of a selfhood which is fashioned out of an existential resolve to be something. Only that something, when clarified, can defeat the meaninglessness or ambiguity of an existence for which there is no explanation. Rebellion is often used as a method for a discovery of self. The rebellion, the anger, is justified on the grounds that one is thrown into existence without so much as a hint of a reason. Why not strike against whatever appears in one's path? By striking, one discovers his hand, his strength, his resolve, and—hopefully—himself. The adolescent in rebellion learns a great deal about himself through the encounter. The metaphysics of rebellion can thus be organized on the theme of self-realization.

Existentialists of the atheistic mode are fascinated by the literature of decision. Choice is the primary method for building personal reality. In a sense a man is the sum of his choices, and choice is everywhere. This ubiquity of choice can be dramatized by imagining one is observing a man beating his wife. Now the observer can intervene and try to stop it—he can go over and try to help. On the other hand he might call the police or decide it is none of his business and pretend it isn't happening. In every case, however, he chooses, and this and countless other choices which make up each day, week, and year consummate his personal essence. More than this, his next choice may be of such magnitude as to alter his reality. It could change his essence completely. Perhaps this is why it is never a good idea to name a school building after a man who still has a capacity for what the world calls mischief. He could make a choice or two such that his essence would be altered.

This happened for the better in the case of Sydney Carton, the *bon vivant* of Dickens' *Tale of Two Cities*. His essence was fairly well established as the narrative unfolded. Nothing much was expected of him. But out of love, sentiment, or propriety he chose to go beneath the falling knife in the place of the fleeing Darnay. That final choice was, as he put it, "better" than any other. There can be no question that by it he was something different to himself and others. Hamlet as a study in choice quite vividly changed his essence as the tragedy unfolded. He became what he became on the wings of his own personal resolve. The great and moving soliloquy depicted a man alone with his personal responsibility to shape his essence. His first alternative was suicide and after this was rejected the agony went on.

All men are Hamlets. If they behave as sheep it is because they choose to. If their being is sheeply, it is because the option of leaving the flock is undesirable. They choose to ignore their individualization rather than to assert it. But this, too, is a choice. Failure in a man is not sheepliness; it is inauthenticity. Some men choose to do things they do not want to do. Or worse, they choose and then try to wade through the consequences of their choice. Consequence is embedded in choice. The chooser who refuses to face this is false to himself.

The theistic tendency of existentialism builds on the Kierkegaardian inwardness. Marcel, for example, appears to be not free of the Thomistic sense of an ultimate being. Existence is awareness of the inner yearning. Conscious life is non-rational, but so also is the inner life. Marcel seems to feel that the growing obsession with technology causes men to lose contact with the interiority of their nature. The hold that "things" have upon men, the extent to which men are managed, have caused the external side of man to dominate his consciousness.

The inwardness can be considered a love of God, which has no explanation and needs none. It can only be experienced. The church can minister to this by becoming a community of inward natures. Such a community is needed in the world to counteract the obsession with externals and the tendency of man to define himself in the vocabulary and syntax of science. He substitutes the pronoun "thou," which depicts the inward self striving for being, for the pronoun "he," which refers simply to the outer man of flesh and things. However, he insists that only faith in God makes love and awareness possible.

Jaspers, on the other hand, indicates that we become aware of our state of being through situations which by their nature compel us to deal with subject matter beyond the boundary of day-to-day existence. Such situations are deaths, struggles, sufferings, guilts, choices vital to determination of one's personal history, and choices which resolve apparent contradictions in the world of things. In such situations a human being explores that which is on or beyond the boundary of existence by *communication*. This is understood to mean the effort of two humans, in union, endeavoring to recognize and experience the deeper personal reality which the boundary situation demands. Participation by another in the joy or sorrow of a boundary situation can be revelational. It can reveal ampler possibilities of being. Through communication the mutually explored possibilities for being can be made real. Such communication is not systematic and is not to be anticipated. Such insights might develop in a seminar. But a teacher would never know in advance that a student might, during the discussion, acquire the insight needed to bring him to a resolution situation with the draft, a recent quarrel with his parents, or the nagging fact that he is cheating on his girlfriend.

By communication one discovers freedom and transcendence. This is taken to mean that freedom itself is something personal and men are free in different ways. Similarly one transcends existential reality in his own way and discovers what lies beyond for him. It is not necessary that God be conceived as a single identity, the same for all men. The issue need not arise. One enters into contact with others in quest of portents or meanings which are beyond the boundary. But because he is bound to observe or to know only from the seat of his personal being, his transcendence will be personal; but in transcendence meanings become shareable.

Jasper's existentialism goes further than others in recognizing man's dependence on social contacts. Indeed, he shows that individual man necessarily has a social side.[24] The individual's knowledge of that which encompasses him is still personal as are the effects of whatever comes of his inward efforts at transcendence. However, the efforts at transcendence as well as the results of those efforts tend to be social. Moreover, it is possible for groups of persons (as, for example, institutions) to attain a spirituality in transcendence which is the totality of intelligible thought, action, and feeling—a totality which is not a closed object for knowledge, but remains idea.

Jaspers' arguments, as translated in English, still have the fatal defect of ambiguity. They are not sufficiently comprehensible for a full assessment of either their rigor or weakness to be made. But there are for students of education attracted to the existentialist posture qualities which invite further exploration. One is his manner of recognizing social institutions and another is his conception of communications. There is also some promise in the recognition of spirit as a way of organizing the components of an idea. Finally, there is the prospect of human optimism which seems, to this writer at least, to be something of a prior commitment in persons who take the profession of education seriously. Somehow it seems that a school philosophy rooted in dread or despair has nowhere to go. If one makes use of Sartre or Heidegger in education some kind of faith must be added to what they give us.

Martin Buber offers another theistic argument which, like the others, might more aptly be termed phenomenological rather than simply existential.[25] This is because he describes all phenomena in terms of relationships. For example, a chair cannot be known as a chair-in-itself. It can be known only as a relationship to the knower. This again is the subject-object relationship common to all existentialist epistemology. The chair as an object can only be known by a person (subject). Without the subject (person) there can be no knowledge of the chair. To put it briefly, no subject, no object. Therefore, the chair in the corner is a-relation-to-me. To avoid confusion with doctrines which endow such things as chairs with separate essences Buber would class the chair as an I-It. All of the objects a person knows about, therefore, are I-Its.

Relations with other persons may or may not be at another ontological level. A person can be treated as an object (an I-It); and in our world of business and technology the tendency to do this is highly pronounced. A waitress, it can be expected, is serving her one-hundredth cup of coffee on any given morning to an object. She may smile and exchange the civilities of common parlance with it. But when that object gets up, pays its bill (and leaves its tip), it is immediately replaced by another object to which the same waitress serves cup of coffee number one hundred one. On the other hand, a relationship with another person can be characterized by a mutual sensibility of feeling. This then is not the same subject-to-object relationship our waitress has with her customer. It is a subject-to-subject relationship; and when such a relationship opens, a new world opens with it. Such a relationship can be termed I-Thou.

> Every relation with a real being of life in the world is exclusive. Its *Thou* is freed, steps forth, is single, and confronts us. It fills the heavens. This does not mean that nothing else exists; but all else lives in its light. . . .[26]

Imagine a young woman whose adolescence was characterized by an interest in art, music, literature, and, of course, young men.

None of the latter, however, was athletic by nature or inclination. So she emerged into adult life knowing little and caring less about baseball. However, her first child was a lusty, brawling boy who in time became a first-rate Little League shortstop. Now we find her on summer evenings alone atop the bleachers shrieking malevolence at umpires, giving advice to everyone, exhorting the team to greater enterprise, and using the jargon of the game as if she had spoken it from birth. What happened? The relationship of mother and son is an I-Thou, a subject to subject. Through the subjective relationship there is an opening through to the other's world. This is not a merging of either, but an expanding of both by which the one encompasses the other in subjectivity.

Now consider once again the I-It, or the subject to object. One can put down a pencil and forget about it because it is an object. Likewise one can read the accidental death of a stranger in a distant city and put the matter out of mind. Although the victim was human, he is related only as an object. But suppose one grows sentimental about his pencil; for some reason the pencil comes to mean a great deal to him. Through him the pencil has been spiritualized and through the pencil some spirit has entered him. Now the pencil becomes an I-Thou because through the object he has encountered a relation to God. All men have such things around them. They have a value which is distinct from what men call commercial. For example, a man will gladly sell a chair which is an I-It at the going price, but if the chair happens to be an I-Thou it simply is not for sale except as a heart-wrenching necessity.

Enspirited relationships whether of things or people are I-Thous and constitute a continuum with individual man on one end and God on the other. Reality is a network of such relationships. One does not turn aside from the course of his life to find God. The divine and the man are related and in communication through any object with which a man has endowed his own self, or through any person with which the man experiences reciprocal subjectivity.

Implications for Schools

This cascade of exciting thought is still too fresh and unrefined for one to make secure predictions on how it will affect American schools. Some assert that schooling as we have known it will soon be ended. They assert that a Copernican transformation in philosophy must inevitably bring a transformation of like magnitude in education. There are some grounds for credence in this prospect. One purpose of a school is to bring each individual into a habitual conformance with whatever ontological structure the community accepts. Now what if the community accepts the proposition that no ontological structure can be sovereign to the individual? What then happens to the school which sets external requirements, requires attendance, exalts some, derogates others, marches people about, limits the being of some, and opens for others it selects by its own special standards the way to privileged stations in life? Clearly, the committed existentialist will come to see such a school as an abomination. So at the very least, the existing order of schools will have to hear this kind of indictment.

Indications abound that existentialist sentiments now exist in American communities, and more of them arrive every day. It can be anticipated that the most immediate result will be a softening of the heartless and oftimes capricious way some schools have handed out life sentences based upon student capacity to perform in certain limited areas of human endeavor. One can presume the school will no longer be permitted to instruct a human being in the eighth or ninth year of his life that he is a failure, a problem, or some other kind of cosmic error. Except in extreme cases the organization of the "special class" will come to be regarded as a transgression upon human consciousness. Prior to the time these troubled or struggling children come fully to examine the majesty of their own being they will have breathed so long and deeply in a "special" atmosphere of convictions about their personal incompleteness that each child's being has been fatefully polluted by a premature commitment to self-abasement. The existentialist will have no more of this. To him such a predatory intrusion upon the person of another can never be justified on the grounds of age, honorific, civil status, or hypothesized social need.

One can see the influence of existentialist thought in the ungraded personalized teaching which now appears to be growing in favor. Theories of education which exalt the natural man are increasingly in vogue. Rousseau, Pestalozzi, and Froebel are fashionable models of pedagogy, and the naturalistic side of John Dewey is increasingly prized in *avant garde* schools. Existentialism is not the only force at work, but sentiments which cohere with existentialist thought are being aired daily by persons who have never heard of Heidegger or Jaspers. Unquestionably, the ontological structures of the past are being dismantled, and children are less often judged on the extent to which they fit into them. This, in part, is the effect of existentialist criticism, and these effects will increase in the years to come.

Educators in the later decades of the Twentieth Century are now in much the same position existentialist philosophers were after the passing of Kierkegaard and Nietzsche. They have a critique but no program. By 1900, the great ontological houses of the past had been shown unfit for habitation by autonomous men, and questions were raised about the divinity which supposedly sanctified such architecture. What now in education? After seven decades of reflection, elements of a strong existentialist tradition in philosophy are apparent in both Europe and America. The struggle for an existentialist pedagogical curriculum and administrative theory in education is just commencing. One noteworthy effort is that of A. S. Neill who since 1921 has operated the widely known Summerhill School in Suffolk, England. His account of the place makes fascinating reading. The school is small and private. So as a prototype of things to come, it has these and other limitations, some of them severe. But as matters now stand, it is a vital example of one man's interpretation of an education in and for freedom.[27]

Of the American educational philosophers, Van Cleve Morris has begun to fashion educational theory from existentialist premises. He has commented upon some engaging ideas; one of them is to take notice of Socrates as a pedagogical model.[28] However, he expresses reservations on the grounds that the Greeks tended to teach that the self was some kind of subject matter and that Socrates apparently knew the answers for some of the questions that he asked. From the context of his constraint one gathers Morris has the Platonic rather than the historical Socrates in view. Not so much is known about the latter. However, we can believe Plato's account of Socrates' trial and accept as authentic Socrates' attitude that the examined life is worth living and the unexamined life is not. This is forthright existentialist posture. Moreover, we can also appreciate whatever may be implied by the emergence of four of his students: Antisthenes, Aristippus, Plato, and Eucleides as founders of divergent schools of philosophy. Plato put answers in the mouth of his Platonic Socrates. But the Socrates of history evidently had not given his students answers. We also have another view of the historical Socrates offered by Aristophanes, who described the Socratic circle as a company in which one learns to prove anything "even though it be false."[29] Whatever the case may be, the historical Socrates appears closer to an acceptable model of existentialist pedagogy than the Platonic Socrates.

Other implications of the Socratic model are clear. Our modern education is answer oriented. American schools and teachers are literally bursting with answers. Where is the American teacher who would stake his professional standing on a proclamation such as: "I know that I know nothing"? Children come to schools with questions. In an existentialist sense these questions are the most precious things children have. The Socratic teacher would not think of taking these questions away by offering dogmatic answers. Children want to know who they are. They want to know about their parents, their friends, their laws; they want to know about justice, love, work, and all of the abstract nouns the Platonists reasoned over.

One can imagine the Socratic teacher would proceed by asking other questions which would bring illumination to the original question, helping each for that moment to come to terms with his question as, in his own way, he must. But the teacher would never take the original question away from the child; instead he tries to teach the child ways of dealing with his questions more satisfactorily. It is tempting to think the historical Socrates taught in just this way, and there is some evidence that he did.

Existentialism and the Curriculum

Morris has developed an existentialist outline of the personal development of children and adolescents.[30] Both Morris and George Kneller have offered views of the curriculum.[31] The existentialist looks approvingly at those parts of the curriculum which seem directly related to personal development. The humanities receive special emphasis because of the potential they hold for personal introspection and the development of self-meaning. But the subject fields ordinarily classified with the humanities do not realize this potential unless taught as introspective disciplines. For example, if one reduces language studies to the examination of grammar *qua* grammar the humanistic value of the course is greatly diminished.

Similarly history can be taught humanely. The existentialist values the work of the critical historian who strives for "objective" knowledge. This knowledge has its place. However, he regards the general student of history as one who is acquiring a sense of his own past. So-called "objective" data has an ontological status similar to physical objects of his own environment. Therefore, a student knows historical events only as he relates to them. For example, there is an objective-thing-in-the-house called a telephone which has a material reality. But one knows it only by how he relates to it or how he feels about it. Similarly, there are events in history which in themselves have an objective reality. However, a person can know these events only by the way he relates to them. Nominally, the event called the discovery of America is a-relation-to-me. One can take the examinations designed to test what one "knows" about America. But the existentialist argues that one does not know America in the way a test score reports. How does one feel about America? Or, more particularly, how does one feel about being an American? This is personal knowledge. Properly taught then, American history demands the student explore his own feelings, examine the boundaries of his own insights, and transcend these boundaries to deeper insights. More than this, one leaves the study of history with a propensity to continue these explorations and examinations both alone and in communication with others. History which is one's sense of his own past, present, and future is never a closed or finished matter, so long as the existentialist is alive and aware.

Probably the best example of this curriculum theory at work is found in the American studies programs increasingly found in colleges and universities. Historians of a positivistic temperament are not, as a rule, congenial to this sort of scholarship. Occasionally this is referred to (and not admiringly) as metahistory. Whatever it is, it appears closer to meeting the requirements of one who is personalizing his selfness as an American than anything else that is currently done in history education.

When the curriculum issue turns to basic skills and vocational skills the answers become more complicated. Given the presuppositions of existentialism, how can one justify forcing children to plow through enormous piles of workbooks, drill sheets, and developmental exercises? One cannot. There are alternatives, and they seem to work fairly well. However, they call for extraordinary skill and commitment from teachers. They also call for parents who do not panic when their own nine-year-old George in his ungraded school hasn't heard of fractions while his neighbor's nine-year-old John in the third grade of another school brings home pages of exercises on fractions to do every night. George's parents, in other words, must be believers. If they are not, his school is in trouble.

Personalized teaching of this kind is costly, and there are other problems. However, there is one fortuitous circumstance. Existentialism and experimentalism, while leagues apart in philosophical method, yield very similar theories of curriculum and method in the area of education in "basic skills." The experimentalist and his "individual" are doing many of the same things as the existentialist (or phenomenologist) and his "person." Perhaps the experimentalist is a little less worried about the effects of educational hardware than is the existentialist. However, the latter would prefer a machine which treats persons as objects to teachers who do the same thing. Still, the advent of educational technology, though anticipated by both, is somewhat feared by existentialist educators. One can guess that disputes between experimentalists and existentialists will one day rage over emphases upon measurement, norms, and schemes for classification of children. The existentialist will probably continue to oppose these and similar educational expedients.

Contrary to what might be expected the existentialist faces right up to the problem of vocational education. Why not? Nothing can be much closer to the center of personal being than the work one does in the world. One must choose it, and when he does he chooses a personal obligation to the skills and paradigms which are associated with that work. He trains willingly (that is to say, on the strength of his own resolve), recognizing that his choice of work includes the training as one of the consequences of the choice. The choice also includes the body of expectations which are held by and of the trained worker. However, these are deeper than anything included in vocational education as presently understood. The existentialist wants vocational education to be humane. He wants the training program to make vivid some of the values and sensitivities which were highly evident in the old apprentice system. Work should mean a great deal more to a person than money. Each worker will want to imbue his work with his personal standards or his personal idea of craftsmanship. His work remains his, even if he is paid for the task and relinquishes existential bond, a bond of being, between artisan and artifact.[32] Vocational education, therefore, is one of the humanities. As one looks at his work, he looks at himself. As he criticizes his work, he criticizes his person. When he excels as a worker, he excels as a person. Thus, existentialism may move vocational education closer to the center of American education than it has previously been in the current century.

Education in the natural sciences would also take a humanistic turn. Current courses in physics, for example, teach Newtonian physics and the relativistic physics of Albert Einstein. The physics taught is the content of what these men saw as they looked upon their world. Now many men have looked at their worlds and have reported their views. Ptolemy, Copernicus, Bacon, Newton, Einstein have presented either different versions of the universe or different versions of how it should be seen. How many more such views will there be? As the historical views are studied humanistically, there will be a much greater need to look at scientists studying the world rather than simply look at the information which is reported by scientists as if the latter were not persons.

Finally, there would be a much greater emphasis on what the schools now call extracurricular activities. These are the school events wherein the intensity of personal experience is high. One presumes that under such conditions internal commitments are formed. Indeed, many graduates of American schools cite their most meaningful and memorable school experience as something which occurred elsewhere than in the regular curriculum. In football, the boy who "blocks" for the ball carrier may have had an even more profound personal experience than the ball carrier who, in scoring, gets praise and recognition. In such circumstances one discovers a great deal about himself. Existentialism recognizes that in these events the personal inclinations of the student are shaped. So existentialist curriculum theory will call for meaningful activities which maximize student interaction and minimize adult domination.

The existentialist sees that the secularization of the school program, while lifting from it the burdens of religious dogmas, has presented American education with a serious anomaly.[33] There can be no question that personal religiousness must be faced as a problem for general education. Education must perforce deal with the struggle of the person to establish cosmic identity. It must also enable the person to develop his religiousness. This is understood as to mean his caring. Every man acquires commitment to an array of persons, objects, and idea. These, of course, are his values. The anatomy of such values is discussed elsewhere in this text.

Returning to Morris, he ties the existentialist theory of education to a theme of responsibility. He suggests that education be the "discovery of responsibility."[34] The kind of responsibility proposed stems from the Sartrean notion that a person is thrown into the world and abandoned there. By this act he thereby becomes responsible for every aspect of his being. He is even responsible for his denials of responsibility. Because personal responsibility is, therefore, ubiquitous, it can become an organizing principle for the educational enterprise.

The merits of this proposition will undergo time and trial. But it is noteworthy that this particular existentialist appeal for responsible men is a marked contrast to the expressed fears that existentialism, as an applied doctrine, would lead immediately to personal irresponsibility and social chaos. Existentialism has yet to convince men that the burden of their own freedom is not easily carried. When a man is alone with his own freedom, then and not before then does he know that awesome thing called personal responsibility. This permits no apologetics; it sanctions no excuses. Perhaps the greatest danger of it is that it may be too much for men to bear.

Notes

1. Jerry H. Gill, *Essays on Kierkegaard* (Minneapolis, Minn.: Burgess Publishing Co., 1969), An essay by Peter Rhode, pp. 6-30.
2. Walter Lowrie, *Kierkegaard* (New York: Harper & Row, Publishers, 1962), Vol. I, p. 55.
3. *Ibid.*, p. 23.
4. Lowrie, *op. cit.*, pp. 29-59.
5. *Ibid.*, p. 235.
6. Soren Kierkegaard, *Either Or, A Fragment of Life*, tr. David and Lillian Swenson (Princeton, N. J.: Princeton University Press), Vol. I, p. 19.
7. Walter Lowrie, *op. cit.*, p. 234.
8. Soren Kierkegaard, *Training in Christianity*, tr. Walter Lowrie (New York: Oxford University Press, 1941), p. 87.
9. Soren Kierkegaard, "Article in *The Fatherland*," included in Walter Lowrie, *Attack upon Christendom* (Boston: Beacon Press, 1944).
10. Soren Kierkegaard, *The Present Age*, tr. Alexander Dru (New York: Harper & Row, Publishers, 1962), p. 63.
11. Ivo Frenzel, *Friedrich Nietzsche*, tr. Joachim Nengroschel (New York: Pegasus, 1967), p. 17.
12. Friedrich Nietzsche, *Twilight of the Idols*, tr. R. J. Hollingdale (Baltimore, Md.: Penguin Books, Inc., 1969), p. 22.
13. Friedrich Nietzsche, *La Gaya Scienza*, tr. Thomas Cannon, *The Joyful Wisdom* (Edinburg: The Darien Press, 1910), p. 168.
14. Friedrich Nietzsche, *Thus Spoke Zarathustra*, tr. R. J. Hollingdale (Baltimore, Md.: Penguin Books, Inc., 1968), p. 10.
15. *Ibid.*, p. 47.
16. *Ibid.*, p. 243.
17. Friedrich Nietzsche, *The Anti-Christ*, tr. R. J. Hollingdale (Baltimore, Md.: Penguin Books, Inc., 1968), p. 149.
18. William L. Shirer, *The Rise and Fall of the Third Reich* (New York: Simon and Schuster, 1960), p. 100.
19. Albert Camus, *The Myth of Sisyphus and Other Essays* (New York: Random House, 1955), pp. 4-5.
20. Jean-Paul Sartre, *Being and Nothingness*, tr. Hazel E. Barnes (New York: Philosophical Library, 1956), p. 104.
21. See *Ibid.*, pp. 107-218.

22. *Ibid.*, p. 430.
23. Jean-Paul Sartre, *Existentialism*, tr. B. Frechtman (New York: Philosophical Library, 1947), p. 61.
24. See Richard F. Grabou, *Communication Through Transcendence*, included in George Schrader, *Existentialist Philosophers: Kierkegaard to Merleau-Ponty* (New York: McGraw-Hill Book Company, 1967), pp. 110-158.
25. Martin Buber, *I and Thou*, tr. R. G. Smith (Edinburg: T. and T. Clark, 1937), p. 3-81.
26. *Ibid.*, p. 78.
27. See A. S. Neill, *Summerhill, A Radical Approach to Child Rearing* (New York: Hart Publishing Co., 1960), 392 pp.
28. Van Cleve Morris, *Existentialism in Education* (New York: Harper & Row, Publishers, 1966), pp. 135-136.
29. Aristophanes, *The Clouds*.
30. Morris, *op. cit.*, p. 113.
31. George Kneller, *Existentialism and Education* (New York: Philosophical Library, 1958), pp. 129-137.
32. John A. Stoops, "Work," *The Education of Inner Man* (Danville, Ill.: The Interstate Printers & Publishers, Inc., 1969), pp. 5-18.
33. John A. Stoops, *Religious Values in Education* (Danville, Ill.: The Interstate Printers & Publishers, Inc., 1967), pp. 97-133.
34. Morris, *op. cit.*, p. 117.

Other Reading

Brie, Germaine. *Camus.* New Brunswick, N.J.: Rutgers University Press, 1964, p. 268.

Camus, Albert. *The Fall.* Tr. Justin O'Brien. New York: Random House, Inc., 1956.

——————, *The Myth of Sisyphus and Other Essays.* New York Random House, Inc., 1955, pp. 1-88.

Frenzel, Ivo. *Freidrich Neitzsche.* New York: Western Publishing Co., Inc., 1967.

Gill, Jerry H. *Essays on Kierkegaard.* Minneapolis: Burgess Publishing Co., 1969. Parts I-III.

Greene, Maxine. *Existential Encounters for Teachers.* New York: Random House, Inc., 1967.

Grene, Marjorie. *Introduction to Existentialism.* Chicago: University of Chicago Press, 1963.

Hillesheim, James W. "Action and Solitude, a Nietzschean View," *Educational Theory*, XIX (Fall 1969), p. 357-362.

Kierkegaard, Soren. *Attack upon Christendom.* 1854-55. Ed. Walter Lowrie. Boston: Beacon Press, 1944, p. 301.

——————. *Either Or.* Tr. W. Lowrie. Princeton: Princeton University Press, 1959. Esp. "Prayer," pp. 343-356.

——————. *The Present Age.* Tr. Alexander Dru. New York: Harper & Row, Publishers, pp. 33-85.

Kneller, George. *Existentialism and Education.* New York: Philosophical Library, Inc., 1958. Chapters I-V.

Lowrie, Walter. *Kirkegaard.* New York: Harper and Brothers, 1962. 2 Volumes.

Morris, Van Cleve. *Existentialism and Education.* New York: Harper & Row, Publishers, 1966, p. 163.

——————. *Philosophy and the American School.* Boston: Houghton Mifflin Company, 1961. Part V.

Neill, A. S. *Summerhill: A Radical Approach to Child Rearing.* New York: Hart Publishing Co., 1960.

Nietzsche, Friedrich. *Twilight of the Idols* and *Anti-Christ.* Tr. R. J. Hollingdale. Baltimore: Penguin Books, Inc., 1969.

——————. *The Joyful Wisdom.* Tr. T. Common. Edinburg: The Darien Press, 1910.

——————. *Thus Spoke Zarathustra.* Tr. R. J. Hollingdale. Baltimore: Penguin Books, Inc., 1968.

Olson, Robert G. "The Anguish of Nothingness in Modern Philosophy," *Antioch Review,* XVIII (1957), pp. 247-254.

Sanborn, Patricia. *Existentialism.* New York: Western Publishing Co., Inc., 1968. Chapters I, II, IV, V, VII.

Sartre, Jean-Paul. *Being and Nothingness.* New York: Philosophical Library, 1956. Parts I-III.

——————. *L'Imagination.* Tr. Forrest-Williams. Ann Arbor: The University of Michigan Press, 1962.

Schrader, George A. *Existential Philosophers: Kierkegaard to Merleau-Ponty.* New York: McGraw-Hill Book Company, 1967.

Ulich, Robert. *The Human Career: A Philosophy of Self-Transcendence.* New York: Harper and Brothers. Chapters I-X.

Warnock, Mary. *The Philosophy of Sartre.* London: Hutchinson and Company, Ltd., 1965, pp. 13-134.

Wirth, Arthur G. "Existentialism, the Emperor's New Clothes, and Education," *Educational Theory,* V (July 1955), pp. 152-157.

CHAPTER XIII

Enspiriting a Civilization of Forms

There is spirit in the world. The world is spiritualized by men. If the ultimate source of spirit is divine then the divine spiritualizes the world through men. Spirit enters the world through beliefs which men hold. Civilization develops and becomes enspirited as these beliefs are made into protocols. So long as men believe in what they are doing and being and so long as their manner of doing and being coheres with held beliefs, their civilization is enspirited.

The feats men perform when developing and enspiriting a civilization include (1) sentimentalization, (2) rationalization, (3) formalization, (4) institutionalization, and (5) conventionalization. Sentimentalization is the acquisition of belief. These activities are, in the general sense, religious and are the essence of education. Rationalization is the organization of sentiment and extension upon its meaning. Formalization is the creation of archetypes or models by which rationalized forms can be known. Institutionalization is the effort of placing these forms in the world of action. Conventionalization is the establishment and enforcement of institutional rules which cohere with the sentiment, reason, and form which brought that institution into being.

When sentiment, reason, form, institution, and convention are in coherence, the institution is enspirited. When any of these fail of coherence the institution is decadent. When many institutions of a civilization are decadent, the civilization is likewise decadent. The purpose of this chapter is to delineate these five activities.

Before starting, however, it is necessary to deliver a complaint about current styles of thought and discussion on social problems. It is becoming increasingly clear that the styles currently in vogue not only are unproductive, but are also misleading. Worse than this, they seem to be bringing on an uncritical demolition of institutions which may be vital to our current civilized order. The implications of this for organized education are ominous.

A Complaint About Social Discourse

In recent years we have become accustomed to using the word *society* in a variety of ways. Philosophers who ground their methods in the ontology of process or action have been prone to identify society as the locus of process or action. The social science disciplines examine these processes or actions to produce knowledge *about* society. This knowledge claim stands on the assumption that both processes and society are real. This assumption and the knowledge claims that it warrants are very appealing. The knowledge has already demonstrated itself, in some respects, to be reliable and useful.

However, one unfortunate outcome of this felicitous development is the increasingly loose usage of the term society by persons apart from the area of philosophy and the most rigorous circles of social science. It is now a journalistic vogue to use the term society in a noumenal rather than phenomenal sense. Volumes of social discourse treat society as if it were a thing-in-itself. Clearly the most frequent incident of loose usage occurs with the creature metaphor. Applications of the metaphor result in society described as if it were a living thing. Frequently, for example, it is said to have needs. Thus, the journalistic vogue is to declare that society needs this or that in order to somehow fulfill itself.

Similarly, one angered at this supposed creature has been heard to remark, "Society is sick." The speaker usually follows this remark by deducing the nature of society's malaise and forthwith prescribes a remedy. This is so often heard as to become tiresome. Another variation of the same theme is to discourse on the "social" or "public mind." Society is described as having a mind, and this opens to speculators a vast range of mental analogs such as: society is ignorant, mad, angry, or confused. Some writers have given society qualities such as intentionality, volition, or ethical judgment. Public figures have proclaimed this or that is done in response to the will of society, or they say that society has ordained this to be good and that to be bad.

Some of the younger generation have been heard to complain of being "captured" by society. This, of course, gives the creature metaphor added dimensions. Among other things it lends itself to a vision of society as a predatory menace whose special villainy is to capture and control all forms of personal autonomy. The furious student demands for liberation confirm their credence to this vision. Indeed, to some this predator is so effective at his work that a special effort must be made to achieve freedom. This "drop-out" as it is frequently called is advertised by affectations of dress, speech, and grooming. Thus, the drop-out dramatizes his thorough rejection of the society which is attempting to control him.

Apologists (and public office holders) assert that society is restless, changing, seeking, or discontented. However, they go on to say that this is healthy. Antagonists (and public office seekers) assert that society is racist, avaricious, violent, and in want of redemption, and they go on to say that this is unhealthy. Apologists take hope in orderly change. Antagonists exalt in the prospect of revolt. In both camps society is something conjectured upon, and in both camps persons appear to derive measures of personal identity and meaning by leaning against this thing they call *society*. Some are attempting to hold it up but both appear to need it for cosmic orientation.

Professor John Dewey, who has done so much to direct our attention to the workings of society, declared ". . . that society is an organic union of individuals."[1] But Dewey tends to diminish his own ontological rigor when, in the same work, he states, "When society once recognizes the possibilities in this direction, and the obligations which these possibilities impose, it is impossible to conceive of the resources of time, attention, and money which will be put at the disposal of the educator."[2] Now one can easily understand why educators would be disinclined to examine such a remark critically. But we are obliged to note that Dewey himself supplies ambiguity to the word society when he bestows upon his "organic union of individuals" qualities of cognition and volition.

It is strange how an obsession of this kind shapes and alters the reality of personal existence. So long as it prevails it works an amendment on every conception and exerts an influence on every thought. Some years ago a man built a privy on the back of his property. Indeed, it was so far back that it edged upon the line which separated his lot from that owned by two elderly maidens. The latter found the structure offensive and when protest availed them naught they adopted the practice of pushing it over. On one nocturnal occasion it was pushed over while the owner was inside, and because it fell doorway to the ground he was reduced to cries for assistance, which finally came from neighbors all of whom kept the problem merrily in perspective. This event was followed by the installation of braces by the owner and the removal of the back wall by the sisters. Finally, the conventions of indoor plumbing ended the contest.

But while it endured there was no question that life on both sides was oriented around that problem. When it vanished the existential world of the disputants soon became grounded on other concerns. The privy, of course, was real. But is this creature called society, which is the object of so much thought and expression, real? Does it exist? Are those who seem to push against it pushing against something that is real? Are those who seem to be bracing it bracing something which exists? Let us suppose that the creature is an illusion. How then would we conduct a dialectic on human relations? If we remove the illusion would our dialectic improve?

Two centuries ago Rousseau began to write of society as if it were a jailer. "Man is born free," he said, "and everywhere he is in chains."[3] Rousseau called for revolution, and revolution came. Voltaire, on the other hand, did not agree. He argued that human institutions are, in part, the result of human nature. If overthrown, new institutions would rise which contain essentially the same defects as those lamented upon priorly. Attention directed to society is, therefore, misdirected. Voltaire concentrated his fire upon the nature of individual man. In the perspective of two bloody and turbulent centuries, Voltaire seems to have won the verdict of history. He, too, knew that revolution was in prospect; but, more than this, he knew that a theory of man must take account of more things than the world of nature or of simple-minded notions about society. He suggested that reason must be established in the minds of leaders; then gradually it descends and, by imitation, at last rules in the people.[4] He did not oppose revolution, but he refused to be sanguine about its consequences. And today we may ask: what has revolt produced? The first cry of the modern protest is, "Man is born free, and everywhere he is in chains."

The creature illusion, pervasive of so much past and modern thought about society, cannot improve or perfect the civilized order because it is in itself deficient. It leaves something out. If we are content to reason our public concerns on the basis that society is some sort of *creature*, if we give credence to notions that the creature is sick, then our thought style takes on the aspect of the medical model. We speculate about remedies. If we are content to reason out public concerns on the basis that society is some sort of *system*, if we give credence to notions that the system is malfunctioning, then our thought style takes on the aspect of a mechanical model, and we speculate about technological repairs.

Something that does not exist in the way a creature exists cannot be healthy in the way that a creature has health. Something that does not exist in the way that a mechanism exists cannot be made into a smooth-running machine. It is sheer nonsense, therefore, to destroy an established society in order that a better one be created which is "healthier" or "better working." This kind of talk spreads confusion and obscures reality.

However, it does offer illustration of one of the major points of this chapter. Men have come to believe in society; they have applied reason to this sentiment and formalized it as a creature. It is in the effort to *institutionalize* society that its absurdity is revealed. How can one institutionalize as an organic whole that which has so many diverse and unrelated parts, all of which are already institutionalized in various ways in response to diverse and unrelated beliefs?

The civilized order really stems from the sentiments that men hold. And the key to understanding change is understanding sentiments that men hold singly and collectively. One examines animal tracks to discover what kind of animal passed that way. Similarly one examines the physical properties of institutions to discover the sentiments which brought them about. When the discerning look at the stone and mortar of institutions they are actually aware of sentiments that, for a time at least, had visited that locality and were enspirited by men. These same sentiments may still preside there; they may have been modified; or they may have expired. Often, the latter is true. The conventions and properties of institutions can, in some cases for centuries, survive the passing of their progenerative sentiments.

Sentimentalization

Plato suggested that forms have an existence independent of man. He believed that through proper exercise of reason forms can be perceived in the minds of men.[5] Thus, the work of reason has been exalted in virtually every tradition of western scholarship. But the product of twenty-four centuries of reason has provided no undisputed representation of form except for those which are bound up in axiomatic systems. What would Plato think of this? Would he reconsider?

Perhaps not. But it is increasingly clear that the towering structure of formal ideas which Plato unveiled in *The Republic* and *The*

Laws was a rationalization of aristocratic sentiments passed along to him by his kindred. Perhaps Socrates taught him the logical methods by which sentiments are made coherent; but, it was Plato's own incomparable pedagogical skill and literary genius which imported to his sentiments persuasive power sufficient to shape two thousand years of western government, religion, and education.

Sentiment is anterior to reason.[6] All thought begins with the raw data of consciousness. These data are encased in feelings. It is often said that a computer cannot know in the way a man knows. It can also be said that a man cannot know in the way a computer knows. A man cannot depersonalize his consciousness. Therefore, all of the data of his consciousness are charged with personal orientation. We refer to this personal orientation as sentiment. Thus, sentiment is ubiquitous.

However, the phenomenology of private sentiments is not within the plan of this chapter. A study of civilization is, perforce, a consideration of public sentiments, their origins and uses. Public sentiment forms on public concerns. There are as many public concerns as there are matters on which men transact. Public sentiment forms on general matters such as justice, trade, governance, love, and education. Each of these general matters has sub-aspects such as laws and courts, work and leisure, control and service, courtship and marriage, authority and freedom. These matters, in turn, have sub-aspects.

In recent years social science has made some progress in understanding the social consensus. Methods have been developed which estimate and record its shifts and turns. Pollsters have discovered how to obtain reliable signals such as might come from a "public mind." Some philosophers have gone so far as to associate this collective valuing with the divine.[7]

One can easily understand why it is that so many accord a high level of reality to society, even to the point of categorizing society as a kind of creature. It does provide a convenient way of talking about public sentiment, but it also provides grounds for error. We see this error in the actions of so many of the young citizens who have, in effect, gone to the whip in order to retrain the beast. Instead of making their own sentiments appealing, they bully, gouge, and pummel institutions into embarrassing concessions. While they win little points they are generating massive antagonisms. They hold to the illusion they are working upon a creature, but in reality they are alienating the large and decisive segment of public opinion which is capable of bringing about social action.

In reality public sentiment is nothing more or less than the effects at any given time of autonomous individuals who reside within the social arrangement constantly affirming, confirming, and re-forming the private sentiments they hold on public issues. This does not mean, for example, that each individual makes a new decision each day about what justice is. But he is alive to the issues which relate to his idea of justice and he is constantly revaluing. His personal orientation may modify from day to day in such a way as to not change much in a year. On the other hand, the modifications may be in a single direction so that the cumulating modifications of a year may in that time bring him to a radically altered view. A married man awakens each day, looks upon his sleeping spouse, and decides again whether or not he will remain married. Theoretically this happens every morning; but, actually, a man does not end one day contented and awaken the next with serious intention of divorce. However, if a large number of consecutive mornings were characterized by antagonism a new sentiment would likely commence to build, and one morning he would awaken and make a new decision.

To understand public sentiment, therefore, one must understand the trends in private sentiment. A collection of barbarians will have sentiments on every general question, but these public sentiments will differ vastly from those of a more reflective class of men. This is because the private sentiment of an individual barbarian is dominated by the materially real and immediately emotional. Justice to a barbarian is simply vengeance. Success to the barbarian is simply winning. Love to the barbarian is simply copulation. The public sentiment in his group would accord with this and support it.

The barbarian, in valuation, moves toward the source of physical sensation, and the public sentiments of barbarian groups reflect this inclination. In reflective groups, the reverse is true. The reflective man moves to the ideational, and the public sentiments of reflective groups correspond. Sensation and idea are not mutually exclusive, but they do reflect opposite tendencies in sentiment.

The cry of the barbarian is, "Tell it like it is!" The comment of the reflective man is, "tell us what it means." The barbarian acts physically upon his sentiments. The reflective man abstracts, then acts upon principles. The barbarian seeks virtue in the exercise of gross animal functions. The reflective man seeks virtue in the exercise of creative potencies. High experience to the barbarian is sensual pleasure ritualized in magic and superstition. High experience to the reflective man is sensual pleasure ritualized in ideality.

Thus, there is no real problem in this distinction. We know the species of sentiments associated with the words barbarism and Philistinism, and we know the species of sentiments associated with reflectivism. In a comparison of the life styles of the two the penalty for barbarism is evident. The barbarian is deprived of distance. He has only the immediate, that which is at hand. The immediate dies every moment. Without a set of derived and believed metaphysical premises he is unable to achieve the "foundation of reverence" which Whitehead described as the "... perception that the present holds within itself the complete sum of existence, backwards and forwards, that whole amplitude of time which is eternity."[8] Reflective men have all that the barbarians have; but they have, in addition, the reverence which stems from this perception.

Clearly, therefore, we do not have a public mind that "thinks." We may have autonomous private minds which form sentiments on public questions. These sentiments move toward the barbarian or the reflective in accordance with the tendencies of the individuals who constitute the public. If it is the wish that our public sentiments become more reflective, and that our civilized order bestow upon us all the ennobling effects of perspective, then our efforts at education must produce reflective men and not barbarians.

Therefore, experiences which have an educative quality strengthen the tendency to sentimentalize in the reflective style. This is a criterion to hold against any educative experience. Reading a newspaper is more than informative, it is educative to the extent that one's experience with the journalism rises to reflection and does not remain merely sensation. Likewise, the theatre, a talk with a friend, or a walk through the city can be educative if it inspires reflectivity. Quarrels are not educative unless they are used as a basis for later reflection. Thirty-two weeks in a social studies classroom is not educative unless some kind of thinking has prevailed persistently. The mere giving and receiving of information has no educative value whatever.

Sentimentalization within a society turns felicitous when it turns reflective. The judgment here rests not upon what public sentiments are or on what they might come to be. It rests upon whether they are consummated in reflection. What is reflection? Reflection is the act of delivering affective interests to the criterion of inner truth. As Saint Augustine said: "... to know intelligible things with our reason we pay attention to the interior truth."[9] Thus, a reflecting man composes reflective sentiments by bringing their subject matter to bear upon his interior beliefs or prior sentiments.[10] In order to do this, however, belief must be converted into form. This is done by rationalization.

Rationalization

The second paragraph of the first formal declaration of American nationhood opens with the sentence: "We hold these truths to be self-evident." The author, Thomas Jefferson, was too much a philosopher to declare: "These truths are self-evident." Indeed, the kind of truths he recorded in the Declaration of Independence must be "held." Then what does it mean to "hold" a truth? There could be at least two answers to this. The first is that one has gone far and wide in an open-minded examination of evidence. After this, and only after this, a self-evident truth of the matter has obtruded upon his mind. He is prepared, therefore, to say that he *believes* in this proposition and uses it to explain all the world. In effect, he says "yes" to this truth and holds it. He does so because this truth *corresponds* to the self-evident state of the world which he has seen. The second answer is that he could have consulted inwardly in search of a paradigm and, finding one to his personal liking, stated it as self-evidently true. In this case a thing is true because some interior moral sense told him it *ought* to be true. Now, if he holds to a sentiment such as "all men are created equal"— a transcending moral force[11] which speaks from within him—such a truth gets believed and in this sense is "held."

Why, one may ask, if you are presented with the evidence of exterior senses, evidence which is overwhelming, is it necessary to believe that the state of affairs is self-evidently true? The answer is that the word *believe* is necessary. In this case it is necessary to believe the exterior senses. One must believe that his exterior senses are reporting truth and that the concepts his mind renders from these data are true concepts. One must believe that his eyes and his mind do not deceive him. These things require believing as much as data from interior senses require believing.

The American philosopher, Charles Saunders Peirce, notes four ways of justifying a belief. The first he calls the method of tenacity; the second the method of authority; the third the method of accepting *a priori* or real causes; and the fourth he calls the method of science, which, in effect, is his now famous "concept of consequences." The import of this observation in regard to belief is that Peirce does not proclaim the method of science as a way of knowing. Instead, he considers it as the best way of four ways of justifying belief.[12]

Philosophically, therefore, all truths based upon the data of external senses or internal senses are believed or held truths. Only analytical truths require no belief. These are the only self-evident truths. Analytical truth is the product of reason alone, unalloyed, uncontaminated by empirical or moral observations. One can say for example, "all red things have color." Here the subject of the sentence is contained in the predicate. This and similar rules furnish syntax for logical or mathematical truth. Logical or mathematical truth is self-evident and is generally called "analytical."

It might be asked: if one need not supply belief to analytical truth, if analytical truth need not be "held," then why do we not build all of our knowledge analytically? If men are *relieved* of the necessity of *belief* would they not be relieved also of the bases for their many quarrels? The difficulty with analytical truth is that it is never *about* anything except possibly itself. In recent years, for example, elementary teachers have learned that one property of addition is that it is commutative. This is to say, among other things, that it does not matter if you add a rational set of 3 to a rational set of 2 or a rational set of 2 to a rational set of 3. The result in both cases is a larger rational set of 5.

But, when dealing with the objects and creatures of the world it does matter how sets are combined. One can say that the sums of rational numbers are, in general, commutative, but one cannot say the same of the cumulative habits or tendencies of the objects and creatures of the world. Analytical truth is neutral. It is without moral or empirical content. By supplying substance to algebraic symbols, men can organize that substance into a bridge or a building, but this does not give moral sanction to the bridge or building. Only men do that. First they must "hold," on one basis or another, a belief that a bridge or a building must be erected.

As Richard Weaver so rightly said, "It appears, then, that culture is originally a matter of yea-saying."[13] It is a matter of believing, or holding, something. Without belief there is nothing. Belief is sentiment. The Jeffersonian sentiment, "all men are created equal," may have originated in Jacobian enlightenment, but it was believed by Jefferson and his colleagues.

Is it a reasoned belief? Again, no. Reason follows belief. We reason *upon* our sentiments, not *to* our sentiments. Our reason is drawn to a matter by an affective interest. Then a belief is established. The next step is to test that belief rationally. If *coherent* logic can be extended from a belief; then the belief (or sentiment) becomes persuading. If not, then it loses persuasiveness.

In a court of equity, the adversaries often produce opposing sentiments, each of them claiming the sanction of law. After stating their sentiments, and presenting the evidence, the adversaries will try to demonstrate with logic the coherence of their respective belief with accepted principles of equity as expressed by law. The more coherent of the two beliefs should win the judgment of the court, if, of course, the judge was not, in advance, possessed of an overriding commitment to one of the opposing sentiments.

What is the role of reason? This is a vast metaphysical issue. Platonists argue for the reality of idea and argue that reason illuminates ideas by demonstrating their good. However, in this view, only one idea of a thing is good; all others are false, or at least less good. Thomists argue that the world can be interpreted as a rational teleology. This view is grounded in the Aristotelian argument that matter behaves rationally (the theory of causes, etc.). Certain pragmatists argue that the processes of the world are rational, using a continuum which moves constantly from need to satisfaction. Reason to them is a procedure which operates in the same fashion.

However, none of these arguments seem adequate. All of them, in one way or another, diminish man as a chooser. All of them depict man, in one way or another, as dominated. In Platonism man is dominated by archetypes. In Thomism, man is dominated by teleology. In pragmatism, man is dominated by process. In all three cases, reason is the method by which man discovers what it is that dominates him. But what of the undominated man? What philosophy explains him?

The undominated man must insist that reason follows sentiment. Reason orders, clarifies, and makes coherent the sentiments men hold. Reason makes sentiment appealing to other men. Continuing the vivid examples Shakespeare offers in his dramatization of Julius Caesar, Cassius uses reason to establish his own sentiment in Brutus. Brutus, in turn, uses his own logic to ennoble these sentiments and raise them to the level of virtue (Caesar was ambitious). On the other hand, the sentiments of Mark Antony are played upon the crowd through an entirely different set of logical propositions (was this ambition?). Here again, both sides use reason to adorn opposing sentiments. Antony wins the crowd by making it seem "reasonable" that Caesar was acting for the good of the common man. As a consequence the assassins are driven from the city.

The question descends through the ages: who was right? Right cannot be determined rationally. Sentiment is the arbitrator. The role of reason is not decisive. However, it is vital because rational demonstrations are used to show if a given sentiment coheres with well established moral insights. Thus, reason illuminates choice, but it does not make choice.

For example, as a moral insight we hold that "all men are created equal." Now this has been held to mean in the world of civil affairs that no one is superior to others in the "eyes of the law." We believe this. Repeatedly it has been rationally demonstrated that denials of public privileges such as going to school, using public facilities, and sharing in corporate benefits because of race, creed, or color, are logically inconsistent with the "created equal" sentiment which was phrased in other language in the Bill of Rights and the Fourteenth Amendment.

Now we do not regard the Bill of Rights or the Fourteenth Amendment as sentiment. These are Amendments to the Constitution. As such they are laws. What is the difference between sentiment and law? Law is a formal expression of a sentiment. How is the formal expression developed? It is developed by a rationalization of a sentiment.

Strong sentiments in and of themselves are not sufficient for institutionalization. Before a sentiment can be institutionalized its form must be developed. This is the work of reason. Without rationalization a clear notion of form cannot be attained. For example, it may be our sentiment to teach American History in school. But before this sentiment can be institutionalized it must be formalized. In order to accomplished this we develop a *rationale*. The curriculum rationale serves as a bridge between a sentiment and its institutionalization. It is often said that one man's history is another man's fiction. In one case men may have differing sentiments about what is historic, and in another where sentiments are similar these can be reasoned into different forms.

Thus, far from being sovereign, reason is probably what Aristotle considered it to be, namely, a tool which must be employed by reflective men. But it is a tool which can be used to serve a variety of ends. It is an essential tool in the work of civilizing because one cannot proceed from the level of sentiment to the level of form without it.

Formalization

Men who associate in their struggle to live in comfort and meaning soon develop a body of collective sentiment. In the fullness of time these sentiments are rationalized into forms. This does not happen quickly. Evidently centuries can pass before a sentiment makes a transition to enduring form. When forms do appear, a civilization is identified. The forms which first distinguish a civilization undergird and sustain its development.

As an example we can consider the ubiquitous presence of the Arthurian legend in the civil forms of the English-speaking people. The legend itself cannot be approached historically. It apparently originated with the exploits of certain celebrities of the Sixth Century, A.D. What exactly they did and, more to the point, how they behaved is beyond the reach of critical scholarship. The earliest written accounts still existing are thought to be substantial elaborations of other written accounts which have been lost. There is some indication that the central figure of the legend was, for a time, deified.[14] Apparently, across the span of years which concluded the first millenium A.D., the legend became enshrined in the sentiments of the people, and the overtones of magic, and suggestion, and sacredotal artifacts gave added authority to the model. It was not until the Eleventh Century that the emerging forms became distinctive. At that time Geoffrey of Monmouth described Arthur as a king. In the next century Wace of Jersey added further detail, including the vital "round table." These elements were mixed with other new romantic details in the history of the noble deeds of England which was written by Layamon in the Thirteenth Century. At last, late in the Fifteenth Century, Thomas Malory composed the classic work. Thus, the forms of stoic sentiments which had been building within this legend for nearly nine hundred years (or possibly much longer) were finally expressed. The work of Tennyson in the Nineteenth Century furnished additional strength.

Did the personalities ever live? Did the events occur? Probably not. But as a consequence of these mature sentiments England had the forms by which its children would learn such abstract nouns as honesty, courtesy, honor, justice, and fidelity. As Arthur presided at his "round table" he became the classic "first among equals." Here then is the suggested form by which knights on the basis of equality could participate with royalty in the formation of policy. This particular form soon found expression in the *Magna Carta*. This form is also expressed in many aspects of English Common law and is reflected in the style of deliberation manifest in English and American rules of public order. And although the Spaniard Cervantes found it possible to laugh at the knight in his quest, he revealed through his work a continuing love of the chivalristic sentiment.

Nowadays the "knight in shining armor" tends to be a term of derision. But this is not the important thing. As our young civilians are educated toward responsibility they are exposed to ideas of manhood and womanhood in the personalities of Gawain and Lancelot, Arthur and Guinevere, Tristram and Iseult. This is the important thing. Therefore, it is also important that these celebrities remain as forms. In Tennyson's *Idylls of the King* the formal image, in general, is sustained. The personalities reflect the delicate blending of form and realism which is styled as classic. Tennyson's Arthur is a classic personality and he does classic things.

The modern stage and cinema do not do this at all. The modern theatre overhumanizes. In this way forms are subdued and only men come before us. Their story has much human interest, but its pedagogical potency is diminished. Camelot becomes "a bright and shining spot." Really, to a thousand years of Englishmen, Camelot has not been a spot. It was never a "spot," and never could have been such. Camelot is a form which rose to formality on the wings of a rationalized sentiment. It still stands as one of the great civilizing influences in western man. No one can say if it has served well or ill; but, indeed, it has served decisively.

The Hellenistic world arrived at its fullest development while under the spell of the Homeric legends. Here in two classic poems attributed to a blind poet of the Ninth Century B.C. mankind is given the sight of forms vital to Hellenistic civilization, and by transference, to English civilization. In the personalities of Helen, Agamemnon, Clytemnestra, Achilles, Hector, and others are discovered, again, the all important forms. Are these personalities historic? Evidently they are. Paradoxically, this great legend of antiquity has better documentation than the legends of Arthur. The time which separated Homer from the events of which he wrote was but two centuries. Malory was much further from Arthur.

It is of some interest here that the sentiments of the Homeric forms were inherited from the earlier Achaean age. But the Greeks of this later time needed the epic in order to build and sustain, and Homer supplied it.[15] When Rome was reaching for the crest of its development, Virgil supplied the *Aeneid.* How important is the poet to a prospective civilization? Without him the civilization is deprived of vital forms. Without these forms the civilization cannot rise from the stage of unorganized sentiment. Its men have not the means for reflection; they cannot achieve distance.

Poetry is not alone. Other arts join in the work. Probably if the vernacular is not suited to poetic forms other arts will be of even higher rank. Mycenaean sculptors of the early state (2500-2000 B.C.) rendered figures of pure formality. Artists of Homer's own time were in the early stage of an obsession with geometry. Egyptian art of several eras depicts life through formal pictures. The Greeks of the classical period combined form with realism in such a way as to create a special epoch in the arts, one which has come to stand as a basic point of reference in human expression. Musical forms are less studied but their importance to the role of balladry is critical.

Thus do we understand the climb of the Mycenaeans, Babylonians, Minoans, Sumerians, and even the Etruscans from primitive states. The efforts of these several groups to civilize themselves have been considered awesome. But the tendency to be civil is achieved by a public commitment to form. In this, of course, is recognition that truth is tribal. Such an admission opens a thesis to several kinds of attack. However, we can do no less than admit that when a group establishes its forms its members establish the way in which they are bound to view the world. As William James remarked, "We carve out groups of stars in the heavens and call them constellations, and the stars patiently suffer us to do so—though if they knew what we were doing, some of them might feel much surprised at the partners we had given them."[16] Indeed, we may name a constellation by different names, depending on our perception of forms. As James indicated ". . . Charles Wain, the Great Bear, or The Dipper. None of these names will be false, and one will be as true as another, for all are applicable."[17]

Thus, the forms which develop within a civilized order become the basis for building out upon reality, ordering reality, and giving meaning to the real. "Our nouns and adjectives are humanized heirlooms, and in the theories we build them into, the inner order and arrangement is wholly dictated by human considerations, intellectual consistency being one of them."[18] Man is not a perceiver of pre-established forms, but rather he is a creator of and believer in forms. Whereas traditional philosophy holds that man's great gift was to see beyond the things of the world to the Real forms, the modern view holds that man's gift is the power to create forms by which he can interpret the things of the world. Man does not simply climb to the Olympian heights. He builds them as well.

Therefore, the barbarian begins his effort at civilization with his first feat of abstraction. From that time onward he is bound to improve the forms by which he views the world about him. Barbaric justice, for example, is rough-hewn, swift, and brutal. Vengeance is its object. Surely, Sophocles, in his comparative studies of Electra and Antigone, suggested a critique of primitive justices. Neither the Mycenaeans nor the Thebians of that period had formalized the problem of justice at a sufficient level to institutionalize the tasks of judgment. In the confrontation of the determined Antigone and the wrathful Creon, denouement is the only possibility, and the City of Thebes stands condemned for the inadequacy of its laws. Orestes of Mycenae, on the other hand, who was indicted by the gods for the murder of Aegisthus and Clytemnestra, reputedly placed himself in the hands of a court in the City of Athens and won acquittal. Although this alleged outcome was not alluded to in the Electra, it was well known to the Sophoclean and Euripedean audiences of later antiquity. In this indirect way the station of Athens on the scale of civilized forms was recognized as above that of neighboring cities.

Among other things, these classic tragedies demonstrate how, when formalized, justice can avoid contamination by vanity or wrath. The Athenean courts, like all courts, failed at times. Our modern courts in many cases may not have done justice to justice. But justice in a formalized state is the mark of civil order. It is worth noting here that Biblical antiquity records the development of judges before kings, and among the royal personalities of that era those most warmly praised for wisdom displayed this quality in judicial roles.

Sentiment rises to form, and form rises to institution. The symmetrical or balanced vision of justice leads to an institutional incarnation which manifests this vision. The rules of evidence, the rules of procedure, and the doctrines of rights that are institutionalized in modern courts reflect the *a priori* commitment to balance a standard of "fairness." Plaintiff and defendant are equal in the eyes of the court, and the ideal of balance demands impartiality in the conduct of proceedings.

But forms, whether of justice, education, commerce, government, or personal affections, cannot be institutionalized until they are believed. This is the role of great human expressions. Paul and Augustine presented Christian forms so coherently that the forms were spiritualized by belief. The purveyors of the Arthurian legends offered intrinsic forms of manhood, womanhood, courage, honor, fidelity, etc., with such an aura that they were spiritualized by belief. The organizers of the Olympic and Pythian games presented the ideal of virtue so persuasively that the best athletes of antiquity endured the discipline and gruel of training in the hope that they might win a laurel wreath or a cup of olive oil. Of all the modes of heroic acts perhaps the one most important to civilization is the act of ennobling form.

The "native hue of resolution" which Shakespeare seems to have understood so well brings men to action. A resolute act is a spirited act. Men who are resolved to act upon the forms they have created do so by erecting institutions. In this way, by the work of institutions, forms enter the world of action.

We should, therefore, be unabashed about spiritualizing our forms. Nationhood, unionhood, brotherhood, freedom, etc., can have no spiritual reality apart from that spirit with which men infuse them. We should not, for the same reason, be too eager to bring these forms into a material or empirical representation. That which is tending to become material is perforce less spiritual. Realism in arts and letters does not ennoble form. Instead it debases form. What is the consequence of reducing form to matter? To understand this we need to examine institutions.

Institutionalization

Men in a state or stage of action are within an institution. Every personal act or public effort is through some sort of institution. Institutions are entities created by man for the purpose of bringing a form to the stage of physical or intellectual action. Institutions are frequently said to have "spirit." This spirit is the basic sentiment or belief which was formalized and then institutionalized. Sentiment progenerates form and form progenerates institution. Wherever sentiment and form are brought to a state of action—there stands an institution. Wherever the sentiment, form, and institution are in coherence, the institution is enspirited.

Any didactical exploration of institutions appears to require taxonomy development. Taxonomy development, seemingly, is a kind of Sisyphean labor. As soon as a major category is identified, the task of demonstrating subcategories and their relationship to the major category and other possible categories begins. Each of these relationships, when clarified, offers self-evident implications which work amendments on all that has gone before. These, in turn, reflect anew upon all that followed. Soon the feeling grows that the taxonomer is like the mythical Sisyphus. Each day he rolls his stone upward to the heights only to discover in the dawn light of each tomorrow that his stone has tumbled back and must be rolled upward again. The work is perpetual.

Even in the best ordered of academic disciplines, taxonomies are constantly reorganized. As long as scholars are actively concerned about how their particular area of knowledge is ordered or arranged the taxonomies of the field will be formed and reformed. Thus do men ever pursue the ideal of greater clarity.

The following taxonomy of institutions is presented with the object of achieving an initial degree of order and clarity about institutions. It is gross. The need for refinement and revision occurred to the writer before ending the first rough cut; as for certain, the need for further refinement and revision would become apparent before he ended the second, and so on.

At first sight, therefore, there appear to be nine major categories of institutional forms:

1. Commercial
2. Procreational
3. Educational
4. Political
5. Hygienical
6. Intellectual
7. Philanthropical
8. Criminal
9. Personal-Interpersonal

Commercial institutions are those created in response to material needs and wants. Included, of course, are basic physical necessities, but beyond these are all of the things that reverie and aspiration contribute to human ambition. Until recent years each American institution of the commercial category tended to be an expression of free enterprise with free utilization of property in a free market. Man's well-being rose and fell with the supposed natural flux of the free market. But since the turn of the century the basic commercial forms have been amended. Keynesian theories place man above the market, and the freedom of the market has been constrained. Property can no longer be freely used. If property usage pollutes air or fouls streams, that property usage is curbed; and enterprise can only be free to the extent that it does not restrain or delimit the enterprise of others.

So the commercial forms so prominent in the development of western material beneficence have been amended as have, in turn, the specific institutions given to capitalizing, planning, manufacturing, producing, distributing, regulating, laboring, and consuming. And, accordingly, the good, the right, or the just in relation to all of these is likewise amended.

Procreational institutions are those that men create to actualize the forms they hold regarding the conception and birth of children and coincidentally the not unrelated matters of sexual behavior, disease, and population control. This institution, of course, is called marriage, but the institution varies according to the form believed in. This in turn varies according to other factors. Nomadic peoples, for example, may be inclined to polygamous forms. Landowners may be inclined to monogamous forms. Where the physiological bases of fertility are unknown or unappreciated, the institution may have variations based on mythological forms which have become traditional.

Educational forms are those created to achieve whatever ends (covert or overt) the educational effort of a civilization has in prospect. In the main, however, educational institutions transmit sentiment and form from the older to the younger. In recent years American institutions have made the error of substituting form alone in place of the necessary combination of sentiment and form. The primary institution in America has been and still is the home. The school and the church are also vital, but in recent years the school has become even more vital. If current trends are grounds for prophecy, the school may one day surpass the home in its importance.

But there are other educational institutions. The neighborhood and the larger community answer constantly to the educational effort. The various communication media when not in pursuit of commercial ends are educative. Indeed, at every point where forces of human tradition play actively upon men an institutionalized educative act is performed.

Political forms are those by which men allocate authority and influence within social arrangements. The ballot box, town meeting, convention, representative assemblies, congresses are all characteristic political institutions which grow from democratic forms. So also are the caucus, the executive session, and the smoke-filled room. Within this category are legal forms and judicial forms. They are considered subordinate to political forms because they are determined through political institutions and given authority by political events.

Legislatures and courts make the law, the former by developing and the latter by interpreting. Each law is itself an institution which has made its way through the stages of sentiment and form.

The strength of democratic institutions is gauged by their capacity to bring the sentiments of the people to the stage of coherent political action. Aristocratic political institutions, on the other hand, are considered strong in the extent to which they can enforce the active obedience of the people to the sentiments of the ruling class. Thus in a true democracy the police and the military are decidedly different institutions than in a true aristocracy even though most of their activities may be similar. Totalitarian regimes of the modern world must be served by the same type of political institutions as once served aristocracy.

Hygienical institutions are those devoted to maintenance of health. Included, of course, are the health professions, hospitals and clinics, and agencies devoted to hygienic standards of food and environment. Of all the realms of value no other is so free of ambiguity. The good in physical health is experienceable and clinically measurable. The forms upon which health institutions stand are reasonably clear. However, there is much ambiguity in our present health institutions. This ambiguity is so potent that recent judgments have been made that these institutions are of a commercial class.

Bifurcation of this sort offers these institutions, for a time, the advantages of both classes. But the danger is that they may have the integrity of neither. Although the forms may be clear, it would be widely agreed that hygienical institutions are in need of intensive study and revision.

Intellectual forms are academic disciplines. These are the forms through which knowledge is produced and validated. Mathematics, physics, history, etc., are institutions. Their incarnation is a learned society of man bound together by shared assumptions, publications, and canons of criticism. An institution such as chemistry has no physical location. Just as marriage is an institution for the procreation of the race, chemistry is an institution for the procreation of knowledge within that phenomenal field.

The form of a discipline provides its structure and syntax. This is nothing more or less than the general rules by which the knowledge a discipline produces is organized and the rational propositions through which knowledge is given meaning. When professional psychologists or geologists debate the structure and syntax of their disciplines, they are really debating upon the authentic form of an institution. Men who are devoted students of any academic area are in continuous contemplation of its form. This, it seems, is never settled.

Unquestionably, the most pervasive intellectual form in human experience is represented in the institution of language. The grammars men have adopted as instrumental to linguistic meaning vary as to form but answer to a single purpose, namely to establish a basis for meaningful organization of words or symbols. Every language which has in it the properties necessary for the transmisson of thought is, in itself, an institution.

The question arises: are aesthetical forms an intellectual property? A very strong case can be made for or against such an organization. Aesthetic ideals, as forms, may or may not be perceived in the same way one perceives the order of mathematics or the grammer of language. To the extent that an aesthetic response transcends the intellectual, artistic forms are alien to the intellectual. However, the discussion of aesthetic forms, to be adequately meaningful, must be ordered in an intellectual context.

Thus, the question is resolved on these grounds; namely, aesthetical forms, when abstracted and shared, are of an intellectual class because abstractions cannot be shared other than linguistically. In other words, we can share an aesthetic response, but we cannot discourse upon its form without resort to language of some kind. This necessity compels that we regard aesthetical forms and their attendant institutions to be of the intellectual class.

The drama, the concert, the art museum are, perforce, intellectual institutions. Their work upon aesthetic forms is in a sense similar to the work mathematicians do upon mathematical forms and historians on historical forms. This argument draws further strength from the fact that the most clear-eyed perceiver of mathematical and historical forms asserts that his perception provides an experience in beauty.

Philanthropical forms are those general ideals which stem from man's interest in helping others. Men of good will seem always inclined toward philanthropy. The ancient argument that altruism is not possible fails of relevance by the strength of the fact that men do give; and the forms of giving are well known, and institutional incarnations of these forms are well known.

The forms of giving and receiving that which is given result in many institutions other than those accorded the respect of mankind. Panhandling has been called a "fine art." There are hobo empires; and the gypsies, who reputedly do not always wait until the giving occurs, have a king and a court. The state of modern philanthropy is in need of much study. So many constantly ask and get who have little need. So much is given in the wrong amounts, to the wrong people, at the wrong time, and by the wrong persons for the wrong reasons. Modern civilization would profit from contemplation of Aristotle's view of liberality as the mean between prodigality and greed. At the end, each reflective man knows that there is nothing to be done except to give all that he has and is to others, but it is not an easy thing to give well.

Criminal forms are the basis for criminal institutions. It seems that each new generation of civilized men must discover anew that crimes are institutions. In our own times we have been astounded at the sophistication and effectiveness of criminal institutions. However, criminal institutions are not simply underworld organizations. Students have been known to cheat in school, according to certain codes. Workmen defraud employers and vice versa by certain generally understood means. Minor offenders are knowingly tolerated by law enforcement officers because they give information.

Formal neglect may be criminal. A law enforcement officer who neglects to apprehend speeding motorists in a school zone soon, in effect, institutionalizes neglect. Speeders cross the area, having learned they will not be apprehended. When the ultimate tragedy ensues, the officer's crime is at least as great as the driver's crime. By his formal neglect the officer created a criminal institution. Institutions like this exist in many places. At any time the expectation is established that malfeasance will be tolerated, a criminal institution has developed.

Personal-Interpersonal institutions are those which are defined by relationships between man, the world, and its things and by relationships between men and men. Much good work has been done in delineating the forms of personal, interpersonal institutions by phenomenologists such as Husserl and Buber. Other contributions of value have come from writers often described as existentialist, such as Sartre, Heidegger, and Camus.

One of the most common of the personal forms is referred to as *being-for-itself*. As it relates to man it refers to his awareness that he supplies reality to the world of objects. In effect, he institutionalizes himself in a world of things. Buber who it seems is willing to make reality solely relationships would conceivably refer to this personal institutionalization as the network of I-It relationships which constitute a man's personal reality.

One of the most common of the interpersonal forms is *being-for-others*. As this relates to man it denotes the special world that attends the relationships between two humans or among more than two humans. In Buber's taxonomy this form is called by the term I-Thou and is not without involvement of the divine. When man and man (or man and woman) are united (or alienated) by sentiment this sentiment takes on form and the form becomes institutionalized. This very definable relationship between humans is in itself an institution, and like all institutions it is enspirited by the beliefs the relating humans have about their relationship.

As we suggested, this relationship could be either of affectionated or alienated sentiments. Both are formalized and institutionalized. Indifference or objectivity is impossible except through an independent institution to which both relate and through which they transact. For example, a doctor and patient are neither affectionated nor alienated. Both relate to each other through the institutionalized practices of the medical profession. Likewise, lawyer and client are related through a similar kind of institutionalized set of practices.

But when friends or lovers relate, a new universe opens. All reality is altered because all is brought within the form of friendship or love and revalued by the special perspective the resultant institution imposes. Similarly, when enemies relate, all is altered by the special perspectives that institution obtrudes upon the sensibilities of those involved. Through each one of his personal loves and animosities a man participates in an institution.

Now, institutions of all kinds are recognized by the conventions that sustain them. Two humans whose relationship has been sentimentalized, formalized, and institutionalized when in the presence of one another (which is to say within the institution) are in a universe of shared conventions. There are special greetings (first names, etc.), special expectations, and mutual understandings. The two, it might be said, have a special way with each other.

Courtship in itself is a social institution. But when practiced by an individual man and woman it is the name given to the active institutionalization of a human relationship. If courtship creates an institution which becomes a matter of great satisfaction, the two may advance their interpersonal institutional form to the procreational form called marriage. This is a new and different institution and, of course, carries within it a new set of conventions.

Conventionalization

It is important for parents and teachers to note that children and youth perceive only the conventions by which our institutions are sustained. Because they are humans and particularly because they are young humans, they press for a fuller accounting for these procedures, processes, or policies. Often this demand for accounting is considered rebellious; and, in part, it is rebellious.

Rebellion is so commonplace in the youth that it requires its own metaphysical explanation. It seems clearly related to the discovery of self. Analogically, one's hand would remain a mystery to him were he unable to strike something with it, grasp something with it, or use it in various other ways. In mid-adolescence a youth discovers himself thrown out into existence. He has existence but the self which exists remains to be discovered or known. So he may strike something with it, grasp something with it, or use it in various ways. In this way the self becomes less of a personal mystery. The youth learns what it does in various circumstances. There is no better target for this self-exploration than the conventions of our institutional order. The youth will tend to view these conventions as *ex cathedra* restrictions upon his freedom; and this, coupled with his tendency to discover a selfhood by striking and grasping, mounts a perennial challenge to institutional conventions. Nowadays these conventions are called by the term *Establishment*.

Those who write in this vein about perennial rebellion of the young are correct in pointing out that the complaints of the older generation about rebellious youth go well into antiquity. Plato complained about the youth of Athens, and the chagrin of the Athenians about the conduct of Plato's generation was, in part, consummated in the martyrdom of Socrates. But one does not ignore a matter simply because it is perennial any more than one can ignore the frost simply because it comes each winter. Pains must be taken to protect both the youth and the institutions they will inherit. Rebellion may be a method of self-discovery, but blind and unguided revolution (or anarchy) is a method of self-destruction.

Our conventions are simply ways of sustaining our sentiments; however, so much stands between convention and sentiment that the connection is not apparent to the neophyte. This disjunction is intensified when the adults have grown weary of the effort of understanding it themselves or are willing to toss it off by using the simplified notions of cultural anthropology. If conventions have no more authority than this, then why are they deserving of fealty? Indeed, why?

The youth asks why he cannot use "four-letter words" in his classroom discussion or in his school newspaper. He asks what kind of authority it is that rules certain words bad and others not bad. He asks what authority makes a certain dress appropriate and another not appropriate. He asks why he should be loyal to his country and participate in its defense, why he should restrain himself in matters relating to sex and drugs, and why he should find remunerative work

when his welfare is sufficiently endowed by his family or his government.

Trouble ensues when the general answer put forward by the
adult is simply, "Because we say so." American youth, in particular,
are not trained in the habits of obedience. On the contrary, they are
informed that some of their most esteemed forebears dumped a ship-
load of tea into the sea, threw out a skirmish line at Lexington, fortified
and defended a hill which rises above the City of Boston, fired upon
Fort Sumpter, marched in Coxey's Army, and repealed the Eighteenth
Amendment. All of this was done by Americans who did not accept
authoritarian pronouncements. Modern teachers and parents can expect the youth to take these lessons seriously.

Indeed, these conventions have no strength *per se*. In and of
themselves they are nothing. But conventions seldom appear in and of
themselves. Almost inevitably they are within a recognized institution.
As such they represent and sustain the beliefs for which that institution was created. When one begins to render offense against beliefs
which men hold he approaches matters of uttermost danger.

For example, men can believe that a campus newspaper *ought*
to be institutionalized in response to reflective sentiments. When they
find such a newspaper uses language which is conducive to barbarian
sentiments, they may rightly reason that it is nullifying its own progenerative sentiment and, correspondingly, its right to exist. One must
examine with the students the sentiments which preside over such an
enterprise before they get started. It is not enough merely to *inform*
them of the conventions of college journalism.

The same applies to all that goes on in school and home. When
the youth believes in what he is doing he will accept, even enjoy, the
conventions which sustain and implement the belief. The attitudes of
youth toward the conventions of military service vary from favorable
to unfavorable in accordance with their beliefs about the mission of
the military service at the particular time in history that it poses an
obligation upon them.

Language is probably the most ubiquitous institution. Its conventions are called grammar and usage. Language conventions vary
from place to place. Carpenters, short-order cooks, lawyers, and
accountants have their own jargons. These vernaculars are separate
institutions which cohere with separate forms and sentiments. A
hospital operating room is imbued with a different sentiment than that
which presides at the family dinner table. Accordingly, the instituted
language conventions are different. Now if an operating room conver-

sation began to lose its terse and precise aspects, the surgeon in charge would be compelled to invoke appropriate discipline. The preservation of proper sentiment is essential to preservation of the patient. Thus, the language conventions in an operating room are critical.

The same can be said of a family at dinner, philosophers in dialogue, advocates in court, and players in huddle. The manner of speech is vital. A bridge table conversation sustains a sentiment that is different from that cultivated on the police radio (or it should). And the sentiments in a barroom result in speech modes unlike those which are generated from the sentiments in force at the stock exchange.

The language conventions of a classroom have the same relation to a sentiment as any other set of language conventions. Indeed, there appears to be a strong association between classroom sentiments and classroom discipline. A teacher's manner in speaking can be vital, and the teacher is as correct in insisting on proper sentiments as the head surgeon of an operating room is correct in his insistence that only conventional modes of speech are acceptable.

A response which must be given to students who wish to use obscenities and vulgarities in the classroom or in student publications is that such are destructive of necessary sentiments. It is reasonable to point out to such students that the destruction of these sentiments takes the *raison d'être* from the classroom or the publication. Different sentiments call for different institutions. One is free, therefore, to alter conventions only if the change is part of an agreed-upon and planned modification in sentiment.

Some persons never use obscenities; others do so constantly. The latter are generally regarded as limited in the range of civil sentiments in which they can partake. Obscenity usually is a lazy form of invective. If one purports to chastise effectively or memorably he does not use obscenity. Profane speech is inexact. Its figures are too general. If one wishes truly to damn an object, idea, or person he turns to language conventions with more profound sentiments. Emerson achieved such a sentiment when he said of Webster that "each drop of his blood has eyes that look downward." Disraeli also achieved this level in responding to the enraged Gladstone who taunted him by saying, "You will die either by hanging or by a loathsome disease" only to receive Disraeli's retort, "That depends, sir, on whether I embrace your principles or your mistress." An American politician once said of a rival, "He has every attribute of a dog except loyalty." In the heat of argument John Marshall said of an opponent, "like a

mackerel in the moonlight, he shines and stinks." Another southern
statesman reportedly remarked of an enemy, "He's like the River
Platte, one inch deep and a mile wide at the mouth." When compared
to these sentiments the sentiments stirred by obscene or profane
language conventions are flaccid and unenduring. If one wishes to
be rough, really rough, he does not bother to "cuss." Instead, he rises to
the art of polemics.

Profanity has its place. There is an oft repeated story of a
profane carpenter who rarely formed a sentence which did not include
one four-letter obscenity as subject, predicate, object modifier, or
simple expletive. Eventually, his scatology became so banal and commonplace that even he never heard it. It got so he could not ask his
helper the time of day without defilement of clock, hour, and calendar.
Finally, there came an occasion which called for him to rise to the
greatest heights of profanity. He cut off a finger. But, alas, all he
could say was "gosh."

We need to understand conventions, and we need to understand
why the young will test them. Rather than despair we must struggle
to achieve in the young a sensibility of the tie which binds convention
to sentiment. The tie is inexorable; therefore, convention and sentiment
must be taught together.

It seems right that this essay should conclude with another
illustration. Athletic games are of the educational class of institutions.
There are sentiments which are taught through games. One of the
greatest is called virtue. The Greeks felt very strongly about this, and
somehow the notion of virtue still attaches even in an era when
winning for its own sake seems to enjoy a powerful vogue.

Some years ago a basketball game was played at a little teachers'
college in western Pennsylvania. It was a close game and the gym was
full. As one might expect, the place was in an uproar. When only
twenty-five seconds remained of the playing time the home team was
ahead by one point, but at that instant one of the visiting players
was fouled in such a way as to give him two free throws. Despite the
uproar from the home spectators he made the first shot good. As he
prepared to shoot the second, which if made would be almost certain
victory for the visitors, the gymnasium become bedlam. Shrieks,
whistles, drums, hoots—nothing was withheld which might serve to
distract his purpose. The ball went up and bounced happily away into
the eager grasp of a home player. He turned to go up the floor and
then came to a complete stop. One by one the players on both sides

did the same. Each of them stared as a great hush settled over the audience and all concentrated on the center of the floor.

For there stood the Dean of Instruction, tall, grim, and in an unmistakable attitude of command. The gym was so silent that not one syllable of his spoken voice was unheard as he said to the referee, "In behalf of the college, I ask that you invite that player to shoot again." The official nodded, bounced the ball once, and passed it to the player. Both teams lined the lanes; and, in continuing silence, the shot was made.

So the game ended in victory for the visitors, and, as the Dean approached the exit, the students parted before him in respect. That night with one sentence the Dean had taught his students one of their greatest lessons. No one who shared that moment would ever forget that sudden exposure to the original and authentic sentiment of athletic games. In defeat the college stood a little taller. Some of the students may since have slipped back, but there were others who never could. It was that memorable.

Somehow we have always known that this is the sort of thing people mean when they speak of quality in education. There are civilized sentiments and men who stand up for them. Civilization does not come easily. A thousand would sit, content to win, and no one would place blame upon even the greatest of them. Yet one man will step forth and he shows others something better, and the others see it is better, and they believe.

If the conventions of modern American basketball games, or for that matter any kind of games, cohere with barbarian and not reflective sentiments, basketball games or athletics in general are not educative and have no place in schools. We must learn to take a hard look at such things.

If the mission of American teachers is to receive into their hands a civilization, improve upon it, and pass it along to others who will receive it with the same inculcation of reverence and obligation to duty, then American teachers must learn to make distinctions of the same sort that a college dean made one night long ago when he rose from his seat, walked to the center of a noisy basketball court, and took his stand.

Notes

1. John Dewey, *My Pedagogic Creed*, Article I.
2. *Ibid.*

3. The bold assertion by which Rousseau began the first chapter of *The Social Contract*.
4. Voltaire, *Age of Louis XVI* (Everyman's Library), p. 415.
5. Plato, *The Republic*, Book V.
6. Richard Weaver, *Ideas Have Consequences* (Chicago: University of Chicago Press, 1948), p. 19.
7. James, Fechner, and Whitehead are among those willing to associate public consensus with the divine.
8. Alfred N. Whitehead, *The Aims of Education and Other Essays* (New York: The Free Press Paperback, Macmillan, 1927), p. 14.
9. J. H. S. Burleigh, *Augustine: Earlier Writings*, contained in the essay *On The Teacher*, included in Herman Shapiro, ed., *Medieval Philosophy* (New York: The Modern Library, Random House, Inc., 1964), p. 35.
10. Weaver, *op. cit.*, p. 20.
11. Kant's *Categorical Imperative*.
12. Charles S. Peirce, "The Fixation of Belief," *Popular Science Monthly*, (1877).
13. Weaver, *op. cit.*, p. 19.
14. Paul Harvey, *The Oxford Companion to English Literature* (Oxford: The Oxford University Press, 1967), p. 43.
15. It is appropriate to recognize here that the authorship of these poems is a matter of dispute.
16. William James, *Pragmatism and Humanism*, included in John J. McDermott, *The Writings of William James* (New York: Modern Library, Inc., 1968), p. 450.
17. *Ibid.*
18. *Ibid.*, p. 455.

Other Reading

Allport, Gordon. *Becoming*. New Haven: Yale University Press, 1955.

Barazun, Jacques. *The House of Intellect*. New York: Harper & Brothers, 1959.

Beard, Charles and Mary. *The Rise of American Civilization*. New York: Macmillan Company, 1936.

Bloom, Benjamin, *et al. Taxonomy of Educational Objectives: The Classification of Educational Goals*. Longmans, Green and Co., 1965. Handbooks I, II.

Cassier, Ernst. *An Essay on Man*. New Haven: Yale University Press, 1966. Part II.

Commager, Henry S. *The American Mind*. New Haven: Yale University Press, 1959.

Drucker, Peter F. *Concept of the Corporation*. New York: The John Day Co., 1946.

Emerson, E. W., ed. *The Complete Works of Ralph Waldo Emerson*. Cambridge, Mass.: The Riverside Press, 1904.

Forester, Norman. *The Humanities and the Common Man.* Chapel Hill: University of North Carolina Press, 1946.

Gardner, John. *Excellence.* New York: Harper & Brothers, 1961.

Hook, Sidney. *The Paradoxes of Freedom.* Berkeley: The University of California Press, 1962.

Karier, Clarence J. *Man, Society and Education.* Atlanta: Scott, Foresman & Company, 1967. Chapters I-VIII.

Kimball, Solon T. and McClelland. *Education and the New America.* New York: Random House, Inc., 1962. Part II.

London, Ephriam. *The Law as Literature.* New York: Simon and Schuster, Inc., 1960.

Marcuse, Herbert. *Eros and Civilization.* Boston: Beacon Press, 1955.

Mead, George H. *The Philosophy of the Act.* Chas. W. Morris, ed. Chicago: University of Chicago Press, 1938.

Morris, Charles, ed. *Mind, Self and Society.* Chicago: University of Chicago Press, 1934.

Mosier, Richard D. *Making the American Mind: Social and Moral Ideas in the McGuffey Readers.* New York: King's Crown Press, 1947.

Piaget, Jean. *The Child's Conception of the World.* New York: Humanities Press, 1951.

——————. *The Language and Thought of the Child.* New York: Humanities Press, 1959.

Snow, C. P. *The New Man.* New York: Scribner's, 1955.

Weaver, Richard M. *Ideas Have Consequences.* Chicago: The University of Chicago Press, 1965. Chapters I-VII.

West, Andrew F., ed. *Value of the Classics.* Princeton, N. J.: Princeton University Press, 1917. Chapters I-V.

Williams, Raymond. *The Long Revolution.* New York: Columbia University Press, 1961.

CHAPTER XIV

Valuation in a Civilization of Forms

Just about every waking moment one is confronted with a decision on what he ought to do. Ought I go to the bank? Ought I call home? Ought I inform the police about that stray dog? Ought I speak to my neighbor about the disgraceful condition of his front lawn? Such decisions—some trivial, others important—are before us constantly. When we are not making decisions of our own we are making judgments about the decisions of others. Ought she have gone to the bank? Ought she have called home? And so on. Deciding and justifying are such vital human activities that students of education *ought* to consider what philosophers have discovered about it. They should also be aware of what kind of work philosophers are presently about.

This chapter will attempt an overview of these matters and will conclude with a proposed standard of morality which appears relevant to a civilization of forms such as that discussed in the previous chapter.

Normative Ethics and Meta-Ethics

It is now recognized that professional students of ethics are of two kinds. The first of the two includes those who look primarily at the ethical problems people have and take a direct hand in the search for moral standards. They are developing *normative ethics*. In order to do this, philosophers work out systems. Such system building requires critical reflection beyond that which is characteristic of ordinary men. This does not mean that the typical man does not reflect and at times reflect critically. The distinction between professional and layman is in the level of rigor. Through rigorous reflection philosophers have produced principles of morality to which men might resort in forming moral judgments. These principles stand independently of the conventions or protocols which the public calls its moral code.

Taylor[1] lists three methods that normative ethicists employ in establishing foundations for morality. The first is to define the ultimate purpose for human existence. The second is to elucidate and examine the moral presuppositions of moral judgments, and the third is to deal with whatever it is that makes a principle moral. Each of these can be illustrated.

For example, St. Thomas went as far as any philosopher can go in establishing the ultimate purpose of human existence. In depicting the "ultimate end of the universe as the good of an intellect,"[2] St. Thomas agreed that the purpose of man is to love intellect or reason as a means of loving Truth which is a means of loving God. Now if man is to reason and is to love reason it therefore follows that reason will tell him what he ought to do. Therefore, in all judgments for which there is not a divine ordinance, reason is used as a standard.

On the other hand, Aristotle, from whom Aquinas drew so heavily, was content to think that the purpose of human life is happiness.[3] This enabled him to establish a hierarchy of means and ends, each of which was evaluated on the way human happiness is strengthened. He ranged throughout man's social affairs, establishing guidelines to all of the moral and intellectual virtues, examining such things as friendship and pleasure, and, of course, terminating his discourse with how all combines in personal happiness. Happiness, he argued, is the ultimate end. It is not a means to anything else. We choose it for its own sake, and we choose everything else we choose for the sake of happiness.

A normative ethicist who employs the second method, that of elucidating and examining moral presuppositions, will begin with a commonly accepted moral judgment such as: It is wrong to bear false witness. Accepting this, questions are asked such as: What acts are right and what acts are wrong? What makes right acts right and wrong acts wrong? What various moral obligations grow out of this judgment? What rules of conduct? What is the role of conscience? As every mature person well knows, the problem of always being a true witness and never a false witness is very complicated. Vast works have been done on each of the Ten Commandments, and each remains as an unexhausted study for further study.

The third method of normative ethics turns aside from ultimates (as is characteristic of the first method) and a priori judgment (as is characteristic of the second method). The third approach is to examine all social operations to discover which is that which produces the moral judgment of the society in question. This presumes that each society, as an organic union of people, has a way of producing moral standards.

These standards may be no more than implied by-laws, customs, economic practices, political regimentation, and the like. Obviously, the social consensus on any standard of morality is constantly changing, and, obviously, it stands sovereign at any moment. Here the task of normative ethics is to discover its signals, read them well, and clarify their meaning.

Regardless of the method, the purpose of normative ethics is the establishment of a guide to the right and the wrong, the good and the bad, the superior and the inferior. The normative ethicist seeks to provide a rigorously derived basis for critical evaluation. "Therefore, he is engaged in moral discourse himself rather than being engaged in talking about or analyzing moral discourse."[4] Or, in other words, he wants to establish a basis for moral action, and his hope is that it will meet the standards of his profession and will be accepted by his fellow men as guides to their action. Therefore, he will advocate his standards in public. Ralph Waldo Emerson, for example, propounded neorational ethical standards to the American public. Many modern social scientists have employed a social consensus theory. Emerson used the first of the three methods most of the time, but on occasion resorted to the second. Social science, of course, has used the third. Normative ethicists all have hoped their methods and conclusions are sound and have represented them persuasively.

When one understands that a normative ethicist seeks defensible moral standards, he is in a good position to make a clear and sharp distinction between the *normative ethicist* and the *meta-ethicist*. The latter does not seek to make pronouncements about what is right or wrong, nor is he attempting by a strict method to find a basis for the good life. This is not his interest. Instead, the meta-ethicist examines the language of those who speak and write about morals. His subject matter is not morals; it is moral discourse. So the *meta-ethicist* analyzes the methods and the language of the normative ethicist. His effort purports to elucidate the meaning of both.

Thus, some meta-ethicists look at the words philosophers use, such as "good," "right," "value," "praiseworthy," and so on. They try to develop the meanings such words have when used in various times and places. What linguistic tasks do they perform? Under what circumstances are such words clear and under what other circumstances are they ambiguous? Other meta-ethicists take sentences from the ordinary language that laymen use, recast them in various ways, classify them, test them against certain criteria, and, thereby, attempt to discover their covert meanings and intentions.

On questions relating to what is good as opposed to what is bad the meta-ethicist is obliged to conduct his examination on neutral grounds. He simply explores the questions to discover, if he can, the full range of their implications. He tries to clarify the questions, clarify alternatives, state the apparent strengths and weaknesses of alternatives, and seek for additional alternatives which can be similarly examined. But he makes no moral pronouncements.

It seems desirable, therefore, that if one proposes to work in the area of normative ethics he first prepare himself in the field of meta-ethics. Normative ethics is the rigorous development of specific moral standards. Meta-ethics is the rigorous examination of the full range of moral propositions. The normative ethicist who has mastered the disciplines of meta-ethics will fare much better when meta-ethical scrutiny is applied to his discourse. To confirm this, it is necessary only to note that the leading normative ethicists of western philosophy have, at one time or another, shown prior qualifications in meta-ethics.

Thus we have these two traditions in the professional scholarship of ethics, the normative and the meta-ethical. Of the two, the meta-ethical comes first. Therefore, we turn to something of a meta-ethical examination of certain well known theories of justification which in one way or another are of influence in moral judgments formed in western civilization.

Theological Ethics

A great portion of all sacred literature is devoted to ethical teachings. The laws, commandments, proverbs, and prophecies of the Old Testament convey the ethical sentiments which had developed among the Judaic Semites during the more than fifteen hundred years their societal identity endured transition from tribalhood to bondage and from nationhood to a theocratic province. The subsequent Judaic, Christian, and Moslem religions have, in general, regarded Judaic literature as law and have accepted its moral subject matter as a basis for righteousness.

There are other recognized expressions of the divine. The New Testament is certainly a major source of law. There are also a number of indirect communications which have been acreeded. For example, the Christian church has been generally accorded supernatural authority. Certain human personalities have been recognized by some as having a special communication with the divine.

Ethical decisions made on the basis of God's will face two distinct challenges. The first is that of establishing acceptable grounds for asserting that the perception in question is, in truth, that of God's will. The second is that of establishing that the interpretation and application are proper and appropriate. In other words: (1) Is God really the source? And (2) How does God's will apply to this or that particular issue?

But the general objection to theological ethics most frequently raised by meta-ethicists is that they may call upon man to perform an act which is morally repugnant. To substantiate this they cite morally repugnant acts which have been justified as "God's will"; and, indeed, God's will has been interpreted in conflicting ways. Thus, it turns out that to determine what is God's will in any number of instances another ethical standard must be employed. Therefore, theological claims very often require justification by an ethical standard which is not attributed to the divine.

Suppose instead of "Thou shalt not steal," or "Thou shalt not bear false witness," the commandments read, "Thou shalt steal" and "Thou shalt bear false witness." These commandments would soon be suspect. Man would hold that they are not "God's will" because they are unsavory and unworkable. However, if God's will as so revealed is to be an uncontested source, one would have to accept these commandments as good regardless of human preference or consequence. Man would not do this for long. Theological ethics, therefore, stand as a good way of expressing ethical standards and securing credence to them; but, again, the moral principles they reveal often must be interpreted and accredited by ethical standards which stem from other traditions.

Utilitarian Ethics

One of these traditions is that which equates happiness with the good. As noted previously, Aristotle consummated his monumental theory of ethics with the notion that "happiness is the end of human life."[5] Epicurus developed similar ethical tradition upon his well known distinction between pleasure and pain.

However, it is reliably reported that Epicurus was not speaking of pleasure as the pleasures of a debauched man or those which stem from sensual enjoyment. He wished the "freedom of the body from pain and of the soul from disturbance."[6]

Neither Aristotle nor Epicurus allowed pleasure or happiness to stand as an undefined term. Aristotle developed a formal definition for happiness which he finally abstracted as a "form of contemplation"[7] and Epicurus joined him in extolling moderation as the proper route to pleasure. His motto was "*Lathe biosas*" (live unobtrusively). If one "controls his appetites, lives without pretense, puts aside all fears, the natural 'sweetness of life' *hedone* rewards him with the greatest of all good which is peace."

Other forms of hedonism in ethics descended from the teachings of Aristippus. These, together with Epicureanism, become imbued in the life styles of eastern Mediterranean peoples, while Stoicism, enshrined in the Christian church, was dominant in the moral standards of Western Europe.[8] This disparity prevailed despite the arrival of Aristotelian thought in Western Europe during the Middle Ages. It seems clear that Aristotle's ethics did not make so strong an impact as his materialism because Aquinas who followed him so closely in other matters subordinated happiness to reason.

Two English philosophers, Jeremy Bentham and John S. Mill, mounted a fresh approach to happiness as a standard of morality. Unlike the philosophers of antiquity, both seemed to hold the view that men do not need to be told when they are happy. So they did not make an elaborate effort to define the term. Instead, they suggested that men look at what it is that gives them pleasure or makes them happy. In other words, men should discover what is useful in producing happiness.

The first of the two, Jeremy Bentham (1748-1832), named his standard as the principle of utility and it rose to general attention as a theme for social reform. It might be termed a form of personal hedonism which in doctrine is related as follows:

> The principle of utility is that principle which approves or disapproves of every action whatsoever, according to the tendency it has to augment or diminish the happiness of the party whose interest is in question, or what is the same thing in other words, to promote or oppose that happiness. I say of every action whatsoever; and, therefore, not only of every action of a private individual, but of every measure of government.[9]

Now insofar as this remains an expression of personal hedonism it stands reasonably clear. One has only to contemplate every potential action in regard to his own personal happiness, and act accordingly. But few actions fail in some way to affect other persons and, of course, their happiness. When other persons are involved the application of the principle of utility becomes more complex and the issues tend to become ambiguous. For example, Bentham immediately comes to grip with the "interest of the community."[10] However, he correctly observes that a community is a fictitious body (a realization lost on many more recent observers). One, of course, can think of a group of happy persons, but one cannot, at the requisite level or rigor, think of a happy group. A group has no way to be happy. Only a person can be happy. (Likewise a society cannot be sick, etc.) Thus, we are bound to understand that the principle of utility determines that an action is good when it maximizes the total pleasure of those persons affected when each person is counted as one person and no person as more than one.

Bentham went to extreme lengths to make this principle explicit in moral choice. To this extent he attempted to define the sources from which pleasure and pain flow. These are his memorable four sanctions (ways in which a man can be bound): (1) physical, (2) political, (3) moral, and (4) religious.[11] Moving boldly from this taxonomy he proposed a method for measuring pleasure and pain which is based on seven factors, defined as follows:[12]

I. INTRINSIC CHARACTERISTICS OF PLEASURE AND PAIN

    1. Their intensity
    2. Their duration
    3. Their certainty or uncertainty
    4. Their propinquity or remoteness

II. CONSEQUENTIAL CHARACTERISTICS OF PLEASURE AND PAIN

    5. Their Fecundity (chance of being followed by kindred sensation)
    6. Their Impurity (chance of being followed by opposite sensation)

III. SUMMATION OF ALL PLEASURE AND PAIN

    7. Their extent

In the literature of philosophy this method is called the *Hedonic Calculus*. It is interesting to pose a hypothetical case which can be examined by the calculus to determine what moral decision is indicated. It must be borne in mind that the calculus must be applied to the pleasures and pains of all persons affected by the action and not simply those of the person who acts.

Bentham's work is original, imaginative, and impressive. In 1808 he met James Mill, and from the association of these two men the organization called Benthamites was formed. As one might expect, when a philosophical system is politicized all sorts of criticism are leveled against it. The Benthamites were a formidable group, and in his final years Bentham found some of his social proposals accepted. But the criticisms of his philosophy were such that a further extension of the principle of utility was clearly needed. This task was undertaken by John Stuart Mill (1806-1873), son of Bentham's great friend and an admirer of Bentham in his own right.

One of Mill's early publications was an essay on Bentham which purported to set the Benthamite image right. He pointed out that Bentham's interest lay "in the direction of jurisprudential rather than ethical inquiry."[13] Bentham, Mill pointed out, developed his system as a necessary foundation for his proposed emendations of English law. Like Plato, in this respect, his primary interest was government and not philosophy, but also like Plato he won an "indisputable place among the great intellectual benefactors of mankind."[14]

Having established this kindly perspective Mill proceeded in a spirit "neither of apology nor of censure, but of calm appreciation," to inquire, "how far this (Bentham's) view of human nature and life will carry one; how much it will accomplish in morals, and how much in political and social philosophy."[15] He immediately perceived that it would not go very far. Although he refused to expiate the deficiencies of Bentham's system he was, doubtless, sensitive to the most telling of the criticisms brought against it. This, after all, was early in the Victorian Age, and the literate Englishmen of that time were of no mood to foster a view that did not discriminate between the gross pleasures of the flesh and the ennobling pleasures of the mind. It seems that Aristotle was speaking to the early Victorians.

Mill's full response did not find public expression until 1863. Then at the peak of his powers, he presented his eloquent essay, *Utilitarianism*. Although his prior writings and those which followed touched on the principle of utility, this must be regarded as his plenary statement on the subject. He met the basic public objections head on. He agreed, for example, that "it is better to be a human being dissatisfied than a pig satisfied; better to be Socrates dissatisfied than a fool satisfied."[16] In response Mill proposed that the *qualitative* basis of the pleasure or happiness be determined by a polity of those with a cultivated taste for the higher pleasures. Thus he moved away from Bentham's *quantitative* determination as illustrated in the hedonic

calculus and embraced a social hedonism based upon a consensus of
the learned or the experienced. Said he, "From this verdict of the only
competent judges, I apprehend there can be no appeal."[17]

Likening the utilitarians to the young Socrates who in his conversation with Protagoras argued down the popular morality of the
so-called sophists, he took up the challenges raised against the principle of utility, leaving the judgment to the "thoughtful reader." He presented a formidable case, subjecting it to various rational tests and
explaining how utility can supplant or improve upon existing ethical
standards. Defining justice as a social utility, he counterattacked at
another point where the principle was found vulnerable. However,
he seemed required to put his argument on the very thin ice of social
expediency with his dictum, "All persons are deemed to have a right
to equality of treatment, except when some recognized social expediency requires the reverse."

Now Mill at this point appears to be giving society a reality
which Bentham suggested it cannot have; namely, a group cannot be
happy, only persons can be happy. His suggestion that the "competent"
judge where happiness lies is a possible, yet dubious, solution. It is
dubious for many reasons, but let it suffice to state here that it is
dubious if for no other reason than it seems a denial of the principle of
utility itself. The discerning group of judges to whom Mill refers are
invited to consult a hierarchy of goods and then name their pleasure.
But when Mill concedes that such a hierarchy is real then he nullifies
utility as the ultimate sanction. This does not suggest in itself that
Mill's system is totally without merit, but it does indicate that it must
be understood and accepted on grounds other than utility.

There are other concerns. One can be understood in terms of the
problem faced by every classroom teacher. This is a special duty. Now
a teacher could maximize the pleasure of the group by giving all good
marks, and by doing other things to promote happiness of every person. But the teacher has duties which stand in the way of this.
Special duties are an objection to utilitarianism. They become a more
serious objection when it is recognized that man at all points in life is
seldom independent of special duty. He lives constantly in a state of
passing from son to father, from brother to uncle, from boarder to
freeholder, from apprentice to master, from suitor to husband, and
so on. Rarely does one man confront another that he is not in some
special duty which must be weighed in contemplation of his actions
to which the other is party. The very fact that we are acknowledged
members of a single civilization imposes the traditional duties of

civility on each of us. We cannot invoke our pleasure as an ultimate sanction.

In addition, many are morally repelled at regarding justice as a social utility. As such, it is a poorly disguised form of "scapegoatism." Let's suppose that a community contains many people who are unhappy about the schools and that the cause of the unhappiness is in the board itself; but the board fires its superintendent. Often this makes the disgruntled gruntled; and, this makes it a social utility, but it is hardly justice. Now one may argue, this is the price we pay for free and democratic institutions, but we don't pay it equally. In fact, the "scapegoat" pays it all. This is neither democracy nor justice, or is it?

Not unrelated to this is the problem of sadism as a form of pleasure. In Marquis de Sade's story of Justine, a room full of men get extreme pleasure from the mutilation of a girl. Similarly, great numbers of persons in communities and indeed in nations have derived pleasure from the torment of others, smaller and correspondingly weaker. It can be argued that these aberrations did not arise from the principle of utility. But what in the principle of utility refutes them? Mill endeavored to answer this complaint, but in the effort to do so he appears to have rejected utility itself.

Finally, there is the commission by both Bentham and Mill of the *naturalistic fallacy* as identified and explained by G. E. Moore.[18] This fallacy is committed by anyone who accepts as *the good* any term which is *descriptive* and *nonevaluative*.

To understand how Mill committed the naturalistic fallacy we must recapitulate part of his argument. Happiness, Mill said, as used in the principle of utility is desirable as an end, and all other things are desirable as means to that end. Mill asserts that the only reason to know that anything is desirable is that people do desire it. Said he, "No reason can be given why the general happiness is desirable except that each person, so far as he believes it attainable, desires his own happiness."

To clarify this, Mill made the point that the only proof of an object's visibility is that people can *see it* and the only proof of a sound's audibility is that people can *hear it*, and therefore, the only proof that a thing is desirable is that people actually *desire it.*[19] The fallacy is this: Visible means able to be seen, but not good to be seen. Likewise, something audible is able to be heard but not good to be heard. Desired is, therefore, able to be desired but *not good to be desired.* The step taken by Mill which is authorized neither by reason nor evidence is that desired means "good." Said Moore, "The fallacy in this step is so obvious that it is wonderful how Mill failed to see it."[20]

Desirable is what it is good to desire. But Mill admitted that certain things desired may indeed be bad. Thus, the question of what ought to be desired cannot be answered by simply asking if it is desired. In classical terms Mill's doctrine consummates in tautology. Instead of the "desired is good" one can say that Mill's statement analyzes out to be the "desired is desired." The same applies to the question about happiness and pleasure so, "happiness is happiness" and "pleasure is pleasure." Accordingly, Mill has said no more than if he said the visible is visible and the audible is audible. Such statements, of course, are trivial. While exposition of the fallacy does not disprove the principle of utility it does demonstrate that, so far, it seems to have brought us only to the question of what we ought to desire; and this, after all, is where we started.

Deontological Ethics

The ethical standard devised by Immanuel Kant has been known by a variety of names, including transcendental, spiritual, and intuitional. The term deontology has nothing special to commend its preference above others except as it dramatizes Kant's decisive break from traditional metaphysics in his search for a highest good and his resolve to conceive a non-teleological ethical standard. Again, as in the case of Bentham, the historical circumstances under which the theory developed must be considered. Kant in his great *Critique of Pure Reason* did not deny the presence of spiritual things. He acknowledged that man could very well be in a world of absolutes, but he demonstrated that man, even through reason, has no way of knowing them as absolutes.

He called this unknowable the noumenal world and indicated that man is given only percepts of the noumenal. But these percepts are unintelligible or meaningless. As such they enter a concept-making faculty called mind. This faculty converts percepts into concepts, and man has only such a view of reality as his concepts yield. It must be emphasized that this view is limited by nature and type of concepts of which the mind is capable. These concepts, as such and only as such, are knowable and those things which are understood as concepts are called phenomena. Man does not know the noumenal, but through concepts he knows the phenomenal. Between noumenal and phenomenal stands the human mind. Its work converts one into the other.

In this way, for example, God comes out as a concept. Whatever God may be, He can be known only as a concept and man's understanding of his being is inevitably limited to the sorts of concepts which man produces. This development in his philosophy brought Kant both great fame and an abundance of personal trouble with both state and church. But of even greater relevance here is the expectation that Kant soon would establish a moral standard consistent with his *Critique.* This he attempted to do in a preliminary essay called *The Foundations of the Metaphysics of Morals.*[21] This was followed by a thorough exposition and analysis in the *Critique of Practical Reason.*

Though much of this was related in the chapter on European idealism, it is worth repeating here that Kant theorized that every man was endowed by a kind of moral intelligence. We could call it a sense of duty or obligation or simply a conscience. In addition to his concept-making capability man has a moral capability. There is no need to explain why man has it. He simply has it.

Now Kant's theory, unlike Bentham's, is non-teleological. That is to say, human action has no preferred destiny such as pleasure or happiness. Instead it is motivated by a good will and a good will is both means and end in moral transactions. Proceeding systematically, Kant eliminated all other possible definitions of the good, and after eliminating all other prospects he was required to conclude:

> Nothing in the world—indeed nothing beyond the world —can possibly be conceived which could be called good without qualification except a good will.[22]

Again, it must be noted that a good will is not good because of what it may accomplish. It is good "only because of its willing, that is it is good of itself."

Now this gave him something out of which to erect a moral standard. All other ethical standards prescribe what acts should be done. This one prescribes what should govern any act, namely, moral law. Thus, all action must be with respect to universal and unconditional lawfulness. The moral law which requires this universal and unconditional obedience is within each of us. Therefore, when Kant cites the first form of the imperative, "Act so the maxim of your will shall hold good as universal legislation,"[23] he is simply putting into language an imperative which in reality is our own moral sense.

So if a man decides to lie, he is deciding at the same time that his action can be universalized. This means that he is willing to say that under the circumstances of his lying, lying should be the rule and men should expect a lie and not the truth. As another example, suppose a man is standing before a counter in a store. All of the clerks are looking elsewhere and before him is a small object he very much wants but cannot afford. Now there is a law which provides he will be punished for stealing, but this is of no consequence because he is certain that he won't be seen taking it. In order to take it morally, he must be able to universalize his action. This means that he must will that all people who are standing before all of the counters of the world can take whatever they want and it would be good if they did. This, however, would not work. His will informs him that it is not good. He, therefore, knows the taking of the object in this way is immoral. Now he may still take the object but he knows he ought not to take it. The imperative does not stop commission of an immoral act; Kant never claimed this. However, it does inform the commissioner that his act was immoral.

Going further, let us suppose there stands before you a man who needs help, and let us suppose you decide not to help him. What moral law have you universalized? Kant would understand the maxim to be that you *shall not help a man who needs help.* This begins to sound unworkable, non-rational, and inhumane. It seems even more absurd when you come to realize that tomorrow you may need help, and yet you are legislating today that no one should help you or anyone else, even when help is needed. Thus, you need consult no ancient code or tribal sage. The moral standard is within you.

Kant's second formulation of the moral law which demands that you "act so that you treat humanity, whether in your own person or that of any other, always as an end and never as a means"[24] is essential to conceiving the good will as it presides over interpersonal relations. In this case, Kant asks us to consider our acts to which another is a party of interest, whether we are valuing that person intrinsically or for his own sake or whether we value him as instrumental to some other end. The good will demands that we regard every person as good-in-himself and not good-for-something or good-for-others.

Both expressions of the categorical imperative are of overriding importance to classroom teachers. The implications of both formulations are obvious. But in present times the second formulation speaks with special urgency. So often the students are seen as the means to a host of institutional, professional, and personal ends. Certainly many classroom teachers and school administrators would be horrified by a suggestion that their dispositions regarding students were immoral. Yet, if the Kantian standard becomes the basis of judgment we can be immoral without violating law, school policy, or conventions of community conduct. You become immoral when you see a child simply as a means to an orderly classroom, or as a means to favorable school publicity, or as a means to gratify some personal urgency of your own.

Kant's theory has had extensive influence on modern thought. At the level of theory there is little fault that can be found. Kant was such a painstaking analyst that even the modern positivist can find little wrong with his methods and fault him only on the form through which his standard is expressed. It is in the world of practical effects that Kant's theory encounters problems, and some of the problems are serious.

For one thing, Kant's ethics go no further than do Mill's in dealing with special duties. It is difficult to imagine that a traffic policeman directing traffic at a busy intersection regards each motorist as an end. Similarly, one cannot imagine an approaching motorist regarding the policeman as an end. In fact, too much of that sort of thing, and traffic would soon be snarled. To be sure, Kant did not have to think about traffic jams and the like, but even in his time there were cooks and carpenters, bakers and barristers, and soldiers and smiths. How does a physician look at a patient, a lawyer at a client, or a banker at a borrower? It is impossible for them to completely depersonalize such encounters. However, they are enjoined by the discipline of their profession from treating those who come to them as ends. Such thought may get in the way of their professional judgment. Kant's ethic does not give the man in a special role an acceptable standard. And, as indicated before, we spend most of our lives in these special roles.

Then there is the problem of conflict of duty. The classic instance of this is the case of eleven men in a lifeboat which, positively, can accommodate no more than ten. A decision is required and no compromise is possible. He who decides is obliged to look upon everyone, including himself, as an end. Does the Kantian standard help there? Someone aboard has got to become a means. How to decide? There is no way to accommodate conscience. Usually it is recommended that all draw straws (or whatever is available to organize a lottery). This leaves it to chance. Kant has given no guideline for a true moral dilemma.

There is also the problem of special need. Suppose the man at the counter in the case cited previously was in desperate need of the object and he was very poor. Now the first formulation of the imperative can take this form:

Whenever anyone is X he is to do Y.

Since the man at the counter is so poor and since his need is most urgent he may well universalize that any man who is as poor as I am and whose need of the object is as great as my need shall steal the needed object. This could very well be, and it is reasonable that the following maxim:

A *poor man, in great need, shall steal what he needs,*

shall be a moral law. But notice, the maxim uses valuated terms. How poor is poor? How great is great? So the universalizer must make a judgment about his resources and his need. This calls for guidelines which are not provided in the categorical imperative.

And this, of course, leaves the way open for the sly universalizer who uses the form:

Whenever anyone is X, he is to do Y,

and in every case of X he defines himself. That is, he makes a special case of himself and universalizes that anyone who is like him in most respects and who is in his circumstances shall do what it is that he does. Now one might argue that his moral intelligence is inoperative and his good will is, somehow, suppressed. And, indeed, this may be true. But everyone is familiar with the man who litters the highway or pushes in at the head of the line. He is convinced that his need or his circumstances are special; and, moreover, it seems that they are constantly so. How shall we deal with him? Kant gives us little help.

Instrumentalist Ethics

John Dewey offers a distinctly different notion of the good which serves as the underlying theory for his view of evaluation. The name commonly assigned to this theory is instrumentalism. In simple expression, instrumentalist ethics holds that when something is evaluated as good, it is evaluated as a means to some desired end. Said Dewey:

. . . the words "valuing" and evaluation are verbally employed to designate both prizing in the sense of holding precious, dear (and various other nearly equivalent activities like honoring, regarding highly), and appraising in the sense of putting a value upon, assigning a value to.[25]

Dewey insists that prizing and appraising are simply modes of valuing based upon a sensibility. For example, if we prize a precious stone we value it not only because we are sensible of the extensive means which were required to obtain it, but because it is a potential means to other ends which may come into view. If we are *appraising* an object we appraise it as a means to some end-in-view. Therefore, both prizing and appraising relate to means.

Traditional philosophy has suggested that prizing is of ends which have intrinsic value. That is, they are in themselves of worth. An example of this would be happiness. Other abstract nouns which might be prized for their own sake by traditional philosophy would be justice, truth, virtue, and so on. As such they are moral absolutes. However, Dewey insists that life is an ongoing *activity*, *without* absolutes or fixed rules of conduct, and these absolutes are nothing more or less than judgments formed when practical problems arise which demand solution. Thus, *justice* is the name we give to the solution of a problem.

Dewey implies that the separation of ends (as prized) and means (as appraised) which occurred in classical philosophy and was repeated in medieval or post enlightenment philosophy has led to confusion in ethical theory. His way of amending the difficulty is to root all valuation in activity of men in relation to ends they have *in view*. Thus, he would put a stop to the means-end style of thought which had enjoyed an unremitting vogue since the days of the Platonists. In its place he would substitute context. This "contextualism" suggests that moral judgments can be neither understood nor justified outside of the problematic contexts in which they arise.

Instrumentalism, therefore, takes its name from the point of distinction in the theory which holds that an object, person, or idea is good to the extent that it is instrumental to some end-in-view. Human interest and activity, being what they are, will always fix on some objective which will represent itself to consciousness as a problem. Once the problem is known all things are more or less instrumental to solving that problem. Turning to examples, water can be good or bad, depending on your problem. If you are very thirsty even a drop is valued; on the other hand, if your basement is flooded you are willing to call anything good that will help you get rid of the water and keep it away. Another kind of example to consider is that of a good horse.

Now what is a good horse? This depends on the problem. Do you want the horse to win a race? Do you want to ride him on a fox hunt? Do you want to ride him on a cattle drive? Do you want him to pull a plow? There are good horses for all four problems, but the horse which is good for one may not be good for the other three. Hence, the good horse is that horse which is instrumental to the end-in-view.

Now let's suppose that the end-in-view for which the horse was selected was simply to pull the plow. As this plowing proceeds the plowman gets an idea that the field would be more farmable if the slopes were terraced. To build the terraces he will need to erect stone retaining walls. Until he had that idea he cursed every stone his plow encountered, but now that he has a new problem he looks upon each stone in a new light. Instead of hoping not to see one, he is eager to see one. Moreover, he values stones with plane surfaces above those with irregular surfaces. Now as he nears the end of his wall-building and terracing another idea occurs to him. His field is more level and this makes it possible for him to use heavy machinery. Soon this is obtained, and now the horse is the problem. It must be fed and cared for; and, after all, it is a plow horse and he no longer plows with a horse. Once the horse was instrumental to his economic survival. He cared for it lovingly. He prized it and constantly appraised it in terms of his need and the horse's capabilities. Now his problem is to find a quick and inexpensive way to get rid of the horse and he looks appraisingly at all the instrumentalities which might serve that end.

According to Dewey, this is the way it goes. We proceed in life with a variety of ends-in-view, but we change them, adapt them, drop some, and add others. This goes on and on. Each man interacts with the opportunities, obligations, and irritations which fall upon him. He determines the ends he will seek when he defines his problems. While he is on the way to solving the variety of problems before him, new ones occur. He is never without problems. Life, to the instrumentalist, is an on-going struggle away from dissatisfaction and toward satisfaction. The distance between dissatisfaction and satisfaction is never fully consummated. Each approaching satisfaction contains within it the seeds of new dissatisfaction.

In sum, Dewey makes three simple points. The first[26] is that men do prize, desire, or value certain objects, acts, or situations. These are simply ends-in-view. The second is that ends-in-view stand as guides to behavior so that prized objects, acts, or situations can be realized. Ends-in-view, therefore, are what traditional philosophy has called means-to-ends. The third simply follows that propositions about such existential means-to-ends are "if-then" in nature and, being hypothetical, are as open to empirical examination as any object of legitimate scientific inquiry. In this way Dewey threw open the prospect that a science of morals can be developed and, ultimately, the hope that such a science could turn out useful knowledge upon which moral standards can stand.

This highly influential essay, *Theory of Valuation*, illuminates Dewey's other works. For example, how does a society decide what is good? In *A Common Faith* he declared, "There are forms in society which generate ideals."[27] In this he stands on grounds very similar to those taken by Mill, namely, that society itself will establish ends-in-view as guides to action. These, of course, will become the means to other socially conceived ends. On matters of taste the public again becomes the ultimate judge of the good. Dewey, as compared to Mill, has a greater faith in an undiluted democracy, but Dewey gave a much more vital role to pedagogy and the school. In the first sentence of his *Pedagogic Creed* he declares, "I believe that all education proceeds by the participation of the individual in the social consciousness of the race."[28] In the last paragraph of that same article he says:

> In sum, I believe that the individual who is to be edu-
> cated is a social individual, and that society is an organic
> union of individuals. If we eliminate the social factor from the
> child we are left with only an abstraction. . . .[29]

In the third article of the same work, that which deals with the subject matter of education, he stated, "Education must be conceived as a continuing reconstruction of experience. The process and the goal of education is one and the same thing." Thus, for Dewey means and ends tend to dissolve into one thing, namely, process. The process is product and the product is process. We are reminded again of Heraclitus' remark that "Man cannot step twice in the same river for other waters are ever flowing on to him."

Instrumentalism, unlike other naturalistic theories (e.g., utilitarianism), does provide for special duties. It is also positive in the sense that once a man or a group can say with certainty what it is that they are trying to do, then they have a basis for declaring what is good. In this respect the good is "good for." In addition, instrumentalism does offer a role to social science. Scientific valuation is a matter of identifying *what objectives* (ends-in-view) that people have and then measuring the effectiveness of activities and resources against the criterion of purpose.

However, there are certain objections. In taking the stand that man is preeminently social, Dewey, by implication, deprives him of his private and being-for-himself reality. He compels a social outlook on every aspect of general concern, and his declaration that a "child is only an abstraction when the social factor is eliminated" is unclear. It certainly can be argued that society itself is an abstraction without the individual persons who compose it. Socialization of classroom teaching may make personal distinctiveness more difficult to attain. This, in turn, may further encourage the "facelessness" and "personal lostness" which nowadays are so frequently condemned.

A second objection to Dewey's theory is its general dependence on epiphenomenalism or extreme materialism as a philosophy of mind.[30] In the fullness of time this may turn out to be a strength, but at the present time the opposing points of view regarding the status of mental events (mind-body dualism vs. materialism) are still, on both sides, matters of faith. An unqualified assertion that all mental events are first of all (and primarily) physical events or, more particularly, brain events is not yet warrantable on empirical grounds. There are still aspects of the mind which are unaccounted for, and the question, as of the present, stands open.[31]

Instrumentalism also draws objection from those who cannot rule out the possibility of valuing things-in-themselves as ends. For example, many persons enjoy the arts, beautiful scenery, friendships, and the like without conceiving them as means to other ends-in-view. Nor does their manner of achieving these situations necessarily affect the extent or nature of their valuation. One may, for example, love the city of Chicago. Long ago it may have taken weeks to get there, but now, with jet transport, it can be reached much more quickly and easily. Does one value Chicago differently as a consequence? It is easy to see how one could valuate the trip differently, but how about the city-in-itself?

Then there is an objection from others who cannot accept desire (of an end-in-view) as a basis for the good. Suppose someone desires to inflict pain upon an animal or another person? Now, in order to know if any of the instrumentalities proposed for this purpose are good we must ask if the desire is moral. In order to know anything at all about this we must invoke a standard from another ethical tradition. Why is it wrong for a man to beat his dog? If he feels better as a consequence or if his dog behaves in a manner more acceptable to society, then is the beating a good thing? In an opposite vein we might view all of the forms of human punishment. If no one really desires to punish criminals then is it bad to punish them? Desire, in Dewey's hands, remains somewhat ambiguous.

In this regard Dewey must answer to a rule which many philosophers call the autonomy of ethics. It is said to have originated with Hume,[32] but it has been reaffirmed in many ways since his time. It holds that no moral judgment can be deduced from a set of premises which does not in itself contain a moral judgment or principle. Dewey, like Mill, seems to challenge this rule in implying that moral judgments can arise from empirical observations. In other words Hume implies that no amount of "is's" can ever determine an "ought," and Dewey suggests here that an "is" when properly understood results in an "ought."

Finally, objection is raised against the suggestion that the satisfaction which can come from the resolution of inner conflict is good. We might believe, for example, that pragmatism can explain the source of inner conflicts, but we cannot believe that the resolution of these conflicts as a definition of human satisfaction is an uncontested good. If the biographers of Paul, Luther, Michelangelo, Kierkegaard, and numerous others are anything near being right, then we can appreciate the fact that they never found the satisfaction perhaps realized by more ordinary men. The beneficence of this to western man needs little elaboration here. On the other hand, Hitler evidently cited his anti-semitism as a way of reconciling the conflict he had between his sentiment and his reason. Thus, Hitler may have found the objective which would "link into an organized whole activities which are now partial and competing." This does not mean that instrumentalism in general, or Professor Dewey in particular, endorses or sanctions un-inhibited brutality. His expressions on record are quite literally to the contrary. But sufficient confusion exists about what satisfaction in all cases might mean that its endorsement as a basis for a theory of the good has not been general.[33]

Existentialist Ethics

It is becoming increasingly clear that existentialist ethics deserves inclusion as a category of ethical thought. Authorized by the deontology of Kant and strengthened by the phenomenological epistemology of Husserl, existentialist morality is highly distinctive. Indeed, it is sufficiently distinctive as to require special consideration by modern students of education.

Existentialism is concerned with *thatness*. An existentialist begins philosophizing on the grounds *that* he exists, *that* he is free, and *that* he is incomplete. This ontological state, however, provides in and of itself nothing from which values can be deduced. In fact, freedom to the existentialist is so complete that it enables him to believe in nothingness. To the existentialist, questions of morality must begin on the grounds of this freedom. On these grounds he can move in either one of two directions. One direction is nihilism and the other direction is belief.

Nihilism presupposes that there is no good or bad except that which man chooses. He endows the quality of goodness by his choice. However, any choice he makes does not bind him to the future. The only consistent good is the freedom to choose, and the absolute nihilist reserves to himself the right to reject even his own freedom, or his own life. It is important to note here that individual actions are right or wrong but no general ethical standard is correct. Nihilism assumes that life is meaningless and is meant to remain so. Efforts at meaning can result only in fraud or inauthenticity. Inner peace is a legitimate motive and can be achieved and maintained by a method of rejection or revolution.

Belief, on the other hand, does not resolve conflict or defeat absurdity, but it does satisfy the human tendency toward consistency and rationality. It can produce a hierarchy of values which, though never complete, and constantly subject to amendment, enables the believer to obtain some measure of personal meaning. Although absolute justification is not possible, elements of justification are. The modes can be as numerous as existentialist thinkers. There is no requirement of a system although semblances of systematic thought have appeared.

Kierkegaard, for example, took on a highly vivid religious belief. Standing on the grounds of his belief, he made resounding judgments about the Church of Denmark and its leadership. Camus, on the other hand, became a friend of rebellion and seemed on the way to building rebellion into a system. Marcel and Jaspers expressed belief in the existence of an authentic self which exists *in embryo*. They argued that it is hidden by inauthentic modes of being. When freed, the real self emerges; when submerged, it is experienced in appeals of conscience.[34] Sartre seems to have developed a psychoanalysis which when applied reveals each human life as having a mission or a fundamental project. By understanding and accepting this project a man can dispose of his inauthentic ways and reject instances of his own bad faith.

The authentic is good and the inauthentic is bad. No external or transcendent mode of justification can be accepted as a basis for knowing the good. The good is entirely personal. Each man's self occupies a seat of observation at the center of an existential world. He can think of his self as a selfhood if he is willing to accept it as primary and pre-existent or he can think of it as selfness if he thinks of it as an essence that is constantly being developed or emerging through choices made.

The existentialist literature of values is varied in forms. Some of it is in conventional philosophical discourse, but the drama and novel are more popular forms of existentialist expression. It is frequently maintained that certain of the existentialists achieve greater clarity and consistency through the literature of feeling than through conventional philosophic discourse. Certainly they have achieved greater influence. Marcel and Camus have been effective playwrights. Sartre has excelled in a variety of genre but his short stories are particularly well known. It is through the personalities of their fiction and through their own autobiographies that such writers have explored the implications of personal freedom and limited meaning through choice. Usually the heroes or heroines are in a process of discovering the falseness and hypocrisy of the institutions men have established to govern themselves. The tone of European existentialists tends to be pessimistic, while that of American existentialists tends to be more hopeful.

Existentialism as it appears in theories of curriculum deplores the imposition, by either overt or covert means, of fixed beliefs on the young. Absolutes are regarded as potential neuroses. By the same token existentialism deplores the denial of opportunities to believe. Existentialism as a mode of being can be developed as a method of education. As such it places a greater stress on *being* than on *doing*. In fact, it emphasizes doing only so far as it is an aspect of being.

Existentialism has played a bold bright spotlight upon all ethical theory. Its primary value seems to lie in criticism although some modern writers such as Kneller and Van Cleve Morris sense that it offers new vistas for educational methods and curriculum theory. It seems to present very little in the way of a social theory of the good because by its very nature it is against such theories as would deny the primary "thatness" of man's life, namely, that he is free and personally autonomous. Social theories, therefore, are simply "pacifiers" which divert a man temporarily from his own anguish (that of not comprehending his own meaning). Man is alone and unaided in the world. And the existentialist calls upon him to be brave, face it, and come to terms with his reality, however he can.

What all of this, placed on a general scale, might do to society or civilization no one can say. Certainly it calls for a political philosophy which maximizes personal freedom. In such an arrangement many of the institutions which now seem important would be eliminated. Some men would perhaps achieve greater fulfillment, but what of the others? Existentialism is not so much a philosophy as it is a denial of philosophy, particularly of those philosophies which assign realities to absolutes, processes, or society. Not only, therefore, does it deny philosophy, it is also a denial of man's historical experience as a collective being whose progress in the world has moved on theories of cooperation, interdependence, and general governance.

European writers who have lived through the tragedy of a world war followed by hope, by a depression, and then by an even more ruinous war have been more forthright in denouncing the whole of the institutional order than have their American counterparts who have been more inclined to depict individual persons who have been trapped in an inauthentic life, and by implication express the hope that such does not become the fate of all.

No one knows what would happen if the existentialist standard would become general. It is possible to assume, however, that our economic and technological progress which is so highly dependent on the existence of a populace willing to bend to their requirements would soon stop. People would tend to be more respectful of personal freedoms, but much of the material abundance which, it is charged, accumulated because some men successfully exploited natural resources and successfully exploited other men will be lost. Are men, particularly American men, willing to adopt a standard which proffers these alternatives?

The Ethics of Civil Formalism[35]

It is conceived that a standard of ethics emerges within a civilization. By such a standard the good is identified by tradition itself. Civil traditions, however, are never static. They are constantly ministered to by the dynamics of human enterprise. Thus, a civil tradition requires constant interpretation. No one can doubt that institutions, and the conventions by which we know them, change. This is because of changes in the sentiments and forms progenitory to the institution. The model of civil formalism, therefore, is somewhat cyclical. Institutions, through their conventions, work upon people; people revise their sentiments and through various rational processes amend the civil forms. The amended forms bring forth amendments in institutions. This, of course, results in altered conventions.

The good is formal, but unlike Platonic forms civil forms change. The source of such forms is not external to the human world as in Plato. Instead, they are produced by man himself. The source, the raw material out of which forms are fashioned, is the active sentiments men direct to the objects, ideas, acts, and relationships of the world by which they are surrounded, and these sentiments are shaped into forms by reason.

The good, therefore, is formal, and the changing forms can represent development or decadence in the civil sense. That is, if the forms are such that they provide increased perspective and increased meanings to the objects, acts, or relationships formalized, then civil development is enhanced. If the forms represent increased immediacy and increased sensuality, then civil decadence obtains. The institutional order takes the direction of the forms.

Likewise the good takes direction from the forms. This, of course, is analytically absurd. How can there be a decadent good? There can be a decadent good simply because a man can say, "I attended a lynching last night, and it was good." Not only can a man say that, but, as the world knows all too well, he can say it and he can be *saying it in truth*. So long as philosophers are unwilling to allow the good, as such, to become the property of those who use the term in conventional reference, so long as some of them tend to cling to the notion that it has an ultimate condition, one cannot deal with it in a context of application.

One may hear with perfect understanding the utterance, "He had a good beating," or "a good dose of heroin." Good is simply a grading word[36] and relates to the extent to which the thing graded approximates the form which stands as paradigmatic in the thought of the speaker. Thus, we must look beyond the word "good" for moral propositions. Depending on the form upon which the grade is based, "good" can be regarded as developmental or decadental. The debate centers upon the style of forms which offer the most to human life.

Now it certainly can be expected that one who has developed such a meta-ethical model will, upon taking a normative position, favor forms which tend to reflectiveness, perspective, and meaning. This is probably because one attracted to meta-ethical concerns is possessed of these propensities. However, this does not give his good ultimate sanction.

Nevertheless, there is one reason, grounded in metaphysics, which at least tends to establish that the reflective forms are more beneficial. Beginning with the ontological state of man as depicted in existentialist theory, one can assert that the anguish and ambiguity of "freedom" entitle man to seek the greatest return possible from human experience. If experience is understood, appreciated, and given meaning through forms, then, surely, the forms which offer both sense and meaning are of greater benefit than those forms which are of sensual phenomena with very limited meaning. In other words, existential man does not have to choose between a life of sense and life of mind. He can, through belief, associate his being with forms which do both. Sense and mind are not mutually exclusive. Therefore, a life which includes rich experience in both is to be preferred.

This, however, is a contradiction of a position taken by certain leading existentialist writers[37] that moral standards cannot be deduced from man's ontological status. However, one does not need to depend on a single philosophical tradition in building a normative standard. Men are free to believe; and they, indeed, do believe. This, then, entitles them to philosophize about the prospects a life-in-belief holds open to them.

How satisfactory a standard is this civil formalism? How does it fare when confronted with the objections raised against others?

Civil formalism does provide for special duties. We are entitled to formalize a conception of an ideal classroom teacher, an ideal school administrator, an ideal student council president. The same, of course, is true of soldiers, priests, jurists, housewives, legislators, and welders. Behind each of these tasks there can be, and there usually is, a formal conception of its rendering. We can rationalize an "excellent" form and believe in it. Although these forms may be as impossible of incarnation as the Platonic archetypes, they represent our standard of "the good" in each case. Therefore, as to special duties, civil formalism offers something which is not offered by utilitarianism or the deontology of Kant.

Civil formalism requires that desire be worked upon by reason. An end-in-view must be rational and formal. Thus, it loses one of the strengths of instrumentalism, but, at the same time, it avoids one of the primary weaknesses. Specifically, it moves the good from the domain of means alone and allows a standing form of excellence to exist apart from what a man thinks he is doing at any given time. In addition, it does not engage the ambiguity of satisfaction. Man, of course, is never satisfied, but in this kind of formalism his dissatisfaction is logical and not psychological. Finally, it depicts man as real and forms as abstract. Dewey's social theory assigned society to a much greater level of reality and made some of man's reality contingent on society. In formalism, society remains an abstraction.

Civil formalism has all of the weakness of a relativistic and intuitionist theory. It relies heavily on phenomenology and makes no pretension of universality. People of differing civilizations are entitled to formalize in different ways. This brings on a host of practical problems. Civilized groups intermingle and conflict results because of the preeminent commitment to different forms. But surely the presence of such dangerous eventualities can itself progenerate sentiment and reason such that forms of tolerance, communication, and governance will emerge, particularly if the civil and not the barbaric forms are in ascendancy.

The question inevitably arises as to how civil formalism can prevent the morally repugnant. How, it can be asked, would such a standard of value making rule out, say, a Hitler. There appears to be no meta-ethical principle which, alone and unaided, rules out a moral repugnancy. No, not even Kant. Camus demonstrated the futility of universalizing in *The Fall* when Clamence pointed out that the general rule that a man does not make love to the wife of a friend did not concern him because the moment he became interested in a woman her husband ceased to be his friend.

However, civil formalism which functions in and for a political system which maximizes individual freedom and which regards the rights of persons as the ultimate sanction, coupled with a program of general education which features a curriculum rationale stressing internal commitment to reflective forms, would give this particular standard the assistance needed. With this standard and with the appropriate political and educational support, a normative system would be developed by the people through their interaction with the institutional order.

This is not a philosophy guaranteed to remove pain, injustice, and hatred. But it does guarantee that these forms will be contemplated as forms and will not be defined as utilities or operations;

nor will there be a tendency toward contemplation of a contextual justification.

How can that which begins in subjectivity end in objectivity? How can that which begins in existentialism end in formalism? First, it must be remembered that existentialism, formalism, rationalism, and the like are simply "tags" or, if you will, "handles" or "harnesses" which students of philosophy have put on traditions which came into existence as products of their own scholarship. Such "tags" do not restrict philosophy from building with assortments any more than the names of substances restrict architecture from composing structures of different materials. One may design a structure of marble, glass, mortar, and iron. But seldom is a suitable structure found which is all marble, all glass, and so on. The question is what goes together in a coherent system.

In this conception of civil formalism existentialism is preeminent, but the existentialist may choose to be part of civilized order. The fact that he has chosen to accept civility and orderliness means that he has chosen to deal with forms. But if he wishes to acquire meaning he will, himself, become religious about some of the forms. It can be summarized by the sentence: *He is free to choose that which will thenceforward enslave him.* Thus, his anguish of freedom is terminated in subjectivity, and, perhaps, another form of anguish supplants it. If inauthenticity, bad faith, and the subversion of his real self are troublesome, it is to be remembered that he is what he has chosen, and he is free to choose again. Choice in a civilization of forms is no less free than in any other, but the consequences of choice seem more evident and more decisive, which makes the choice itself less ambiguous.

Thus, this proposed standard contains elements which are derived from traditions which carry labels such as existentialism, formalism, personalism, subjectivism, and so on. Its merits do not rest upon its unity with a single established tradition. Rather, they rest upon the extent to which they describe the way humans in a civilized order work upon the interval called life to make it into a thing of meaning and of worth. Its purpose, in a time when long-standing religious forms are losing strength, is to establish a basis for fuller meaning and greater worth through education.

Notes

1. Paul W. Taylor, *The Moral Judgment* (Englewood Cliffs, New Jersey: Prentice-Hall, Inc., 1963), p. XII.

2. Thomas Aquinas, *On the Truth of the Catholic Faith (Summa Contra Gentiles)* (Doubleday & Company. Image Book Ed., 1955), Book I.
3. Aristotle, *Nicomachean Ethics.* See Book X.
4. Taylor, *op. cit.,* p. XIV.
5. Aristotle, *op. cit.*
6. Diogenes Laertius, *Lives and Opinions of the Eminent Philosophers.*
7. Aristotle, *op. cit.*
8. Will Durant, *The Life of Greece* (New York: Simon and Schuster, 1939), p. 648.
9. Jeremy Bentham, *An Introduction to the Principles of Morals and Legislation,* included in Edwin Burtt, *The English Philosophers from Bacon to Mill,* (New York: Random House, Inc., 1939), p. 792.
10. *Ibid.*
11. *Ibid.,* ch. III.
12. *Ibid.,* ch. IV.
13. *Ibid.*
14. *Ibid.*
15. *Ibid.*
16. John Stuart Mill, *Utilitarianism,* included in Albert Levi, ed., *The Six Great Humanistic Essays of John Stuart Mill,* (New York: Washington Square Press, Inc., 1963), p. 252.
17. *Ibid.*
18. G. E. Moore, *Principia Ethica* (Cambridge University Press, 1903), included in part in Paul Taylor *The Moral Judgment* (Englewood Cliffs, New Jersey: Prentice-Hall, Inc., 1963), pp. 5-21.
19. *Ibid.,* p. 21.
20. *Ibid.*
21. Emmanuel Kant, *The Foundations of the Metaphysics of Morals* (New York: Liberal Arts Press, 1959).
22. *Ibid.*
23. *Ibid.,* p. 9.
24. *Ibid.,* p. 10.
25. John Dewey, *Theory of Valuation* (International Encyclopedia of Unified Science II, No. 4).
26. *Ibid.*
27. John Dewey, *A Common Faith* (New Haven: Yale University Press, 1934), p. 51.
28. John Dewey, *My Pedagogic Creed,* Article I.
29. *Ibid.*
30. See Chapter XI, *Mind and The Phenomenological Method.*
31. John Dewey, *The Quest For Certainty* (London): George Allen and Unwin, 1930), p. 225.
32. Hume, *A Treatise of Human Nature,* L. A. Selby-Bigge, ed. (Oxford: Oxford University Press, 1960), p. 469.
33. Brand Blanchard in *Reason and Goodness,* as part of a critique of Dewey's *Theory of Valuation,* pointed out that Hitler in Chapter II of *Mein Kampf* resolved an inner dilemma in just this way. Quote is from Dewey, *Human Nature and Conduct,* p. 229.

34. Patricia F. Sanborn, *Existentialism* (New York: Western Publishing Co., Inc., 1968), p. 109.
35. See Chapter XIII for a fuller exposition of a civilization of forms.
36. J. O. Urmson, "On Grading," *Mind*, LIX, No. 234 (1950), 145-169.
37. Jean-Paul Sartre, *Being and Nothingness*, tr. Hazel E. Barnes (New York: Philosophical Library, 1956), p. 625.

Other Reading

Aiken, Henry D. *Reason and Conduct: New Bearings in Moral Philosophy.* New York: Alfred A. Knopf, Inc., 1962.
Bentham, Jeremy. *An Introduction to the Principles of Morals and Legislation.* New York: Doubleday & Company, Inc., 1961.
Braithwaite, R. B. "Critical Notice of *The Language of Morals*," *Mind, LXIII* (April 1954), pp. 249-262.
Butler, Joseph. *Five Sermons.* New York: Liberal Arts Press, 1950, pp. 1-65.
Chandler, Robert W. "A Revised Conception of Ethical Analysis," *Journal of Philosophy*, XLIII (August 5, 1954), pp. 464-474.
Dewey, John. "Theory of Valuation," *International Encyclopedia of Unified Science* II, No. 4. Chicago: University of Chicago Press, 1939.
Ewing, A. C. *The Definition of Good.* New York: The Macmillan Company, 1947.
Flew, Antony. "On Not Deriving 'Ought' From 'Is,'" *Analysis*, XXV (December 1964), pp. 25-32.
Frankena, William K. *Ethics.* Englewood Cliffs, N.J.: Prentice-Hall, Inc., 1963.
Gewith, Alan. "Meta-Ethics and Normative Ethics," *Mind, LXIX* (April 1960), pp. 187-205.
Hancock, Roger. "A Note on Hare's *The Language of Morals*," *Philosophical Quarterly*, XIII (January 1963), pp. 56-63.
Hare, R. M. *The Language of Morals.* Oxford: Oxford University Press, 1952. Chapters V-IX.
Kerner, George C. *The Revolution in Ethical Theory.* Oxford: Oxford University Press, 1966.
_____. *Logic and Language of Education.* New York: John Wiley & Sons, Inc., 1966.
Mill, John S. *Utilitarianism.* In Albert Levis ed. *The Six Great Humanistic Essays of John Stewart Mill.* New York: Washington Square Press, Inc., 1963.
Moore, G. E. *Principia Ethica.* Cambridge, England: The Cambridge University Press, 1903. Chapters I-III.
Nowell-Smith, P. H. *Ethics.* Baltimore, Md.: Penguin Books, Inc., 1969. Parts II, III.
Perry, Ralph B. *Realms of Value.* Cambridge, Mass.: Harvard University Press, 1954.
Peters, R. S. *Education and Ethics.* Atlanta: Scott, Foresman & Company, 1967.

Phenix, Philip. *Education and The Common Good.* New York: Harper and Brothers, 1961. Parts II, III.

Ross, D. *The Right and the Good.* Oxford: Oxford University Press, 1955. Chapters I-III.

Scarrow, David S. "Hare's Account of Moral Reasoning," *Ethics,* LXXVI (January 1966), pp. 137-141.

Stevenson, C. *Ethics and Language.* New Haven: Yale University Press, 1963. Chapters I, II.

Taylor, S. E. *The Moral Judgment: Readings in Contemporary Meta-Ethics.* Englewood Cliffs, N.J.: Prentice-Hall, Inc., 1963. Parts I-V.

Toulmin, S. E. *An Examination of the Place of Reason in Ethics.* Cambridge, England: Cambridge University Press, 1950. Chapter II.

Urmson, J. O. "On Grading," *Mind,* LIX No. 234 (1950), pp. 145-169.

Westermark, E. A. *Ethical Relativity.* London: Routledge and Kegan Paul, Ltd., 1932. Chapters III-V.

Zink, S. *The Concept of Ethics.* New York: St. Martin's Press, Inc., 1962.

Applications of Meta-Ethical Theory in Education

Gertenbach, Donald. *An Analysis of the Discourse of Justification of Educational Decision Makers.* A dissertation in education. Bethlehem, Pa.: Lehigh University, School of Education, 1970.

Leight, Robert L. *Application of Meta-Ethical Theory and Technique to Discourse on an Educational Value Problem.* A dissertation in education. Bethlehem, Pa.: Lehigh University, School of Education, 1966.

CHAPTER XV

Religiousness in a Civilization of Forms

Histories which describe the formative eras of American civilization quite rightly depict the religious nature of the early American as churchly. The neustic force of churchness in the common usage of the word religion was, in those times, so compelling the authors of the *Bill of Rights* proclaimed in the first phrase of the first amendment, "Congress shall make no law respecting the establishment of a religion." These words and their obvious intent (that government may not establish a church) have created much irony and greatly confused our contemporary efforts to understand the essential nature of education. The historical consequence of this association is such that the word religious and its cognates are withheld from our conceptions of secular education.

The Ambiguity of the Word Religion

Writing in the tenth book of his general treatise called *The City of God*,[1] St. Augustine gives a convincing account of the difficulties both the Greeks and the Latins had with the words cult, religion, service, worship, and piety. He said the word religion "... might seem to express more definitely the worship due to God alone .... Yet, as not only the uneducated, but also the best instructed, use the word to express human ties, and relationships, and affinities it would inevitably produce ambiguity to use the word religion in discussing the worship of God. ..." We, in America, for three centuries have used the word in this way; and, as a consequence, the American people, and especially their courts and their educators, bear this burden of ambiguity which Augustine prophesied.

The ambiguity of the word religion seems to account for three fictions which confuse the thought of the American public about edu-

cation in general and the public schools in particular. The three fictions
are:

1. *Education is one thing and religion is another.*
2. *Quality education can be devoid of religious content.*
3. *Education as now offered in American public schools is devoid of religious content.*

These three fictions are of concern in the issues of religiousness
at the level of meta-religion.[2] There is also a fourth fiction: It is that
certain values strongly evident in American civilization can survive
current interpretations of the separation of church and state. Because
discourse on this opinion would perforce include issues in normative
religion it is not presented here.[3]

The *first* of the three *fictions* appears to be mainly the consequence of a language tradition, and this particular tradition is a circumstance of American history. Culture can blind men to certain
realities. In this case the cultural "press" is so strong that even a determined meta-religionist feels a pause when simply noting that religion is much more than something that goes on in churches and
synagogues, let alone going even further to suggest that the major religious aspects of American civilization are now apart from nominally
religious institutions. The American citizen is no less spiritual than he
ever was. But the things he now cares about most of all are different
from those matters which characterized the spirituality of his forebears. It is not the task of meta-religion to recognize this as good or
bad but simply to recognize it.

Unless one is content with only a severely restricted meaning for
the word education, it would be absurd to argue that education is one
thing and the things a person cares most about or feels deeply about
are something else. Learning involves caring and caring involves learning. To learn anything one's attention must be drawn to it by an
affective interest. The greater the caring, the better the learning.
Things not cared about in any way are soon forgotten. This is not
simply an aphoristic argument. The religious side of man is inexorably
related to his educational development. This has been amply demonstrated in both the empirical and rational philosophical systems, and
the modern philosophical traditions of pragmatism and existentialism
are, if anything, more positive in this regard. Thus, the common
parlance (for that is what it is and nothing more) that education is one
thing and religion is another is a fiction.

In regard to the *second fiction* which suggests that quality education can be devoid of religious content, it is well to consider as an example Alfred N. Whitehead's definition of education. Said he:

> We can be content with no less than the old summary of educational ideal which has been current at any time from the dawn of our civilization. The essence of education is that it be religious.
> Pray, what is a religious education?
> A religious education is an education which inculcates duty and reverence. Duty arises from our potential control over the course of events. Where attainable knowledge could have changed the issue, ignorance has the guilt of vice. And the foundation of reverence is this perception, that the present holds within itself the complete sum of existence, backwards and forwards, that whole amplitude of time which is eternity.[4]

"Pray, what is a religious education?" Whitehead precedes the question by saying that "the essence of education *is that it be religious.*" He follows his question with an answer which contains none of the notions about religious education which dominate American thought on the same matter.

Whitehead speaks of duty and of reverence, but it is neither the duty to nor the reverence of the God of our conventional reference. Neither is it duty to or reverence of an established mode of institution of worship. Whitehead recognizes that men can control events. Man is not helplessly adrift. He has navigational powers. This being the case, *duty* falls upon him, and his responsibility is one of informed action. *Reverence* comes from recognizing that when one looks at the present he is observing a process, and the process carries in itself all that has been and all that will be.

This, as it turns out, is a modern religious position. Man is responsible because he has a certain control over events. His life is not fated. One can feel very deeply about the *duty* this imposes and at the same time *revere* the process which brought the world to its present and will take it on into its future. This is simply an example of how a clear-thinking philosopher defines quality education. Whitehead readers constantly rejoice in his habit of offering a polemical sentence which makes his reasoning even more clear. In the same essay, almost as if in anticipation of the plenary statement quoted above, he said, "A merely well informed man is the most useless bore on God's earth."[5]

Quality education involves caring deeply. Or, to put it in other words, it involves internal commitment. Now this does not mean zealousness alone. One does not like to think that Adolph Hitler and his circle were recipients of quality education simply because they cared deeply enough about a social ideology to undertake mass murder in its behalf. Indeed, such repugnant episodes in the history of man's effort to civilize himself do involve committed men. So there must be something more edifying in quality education than just its capacity to develop commitment.

But there must be commitment. Life must have meaning and there is no source for meaning other than commitment. A man devoid of a sovereign intention has no basis to organize his own life. There must be something he feels should be done, something he cares about, something which he is willing to give himself to. It is this "giveness" of himself which acts against the absurd. If he emerges from his education without a tendency to care, he is a bore both to himself and to others no matter how well informed he may be on sundry matters of the present and the past.

This commitment can arise in a number of ways. And it is of relevance and interest to note that variant types of schools seem able to build it. How can this be? What is it that these variant schools have in common? It cannot be method, nor can it be purpose. By deduction it is apparent that they have school activities which build commitment and which are under the direction of teachers who inspire commitment.

The religious content in any education of quality is that which inspires *duty* and inculcates *reverence*. This may be done in a variety of ways, including those ways in which churches have done it. *But it must be done.*

The *third fiction* offered here for examination is that education as now offered in American public schools is devoid of religious content. Again, resorting to common parlance, a religious experience is a "moving experience." A perfunctory experience cannot be religious no matter what its subject matter is or where it occurs. A church service which bores an adolescent boy is not a religious experience. A school experience which inspires him is a religious experience. The difference between the two is that the latter touches and moves the boundary of his personal being and the former does not.

We do not necessarily have to turn aside from life to have such boundary experiences. Life is full of them. Life offers them almost everywhere, but in some schools and in many churches the adult generation conspires to bore the younger generation into states of near desperation. It is commonly noted that children and youth seek excitement. *But this is simply a yearning for a moving experience.* The urban boy who does not find it in school may very well find it in the streets. The suburban boy who does not find it in school may find it in drugs.

However, we can be thankful in these times that some schools do provide religious experiences. Drama, athletics, art, music, and the experience of learning through a gifted and beloved teacher can be what is needed. Many public schools do this and do it very well. The irony is that the small schools, and the large schools organized in small units, apparently do it better than the large "educational factories" with top-down management. Many students in such places have, in recent years, been in revolt. The revolution is, to them, meaningful and moving. It throws them into a commitment. It is not a commitment which seems wholesome to many adults, and in the end it may bring on grief and travail, but it is better than the nothing that all too many such schools offer to their students. Make no mistake, a vigorous student rebellion is as much a religious experience as any of the participants are likely to have in education.

The Anatomy of a Value

Critics of American education are frequently heard to say that our schools do not teach values. An alternative expression of this, which is often heard, is that young people do not have *a sense of values.* Neither of these things is true. What these observers mean is that schools do not inculcate the attitudes of the older generation, and the attitudes which students seem to have are not those of which many adults approve. Some adults say religion is the answer, and they are right. But what they fail to recognize is that religion is already present.

One who sets about to look intently at the question of values could reasonably begin by asking: What kinds of values are there? This, of course, calls immediately for taxonomy development. One might start by naming health values, civic values, vocational values, moral values, democratic values, etc., etc. A list of ten or twelve "affective realms" of this kind would soon be assembled. But such a list is simply a conglomeration of forms. Forms are not values. They are things valued. Rather than being value in itself each of these forms is something of which value is. One may value his health but this is not the same thing as saying health is a value. One may value democracy, but this does not imply that democracy itself is value. Chicago may be a windy city, but this does not mean Chicago is wind. Puerto Rico may be called a sunny island without suggesting that Puerto Rico is part of the sun.

The wind pervades Chicago and the sun illuminates the Carribean in the way a man will pervade or illuminate an idea such as health, democracy, scholarship, family, nation, etc., with value. What is to be done therefore, is to induce each student to *envalue* moral form. A moral form in and of itself *does not* contain value any more than Chicago in and of itself contains wind. Wind is given to Chicago to make it the windy city. Sun is given to Puerto Rico to make it an island of sunshine. Similarly, a man gives value, say, to democracy, and thereby it becomes a democratic value. It is a believed form.

This is a subtle point, but one which must be grasped if there is to be understanding of the anatomy of a value. To be valued an object, idea, process, or person must first be "prized." This act of prizing is that of becoming religious. It is at this point that religiousness as an educational end must be understood. The experience which moves a student to prize something must be at a religious and not at an academic level. Academic experiences cultivate attitudes; academic experiences do not cultivate religiousness. But the two go together in valuation.

Indeed, the anatomy of a value includes two aspects. The external aspect we call an attitude; the internal part we can call a religion. These two aspects of value have the same dynamic relationship as the interior of an egg to its shell. We know, however, that you can put a pin-sized hole in the shell and the contents will drain out. What remains looks like an egg, but it is not. Similarly, you can cultivate a mere attitude which looks like a value, but it is not a value because the religious content is simply not within it.

One can have attitudes toward conventional forms called friendship, justice, and honesty which appear admirable. But he can have these attitudes and not be a friend, not be just, and not be honest. Attitude alone is simply a shell. Alone, it does not constitute a value. Religion is the indispensable inner aspect of valuation.

When rigorously considered, all valuation is found to have religious aspect. There can be no such thing as a non-religious value. If one values health then there is a religiousness within his health attitude. If one values democracy there is religiousness within his attitude toward democracy. In fact, any notion of a non-religious value is nonsense. A value *per se* is not an ostensible nor a formal quality. It is heuristic; that is, it is a quality of experience-in-belief. Something becomes valued by force of a person's act of believing, prizing, or finding it of worth. Properly speaking, all values are religious, and the term religious values is really a redundancy.

The Value Hierarchy

We care more about some things than others. The more strongly one values an object or idea the greater his religious sensibility of it. Put in other words, some of my values I am only mildly religious about. Other values, as we move along the scale, increase in the religiousness until we approach those I am deeply religious about. Finally, we will come to the sovereign religious value which *may* be the Judeo-Christian God and the theological ethics revealed by the literatures of Biblical antiquity. But then again, the sovereign value *may not be that*, and in the case of many Americans it is not that, even though most of them still attend churches and tell themselves (and each other) that it is.

Indeed the religion in the life of most Americans at any given time may be a successful profession or business, college diploma, professional license, healthy body, rewarding talent, and so on. No one can watch such persons in action and question that they are devout. From time to time a man may change his religion. Some do believe in God and are religious in the traditional way. Some accept emanational ideas of God which interpret God as existing, but indifferent to men, and as men they are indifferent to God. So even though they do believe in the existence of God they don't care one way or another and are religious about other things.

We are indebted to William James for reporting to us the ancient story of an old woman who, in speaking of cosmic reality, asserted that our world rests on a large rock and is thereby prevented from falling into emptiness. When pressed to explain what the rock is supported by she indicated this support to be another rock, "a bigger one." When further plied with questions along this same line she declared, "Well, it is rocks all the way down!"[6]

This figure has two merits. The first is that it helps envision our existence. We are thrust into it, aware. Our awareness is unsupported by anything of certitude. We don't know why we exist or what existence means, and the painful part of this is that we are aware that we don't know. When an existentialist suggests that this situation is meaningless or absurd he is sort of imagining himself as a man with his two feet dangling in midair and a great yearning to ground them upon something in order that he can overcome what to him is a patently ridiculous situation. So he "intuits" rocks and puts his feet down upon them. The act of intuiting is the act of experiencing religious ideas (or phenomena). The act of putting rocks under his feet is analogous to *believing*. There is not a single rock. By the time a man is mature he stands on a pile of rocks. *These are his values,* and they keep him from being suspended in mid-air, without personal meaning. So long as he has these to stand upon, he is not absurd.

Let us say then that my religious nature is a pile of rocks that goes all the way down to a bottom rock. And let us say all of those rocks are values; therefore they are religious commitments. They are religious because I hold them in belief. Now the second merit in this metaphor of a "world on the rocks" is that it depicts *that bottom rock* (that sovereign religious value) in such a way as to show the dynamic it contributes to all above. The shape and the size of the bottom rock imparts inclination, organization, and sway to all above.

This envisions the value hierarchy as having a one-way dynamic, from bottom to top. The metaphor cannot be pressed too far, but we can use it to conceive that our more basic values alter the less basic, and when a value at or near the base is destroyed chaos results for a time. Anyone who lives in an academic environment has seen this occur when clever young professors make use of their academic forum to conduct a general assault on the value hierarchies of freshmen. One supposes that the theory behind creating disarray in the personal values of young scholars is that it sets the young men free to form something better. But do they?

Moving away from metaphors, a religious education is the acquisition and organization of the sentiments by which a man formulates his personal meaning and determines his personal choices. Note that more is involved than simply the acquisition of beliefs. Organization is also involved. This means the development of the sovereign values which in turn works its own amendments upon all of the others. You can picture it in a variety of ways, even write it in mathematical sentences, but a man's religious nature has only one way of appearing in the world of action. We know a man's values by examining the choices he has made.

Religious education is the acquisition and organization of the personal sentiments which govern our choices. It seems that in some remote part of our conscious reflection we have always sensed that this is the central mission of "quality education." A quality education produces powerful sentiments, and as Whitehead rightly insists, the essence of this is religious, and he rightly calls it by this word.

Quality in Education

What quality in education is, is a perennial question. The American passion for quality is in itself a religious quest. One cannot say that our notions about what this is are any clearer than in former times. But some bold suggestions have been offered. For example, some now suggest that not only does a quality education give Johnny a meaning for friendship; it also makes him a good friend. Not only does it teach him justice; it also makes him a just man. Indeed, it is one thing to teach a boy a meaning for honesty and quite another thing again to develop him to be an honest man. This can result only if his orientation toward honesty is in the nature of a religious commitment to be an honest man.

Recalling that the anatomy of value has two aspects—attitude and religiousness—it can be shown that one can have an attitude toward friendship, justice, and honesty which in the eyes of his civilization appears admirable. He holds a paradigm for each of these things which is articulated smoothly in his conversation. But when the test of commitment is applied it is found that he is incapable of incarnating his paradigm of friendship, he will not sacrifice anything of himself in behalf of his model of justice, nor would he be honest in the way he knows how when strongly tempted.

The exterior of value is attitude; but the interior, that which makes it a value, is religiousness. Therefore, one important distinction which characterizes that which we call quality in education is that a quality education goes beyond attitude and develops the religiousness which valuation requires. What sort of pedagogy produces religiousness? The sage who proclaimed that the British empire was formed on the playing fields of Eton had a point. Religiousness develops in experience. Experience in this instance is overt and intense, not covert and detached.

If religiousness develops in the heat of experience, then a personalized and activity-centered humanities education should be prominent in elementary school classrooms. The humanities curriculum appropriate for this style of education at early school levels is that which generates vivid internal experiences. A humanistic experience which does not excite the student fails in its educative mission. The phenomena it renders into the child's life world must be such that the child's experience of it afflicts his pattern of intentionality. The core of such education might include poetry, drama, games, art, dance, music, and other forms of literature. But it should be *experience* and not analysis. Analysis is an experience in itself. The child can get that later. With appropriate modifications, this curriculum would extend into secondary education with continuing intensity but increasing sophistication. This is not religious subject matter. It is a humane pedagogy designed to develop religiousness. It is anticipated that as a consequence a strong religious nature will start to develop within each person.

Nor should we rule out, as have our courts, our conventional and commonly understood religious experience. It may add to our understanding if, for just a moment, we examine the church simply as a teacher of religiousness. The church as a teacher of religiousness does not proceed by direct narration or formal analysis. It does not communicate through the syntax of ordinary speech. Ordinary conversation, appropriate as it is for communication, does not develop religious sentiments. Instead the church relies on prayer, poeticized maxims, hymns, chants, physical gestures, symbolized rituals, and in some cases special sound effects and exotic smells. Byzantine chapels are treasure houses; Quaker meeting houses manifest rigorous simplicity. Both are spectacular in their own way, and each is designed to produce special effects in the religious learner. The church itself, therefore, has learned much about the development of religiousness. Its modern problems should not lead us to overlook its pedagogical capabilities which have been developed across centuries of successful teaching.

The academic world is not without its sentiment-building occasions. The university convocations are conducted in accordance with pristine conventions of the academic world. When done propitiously and gracefully they can be very moving. A convocation is not simply a group of professors observing or acknowledging the ties they have with their heritage. It is an affirmation or reaffirmation by the internal person of his commitment to the forms with which the academic profession has long been associated. The religiousness by which these forms are embraced needs occasional reinforcing or rebonding. Occasions of sentiment do that. No matter how much the empirical man may wish to disparage or discount such occasions of general sentiment, that inner monitor (to paraphrase James) informs him—"bosh." It does mean something important to him, and he knows it does.

Emendating the Religious Experience

Much of the American academic world, ably assisted by American jurisprudence, has fostered an illusion that men can be religiously neutral. The vast majority of the American public is imagined as pacific while heretics storm on the fringes. Each year the fringe elements, composed largely of people whose feet seem to be in mid-air, appeal to increasingly larger segments of the young. People in fringe elements, vexed by their own personal needs, seem to draw such satisfaction as life offers them by mutilating the forms of the civilization which supports them. However, in the frenzy of his own problems the man of the fringe offers the kind of religious experience which the established institutional world now withholds. This poses an issue for those who sense in their own nature a duty to communicate more effectively to the young the forms of contemporary civilization. It can only mean that there must be more religiousness in schools and churches in regard to those forms. In other words, our conventional pedagogy must offer an improved religious experience.

If we wish to improve the quality of religious experience in American life and eliminate the recurrence of mob catharsis, we must embrace and not reject conventional wisdom. This means encouraging loyalty and belief rather than detachment and doubt. An institution, either a school or a church, which seeks to foster loyalty must create an environment in which loyalty is learned. Student activities in this light are not incidental diversions from academic experience, but vital educational enterprises in their own right. We must not go on streaming our children through these incredibly faceless and impersonal systems with contrived standards and invented categories which take the place of human interaction and judgment. Our magnificent effort at public education has left us with a plan for elementary education which does not permit us to look at children as children. Instead they are treated and discussed as mechanisms which must acquire skills. This same massive effort has left us with a secondary education which equates the acquisition of cognate knowledge with education itself. Higher and graduate education increasingly wear this same aspect. Student disorders at this higher level frequently involve persons who are desperately seeking forms to which they can be loyal. Not finding it in the institutional order, they seek and find it outside of order.

This is not a polemic against schoolmen and churchmen. If anything, the majority of those who now lead our schools and churches recognize the problem all too well. They want reform, but the word has yet to go out with sufficient strength to summon the public to acceptance of reform. If clergymen who lead congregations continue to be judged by the quality of buildings, the size of congregations, or the amounts which gather in collection plates, they cannot be blamed for trying to make a good showing in these things. Likewise a school-man who runs his system well knows the system rewards slavishness; and, indeed, he also knows it punishes heresies. But, in the fullness of time, the very obvious need for reform will result in a public demand for reform. Schoolmen and churchmen then should proceed with reform rather than submit to or suffer revolution. Reform for the most part remains under the control of civil sentiment. Revolution starts that way but civility soon leaves, and in the interval of its absence destruction reigns. Man's capacity for destruction has now grown so great that revolution is no longer a responsible approach to change.

Two centuries ago Rousseau began *The Social Contract* with the words, "Man is born free, but he is everywhere in chains." This sentiment and those which followed it presented the world with two centuries of bloody and turbulent revolution. It is not over yet. There are places in the world where revolt is still needed. Even so, one would think that after two centuries of this sort of thing mankind would have learned something about man. Even after two centuries and the development of democratic institutions we still place our young civilians in chains and expect them to grow up loving them. If we allow our children to experience the same excitement of discovering our civil forms as our forebears experienced when they first discovered them, the possibility stands that the ideas of the republic will remain forever young and the civilization of which it is part will constantly regenerate. We must not, therefore, continue presenting these forms as dry abstractions to be remembered for testing. As such, the forms are as much manacles as those of which Rousseau complained. Only an education which offers an emendated religious experience can prevent revolution from becoming a violent and debilitating habit.

Clearly, therefore, much can be done to improve the quality of regular and frequent religious experiences in America, and it follows that men who have regular and frequent significant religious experiences are more stable, contented, and assured in their lives. They are not confounded by meaninglessness or absurdity. It is not too much to say that they are better men. The conversation of modern times is heavily burdened with prescriptions for the improvement of society. Society, as some think of it, may exist or it may not. There can be no reasoned assurance that improved social processes or systems improve either society or men. But in the mass catharsis, we have seen again and again that in those shining moments when men are better, society is better. Therefore, there can be a reasoned assurance that better men compose a better society. The business before us, then, is the making of better men. The splendid hope of western civilization is in recognizing that we have made so many; therefore, we must know how it is done.

The Humane Pedagogy

If humanities activities are not stirring to the inner man; if they do not generate a yearning by the inner man; if they don't produce commitment within inner man, then their outcomes will be neither an inclination to duty nor an inculcation of reverence.

By these standards much of our present humanities education fails. Too many students are touring museums and too few are painting; too many are attending plays and too few are writing, directing, and acting; too many are collecting pop records and too few are in choruses and playing in bands and orchestras. Too many are expressing and experiencing sensuality in dance and too few are expressing and experiencing form. Too many are developing student publications by paste-up formulas and too few are developing a tasteful literature of authentic student expression. Yes, and we must admit that too many students are watching athletic games and too few are playing. Too many industrial arts classes are devoted to learning operations and too few provide a boy opportunity to extend himself through an enterprise of free creation. Too many students come to instructors at the end of graduate seminars and say, "You know I have been all the way through the American system. I have been what the system calls a good student. I am now working for the doctorate degree. And, you know, aside from simply succeeding in what passes for success, nothing else has happened to me in school which really mattered." Not all of them say this, but too many of them do.

A few years ago a young teacher gave a true and false test of twenty questions to sections of high school freshmen, sophomores, juniors, and seniors. He graded the results but put no marks on the papers. Returning them to the class he appealed to their integrity and announced that they could grade their own papers. When he re-collected the papers he found that more than a third of the freshmen had raised their marks as had half of the sophomores, more than half of the juniors, and almost seventy percent of the seniors.

When the students were informed of this they were full of in-dignation at the trick that had been "pulled." The teacher had not played the game properly! Were these youngsters dishonest? No indeed. Many of them now occupy stations of trust and responsibility with distinction and honor. But to them, at that time, as they reported in follow-up interviews, the school was a kind of game which no one could afford to lose because of the crushing consequences which the civilized order metes out to academic losers. What is more, the further they went along in the system the more they found this to be, and so even the honest accepted the moral—get through it, never mind how, just get the passport which intitles you to have a try at succeeding in America. Without it you are nothing!

This paradox was dramatized again in a scene witnessed by this author just a few hours before recording these final sentences. A big yellow bus discharged a kindergarten child. As she ran the few steps to her home she called several cheerful goodbyes to the driver and her companions. She gave a quick knock on the front door and turned. As the bus pulled away she stamped her foot and put out her tongue.

Thus, this curious paradox is still visible at all points on the educational continuum. A review of the philosophy and education of western man shows rather decisively that the American effort at education in regards to magnitude and accomplishment overshadows any which preceded it. So much has been achieved that this effort deserves to be called mankind's greatest human enterprise. But all that has been done is just a beginning. We have accomplished an unprecedented social commitment, assemblage of resources, and felicity of organization. In the fullness of time public education may be seen as America's distinctive contribution to civilized enterprise. All that stands in the way of even greater achievement is a failure of vision or of nerve. It will require both for American educators to recognize our young not only as *individuals* who require training but also as *persons* in quest of *meaning*.

Notes

1. St. Augustine, *The City of God* (New York: Random House, Inc., The Modern Library, 1950), p. 304.
2. Meta-religion as used here relates to religion *qua* religion. It means no consideration is given the content of the normative religions which are mentioned.
3. The author's opinion on this "fourth fiction" is explored in *Religious Values in Education* (Danville, Ill.: The Interstate Printers & Publishers, Inc., 1967). There have been several refinements since.
4. A. N. Whitehead, *The Aims of Education and Other Essays* (New York: The Macmillan Company, Free Press, Paperback edition, 1967), p. 14.

5. *Ibid.,* p. 1.
6. William James, *Essays on Faith and Morals* (New York: Longmans Green and Co., 1943), p. 82.

Other Reading

Arisian, Khoren. "Ethical Humanism and the Death of God." *The Humanist.* (March, April 1970) Vol. XXX, No. 2, pp. 27-30.

Borne, Etienne. *Atheism.* Tr. S. J. Tester. New York: Hawthorne, 1961.

Butler, Richard O. P. *God on the Secular Campus.* New York: Doubleday & Company, Inc., 1963.

Butts, Freeman. *The American Tradition in Religion and Education.* Boston: Beacon Press, 1950.

Cox, Harvey. *The Secular City.* New York: The Macmillan Company, 1965.

Flint, Robert. *Anti-Theistic Theories.* London: William Blackwood and Sons, 1879.

Hartshorne, Charles and William Reese. *Philosophers Speak of God.* Chicago: The University of Chicago Press, 1963. Phoenix Ed.

James, William. *A Pluralistic Universe.* New York: Longmans Green and Co., 1909.

——————. *Essays on Faith and Morals.* New York: Longmans Green and Co., 1943.

Keyser, Cassius. *The Rational and the Supernatural: Studies in Thinking.* New York: Scripta Mathematica, 1952.

Marty, Martin E. *Varieties of Unbelief.* New York: Holt, Rinehart & Winston, Inc. 1964.

Mason, Robert E. *Moral Values and Secular Education.* New York: Columbia University Press, 1950.

McClusky, Niel G. S. J. *Catholic Viewpoint on Education.* New York: Doubleday & Company, Inc., 1959.

Piaget, Jean. *The Moral Judgment of the Child.* New York: Harcourt, 1932.

Royce, Josiah. *The Conception of God.* Berkeley: Executive Council of the Philosophical Union of the University of California, 1895. New York: The Macmillan Company, 1898.

Sizer, Theodore, ed. *Religion and Public Education.* Boston: Houghton Mifflin Company, 1967.

Soltis, Jonas. *An Introduction to the Analysis of Educational Concepts.* Reading, Mass.: Addison-Wesley Publishing Co., Inc., 1968.

Stoops, John A. *Religious Values in Education.* Danville, Ill.: The Interstate Printers & Publishers, Inc., 1967.

Tillich, Paul. *The Courage to Be.* New Haven: Yale University Press, 1952.

——————. *Theology of Culture.* New York: Oxford University Press, 1959.

Trilling, Lionel B. *Beyond Culture.* New York: The Viking Press, 1965.

Ulich, Robert, ed. *Education and the Idea of Mankind.* New York: Harcourt, Brace, & World, Inc., 1964.

Weiner, Norbert. *God and Golem, Inc.: A Comment on Certain Points*

Where Cybernetics Impinges on Religion. Cambridge: M.I.T. Press, 1966.
Whitehead, Alfred N. *Religion in the Making.* New York: The Macmillan Company, 1926.
_____. *The Aims of Education and Other Essays.* New York: The Macmillan Company, 1929.

Name Index

A

Abelard, Peter, 152, 165, 166
Aeschylus, 29
Agathon, 11, 12
Albert the Great, 167
Alcibiades, 48, 53, 107
Alexander, 46, 86, 88-89, 110, 114
Amyntas, 86
Anaxagoras, 43
Anaximander, 32-33, 123
Anaximines, 33
Anselm, 130, 147-153, 163, 175, 211, 214
Antisthenes, 44, 53, 107-109, 114, 123, 126, 330
Anytus, 50
Appollodorus, 53
Aquinas, Thomas, 3, 9, 85, 153, 167-183, 211, 288, 305, 370
Arete, 113
Aristippus, 53, 112-114, 123, 330
Aristophanes, 129, 330
Aristotle, 7-12, 19, 46-48, 83-108, 114-115, 123-130, 164, 172-175, 185, 250-251, 269, 275, 288, 370, 372
Athena, 54
Augustine, 84, 130, 139-145, 174, 180-181, 214-215, 303, 307, 346, 399
Aurelius, 120, 126-127, 211
Averroes, 147, 164, 170-172
Avicenna, 147, 164

B

Bacon, Francis, 3, 249-251
Bancroft, George, 239
Bentham, Jeremy, 12, 117, 260, 374-380
Berkeley, George, 68, 191-193, 199, 215, 307
Boethius, 145, 160

Bolte, Marie, 205, 219
Bonaventura, 153, 167, 171-172, 185
Brentano, Franz, 292
Buber, Martin, 327-328, 360

C

Calhoun, John, 219-221
Camus, Albert, 319, 360, 389-394
Carlyle, 199, 228
Celsus, 120
Chaucer, Geoffrey, 85
Cicero, 19, 124-125
Cleanthes, 118-119
Coleridge, 199, 223, 228
Comenius, John, 19, 251
Comte, Auguste, 259-261
Coombs, 299
Copleston, 182
Crates, 107, 109, 117
Cratylus, 36

D

Democritus, 44, 123
Descartes, René, 9, 140, 151, 185-191, 199, 215, 251, 288, 290
Dewey, John, 9, 13, 18-19, 100, 205-206, 210, 242-244, 268, 270-278, 329, 341, 383-388, 394
Diogenes, 30, 107-114, 154
Dionysius of Syracuse, 54, 112-113
Dionysus, 315
Dupont, Pierre, 217
Durant, Will, 126

E

Edwards, Jonathon, 214-216, 220
Elizabeth, the Queen, 212-214
Emerson, 199, 215, 228-235
Empedocles, 43, 66

Subject Index

A

Above-Being, 128-129
absurd, 308
Academy of Plato, 54, 87
Achaeans, 23, 27
actuality-potentiality:
    Aquinas on, 173-174
    Aristotle on, 92-93
Aeneid, 352
Ahriman, 25
American studies, 211
analogy of cave, 60
angst, 311
apodictic, 294
Apollo, 25
Apollo Lyceus, 88
Apology, 55
apperceptive mass, 266-267
archeological expeditions, 21
Argos, 24
atheism, 323-325
Athens and philosophy, 30, 31, 43
authority of state, 72
axiology, 8-13:
    of Aristotelian realism, 98-102
    Augustinian, 141
    Bentham's hedonistic calculus, 374-376
    of civil formalism, 391-395
    deontological ethics, 379-383
    existentialist, 318f., 388-391
    of formal idealism, 67-70
    of Hegelian idealism, 204-205
    Hume's is/ought distinction, 258, 388
    of Kantian (spiritual) idealism, 197-199, 379-383
    Mill's hedonism, 376-379
    Nietzschean, 317
    of pragmatism, 275-277, 383-388
    of Spinoza, 190-191
    theological ethics, 372-373
    Thomistic, 177-180
    utilitarian ethics, 373-379

B

Babylon, 22
beauty:
    Aristotelian, 100-101
    Kantian, 198-199
    Platonic, 69
    Plotinus on, 129-130
    Thomistic, 179-180
    (*See also* axiology)
Being, Plotinus' conception of, 128-129
being, 307-308:
    and becoming, Aristotle on, 92
    modes of, 321-323
being-for-itself, 322
being-for-others, 322
being-in-itself, 321
Beyond Good and Evil, 316
Birth of Tragedy, The, 314
bracketing, 293
Brahmanism, 24, 36

C

Calvinism, 214-216
change, metaphysics of, 31-36
choice, 319, 324-325
Christians, 25
Christian idealism, 135f.:
    in America, 212-216
Christian Science, 226
Christianity, Kirkegaard's attack, 310-313
City of God, The, 142-144, 399
civil formalism, 339-366:
    ethics of, 391-395
    religiousness in, 399-412